Constitutional Economics and Public Institutions

NEW THINKING IN POLITICAL ECONOMY

Series Editor: Peter J. Boettke, *George Mason University, USA*

New Thinking in Political Economy aims to encourage scholarship in the intersection of the disciplines of politics, philosophy and economics. It has the ambitious purpose of reinvigorating political economy as a progressive force for understanding social and economic change.

The series is an important forum for the publication of new work analysing the social world from a multidisciplinary perspective. With increased specialization (and professionalization) within universities, interdisciplinary work has become increasingly uncommon. Indeed, during the 20th century, the process of disciplinary specialization reduced the intersection between economics, philosophy and politics and impoverished our understanding of society. Modern economics in particular has become increasingly mathematical and largely ignores the role of institutions and the contribution of moral philosophy and politics.

New Thinking in Political Economy will stimulate new work that combines technical knowledge provided by the 'dismal science' and the wisdom gleaned from the serious study of the 'worldly philosophy'. The series will reinvigorate our understanding of the social world by encouraging a multidisciplinary approach to the challenges confronting society in the new century.

Recent titles in the series include:

Media, Development, and Institutional Change
Christopher J. Coyne and Peter T. Leeson

The Economics of Ignorance and Coordination
Subjectivism and the Austrian School of Economics
Thierry Aimar

Socialism, Economic Calculation and Entrepreneurship
Jesús Huerta de Soto

The Political Economy of Hurricane Katrina and Community Rebound
Edited by Emily Chamlee-Wright and Virgil Henry Storr

Robust Political Economy
Classical Liberalism and the Future of Public Policy
Mark Pennington

Good Governance in the 21st Century
Conflict, Institutional Change, and Development in the Era of Globalization
Edited by Joachim Ahrens, Rolf Caspers and Janina Weingarth

Institutions in Crisis
European Perspectives on the Recession
Edited by David Howden

Constitutional Economics and Public Institutions
Edited by Francisco Cabrillo and Miguel A. Puchades-Navarro

Constitutional Economics and Public Institutions

Essays in Honour of José Casas Pardo

Edited by

Francisco Cabrillo

Department of Applied Economics, Complutense University, Madrid, Spain

Miguel A. Puchades-Navarro

Department of Applied Economics, University of Valencia, Spain

NEW THINKING IN POLITICAL ECONOMY

Edward Elgar

Cheltenham, UK • Northampton, MA, USA

Published by
Edward Elgar Publishing Limited
The Lypiatts
15 Lansdown Road
Cheltenham
Glos GL50 2JA
UK

Edward Elgar Publishing, Inc.
William Pratt House
9 Dewey Court
Northampton
Massachusetts 01060
USA

A catalogue record for this book
is available from the British Library

Library of Congress Control Number: 2012947119

This book is available electronically in the ElgarOnline.com
Economics Subject Collection, E-ISBN 978 1 78100 397 8

MIX
Paper from
responsible sources
FSC® C018575

ISBN 978 1 78100 396 1

Typeset by Servis Filmsetting Ltd, Stockport, Cheshire
Printed by MPG PRINTGROUP, UK

Contents

Contributors

Peter Bernholz, Center for Economics and Business (WWZ Universität Basel), Switzerland

Vani K. Borooah, School of Economics, University of Ulster, Northern Ireland, UK

Geoffrey Brennan, Research School of Social Sciences, Australian National University, Canberra, Australia, The University of North Carolina at Chapel Hill and Duke University, US

Giorgio Brosio, Department of Economics, University of Turin, Italy

James M. Buchanan, Nobel Laureate – 1986, Distinguished Professor Emeritus, George Mason University and Virginia Polytechnic Institute and State University and Advisory General Director, Center for Study of Public Choice, George Mason University, US

Francisco Cabrillo, Departamento de Economia Aplicada IV, Universidad Complutense de Madrid, Facultad de Derecho, Ciudad Universitaria, Spain

Roger D. Congleton, BB&T Professor of Economics, College of Business & Economics, West Virginia University, Morgantown, US

Giuseppe Eusepi, Faculty of Economics, Sapienza University of Rome, Italy

Silvia Fedeli, Dipartimento di Economia e diritto, Facoltà di Economia, Sapienza – Università di Roma, Italy

Mario Ferrero, Department of Public Policy and Public Choice (POLIS), University of Eastern Piedmont, Italy

Sean Fitzpatrick, Consultant at the Economic and Social Committee, Regional Government of Madrid, Consejo Económico y Social, Comunidad de Madrid, Spain

Francesco Forte, Dipartimento di Economia e diritto, Facoltà di Economia, Sapienza – Università di Roma, Italy

Bruno S. Frey, Institute for Empirical Research in Economics University of Zurich, Switzerland

Juha Helin, Department of Political Science, University of Turku, Finland

Manfred J. Holler, Institute of SocioEconomics, University of Hamburg, Germany

Juan D. Montoro-Pons, Departamento de Economia Aplicada, Universitat de Valencia, Spain

Susanne Neckermann, Institute for Empirical Research in Economics, University of Zurich, Switzerland

Hannu Nurmi, Department of Political Science, University of Turku, Finland

Martin Paldam, School of Economics and Management, University of Aarhus, Denmark

Miguel A. Puchades-Navarro, Departamento de Economia Aplicada, Universitat de Valencia, Spain

Gian Cesare Romagnoli, Università Roma Tre, Italia

Pierre Salmon, Laboratoire d'Economie et de Gestion, Université de Bourgogne, France

Viktor J. Vanberg, Walter Eucken Institut, Freiburg, Germany

Bengt-Arne Wickström, Institut für Finanzwissenschaft Wirtschafts-wissenschaftliche Fakultät, Humboldt-Universität zu Berlin, Germany

Foreword

It is a great honor for me to see this volume edited by Francisco Cabrillo and Miguel Puchades-Navarro, *Constitutional Economics and Public Institutions*, published in the book series that I edit 'New Thinking in Political Economy'.

The field of constitutional economics, or my preferred label, constitutional political economy, is underappreciated in the profession. There may be more attention paid to institutions and political structure today than there was a quarter century ago, when Professor Buchanan was awarded the Nobel Prize (1986). But the analysis in mainstream economics has not yet caught up completely with Buchanan. Professor Buchanan was the pioneer in moving economic thinking from the analysis of the logic of the situation given a set of well-established and well-enforced rules of the game, to the analysis of the logic behind the selection of the rules of the game themselves. Buchanan's relevance to the examination of our current situation – whether we are talking about the financial crisis in the US, the debt crisis in Europe, the plight of underdevelopment, or the difficulties that are still being dealt with in the transition from the failed communist model – should be immediately obvious to all students of political economy. These problems are not fixed via various technocratic solutions within the existing political/legal structure of rules of the game, but require a change in the rules. Same players, but different rules, will produce different games people play.

The various chapters in this volume address this theme of the examination of the choice between rules, as well as the more conventional analysis within rules, across historical time and place, and in various thought experiments and conceptual situations. It is my hope that this will inspire readers not only to think along these lines, but to engage in their own inquiries at the constitutional level of analysis.

It is my pleasure as well to join with the editors and various authors in honoring José Casas Pardo, who has been a great champion of constitutional political economy and public choice throughout his career.

Peter Boettke
Professor of Economics
George Mason University, Fairfax, US

Introduction

Francisco Cabrillo and Miguel A. Puchades-Navarro

In the development of public choice and constitutional political economy in Spain the name of Professor José Casas Pardo is a necessary reference. Born in Granada in 1938 he studied law and economics at the University of Granada and London School of Economics. He was Professor of Economics at the Autonoma and Complutense Universities in Madrid. In 1981 he moved to the University of Valencia where he was a Professor until his retirement in 2008.

As a Public Choice Scholar he has been President of the European Public Choice Society (1994–95) and member of its Executive Board (1995–97). He was also the conference organizer of the very successful Annual Meeting of the European Public Choice Society (EPCS) that was held in Valencia in 1994. He has served as a member of the editorial board of *Public Choice*, and since 1990 has been member of the editorial board of *Constitutional Political Economy*. He was co-director with Professor J. Buchanan of a research project on the Spanish Constitution of 1978 financed by the Joint Spanish American Committee for Educational and Cultural Affairs. Professor Casas Pardo has written widely on these topics. But his main ideas on the role of Public Choice in modern economics can be found in his Presidential Address of EPCS, delivered in Saarbrücken in 1995.

One of his most interesting contributions to this field deals with the performance of institutions. This is an important topic for public choice theory, mainly because many collective institutions perform poorly to various degrees. One reason for this may be that many institutions are organized on the assumption that individuals behave ideally and their bodies of government or directors always pursue public welfare. Some think that institutions work better the more 'democratic' they are; even – it is argued – technical institutions that provide services such as education, transportation or medial assistance should be more open to democratic decision making procedures.

Experience shows us, however, that these so-called democratic institutions lose a great deal of their efficiency. Some individuals, pursing their own interests, take the opportunity to play politics through assemblarian systems of decision making. So the quality of decisions is reduced and the system of rewards and penalties is perverted. This happens more often with public institutions than private ones. In the public sector property rights and obligations of individuals are less clearly defined, so the room for politicking by individuals within the institution increases.

The conclusion is that collective institutions should be organized in such a way that individuals working in them are positively interested in behaving so as to enhance the efficiency of these institutions.

In recognition of his efforts to introduce the study of public choice theory to Spain, his contribution to its diffusion in Europe, and his whole career, a number of colleagues would like to pay tribute to José Casas Pardo upon his retirement as university professor. To this end we have written this collection. Participants are colleagues who have been his friends throughout his career and membership of the EPCS. Contributors include prominent professors of economics, and prestigious public choice scholars from several European, Australian and American universities. It is particularly worth noting the participation in this festschrift of Nobel Laureate James M. Buchanan, whose friendship Professor Casas Pardo has always appreciated so much.

This volume covers a wide range of topics within the public choice and constitutional political economy tradition. But they are not unrelated, and the collection as a whole can provide an overview of current work across the field. To give coherence to this volume, chapters have been arranged and grouped into five parts: Foundations of Constitutional Economics; Constitutional Political Economy: Case Studies; Political Competition and Voting; Public Choice and Public Policy; and Extensions in Public Choice Theory.

Part I, 'Foundations of Constitutional Economics', includes two chapters, one by James M. Buchanan and the other by Geoffrey Brennan and Giuseppe Eusepi. In his chapter, 'Presuppositions in the evaluation of rules', Buchanan encourages economists to pay more attention to the rules, and the constitution, that define the order within which economic and political behaviour takes place. Professor Buchanan points out two separate but related logical mistakes as the origins of the reluctance to examine the rules of political-legal order. The first one is the apparent failure to recognize the public characteristic of laws and institutions, and the second is the attribution of an efficient criterion to the existing institutions. The present financial crisis shows that economists have been negligent when examining, at various levels of abstraction, how institutional structures emerge in different settings. And Buchanan concludes that the folly of overextending the 'markets work' attitude to anything that emerges in an institutional setting is amply demonstrated by the observed events of the crisis.

In the second chapter, 'Buchanan, Hobbes and contractarianism: the supply of rules?', Geoffrey Brennan and Giuseppe Eusepi revisit two seminal works of Buchanan: *The Calculus of Consent* and *The Limits of Liberty*. They assert that there are significant differences between the approaches taken by Buchanan in his two books, and focus on the change in his perception of the 'constitutional political economy' project. To this aim, the authors juxtapose the central elements in the appendix of *The Calculus* ('Marginal Notes on Reading Political Philosophy') with key passages of *The Limits of Liberty*. *The Calculus* is a normative theory of political organization, not a theory of political obligations; and it is a marginal, not a total theory. By contrast, in *The Limits* Buchanan quite explicitly embraces a revolutionary project and for this he requires a more ambituous, a more 'total' analytical scope.

The second part of the volume includes four chapters under the heading 'Constitutional Political Economy: Case Studies'. In the first one, 'Economics governance in the European Union: a problem of legitimacy', Francisco Cabrillo and Sean Fitzpatrick discuss some aspects of the Lisbon Treaty and assert that this treaty – like the European Constitution before it – increases the gulf between citizens and decisions that affect their lives. Movements in Europe towards greater centralization are inefficient and bridging the gulf between citizens and decision makers does not involve awarding greater responsibilities to the European Parliament as a supervisory body over other institutions. Their thesis is that the European Union could best mitigate its legitimacy problems by concentrating on achieving better results in core areas in which its institutions are best able to serve, i.e. by respecting the principle of subsidiarity, which should be the basis of European integration.

The chapter 'Early Spanish liberalism and constitutional political economy: the Cádiz Constitution of 1812', by Roger D. Congleton, focuses on political and constitutional developments in Spain, and uses the Constitution of 1812 as a window into Spanish political liberalism in the early nineteenth century. Liberalism had an early start in Spain, but it was pushed underground during the seventeenth and eighteenth centuries. The Constitution of 1812 shows that Spanish liberal thought was more sophisticated and influential at the beginning of the nineteenth century than might have been expected. Although Spanish scholars produced relatively little written liberal political theory, Spanish political liberals did exist and were organized and influential. The subsequent process of constitutional negotiation and exchange did not fully deliver on its potential, leading to the turbulent constitutional and political history of nineteenth-century

Spain. However the 1812 Constitution continued to influence politics both in Spain and in America.

The chapter by Pierre Salmon, 'Reforms and decentralization: friends or foes?', addresses the significant relationship between economic systems and the architecture of government. Historical experience suggests that large-scale reforms of economic and/or social arrangements are often associated with changes in the architecture of government. This chapter deals with the relationships between public intervention and income redistribution on the one hand and political centralization on the other. Large-scale reforms of the economic system typically occur in political environments in which the central governments can reshape institutional arrangements with subcentral governments. The first part of the chapter is based on a design perspective. Reform is perceived as the replacement of one model by another. The second part is devoted to reform processes. Integrating decentralization into an analysis of reforms as they are being implemented seems more promising, since it allows one to formulate hypotheses about the relationship between economic performance over time and changes in decentralization.

In his chapter 'Democracy-preserving institutions: the quasi-federal system of South Africa', Giorgio Brosio analyzes the process of decentralization carried out in South Africa after the 1996 Constitution. The case of South Africa is one of the most interesting among the current decentralization processes. This interest stems from the peculiarities of fiscal institutions, such as the peculiar sociopolitical framework in which the process is taking place. International experience shows that decentralization and equitable provision of services can coexist. On the other hand, a decentralized or federal system is a fundamental checks and balances mechanism. The conclusion is that a well-designed decentralized system is essential for enhancing democracy in a country with the economic and political features of present day South Africa and for the equitable and efficient provision of public services.

'Political Competition and Voting' is the title of Part III of the volume. Conspiracy has often been used in history as a strategy to acquire or increase political power. Manfred J. Holler, in his chapter 'On Machiavelli's conspiracy paradoxes', analyzes how to plan and execute a successful conspiracy and how to prevent its success. He discusses inherent strategic relationships in conspiracy from the perspective of rational agents. The analysis is based on Machiavelli's very informative and highly competent writings on this subject. Holler points out that Machiavelli developed a rational theory of conspiracy that follows the pattern of a cost-benefit analysis. He also discusses some paradoxes in Machiavelli's writing on conspiracy, revisits his treatment of conspirator strategies, and his advice to the Prince on how to counteract conspiracies and use them to increase power. The chapter includes an appendix illustrating the behaviour of a rational conspirator.

Vani K. Borooah, in his chapter 'A general measure of the "effective" number of parties in a political system', proposes a measure based on the family of generalized entropy inequality indices. The main problem of measuring the effective number of parties is how to count parties of a different size; in the literature it is assumed that some kind of weighting is required. Calculating the effective number of parties in a system involves assigning a scalar value to a vector of inter-party distribution of seats or votes. The central message of this chapter is that the construction of indices or measures which purport to give scalar representation to vectors of distributive outcomes cannot be wholly based on objective considerations. This observation applies fully to the measurement of the effective number of parties in a political system.

Explaining the act of voting is the focus of the chapter 'Party competition and electoral turnout: Downs's calculus in a multiparty system', by Juha Helin and Hannu Nurmi. In many countries in Western and Northern Europe, the overall trend in electoral turnout has been declining over the past few decades, reflecting an apparent lack of interest by the electorate in expressing their opinions. Majoritarian systems are, in general, associated with lower voter turnout than proportional ones. This chapter focuses on the possible effect that the closeness in an electoral race has on turnout in majoritarian and in proportional electoral systems. Downs's voter calculus indicates that, ceteris paribus, voters' turnout should be higher in closely contested elections. This hypothesis is tested looking at evidence from two very different political systems, the British and the Finnish. The former is based on majoritarian principles, while the latter is a proportional representation system. In the Finnish proportional system evidence seems to contradict the voter calculus prediction. With regard to the British election data, conclusions are less clear-cut. In general, it seems that turnout is not higher in high competition constituency clusters.

Part IV, 'Public Choice and Public Policy', includes four chapters that have a clear connection with public policy. 'The political economy of Dutch Disease: a survey', by Martin Paldam, is the first one. It is well known that countries rich in natural resources become wealthy in the short run, but grow less than other countries in the longer run, so that the long term effect is ambiguous. This chapter presents the basics of the Dutch Disease model, looks briefly at OPEC, and provides a stylized picture of policy reactions to discovery of one resource. A resource specific sector is normally a small enclave in the economy that mainly 'produces' a resource rent, which is appropriated by the state as a tax paid by the rest of the world. The resource thus causes an inflow of foreign exchange to the state. The new income flow raises expectations, decreases the labour supply and forces the state to spend the new rent. Given that resources run out, it is essential that spending programs are long term economic investments. In this vein, it is possible to do a great deal to mitigate a 'disease' element from eating at societal gain. It would also appear to be prudent to invest a considerable amount of resource rent abroad, with the aim of generating a permanent income stream instead of a temporary resource rent.

The chapter 'Higher education as private good and as quasi public good: the case of Italy', by Silvia Fedeli and Francesco Forte, focuses on higher education as the key means to increase human capital. It distinguishes private human capital – whose returns are mostly in the market economy – and public human capital, which has larger non-market returns and therefore characteristics of a quasi public good. The position that there is generally an excess of higher education in developed countries is not warranted for Italy. The flow of graduates in Italy is constantly increasing at an important rate, but the share of those contributing mainly to human capital is declining; and education in the family is very important in determining public human capital in higher level education.

Gian Cesare Romagnoli, in his chapter 'The actual role of government intervention for the recovery of the Italian economy', points out ideas that would support State intervention. In the years 1993–97 some relevant corrective policy measures were taken, leading to social security reforms, fiscal decentralization, privatization and reforms of the labour market. Nonetheless, they were inadequate to improve competitiveness. This chapter presents a discussion on the economic role played by the State and the market in the economy, a reconsideration of the theoretical conclusions on the merits of nationalization and regulated privatization, and some suggestions of institutional reforms required for the recovery of the Italian economy. Professor Romagnoli thinks that the ill-functioning of the Italian State has impacted negatively on the national economy. He provides evidence that institutions matter and consequently that Italy needs substantial institutional change to reverse the economic decline which is taking place across the country.

The last chapter in Part IV, 'Government bankruptcy of Balkan nations and the consequences for money and inflation before 1914: a comparative analysis', by Peter Bernholz, deals with government bankruptcies in countries of the so-called 'periphery' during the gold standard. Studying the Balkan countries and the Ottoman Empire, this chapter shows that high inflation levels were usually caused by financing excessive government deficits with the printing of money. All inflation in Balkan countries before 1914 and that of the Ottoman Empire, as well as the abolition of fixed exchange rates corresponding to monetary regimes based on gold or silver standards, was caused by veiled government bankruptcies. This usually led to an undervaluation of respective currencies. If, however, fixed exchange rates were maintained or restored, a tendency towards overvaluation of the currency or a removal of earlier undervaluation took place. Open bankruptcies also occurred on numerous occasions because of excessive deficits financed by foreign debt denominated in stable currencies.

Part V, 'Extensions in Public Choice Theory', includes chapters dealing with traditional issues of public choice theory and with other non-market decisions. The standard public choice analysis of contests deals with situations in which outcomes are related to lobbying resources invested by competitors in a rent-seeking contest. The chapter 'Regulator preferences and lobbying efforts in rent-seeking contests', by Juan D. Montoro-Pons, discusses rent-seeking activities and ideological preferences to explain allocations of rents in a contest. Both the groups competing for rents and the regulator are included in the model. The chapter analyzes how the standard rent-seeking process is affected by the explicit introduction of a dissipation maximizing regulator, who has preferences over potential outcomes, and by the introduction of information by interest groups.

The chapter by Victor J. Vanberg, 'Cooperation in multilateral PDs: self-selected vs pre-defined groups', deals with the issue of cooperative behaviour in settings where adverse incentives exist. This is the case, for instance, in social dilemma situations of the prisoner's dilemma type. The specific focus of this chapter is on the issue of cooperative behaviour in bilateral and multilateral PDs. The multilateral PDs, which cannot be factored down into elementary bilateral relations between agents, are exemplified by the kind of collective goods problems involved in team production that, for instance, private firms, cooperatives, and clubs must overcome to be successful enterprises.

The chapter 'Voluntary provision of public goods', by Miguel A. Puchades-Navarro, highlights that voluntary supply is a real alternative to public compulsory provision of public goods. Unlike the standard theory of public goods, historical evidence shows that goods such as charitable services, medicare, education, and so on have been supplied through non-governmental, non-profit institutions – mainly religious institutions. In this model, voluntary funding of public goods is not grounded on altruism but on honesty as a behavioural pattern. A set of ethical and moral rules constrain individuals' behaviour and make cooperation possible. Consumers reveal their preferences for public goods through voting to determine taxes and public supply, and by funding non-profit institutions.

Provision is either governmental or voluntary depending on the position of the median voter in relation to the distribution of consumers' preferences for the public good.

Bruno S. Frey and Susanne Neckermann are authors of an interesting chapter entitled 'Awards play an important role'. Awards in the form of orders, decorations, prizes, and titles, are predominantly non-material incentives. They thus differ from both intrinsic incentives and extrinsic incentives in the form of money. The chapter analyzes the nature of awards and beliefs about them. Awards have existed for centuries, and are used in all countries and in all areas of society. The statistics presented in this chapter offer interesting and unexpected insights. Awards are widely used in modern society, not just in monarchies; they are relevant in the civil sector and are not mainly a military affair; and they are also important in academia. Hence awards are worth studying as they present a widespread phenomenon that we currently know little about.

The chapter 'The optimal Babel: an economic framework for the analysis of dynamic language rights', by Bengt-Arne Wickström, analyzes various normatively determined distributions of language rights in multilingual settings. A general model with overlapping generations is developed for the analysis of language rights over time. This model is first used to find an efficient allocation of rights, in the tradition of Wicksell. It is shown that, when present rights influence the status of a language in the future, 'naive' static analysis has to be abandoned in order to take into account the dynamic aspect. It is then demonstrated that a traditional welfare-economic analysis generally goes even further in support of minority rights. If possible externalities on other communities are taken into account, however, these results are reversed. When redistribution arguments are included the opposite may again be true.

Mario Ferrero is a renowned European researcher on the economics of religion from a public choice perspective. His chapter 'A theory of conversion to exclusive religious and political faiths' presents a theory of conversion to exclusive faiths grounded in rational choice. He argues that exclusivity is a signal that consumers can trust, since it entails an opportunity cost to those consumers that would like to diversify their portfolios. Signalling theory is applied to the rise of Christianity in the Roman Empire and to the rise of socialism in nineteenth-century Europe.

PART I

Foundations of Constitutional Economics

1. Presuppositions in the evaluation of rules

James M. Buchanan

1. INTRODUCTION

I have often asked my fellow economists to pay more attention to the rules, to the constitution, that define the order within which economic and political behavior takes place, and from which end-states emerge. I have been continuously disappointed by the failure of my peers to express an interest in, or even to understand the presuppositions of, my argument. The separation between constitutional politics and ordinary politics is seldom recognized; hence, the important implications of the distinction are not examined.

Politics, as observed and widely interpreted, readily becomes an arena of conflict, with winners and losers identified. By contrast, the setting for constitutional politics involves the search for agreed-upon rules that define 'games' from which mutual gains are anticipated by all participants. Failing some presupposition that members of the body politic agree on the ultimate rules, how can the polity, as a collective entity, be legitimized at all?

I shall not, in this chapter, make yet another effort to convince my peers to change their focus of inquiry. Instead my aim here is to clarify elements of confusion that may have influenced the analysis. Specifically, the seeming reluctance to examine the rules of political-legal order may find its origins in two separate but related logical mistakes. The first of these is the apparent failure to recognize the publicness characteristic of the laws and institutions of social order. The second, and more general, error involves the putative attribution of an efficiency criterion to the observed continuing existence, as such, of these institutions.

These two mistakes or oversights are discussed in Sections 2 and 3. Section 4 relates the arguments, one to the other, and Section 5 applies the analysis to an understanding of the events of the 2007–09 crises. Section 6 offers a summation.

2. THE PUBLICNESS OF INSTITUTIONS

For public finance scholars, Paul Samuelson's short 1954 paper on the theory of public expenditure was a seminal breakthrough. By using the newly familiar formal tools, Samuelson was able to clarify much prior analysis that had remained, at best, conceptually fuzzy, even if basically correct in essentials. His formalization involved the taxonomic step of modeling the set of goods valued by individuals in two subsets, the private and the public. In the first subset, Samuelson placed goods that are fully partitionable among end-users, embodying both excludability and rivalry. In the second subset, Samuelson placed goods that are described by neither of these attributes. Goods in this subset are non-partitionable, embodying both non-excludability and non-rivalry.

Using these stylized models, Samuelson was able to lay out the necessary conditions for allocative efficiency or optimality. The follow-on normative corollary was that the idealized competitive market could be expected to satisfy these necessary conditions for partitionable goods, but that the market fails for non-partitionable, or 'public,' goods. The incentive structure is such that persons will not invest in the provision of goods in this subset despite the potential value surplus.

In public finance, the conflict here between individual and collective interest was summarized under the 'free rider' rubric, but economists more generally came increasingly to recognize that the setting becomes widely descriptive over many areas of social interaction. Interestingly enough, the predicted failure of markets in the presence of non-partitionable goods did not lead to exhaustive analyses of the institutional consequences. Samuelson's contribution was seen as a part of the corpus of theoretical welfare economics, from which exhibition of market failure led more or less directly to the inference that political or collective correction was indicated. Little or no attention was given to prospects for incentive incompatibility in politics. The public choice research program remained to be developed.

What does emerge in the absence of stylized collective correction for market failure in the public goods setting? The default option need not be some total absence of investment in efforts to capture the potential value surplus. Rents are there and these prospects attract investment. But because of the non-partitionability of the goods, as defined, these efforts may involve the construction of artificial barriers to access aimed at some concentration of rents to members of coalitions. The activities of rent-seeking coalitions directed at capture of differentially higher benefits for members may impose spillover damages on those outside the relevant coalitions. In net, the institutions that emerge may be utility-reducing rather than utility-enhancing. And there may be no market-like adjustment that will insure movement toward, rather than away from, the utility frontier.

A whole research program seems to have been largely overlooked. The welfare economists of mid-century were apparently satisfied with market failure demonstrations while, at the same time or shortly thereafter, the Chicago price theorists who extended the rational choice models neglected the empirical reality and relevance of the Samuelson taxonomy. The economists who developed the efficient markets-rational expectations stylizations provided the basis for the generalized thesis that 'markets work.' The research program was developed under the implicit 'as if' presumption that all valued goods are partitionable.

A critical mistake was made, perhaps unconsciously, when the 'markets work' mindset was extended to apply to the institutions or rules within which exchanges in goods take place, including new institutions that may be invented. Several contributors who worked in the intersections of economics, politics, and law, myself included, recognized and called attention to the applicability of the Samuelson taxonomy to law, or, more generally, to the framework institutions that constrain market behavior. We did not, however, develop the implications of this classificatory understanding for the normative evaluation of either the institutions in existence or possible alternatives. We were, indeed, remiss in our oversight of this important next step.

By inference, we summarize a half-century by asking the question: Where were the market failure welfare economists when we needed them? Did they, too, along with the Chicago rational-choice modelers, fail to recognize that the institutions of the market, rather than the market itself, may be inefficient, by standard criteria, hence allowing for the generation of 'public bads' rather than 'public goods'?

3. EFFICIENCY, EVOLUTION, AND EXISTENCE

The oversight discussed above may have been reinforced by an accompanying transference of a mindset from biology. The theory of evolution may have been introduced, implicitly or explicitly, into the normative evaluation of the economic, legal, and political institutions that define the 'playing field' within which transactions between and among persons and organizations take place.

An institution (or rule), convention, or practice that is observed to be in existence is, often by its very existence, as such, given a normative 'pass.' The fact of existence itself creates a bias or prejudice. That which 'is' becomes 'efficient,' or, minimally, the burden of proof rests on the alternative to be examined.

My point of emphasis is that the observed existence and survival of the components of the institutional framework within which simple and complex exchanges are made cannot legitimately be defended on efficiency arguments. There is no presumption that what is is efficient when the criterion is, itself, defined as survival. The institutions of a status quo may be privileged in comparisons with alternative arrangements by invoking transitional costs of change. But this possibly valid conservative bias is quite different from any implicit claim that existence and survival, as such, pass muster on standard efficiency norms.

4. THE WORKING OF THE MARKET: FAILURE OR SUCCESS

Fully two generations after the dominance of the market failure theses of welfare economics, the normative thrust was reversed in what is often referred to as 'Chicago School Thinking' – the attitude, again often implicit, that markets work, anywhere and everywhere, and despite the stylized models that suggest the opposite. To my knowledge, there have been few attempts at reconciliation of these conflicting visions of the economy. Market failure analysts shifted their attention to informational asymmetries rather than any continued emphasis on the relevance of the Samuelson taxonomy. And normative policy arguments were concentrated on emergent end-states rather than on the rules and institutions that generated such results. The 'market works' analysts continued to ignore empirical reality that should have identified rules as necessarily exemplars of Samuelsonion publicness.

Elementary logic forces a recognition that the normative defense of the market order is overextended when applied to the rules or constraints of this order. And this principle holds regardless of the success or failure of markets in partitionable goods and services in meeting independently defined criteria for efficiency. Such recognition requires an acknowledgment that the rules that are observed to exist, 'the constitution,' carry no efficiency loaded normative weight. These institutions may or may not be efficient or optimal in some Pareto sense. Any effective reform in market processes must commence with efforts to analyze the predicted working of these institutions and possible alternatives. Constitutional political economy, as a research program, must command center stage.

5. THE CRISES OF 2007–09

The crises in financial structures that occurred in 2007–09 offer an opportunity to apply the discussion sketched out above. I identified two critical mistakes or oversights that were influential in creating an intellectual-scientific mindset that fostered the 'markets work' attitude. But why were the institutional changes allowed to develop without more discussion of the possible incompatibility with widely shared objectives? Return to the Samuelson taxonomy and its implications. Why does the market fail in the presence of valued goods that are non-partitionable? There is the value surplus that beckons, but this surplus cannot be captured successfully by rent-seeking arbitrageurs because of the necessary commonality among users. By definition, differentially valued shares cannot here be 'sold' to users. Instead, all potential users are locked in, so to speak, to whatever quantity of goods becomes available.

Apply this basic logic to the empirical reality of the modern economy. Participants do not, indeed cannot, have access to differing financial-monetary structures, that qualify as public or collective use goods in the full Samuelson sense. Units of money, as designated and accepted, are, of course, partitionable among holders-users. (I cannot claim possession of the bill in your wallet.) But the institutional framework that defines the parameters within which holders-users organize transactions, these can only be analyzed in a model embodying 'publicness.' Acknowledgment of this elementary understanding implies that there can be no presumption that any of these relevant institutions can be assigned a positive normative weight because they may have been generated in some market-like process independent of explicit collective action.

The crises of the early years of the century demonstrate that economists have been woefully negligent in their failure to examine, at various levels of abstraction, the institutional structures predicted to emerge in settings that cannot accommodate the activity of potential arbitrageurs, at least to any full extent – activity that is analogous to that which promotes 'the invisible hand' in markets for partitionable goods. The presence of the potential surplus value from institutional order will, predictably, attract investment by rent-seekers. But the structures that emerge will be designed in the interests of members of particular coalitions, with possible spillover damages to nonmembers, who remain within the economic nexus. The omnipresent free-rider barrier prevents representation of the inclusive, or general, interest in the absence of explicit collective action. The folly of overextending the 'market works' attitude to anything that emerges in the institutional setting is amply demonstrated by the observed events of the crises.

6. SUMMATION

There are no extensions of the rational actor models that establish grounds for a presupposition that existing rules (institutions) meet standard criteria for efficiency in the generation of economic value. And the facts of existence, as such, offer no independent criterion for prejudiced normative judgment. Critical analyses must commence without presuppositions concerning the comparative performance of alternative sets of rules. As attention is shifted from end-states to process, political economists must avoid the false trails suggested by the extended models of rational choice as well as any simplistic application of evolutionary arguments. Both incentive compatibility and historical evidence may, of course, be used in the unbiased evaluation of alternative structures.

Finally, however, the economist must confront the task of evaluation head on. We did not get to where we are through institutional arbitrageurs whose actions worked as if guided by an invisible hand. The institutions that we observe were generated, at least in part, by the rent-seeking behavior of those persons and organizations whose interests were limited to the opportunities presented. Any Panglossian presupposition that existing structural rules are somehow 'best,' can only be defended by reckoning on the costs of transition. The public nature of rules insures that individuals, in their totality of actions, do not act as an inclusive body politic. Nor are rent-seeking coalitions necessarily contestable to the extent required to allow simple acquiescence and acceptance of the rules that happen to exist.

REFERENCE

Samuelson, Paul (1954), 'The pure theory of public expenditure', *Review of Economics and Statistics*, **36** (November), 387–9.

2. Buchanan, Hobbes and contractarianism: the supply of rules?

Geoffrey Brennan and Giuseppe Eusepi

1.

José Casas Pardo has been for many years Spain's most distinguished scholar in the 'constitutional political economy' tradition and in that sense the most faithful Spanish disciple of American Nobel Laureate James Buchanan. Accordingly, it has seemed to us that, in seeking to honour our Spanish colleague, it would be appropriate to revisit two of the Buchanan classics in the field – *The Calculus of Consent* and *The Limits of Liberty*. The former is now hovering on its fiftieth anniversary, the latter well beyond its thirtieth, while Buchanan himself celebrates his ninetieth birthday this year.

The particular aspect of the two works on which we seek to focus is the change in Buchanan's perception of the 'constitutional political economy' project between the two works, occurring over the space of a dozen or so years. We are inclined to think that there is a quite deep shift in Buchanan's views about what the CPE project entails. In what follows, we shall attempt to track that shift, lay open its central features via documentary evidence, and offer some remarks on its significance. Although we do not advance a 'two-Buchanans' thesis of quite the kind that has figured in Smith scholarship over differences between *The Wealth of Nations* and Smith's earlier *Theory of Moral Sentiments*, we do think that there are very major differences between the approaches taken in Buchanan's two major books, amounting to something like a major discontinuity on several major points.

However, this discontinuity claim is not entirely uncontentious. Specifically, the impression one gets from reading the first chapter of *The Limits of Liberty* is that Buchanan (at that point) saw his second book as essentially a development of principles outlined in *The Calculus*, as if the two works were part of a more or less seamless web of analysis. Specifically:

> . . . The approach taken in *The Calculus of Consent* might be described as the extension of the 'theory of public goods', interpreted in a Wicksellian setting, to political structures and to the formation of political decision rules. In similar usage, the approach taken in this book [*The Limits of Liberty*] might be described as an 'extension of the "theory of public bads"' to explain apparent failure in political and institutional structure. In this respect, I hope that this book will be complementary to the earlier one. In a broad sense, both are contractarian. In *The Calculus of Consent*, existing and potential institutions were conceptually explored as having emerged from contractual arguments among participating and rational individuals. In this book, by contrast, existing and potential institutions, as well as behaviour with certain institutional constraints, are explained in terms of the failure of potentially viable contractual agreements to be made or, if made, to be respected and/or enforced. Political-legal order is a public good; disorder is a public bad. There are two sides to the coin.

True, Buchanan goes on to note the differences between this book and the earlier work – specifically, differences of emphasis that relate to the different focus of attention in each case. There must, in the 'public bads' version, be explicit analysis of 'the working properties of anarchy in an organizational system', and more attention given to '. . . the initial assignment of rights'; and there can no longer be '. . . neglect [of] the problems that arise in controlling the self-perpetuating and self-enhancing aims of the collectivity itself'. But there is little sense in Buchanan's remarks here that these differences amount to much. The impression is rather that *The Limits of Liberty* represents merely a more detailed working out of aspects of constitutional analysis that in *The Calculus* were set on one side.

We are inclined to think that there is considerably more at stake. In part, our authority for thinking this derives from Buchanan's own interpretation of the 'constitutional project' as set out in his Appendix to *The Calculus*. We take it that that Appendix ('Marginal notes on reading political philosophy') is an accurate reflection of Buchanan's interpretation as at 1962. And his strategy in this Appendix of lodging his assessment of *The Calculus* enterprise within the broad tradition of political theory provides reference points against which later developments in his own thinking can be set.

The point of departure for our own exercise is, then, to juxtapose the central elements (as we identify them) in this Appendix to *The Calculus* with what we take to be key passages from *The Limits of Liberty*. This occupies Section 2 of the chapter. In Section 3, we focus on one apparently major aspect – namely, Buchanan's attitude to Thomas Hobbes – which seems to shift quite radically between 1962 and 1976. We go on, in Section 4, to underline what we see as the analytic and conceptual significance of the changes we identify. Section 5 offers a brief conclusion.

Two final preliminary remarks. First, it is well known from autobiographical accounts that Buchanan's own attitudes underwent a significant shift over the relevant period. The natural 'optimism' that pervades the contractarian evaluation of collective decision procedures in *The Calculus* gives way to a deep anxiety about the potential fragility of political order, as a result of the 'decade of the sixties' and the anti-Vietnam movement. The anarchic face of those developments was perhaps more notable within the university than elsewhere – and perhaps more so in Los Angeles than in Blacksburg, Virginia. In any event, *The Limits of Liberty* was clearly written under the shadow of these influences. By 1975, Buchanan sees *The Calculus* as embodying an excessively 'optimistic ontology' with which he has 'come to be increasingly disturbed'. For present purposes, this shift in mood is not of particular interest in itself; but it *is* interesting in terms of the analytical presuppositions and implications to which it gives rise. Only by going back to the express claims – and disclaimers – of the 1962 self-interpretation can we identify what the retreat from optimism amounts to. And that is our interest here.

Second, it is worth emphasizing that the issues are of some importance. The 'constitutional political economy' project has come to occupy an increasingly significant place not only in economics but also in political science and political philosophy. Much of this growth reflects the major intellectual influence of Buchanan. Just what the project *is*, how broadly its scope extends, and how it connects with apparently related enterprises in traditional political theory are all important matters. Tracing Buchanan's own views on such questions by means of a little exegesis seems to us to be a worthwhile exercise – and not least if those views have themselves been subject to significant and only partly acknowledged changes.[1]

2.

In his Appendix to *The Calculus*, Buchanan attempts to appraise the exercise that he and Tullock have just completed, by setting it within a broader frame of political theory.[2] In doing so, he makes two distinctions that he considers relevant in placing his own work (and in distancing that work from most other, more conventional, political theory). These two distinctions are:

(i) that between a theory of political obligation and a normative theory of political organization; and
(ii) that between a 'marginal' and a 'total' theory of political institutions.

Both these distinctions are, in different ways, relevant to the shift that occurs when Buchanan comes to write *The Limits of Liberty*, and it will be necessary to attempt to amplify them a little. Before doing so, however, we should be clear as to where Buchanan locates *The Calculus* in this typology: as he sees it, *The Calculus* is a normative theory of political organization, not a theory of political obligation; and it is a *marginal* not a total theory. That categorization needs to be borne in mind in the ensuing discussion.

As it happens, we think the first of these distinctions is somewhat unclear in Buchanan's presentation. We want to say something briefly about the ambiguities; but we should emphasize that this aspect is not especially important in the shift between the *Calculus* and the *Limits*. What is important in that connection is the marginal/total distinction, to which we shall shortly turn.

The distinction between political obligation and a (normative) theory of political organization is initially set out as a distinction between personal morality and the 'normative aspect of political theory, quite apart from morals'.[3] The normative question in the latter connection is: What ought the State to be? The analogous question in a theory of political obligation is: how should the individual act? – with the individual in question conceived either as 'ruler' or as 'subject-citizen'.

If the State is organized as a single ruler, the ultimate location of sovereign power, the only questions of relevance, Buchanan claims, are ones of personal morality – either the ruler's, in deciding what policies to put in place; or the citizen's, in deciding whether to obey the ruler's dictates. In such a setting, 'any "improvement" or "reform" can only come through some change in the behaviour of individuals'. Under this conception of political order, 'it becomes impossible to separate politics from morals'.[4]

Things are different, however, once we move 'away from absolutism and toward democracy'. Here, a

> genuine 'science of politics' can be developed that is almost wholly independent of moral philosophy. This 'social science' can include both positive and normative elements, but the variables with which it deals are social institutions, rules of the political game, not human motives. In so far as this science becomes normative, ethical questions must remain, but these do not pertain to precepts for ordering individual behaviour in acceding to or participating in collective decision-making . . .

The political scientist may try, as best he can, to develop the normative implications of a set of ethical standards, but whatever those standards, 'he must take men as they are, not as he would like them to be'.[5] And in taking men as they are, the analysis adopts the *Homo economicus* (rational, egoist) assumption – essentially to 'serve an empirical function'.

There are, in fact, several puzzles in this formulation. It seems to us that the central distinction at stake here is between normative questions relating to 'in-period politics' and normative questions arising when the domain of evaluation is the rules of the political game. That distinction, at least, is the one that the CPE tradition has taken to be crucial, and we are following the tradition in this regard. But if this is so, then distinctions between personal morality and normative considerations of other kinds – and between democratic and non-democratic institutional forms in this regard – are red herrings. So is the requirement that the analyst '. . . must take men as they are'. Indeed, these elements merely run the risk of muddying the waters. Consider the 'personal morality' aspect first. Note that within the individualist method that the analysis assumes, '. . . all theorizing, all analysis, is resolved finally into considerations faced by the individual person as decision-maker'.[6] Normative theorizing presupposes an audience of some kind, and if the theorizing is to have any effect, that effect must be brought about through a change in the behaviour of *some* agent or agents. Ultimately, normative reasoning collapses to 'personal morality'. This is not to question the perfectly valid distinction to be drawn between various kinds of 'personally moral' questions: Should I or should I not comply with this law? How should I vote, at the in-period level? How should I vote on proposals to change political institutions? Buchanan is surely correct to distinguish the latter two questions sharply. But it is a mistake to think that the one is a matter of 'personal morality' and the latter not.

Moreover, we think it a mistake to think that the relevant distinction is not also present for the single ruler. The single ruler may decide on policy issues at the in-period level, or may decide on institutional arrangements of various kinds. It seems likely that the incentives of the individual agent as citizen in a broadly democratic polity would differ from those of the individual agent as ruler. But it should not be assumed that constitutional rules are of no interest in the despotic setting – that it would never be attractive to the ruler to seek to limit his own discretion. Of course, the ruler may not be able to limit his own discretion. he may not be able to make credible commitments. But if that is the case, such considerations will be no less a problem for the democratic citizen. These are, of course, matters that the more Hobbesian style of analysis in the *Limits of Liberty* brings into sharp relief. At this point, we simply note that 'constitutional' reasoning, as distinct from 'in-period' reasoning, is no less accessible to the single ruler than to the democratic citizen. A concern to distance himself from issues of 'personal morality' causes Buchanan to downplay the possible relevance of 'constitutional choice' in the despot context.

Further, Buchanan must also be wrong to insist that we must '. . . *take men as they are*', unless that is understood to incorporate a capacity in '*men as they are*' to respond to the normative theorizing about alternative political institutions that the *Calculus* offers – something that the strict *Homo economicus* construction as such denies. If that modification is made, however, may there not be consequent behavioural changes at the level of in-period politics? Are there, in other words, feedback loops that will require some modification to the positive analysis of alternative institutional forms, of the kind *The Calculus* develops? In fact, these are issues that the approach taken in *The Limits of Liberty* brings to central stage.

In any event, as the CPE tradition has come to recognize, the critical distinction at stake in Buchanan's framework is that between 'in-period' and 'constitutional' decision-making – between choices exercised within a set of rules and choices exercised over alternative rules. But whether 'in-period' choices concern 'political obligations' or invoke issues of 'personal morality', and whether they are exercised 'democratically' or by a single despot, are side issues. The *level* distinction applies, and it is that level distinction that is characteristic of *The Calculus* method and the ongoing CPE tradition. Certainly, there is no significant change between *The Calculus* and *The Limits of Liberty* in this respect. The later book includes a wider range of institutional options[7] – but the 'constitutional orientation' remains.

The chief difference between *The Calculus* and *The Limits* surrounds the second of the distinctions Buchanan offers in his Appendix – that between 'total' and 'marginal' explanation/evaluation. In drawing this distinction, Buchanan seems to reject totally the 'total' approach. 'Both the contractarians and their critics', he observes, 'have been too much concerned with the origins of government. . . . The relevance of the contract theory must lie, however, not in its explanation of the origins of government . . . The origin of civil government and the major influences in its development may be almost wholly non-rational . . .' (*The Calculus*, p. 319). Discussion must rather be concentrated on the 'margins' of variation in political institutions, not on the 'totality' of such institutions, and the relevant question becomes one of the criteria through which the several marginal adjustments may be arrayed.[8] In short, then, Buchanan conceives the central task in *The Calculus* as being the 'contractarian' evaluation of alternatives all of which differ only 'marginally' from the prevailing set of arrangements, and hence can be construed as falling under the rubric of 'existing institutions'. The deliberate modesty of this task enables Buchanan to finesse a range of questions which would have to be engaged in a more 'total' enquiry. In particular, there need be no consideration of the 'feasibility' of alternative institutional structures. The analyst can examine the working properties of alternative institutional arrangements within the broad category of 'marginal adjustments' without having to engage with the question of whether rule-governed social life is itself feasible, and if so, on what terms. The origins of social order – both temporal and logical – are not issues on the table. Whatever processes – whether obedient to the logical structure of rational agency or not – generated the institutional *status quo* can be presumed to remain applicable, provided the changes in institutional arrangements are 'marginal'. Put another way, the choice among institutional arrangements can be conceived as the prevailing meta-rule. A more 'total' analysis would include the possibility of choices without rules – which could be thought of as the point of departure for *The Limits of Liberty*. And this more 'total' treatment would have to contend quite explicitly with the possibility that no rules at all are feasible – or at least that no explanation of the possibility of rules being feasible is available within the analytic repertoire that CPE offers. In fact, we would be led back to matters of 'political obligation' which, at least in 1962, Buchanan takes explicitly *not* to be part of the CPE program.

However, for the purposes envisaged in *The Calculus*, the observation that we are already actually operating within an existing regime of broadly democratic rules, and under a formal Constitution that admits, both in theory and practice, the possibility of amendment, is itself sufficient to legitimize the exercise. Perhaps the prevailing set of rules is the only set that is feasible. If so, this fact would perhaps make even the modest exercise of 'marginal perfection' envisaged in *The Calculus* infeasible or in the terms of the analysis in *The Limits of Liberty* even attempts at 'marginal' reform might threaten to plunge the social order into either anarchic chaos or Hobbesian despotism. However, there does not seem to be much evidence to support such a radically conservative claim. *Some* tinkering along contractarian lines seems likely to be feasible: to assert the contrary would stretch credulity. Just how extensive such tinkering can be must be an open question. Yet, as we see it, feasible and infeasible change sets precisely the boundary between 'marginal' and 'total' explanation/evaluation – and analogously, the boundary between the domain of enquiry engaged in *The Calculus*, and that engaged in *The Limits*. What is striking is that, in *The Calculus*, Buchanan explicitly repudiates the application of the CPE program to 'total' explanation/evaluation – whereas in *The Limits of Liberty* he seems to embrace that application no less explicitly.

Consider, for example, Buchanan's final chapter in *The Limits*, provocatively (and instructively) entitled 'Beyond pragmatism'. Here, Buchanan's radical purpose is laid out clearly.

> The time has come to move beyond . . . the pragmatism that has characterised the American mind-set on social policy reforms . . . and to make an attempt at reconstruction of the basic constitutional order itself. My analysis suggests that there are structural flaws in the socio-political system which can scarcely be remedied by superficial tampering [!] . . . I am convinced that the social interrelationships that emerge from continued pragmatic and incremental situational response, informed by no philosophical precepts, is neither sustainable nor worthy of man's best efforts. (p. 167)

Buchanan also makes a direct comparison of John Rawls and *The Calculus*:

> My efforts in this book are simultaneously more and less ambitious than those of John Rawls, or some of my own earlier works . . . Rawls does not discuss the critically important bridge between such an idealised setting and that within which any discussion of basic structural rearrangement might, in fact, take place . . . In this respect, my approach is more ambitious . . . [and] it is for this reason that the return to the conceptual emergence of contract from Hobbesian anarchy has been necessary to develop my argument. (p. 176)

The sense in which Buchanan's project is *less* ambitious than Rawls's (though not than that in *The Calculus*) lies in the absence of any specification of where the trade-off between 'liberty' and 'order' should be set. He attempts no specification that might be 'debated in the pragmatically oriented arena of day-to-day politics' (p. 176). In *The Limits*, Buchanan quite explicitly embraces a 'revolutionary' project – and for this, he requires a more ambitious, a more 'total' analytic scope. It simply needs to be acknowledged that this is a level of ambition that in *The Calculus* he quite explicitly repudiates.

3.

One of the most notable contrasts between the Buchanan of *The Calculus* Appendix and the Buchanan of *The Limits of Liberty* resides in the changed attitude to the work of Thomas Hobbes. In *The Calculus* Appendix, Buchanan acknowledges that the *Homo economicus* behavioural assumption and the general spirit of the analysis connect poorly with the 'so called idealist theory-philosophy of political order', and more naturally with the '. . . "realists" in the history of political doctrines' (p. 312). In this context, Buchanan mentions Glaucon in Plato's Republic, Thomas Hobbes and Benedict Spinoza. But of these '. . . only Spinoza's work seems to have much in common with our approach and only his seems deserving of special comment' (p. 312). Indeed,

> . . . although Spinoza is often described as a follower of Hobbes, we do not find Hobbes' work at all similar to Spinoza's in relation to our own construction. The contractual apparatus, to Hobbes, becomes an excuse or a justification for political obedience of the individual and little more. Hobbes' construction is aimed at establishing a basis for political obligation whereas Spinoza's construction becomes a genuine theory of political order that, more than most others, is largely divorced from all issues of obligation. (p. 313)

It is not central to our argument whether Buchanan's interpretation of Spinoza is valid. All we need to observe is that in *The Limits of Liberty* Spinoza receives only one reference in passing in the entire book, whereas Hobbes receives a round dozen, as many in the text as Frank Knight and Knut Wicksell combined.[9] Not surprisingly – for a central element in *The Limits* project is Hobbesian in character. Although Buchanan makes no attempt at textual exegesis, there is a sense in which *The Limits* is a kind of rationalist reconstruction of Hobbesian analysis. That is, *The Limits* accepts the Hobbesian starting-point – an anarchy that is nasty, brutish and short – and uses what seems like the Hobbesian account of agent motivation. Yet Buchanan appears to derive from his analysis, possibilities that Hobbes believed infeasible. For Hobbes, there was no space between anarchy and Leviathan – no logically possible continuum of possible trade-offs between those logical extremes over which subject-citizens might conceptually choose (whether unanimously or not). In short, Buchanan puts into his basic analytic model all the Hobbesian inputs – but manages to extract non-Hobbesian outputs. Or at least he implies that non-Hobbesian outcomes *might* be available. He freely acknowledges that '. . . after examination and analysis . . .' there may be '. . . no such potential for change,. . . despite the possible presence of discontent among specific numbers of the body politic', but this is because of failure to meet the normative test – because agreement cannot be secured – rather than because the option set turns out to be empty.

In this connection, it is instructive to note the quotation from Frank Knight that stands as the epigraph to the whole book:

> And the main, most serious problem of social order and progress is . . . the problem of having the rules obeyed, or preventing cheating. As far as I can see there is no intellectual solution of that problem. No social machinery of 'sanctions' will keep the game from breaking up in a quarrel. Or a fight (the game of being a society can rarely just dissolve!) unless the participants have an irrational preference to having it go on even when they seem individually to get the worst of it. Or else the society must be maintained by force, from without – for a dictator is not a member of the society he rules – and then it is questionable whether it can be called a society in the moral sense. (*The Limits*, p. vi)

Buchanan's decision to include this quotation as the point of departure for *The Limits* raises the obvious question as to what Buchanan perceives *The Limits* to be doing. Does he see the analysis as endorsing Knight's claim – that there *is* no intellectual solution to the puzzle of social order? That unless there is some element of irrationality, nothing between anarchy and Leviathan is possible? If so, what is the obvious normative conclusion? Presumably, one might think, that if we find ourselves, by luck or by dint of some mysterious process inaccessible to the economistic method, landed in some hinterland between anarchy and Leviathan, we should simply thank our lucky stars and not rock the boat too much. 'Marginal adjustment' in our institutional arrangements might be possible via constructivist endeavour – but, though 'life in the here and now may be more brutish . . . and certainly more nasty' (*The Limits*, p. 169) than we might prefer, hope for something significantly better via total analytical reconstruction of our political institutions is an idealist's delusion. In short, if we take the Knight quotation and its conspicuous location in *The Limits* at face value, does not the logic propel us back to the explanatory and reformist modesty of *The Calculus*?

Central in answering these questions is, of course, an appraisal of the success of *The Limits of Liberty* as an intellectual enterprise. If Buchanan's analysis there succeeds in showing that some institutional order 'between anarchy and Leviathan' is capable of being secured and enduring, and that indeed there is a more or less complete set of options over this range that citizens may profitably consider and ultimately choose among, then this would not only be a major intellectual accomplishment (against both Hobbes and Knight) but it would also put paid to the more timorous stance of *The Calculus* Appendix. But perhaps this is to mistake Buchanan's enterprise in *The Limits*. Perhaps the intention is to expose the magnetic force of the two Hobbesian extremes, to underline the fragility of tolerable constitutional order – not just to a declining sense of 'political obligation' but also to an individualist rationalist analysis. In that case, the rhetoric of the final chapter may be misplaced; but the essential caution of *The Calculus* Appendix would be vindicated.

4.

Constitutional political economy, it may be said, concerns the demand for, and supply of 'rules' – where rules are understood as the institutional framework within which ordinary choice behaviour proceeds. Ordinary choice takes place within some institutional setting – say within a market structure with more or less well-defined property rights and arrangements for exchange, or in a political setting with a particular set of arrangements concerning elections and the particular powers assigned to electorally successful practice or candidates. Much of what passes for 'constitutional analysis' involves working out the equilibrium that emerges from the interactions of rational individuals within such an institutional setting – and then comparing the equilibria for the variety of institutional settings as an input into a meta-level institutional choice. The simplest and most familiar such exercise in economics is the comparison of competitive and monopoly markets; but over the last forty years or so, 'public choice' scholarship has extended the range of such comparisons widely – so as to include in particular comparisons of market provision with democratic political provision under a variety of specifications.

The comparative evaluation of alternative possible institutions within the CPE scheme is typically normative in character, with the evaluative norm in question being broadly contractarian in a style reflecting Buchanan's influence. Individuals are conceptualized as making a choice from within the set of institutions or possible 'rules', under 'veil of ignorance' conditions that serve to detach each individual from his own location in the prevailing social order and serve to obliterate any disagreements on the basis of rival interests. In these conditions, what is best for each is best for all. Wicksellian (virtual) unanimity can be expected to form around a single preferred institutional order, a single 'best' set of rules for the socio-politico-economic game that is to ensue. All this is totally familiar. And the Buchanan-Tullock exercise in *The Calculus* of comparing in-period collective decision-making procedures under varying decision-rules (from simple majority up to total unanimity) exemplifies it perfectly. Within this general setting, there are no boundaries set on the variety of institutional arrangements envisaged, except those imposed by the limits of the analyst's imagination. *Within* any particular set of rules, the equilibrium outcome that attaches to that set is worked out under the assumption of *Homo economicus* motivations on the part of all relevant actors; but the rules themselves are taken as given and exogenous to that exercise. The issue of the feasibility of rules as such – the question as to why any agent would rationally abide by the rules of the game in any particular case – is simply assumed away. In *The Calculus* Appendix, that issue is essentially assigned to the 'too hard' basket. As in the Knight quotation at the beginning of *The Limits*, it is taken that there is '. . . *no intellectual solution of that problem*' – not, at least, unless we seek to invoke some form of '. . . *irrational preference*' on the part of relevant agents. But *The Limits of Liberty* takes up the challenge here, recognizing (as we think one ultimately must) that *some* effort at explaining the demand and supply of rules at a more basic level is necessary.

On the 'demand' side of this agenda, Hobbes provides an obvious starting point – though a slightly treacherous one, since the coherence of Hobbes's own account has long been a matter of contention. Conceptualizing the state of nature, with all the nasty Hobbesian attributes, as the outcome of an n-person prisoner's dilemma as Buchanan does, it is self-evident that everyone stands to gain from a 'rule' of no predation. Put another way, it is an axiomatic feature of the prisoner's dilemma structure that all would be better off if all co-operated. And we might loosely describe that fact as constituting a *prima facie* case for appropriate 'rules'. But the 'rules' terminology here is loose, unless it can be established that there exists some feasible institutional arrangement that will actually deliver the co-operative outcome. Unless there is some prospect of a *supply* of rules (understood as arrangements that agents will actually follow in sufficient numbers to make the rule-governed outcome a tolerable approximation to the actual outcome), the *demand* for rules is just wishful thinking, along the lines of the pauper's 'demand' for a castle, or (more to the point, perhaps) the public economist's 'demand' for a benevolent despot. Even Hobbes's own 'solution' to the n-person prisoner's dilemma (if that is how we are to conceive the problem) seems precarious here. Players might appoint some agent to enforce co-operative behaviour, but how is that enforcement power constructed? If agents in general follow the enforcer's dictates, then it may well be rational for each to follow those dictates: the enforcer will have the advantage of numbers. But why *should* agents in general follow the enforcer's dictates? To assume that they will is to assume what needs to be proven – namely, that 'co-operation' (whether under an enforcer or not) among at least some is rational. Long before we get to the question of the enforcer's incentives – a question that has long concerned political philosophers (and long before Hobbes) and a question that naturally arises within the agenda of CPE more narrowly construed – there is the logically prior question of how power is *possible* in the Hobbesian scheme. Or at least there is the question as to how power is possible in the Hobbesian scheme as modelled in *The Limits*, in which the prisoner's dilemma is the essential modelling tool. Other political theorists using game theoretic categories (Hardin, 1995 and Hampton, 1997, for example), have been inclined to insist that the proper model for Hobbesian analysis is the 'battle' of the sexes or some similar multiple equilibrium coordination game. As far as we can see, however, this formulation simply fails to engage the question that Buchanan (and Hobbes perhaps) are posing. Either Buchanan is posing a deeper problem than Hobbes, or there is a conflict here about Hobbesian interpretation, or both. In short, it is the issue of whether rules are *feasible* – the issue of the *supply* of rules – that needs to be engaged. And whether there are many rulers or only one (as in the Hobbesian case) does not seem to solve the issue – or even bear on it in any direct way.[10] Note the implication of this last remark. Buchanan seems to more or less accept the Hobbesian dichotomy between anarchy and Leviathan. These become the two logical end-points between which the relevant trade-off between liberty and order is to be set. And each is conceptualized not just as a notional benchmark, but as a kind of rational attractor, a source of magnetic force, to which any institutional order is logically driven. But if, as we have suggested, Hobbes's own solution to the 'Hobbesian problem', as Buchanan identifies it, is problematic (or radically incomplete), then it may well be that there is, within the Buchanan scheme properly understood, only one magnetic attractor, only one polar case – that of anarchy.

Let us, however, set that issue aside, and suppose – for the sake of argument – that the Hobbesian-Buchanan polarity is appropriate. That is, we take it that there *is* one institutional order that will be a possible solution to the n-person prisoner's dilemma. This is the single dictator solution. The question then arises as to how any other institutional order is feasible. How can Buchanan find some logically coherent space between anarchy and Leviathan in which a liberal constitutional order can take a stand? Buchanan's own answer seems to involve a combination of ethics and habit:

> There are countless activities that require persons to adhere to fundamental rules for mutual tolerance, activities that may be observed to go on apace day by day and without formal rules . . . There does exist a sense of ordinary respect for his fellow man in the ingrained habit pattern of the average American . . . Whether this reflects a heritage of Christian or Kantian ethics that were once explicitly taught or whether such habit patterns are over more basic to the human psyche, their existence cannot be denied. (p. 5)

> . . . The reconciliation of individuals' desires to 'do their own things' with the fact that they live together in society is accomplished largely by mutual agreement on spheres of allowable or tolerated activity . . . The act of manners, the customary modes for personal behaviour . . . reflects the mutual acceptance of [such] limits. (p. 20)

> . . . To the extent that ethical precepts are widely shared, and influence individual behaviour, there is less need for the more formal restrictiveness of legally imposed standards. (*The Limits*, p. 117)

Equally, however, there will also be less anxiety over the question of the coercive powers held by the agents of the state. Buchanan's claim that ethics and law are substitutes seems to overlook that dimension of the relation between ethics and legal institutions.[11]

> At any point in time, behaviour that may be observed in a community reflects individual utility maximisation, and the pattern of behaviour is reinforced by the arguments in the preference functions of participants, along with the internal and subjective trade-offs among those arguments, and by the formally imposed legal constraints on behaviour that participants confront, constraints that are nominally embodied in formal rules accompanied by enforcement instruments and by constraints imposed by custom and tradition which, although non-formalised, remain external to the individual and carry their own enforcement processes. (*The Limits*, p. 118)

Here, then, is the 'supply of rules' issue squarely faced.

> The individual who restricts his own behaviour voluntarily, who limits his own freedom of choice because of built-in ethical standards, who acts in accordance with something like a Kantian generalisation principle, is continually confronted with a dilemma of sorts. His narrowly defined self-interest may dictate departures from that pattern of behaviour required by adherence to his ethical-moral standards. So long as a significantly large proportion of the community's total membership abides by the same standards, the temptation placed on any individual, although always present, may not be sufficiently great to cause him to modify his cooperative behaviour. However, if . . . a critically large minority of persons are observed to violate ethical precept,. . . the standards may erode rapidly as more and more individuals revert to narrowly defined self-interest. (*The Limits*, p. 118–19)

In fact, the stated objective in *The Limits* is '. . . to offer procedural diagnosis' – to underline both the fragility of liberal order and the limits of collective action to compensate for the 'erosion of the . . . unenforced rules . . . on which society depends' (p. 14). Such procedural diagnosis is, as Buchanan rightly claims, 'required before we can begin to answer the larger questions' (p. 15). But, as it stands, the procedural diagnosis seems to offer little more than Buchanan (in the *Calculus* Appendix) accuses Hobbes of offering – namely, '. . . a justification for a political "personal morality"' which the Buchanan of *The Calculus* considered does 'not belong properly in political theory' (*The Calculus*, p. 310).

In terms of the *economic* theory of rules, however, there is an obvious further question to be posed. Namely, to what extent do different 'institutional structures' affect the trade-off between the requirements of ethics and self-interest? To what extent do different arrangements increase the incentives for particular players to break the rules, under any given rule regime? Buchanan addresses one aspect of this question when he investigates the effect of changes in the underlying 'natural distribution': those who stand to lose least by actions that threaten to return the social order to Hobbesian anarchy are those who may have to be 'bought off'. But it is doubtful whether any individual rule-breaker weighs the individual (expected) costs of anarchy very heavily in her calculations. Much more relevant are the individual gains she stands to make if she alone breaks the rules.

For example, when individual taxpayers decide whether or not to comply with the tax law, they rationally look to the tax-savings they stand to make rather than to the foregone value of the public goods that the taxes finance. The logic of the free-rider incentive makes it clear that the self-interest of each taxpayer is almost totally divorced from the public goods increment his particular tax contribution pays for. Much more relevant in taxpayer calculus are his ethical precepts about the legitimacy of his paying taxes, his subjective estimates of the likelihood of being caught, and the costs he endures if he is caught.

The tax example is instructive here, because it can be used to illustrate the distinction between 'marginal' and 'total' analysis as Buchanan's *Calculus* Appendix seems to pose it. One analytic exercise would be to examine alternative tax rules or regimes on the assumption that each individual, while exploiting all opportunities for tax minimization within the rules, will nevertheless obey the rules themselves. Evaluation of those alternative tax regimes might follow a broadly contractarian line, asking which regime rational citizens would choose (from behind a veil of ignorance, perhaps), allowing for all the aggregate feedback effects between tax institutions and expenditure levels. An alternative exercise would explicitly allow for the fact that individuals will not fully comply with the tax law that some tax regimes will predictably prove more robust to non-compliance than others. This compliance dimension will require us to examine not only the economic incentives associated with compliance, but also prevailing taxpayer ethics, and the apparatus of resolving disputes between taxpayers and government agencies.[17] What is at stake in the second institutional comparison is an additional, different, margin of adjustment from those included when compliance issues are assumed away. But clearly all relevant margins ought to be included in the ultimate institutional comparison. We might term the latter comparison 'total' in the sense that it includes all relevant behavioural margins: but it remains 'marginal' in the sense that there is a conceptual continuum of institutional forms over which the citizen may be deemed to choose.

The foregoing tax example is limited, because there are many more dimensions of non-compliance at stake in the more global institutional comparisons that are envisaged in *The Limits of Liberty*. There can be 'non-compliance' by tax authorities, in the form of either self-aggrandizing or lax enforcement procedures. Political agents may use all the tax revenue for their own private use, rather than for public goods; and so on. The economic incentives, and the nature and strength of countervailing ethics, and the effect of (doubtless imperfect) enforcement procedures are relevant at all these levels. The analyst must make choices as to where to focus (intrinsically limited) analytic attention. In that sense, it is entirely proper to distinguish the intellectual agenda of *The Calculus* from that of *The Limits*, and entirely legitimate for Buchanan to abstract from the broader issues in the earlier work. What is puzzling, however, is the suggestion in *The Calculus* Appendix that the broader agenda is inappropriate.

Finally, it should perhaps be emphasized that, in engaging that broader agenda, we need to specify in some detail the precise content of the ethical norms that restrain rational defection; and precisely what are the internal enforcement processes attached to the ethical norms and how these latter processes may be reinforced and supported.[13] These matters are not, contrary to the suggestions of the Knight quotation, beyond the reach of 'intellectual' enquiry – even within a broad rational actor tradition.

Perhaps we should emphasize finally that none of this ethical enquiry is concerned with the sort of ethics that agents 'ought to have'. Specifying the ethics that would be most congenial to liberal constitutional order may be an interesting and worthwhile endeavour, but it is not the exercise we have in mind. In the spirit of 'taking men as they are', we need to understand the content of the *prevailing* ethical 'constraints'. Economics may have less to contribute to this exercise than anthropology, social psychology, and perhaps criminology; but disciplinary boundaries fail us when they serve to insulate analysis from obviously relevant questions.

5.

The central aim of this chapter has been to expose something of a divide in Buchanan's attitudes to the CPE project, as revealed first in his Appendix to *The Calculus* and then subsequently as engaged in *The Limits of Liberty*. In the former exposition, Buchanan draws a distinction between 'total' and 'marginal' constitutional analysis, and between the working properties of attractive institutional arrangements and personal ethics/morality. He uses those distinctions to specify where he sees the exercise of *The Calculus*, and by implication the whole CPE project, properly to lie. *The Calculus* is a 'normative theory of marginal institutional adjustment/evaluation', almost totally divorced from personal morality, and questions of political obligation. In *The Limits*, by contrast, the 'total' theory is engaged with enthusiasm. And in that 'total' theory, personal ethics – in particular those surrounding questions of political obligation – turn out to be quite central. One aspect of the contrast between the two Buchanan works revolves around the appreciation of the work of Thomas Hobbes.

In *The Calculus*, Hobbes is seen as a somewhat kindred spirit in method, but ultimately of very little use in the CPE exercise. In *The Limits*, Hobbes plays a central role, both in determining the domain of enquiry, and in specifying its analytic focus.

The issues at stake here seem important in identifying the precise ambitions of the CPE enterprise. In particular, at stake are critical issues about the supply of rules – about the feasibility of alternative rule regimes, and the extent to which the relevant ethical 'constraints' that are seen to make such regimes feasible are capable of withstanding possible regime changes.[14]

It is no criticism of *The Limits of Liberty* that it does not complete the project it lays out. There is a great deal more to be done here. Buchanan's 'procedural diagnosis' aims to do little more than gesture at what that 'great deal more' may be. But, despite the ambitiousness of that project, and the far-ranging enquiry that it invites, there is nothing to suggest that it lies beyond the scope of rational analysis – still less, beyond the possibility of 'intellectual solution'. In that sense, neither the essential modesty of the CPE project as envisaged in Buchanan's Appendix to *The Calculus*, nor Knight's intellectual nihilism as revealed in the epigraph to *The Limits*, seems at all appropriate.

NOTES

1. Buchanan himself is temperamentally ill-disposed to much in the way of self-exegesis. He has never shown much interest in reworking 'old stuff', and never seemed to regard inter-temporal consistency as a virtue to be cultivated. Nevertheless, external observers are often struck by how coherent the whole 'Buchanan project' is. The work comes across very much as a single intellectual scheme. Much more than others who have won the Nobel Prize in Economics, Buchanan's work reflects a unity of interest, purpose and approach. It is therefore of some special interest to investigate whether and to what extent, within the framework that is distinctively Buchanan's, there are nevertheless very significant revisions of what the CPE project amounts to.
2. We consider Buchanan's Appendix to *The Calculus* to be an especially interesting and important piece – more interesting and important than is suggested by the fact that it does not seem to have received very much explicit attention – from either CPE scholars or political philosophers of other traditions.
3. *The Calculus of Consent*, p. 310.
4. Ibid., p. 310.
5. Ibid., p. 311.
6. Ibid., p. 315.
7. Or at least seems to, in that the possibility of anarchy is included explicitly within the institutional array. There is an issue, however, as to whether incorporating anarchy in the way that Buchanan does, does not simultaneously raise questions about other institutional options – questions that in *The Calculus* Buchanan is able more or less satisfactorily to finesse.
8. *The Calculus*, pp. 318–19.

9. This comparison is worth making only because Buchanan himself has routinely recognized Knight and Wicksell as the two most significant influences.
10. We thank Hartmut Kliemt for forcing on us, over many years, a view of the Hobbesian challenge in such terms.
11. See Brennan et al. (2003) for relevant discussion.
12. In Tyler's interesting work on *Why People Obey the Law*, procedural justice seems to be an important, perhaps predominant, influence.
13. We have in mind especially the forces of esteem, following Smith's *Moral Sentiments*; and Brennan and Pettit (2004).
14. Actually, the language of 'feasibility' and of 'ethical constraint' may be misleading here. Both carry the sense of non-continuity. A regime is either feasible or it is not. A constraint is either met or it is not. It may be in this sense that the enterprise in *The Limits* appears as a 'total' rather than a 'marginal' exercise. But different regimes can be more or less likely to be feasible: the 'economic' incentives that various players have to abide by ethical norms or not are a continuous variable. And the individual's demand curve for ethical compliance is downward-sloping: there will, *ceteris paribus*, be more compliance when temptations are smaller. In short, the 'total' dimensions of *The Limits* project admit a more or less continuous measure of likely institutional feasibility, and admit marginal choices over institutional forms with an eye not just to their contractarian attractiveness but also to their likely 'robustness'.

REFERENCES

Brennan, G., W. Guth and H. Kliemt (2003), 'Trust in the shadow of the courts', *Journal of Institutional and Theoretical Economics*, **159**, 16–36.

Brennan, G. and P. Pettit (2004), *The Economy of Esteem*, Oxford: Oxford University Press.

Buchanan, J.M. and G. Tullock (1962/1999), *The Calculus of Consent*, Indianapolis, IN: Liberty Fund Inc.

Buchanan, J.M. (1976/1999), *The Limits of Liberty*, Indianapolis, IN: Liberty Fund Inc.

Hampton, J. (1997), *Political Philosophy*, Boulder, CO: Westview Press.

Hardin, R. (1995), *One for All: The Logic of Group Conflict*, Princeton, NJ: Princeton University Press.

Tyler, T. (2006), *Why People Obey the Law*, Princeton, NJ: Princeton University Press.

PART II

Constitutional Political Economy: Case Studies

3. Economics governance in the European Union: a problem of legitimacy

Francisco Cabrillo and Sean Fitzpatrick

1. INTRODUCTION

The central thesis of this chapter is that the Lisbon Treaty – like the European Constitution before it – serves as a further step along an already well-established path towards increasing the gulf between citizens and decisions that affect their lives. Efforts aimed at reducing the democratic deficit via furthering the role of the European Parliament and increasing the role of majoritarian preferences are misplaced and inefficient. The European Union is becoming increasingly centralist and its allocation of competencies violates both economic principles and the democratically expressed volition of the citizens of Europe.

2. TROUBLING TIMES

These are troubling times for free-market economics. President Sarkozy – himself oftentimes considered too pro-market in his own country – recently proclaimed 'Laissez-faire is finished, the all-powerful market that is always right, that's finished.' He continued by suggesting it 'necessary to rebuild the entire global financial and monetary system from the bottom up, the way it was done at Bretton Woods after World War II.'

Getting in on the act, the current German Finance Minister, Peer Steinbrück, suggested: 'The US will lose its status as the superpower of the world financial system' with the emergence of stronger, better capitalized centres in Asia and Europe. He further professed: 'The world will never be the same again.' These comments, according to the *Financial Times*, 'echo deep anger in Germany at the perceived recklessness of Anglo-Saxon financial engineering and a feeling that the US model of economic liberalism has failed while the more regulated, long-term oriented, and industry-based German economy has proven resilient.'[1] Troubling times indeed!

There can be little doubt that the institutions of the European Union – primarily the Parliament and the Commission – have been treated as largely inapposite during the current financial crisis, as has what the *Financial Times* dubbed 'the mighty body of EU law'.[2] The current crisis has shown that economic governance at an EU level is a paper tiger in the face of serious national interests.

One can hardly speak of a return to protectionism in Europe, given that Europe has presented itself as staunchly protectionist to the outside world, but rather that there is a force of moral authoritarianism behind this position unseen in recent years. It would appear that the dirigiste-inclined political leaders in states such as France and Germany will further seize their opportunity to triumph over those with a more free market approach.

3. THE INEXORABLE RISE OF EUROPEAN INTEGRATION

There can be little doubt that Europe's greatest achievement has been the establishment of a single European market. The Treaty of Europe put forth the vision of a Europe of freedom and competition, and the 'four freedoms' – of persons, goods, services and capital – made individual choice a key component of the unification process. But for much of the last 15 years, European integration has moved beyond enforcing peace and security and the common market. European institutions have increasingly acquired responsibilities that have heretofore been considered the domain of national governments.

But, let us be clear about the fact that the inexorable involvement of the European Union in numerous policy areas runs counter to economic theory. In particular, the economic literature on federalism provides us with a clear guideline on the allocation of responsibilities between the EU and national governments. The European Union should be active where heterogeneity of preferences in member States is very low and there are sizeable economies of scale and externalities.[3] The EU is, nonetheless, increasingly active in numerous areas where preferences are clearly heterogeneous, there are virtually no economies of scale and externalities are low, such as agriculture, welfare policies and consumer protection. However, theory also suggests that there are areas in which the EU is possibly not active enough. These include defence and foreign relations.

Similarly, international crime and immigration may warrant a stronger role within the EU, as may environmental protection.

4. PATERNALISM

Critical voice has been stifled in the European integration process. A favourite tactic of politicians is that criticism of the process is considered un-European. Nowhere was this more apparent than in the accusations voiced from Brussels and national parliaments Europe-wide, concerning the referendum in Ireland on the Lisbon Treaty. All evidence suggests that the document was too complex for even the most educated members of Irish society to read and fully fathom; and this was reflected in the reasons for voting no to the treaty. Irish politicians of the two largest political parties, in an expression of pure hubris, advanced the doctrine: 'Trust your government, don't worry about the Treaty, we have read it and it is good for the country.'

Most European politicians and senior bureaucrats seem to think that people should be allowed to vote only if they vote what they want. For instance, to vote 'yes' in a national referendum to approve the new Treaty is democratic. To vote 'no' is a mistake that shows that people have not understood the benefits of the proposal. It is democratic to repeat a referendum if people voted 'no', but not if citizens voted 'yes'.

The colourful former Irish Prime Minister, Bertie Ahern, was clear in this respect, stating that the Lisbon Treaty was simply a rehashed version of the Constitution. When asked about the differences between the Constitutional Treaty – which was torpedoed after 'no' votes in the Netherlands and France – and the Lisbon Treaty, he responded to an audience at the John F. Kennedy School in Harvard, 'We changed the name, and as with all great agreements, took a few sections out of it, turned it around a bit, and called it the reform treaty.'[4]

Worse still was the nature of the attacks on the Irish after the referendum. One can give some credence to the accusations that the Irish were ungrateful, given that Ireland was a net recipient of European funds for such a long period of time. However, accusations of the nature that the Irish were un-European are populistic, polemical and clearly untrue. A Eurobarometer survey conducted in the aftermath of the Irish rejection of the Lisbon Treaty suggested that support for the European Union among 'yes' voters was 98 per cent, and among 'no' voters 80 per cent (European Commission 2008). A similarly high percentage of French and Dutch voters – who rejected the European Constitution – also voiced their support of the European Union. According to a Eurobarometer post-referendum survey conducted in France, French citizens are still in favour of the European Union, with 88 per cent of respondents considering that France's membership of the European Union is a good thing. This positive view is shared not only by nearly all the 'yes' supporters (99 per cent) but also by a very large majority of 'no' voters (83 per cent (European Commission 2005a)). Similarly, there is strong support for the European Union in the Netherlands, where 82 per cent consider membership of the EU to be a good thing. Even a clear majority (78 per cent) of those who voted 'no' to the Constitution support the European Union (European Commission 2005b).

Thus, the tendency for the EU to extend its involvement into areas in which it is not best designed to do so has not gone unnoticed by citizens of member States, who have consistently been more reticent than their political leaders to approve of issues that involve greater integration and coordination of policies.

Interestingly, when the Dutch rejected the European Constitution and the Irish the Lisbon Treaty, the first reason they gave was that they did not have enough information or that they did not understand the Treaty well enough; the second, in both countries, was related to the protection of national sovereignty. In the French case, however, the first three reasons for rejecting the Constitution were respectively: it will have negative effects on the employment situation in France/relocation of French enterprises/loss of jobs (31 per cent); the economic situation in France is too weak/there is too much unemployment in France (26 per cent), and that the draft is too liberal, economically (19 per cent).[5] This divergence in the reasons for rejecting the Constitution/Treaty may be indicative of the cultural division within the European Union.

5. DRAFTING THE CONSTITUTION

The movement towards forming a Constitution for Europe was clearly a missed opportunity to limit the power of government, delineate the competencies of member States and the Union, and clear up what can only be described as the abysmal separation of powers within the institutions of the European Union. Properly designed, a Constitution could have clarified confusion concerning the prerogatives of EU institutions and mitigated their ability to encroach into national competencies.

There was nothing, however, more undemocratic than the way in which the members of the convention that wrote the draft of the Constitutional Treaty were appointed. As Otto Graf Lambsdorff (2002) reminds us:

> The question who should write a constitution is as old as the idea of constitutionalism itself. There was – since the days of the Roman republic – always a consensus, that constitution makers and policy-makers should be separated. Those who already have a vested interest in politics should not be the rule-makers of politics. This certainly is a wise maxim. I really wonder whether in a distant future some historian will describe the members of the new European Convention under former French president Giscard d'Estaing as 'giants', but one thing can be said already. These members do not stand outside the political process and its vested interests. Most of them by far will be people who come from the 'establishment' of the European Union. Most of them will find that the real issue – whether we need more integration and centralisation or not – is no issue at all. There seems to be a general agreement that integration and centralisation are to be re-enforced. (p. 1)

5.1 Chief Errors

As has been identified by the European Constitutional Group, the Lisbon Treaty repeats the errors of the Constitutional treaty and fails to clarify these and other issues. In particular, 'It gives the Union still more competencies; it extends the general empowering clause from common market matters to all EU policies, it lowers the upper majority requirement in the Council from 73.9 per cent to 65 per cent; it abandons unanimity in fields in which this is dangerous; it leaves the national parliaments powerless in EU legislation. All these amendments, and several others, will reinforce the centralisation of Europe.'[6]

There is one potentially treacherous difference between the EU Constitution and the Lisbon Treaty. The EU Constitution would have set the furthering of 'free and undistorted competition' as an objective of the European Union. Following efforts from the French government, this phrase was removed from the Lisbon Treaty. Instead, the text relating to free and undistorted competition in Article 3 of the EC Treaty was moved to Protocol 6 ('On the internal market and competition'). There has been much debate over whether this will have an impact on EU competition policy in the future. On the one hand, French President Sarkozy has declared: 'We have obtained a major reorientation of the union's objectives. Competition is no longer an objective of the Union or an end in itself but a means of serving the internal market.' On the other, the EU Competition Commissioner Neelie Kroes strongly refuted these claims, affirming that:

> The protocol to the Treaty is a legally binding confirmation that the system of undistorted competition is part of the internal market. Of course, competition is not an end in itself, but it is one of the best means to create conditions for growth and jobs. Putting it in a Protocol on the internal market clarifies that one cannot exist without the other. They have moved the furniture round, but the house is still there. The Protocol is of equivalent status to the Treaty.[7]

Whether or not this change will make a real difference in the long run may be left up to judicial discretion.

6. INCREASING LEGITIMACY AND CURBING THE DEMOCRATIC DEFICIT

For decades now, politicians have engaged in numerous attempts to have citizens of member States warm to the European integration process; most notably via the Common Agricultural Policy, numerous social policy measures, policies of regional aid and social cohesion, and the direct election of the European Parliament. Efforts towards improving legitimacy and curbing the democratic deficit almost invariably, however, focus on increasing the role of the latter, as it is the only directly elected body within the European Union.

The European Parliament has consistently seen its powers increased in recent decades.[8] Thirty years ago the only important powers of the European Parliament were the right to reject the budget and propose some amendments. Prior to Maastricht, it enjoyed the new cooperation procedure in various policy fields and a more substantial consultative role. It also had veto power over the accession of new member States and over the conclusions of agreements with associate States. Following Maastricht, the EP had the right to vote on the Commission before it took office; it had the power to appoint a European Ombudsman and establish committees of inquiry, as well as power to request the Commission to present a legislative proposal. Of particular importance was the fact that Maastricht granted the EP the power to adopt legislation jointly with the Council of the European Union in numerous Treaty areas, thereby obliging the two bodies to agree on an identical text before a proposal became law. The Amsterdam Treaty extended this power to other Treaty areas. Under the provisions of the Treaty of Lisbon, co-decision would become the ordinary legislative procedure in the work of the Council and the Parliament. In addition, the Parliament would also acquire greater powers over the entirety of the EU budget.

But there can be little doubt that the European Parliament has failed to improve the legitimacy of the European Union. Interestingly, Majone (2006) has pointed out that there is a negative correlation between the constant decrease in voter turnout in European elections and the expanding of powers of the European Parliament.

Citizens of member States clearly do not see members of the European Parliament as their representatives. Suggestions that the only means to mitigate the democratic deficit involve furthering the role of the European Parliament are both misleading and wrong.

7. ECONOMIC GOVERNANCE AND THE EUROPEAN PARLIAMENT

So, given that the European Parliament has done little to improve the perceived legitimacy and accountability of EU institutions, to what extent should efforts be made to further increase the role of the European Parliament?

Economic governance in Europe is based on two non-democratic institutions – the Commission and the European Central Bank. What are the dangers of increasing the role of the Parliament in the Commission? As Alesina and Perotti (2004) note, this depends on what activity within the Commission we are talking about.

> If one focuses on its 'think tank' role, one would want to make it as independent as possible from the EP: there is nothing wrong with a technocratic think tank – indeed, this is part of the definition itself of a think tank. But if one focuses on the executive role of the Commission, clearly accountability becomes an important issue. Depending on which side of the Commission one considers the most important – the executive, regulatory, or legislative – more accountability, politicization and legitimacy can be good or bad. (p. 6)

Now consider the role of the European Central Bank. In the United Kingdom and the US, the central bank enjoys instrumental independence. Accordingly, the governments set a target, such as an acceptable level of inflation, leaving the central bank with discretion over how to achieve this target. The European Central Bank, however, enjoys both instrumental as well as goal independence. As such, it is free to set its own targets. This has led some to decry a democratic deficit in the role of the ECB. To overcome this perceived democratic deficit, it is argued, governments or the European Parliament should have the option of overriding the ECB's decisions in certain matters. But there is no governance structure within the EU that could effectively and credibly assume this role, and it is difficult to see how one could be established in practice. Heterogeneous preferences and poor governance structures suggest that granting the ECB this independence was an effective means to credibly commit to stable long-term economic policy.

8. REGULATORY AND FISCAL COMPETITION

Better regulation and lower taxes in a European country can produce positive externalities. In addition to furthering the welfare of citizens and companies of that specific country, the measures may also benefit the economies of other member States of the Union. This occurs because governments in other countries are forced to improve their fiscal and regulatory models, in order to prevent their own firms and citizens – who support such regulations and levels of taxation – from 'voting with their feet' and leaving a country or region.

Fiscal and regulatory competition is the basis of fiscal federalism. Taxes and regulations should be harmonized in Europe only in those cases in which they may harm the principles of the single market. To further the powers of the European Parliament in these fields, would surely result in higher taxes and insufficient regulatory competition.

Opponents of fiscal and regulatory competition sometimes argue that European economic integration has tied the hands of national governments when it comes to responding effectively to the demands and expectations placed on them by their citizens. Accordingly, European leaders have been forced to accept conditions of regulatory and tax competition that affect 'market correcting'. Fiscal and regulatory competition thus leads governments to a 'race to the bottom', whereby countries offer tax rates that are too low, accompanied by inadequate levels of public services and regulation. Thus, to effectuate real responses to the problem, Europe would need to move further away from its present constitution as a confederacy of individual states towards that of a federal state. In an ideal situation, 'the Commission would become more like a European Government that is politically accountable to the European Parliament; there would be legislation by simple majority in both chambers, and the European Union would have the authority to raise its own taxes (preferably taxes on business profits and capital incomes that member states have difficulty collecting' (Scharpf 2000, p. 11).

Whilst this 'vision' is generally acknowledged as being unrealizable, so the argument goes, one should make real efforts towards harmonization and coordination in these areas to facilitate national responses by reducing the pressures, and regulating the practices of regulatory and fiscal competition among EU member States.

We argue, however, that there is not much weight to these arguments. For one, fiscal and regulatory decentralization reinforces democracy, as governments are better able to respond to citizens' preferences. In Europe, where preferences are highly heterogeneous – and even more so following recent expansion – coordination comes at serious democratic costs.

In addition to the democratic gains to decentralizing fiscal and regulatory competition, there are also substantial economic gains to be enjoyed. As Gary Becker (1998) put it, 'Competition among nations tends to produce a race to the top rather than a race to the bottom by limiting the ability of powerful and voracious groups and politicians in each nation to impose their will at the vast expense of the interests of the vast majority of their populations' (p. 22).

Whereas it is true that economic competition between member States may reduce the capacity of national governments to implement welfare programs, it is more likely that the efficiency gains from inter-jurisdictional competition would more than offset these losses.

In practice, within the EU there is little evidence of any race to the bottom occurring as a result of fiscal and regulatory pressures. One suspects that these arguments have grown substantially due to preferences for protectionism by certain interest groups and the usual opposition to the disciplining powers of market forces.

9. CONCLUSION

Movements towards even greater centralization of the European integration process in many activities are unwarranted and inefficient, and they are further distancing citizens of member States from decisions that affect their lives.

Bridging the gulf between citizens and decision-makers does not involve awarding greater responsibilities to the European Parliament as a supervisory body over other institutions, but rather preserving national sovereignty over issues which it is best able to decide.

The European Union could best mitigate its legitimacy problems by concentrating on achieving better results in core areas in which its institutions are best able to serve, i.e. by respecting the principle of subsidiarity that should be the basis of European integration.

NOTES

1. 'Sarkozy says era of laisser faire is finished', *Financial Times*, 26 September 2008.
2. 'Super-Sarko's plans for the world', *Financial Times*, 20 October 2008.
3. Alesina and Perotti (2004); Alesina et al. (2005); Cerniglia and Pagani (2007). See also Oates (1999).
4. 'Taoiseach warns of greatest act of lunacy if treaty rejected', *Irish Independent*, 3 May 2008.
5. Compare Flash Eurobarometer 172, p. 15 and Flash Eurobarometer 245, p. 19 with Flash Eurobarometer 171, p. 17 (European Commission 2005b, 2008 and 2005a respectively).
6. European Constitutional Group, letter to *Financial Times*, 2 December 2007.
7. Euractiv.com, 'Brussels plays down EU Treaty Competition Fears', 27 June 2007.
8. See Majone (2006) for discussion.

REFERENCES

Alesina, Alberto and Robert Perotti (2004), 'The European Union: a politically incorrect view', NBER Working Paper 10342, also published in *Journal of Economic Perspectives*, **18** (4), Winter, 27–48.

Alesina, Alberto, Ignazio Angeloni and Ludger Schuknecht (2005), 'What does the European Union do?', *Public Choice*, **123**, 275–319.

Becker, Gary (1998), 'What's wrong with Centralized Europe? Plenty', *Business Week*, **29**, 22.

Cerniglia, Floriana and Laura Pagani (2007), 'The European Union and the Member States: which level of government should do what? An empirical analysis of Europeans' preferences', CESIFO Working Paper No. 2067.

European Commission (2005a), Flash Eurobarometer 171, 'The European Constitution: post-referendum survey in France', June.

European Commission (2005b), Flash Eurobarometer 172, 'The European Constitution: post-referendum survey in The Netherlands', June.

European Commission (2008), Flash Eurobarometer 245, 'Post-referendum survey in Ireland: analytical report', July.

Lambsdorff, Otto, Graf (2002), 'Europe and the Constitutional Treaty', European Constitutional Group.

Majone, Giandomenico (2006), 'Is the European constitutional settlement really successful and stable?', *Notre Europe*, October, 1–10.

Oates, Wallace E. (1999), 'An essay on fiscal federalism', *Journal of Economic Literature*, **37**, 1120–49.

Scharpf, Fritz W. (2000), 'Democratic legitimacy under conditions of regulatory competition: why Europe differs from the United States', Estudio/Working Paper 2000/145, also published in *The Federal Vision*, **21**, 355–75.

4. Early Spanish liberalism and constitutional political economy: the Cádiz Constitution of 1812[1]

Roger D. Congleton

> Freedom, Sancho, is one of the most precious gifts that heaven has bestowed upon men; no treasures that the earth holds buried or the sea conceals can compare with it; for freedom, as for honour, life may and should be ventured . . .
> *Don Quixote de la Mancha*, Chapter LVIII, Miguel de Cervantes (1620).

1. INTRODUCTION

The history of Spain is not usually associated with liberalism or constitutional innovation by most English or American historians. That is partly because other aspects of Spain's history attract the most attention. American historians tend to focus on Spanish exploration and settlement in the New World. European historians tend to focus on wars against the remnants of the Islamic empire to the south, Turkish Empire to the east, and the roles that Spanish rulers, such as Charles V (Carlos I) and Philip II, played during the Protestant Reformation. Spain's international policies had major impacts on Europe and the New World during the late Middle Ages and early modern period.

The neglect of early Spanish liberalism is also partly a consequence of the infamous Spanish Inquisition developed during the sixteenth and seventeenth centuries. The Inquisition was used to curtail the rise of Protestantism throughout the Hapsburg territories and also to suppress political dissent. The failure of the Inquisition and related military efforts weakened the Catholic Church in Northern Europe. It also led to the emergence of the Dutch Republic, which subsequently played important roles in the rise of liberalism (Congleton 2008). In these contests, the Spanish could be said to be the conservatives against whom early liberals rebelled, especially in the Netherlands. Yet both liberalism and liberal constitutional innovations had a relatively early start in Spain and played important roles in its history.

That liberal strands existed in Spanish thought is evident in many literary pieces written in the seventeenth and eighteenth centuries, as in the quote above from *Don Quixote*. However, political and religious censorship evidently pushed most liberal thought underground into private conversations and most writing into fiction, rather than academic works or political pamphlets. Liberal proposals for reform of Spain's constitution(s) were rare during the seventeenth and eighteenth centuries.

The Constitution of 1812, as developed below in this chapter, demonstrates that liberal constitutional political theory, nonetheless, was relatively advanced and that liberalism had penetrated into relatively high levels of government and society in Spain. The 1812 constitution is clearly a liberal document and shows a sophisticated understanding of constitutional designs. Indeed, it provides the first written liberal constitutional framework for monarchy in Europe.

Liberalism emerged gradually in Spain, as also true elsewhere in Europe. The Enlightenment and liberalism were consequences of new rational perspectives on society, life on earth, and the natural world that emerged at about the same time as the Protestant Reformation. These secular theories challenged medieval views in many areas, including political and economic views that had long been espoused by the Catholic Church. This made the new perspectives congenial to Protestants, but did not prevent Catholics from contributing to their development or from incorporating the new ideas into their own world view. Moreover, the discovery of the New World by Catholic sailors from Italy, Spain, and Portugal clearly helped launch the Enlightenment by demonstrating that many long-held ideas about the world were incorrect. Liberalism emphasized reason over tradition, and civil equality over privilege. These general ideas had broad implications for economic, education, and political reform.

Contemporary Protestants often argue that the Enlightenment and liberalism were Protestant phenomena, but this claim has little basis in fact, as the Spanish case demonstrates. Indeed, the use of the term 'liberal' as a description of a political reform agenda is of Spanish origin (Payne 1984: 71). Spanish constitutional political economy and Spanish liberalism did not suddenly spring forth as a consequence of the king whom Napoleon imposed on Spain or the inspiration of the French or American Revolution, although these naturally had effects on Spanish liberalism, as elsewhere in Europe.

Liberals were a minority in Spain during that period, as elsewhere, but they were clearly politically active and influential. Of particular interest are their theories of sovereignty, citizenship, rights, and institutional design. These are analyzed from the perspective of contemporary constitutional political economy and from the perspective of nineteenth-century liberalism as developed in Congleton (2011).

This chapter provides a brief history of the rise of liberalism in Spain and uses the Constitution of 1812 as a window into the political liberalism of Spain in the early nineteenth century. Section 2 of the chapter provides a brief historical overview of constitutional developments in Spain before 1800. Many readers will not be familiar with the political institutions of medieval Europe or the great transformation of those institutions that produced democracy in Europe. For example, Spain, as such, did not exist during the late Middle Ages. Governance in the Iberian Peninsula was highly decentralized. There were several small independent kingdoms and governance within each kingdom was substantially a local affair. Spain as a territory ruled by a single king or queen emerged gradually through marriage and conquest during the fifteenth, sixteenth, and seventeenth centuries. Spanish government emerged somewhat later. It was not until the eighteenth century that most of the regional parliaments of the formerly independent kingdoms were eliminated.

Section 3 provides a brief overview of the emergence of Spanish liberalism. Liberalism had an early start in Spain, but it was pushed underground during the seventeenth and eighteenth centuries. Section 4 uses the Constitution of 1812 as a window into the political and constitutional theories of Spanish liberals in the early nineteenth century. That document demonstrates that Spanish liberal thought was more sophisticated and influential at the beginning of the nineteenth century than might have been expected.

As in Congleton (2011), the historical analysis undertaken in this piece focuses on political and constitutional developments and neglects international entanglements and wars, except as necessary to shed light on those developments. Constitutional developments in late medieval Spain, as elsewhere, reflected internal bargaining among privileged families, which were influenced by preexisting political and legal institutions and by new ideas, interests, and external threats.

2. SETTING THE STAGE: LATE MEDIEVAL GOVERNANCE IN SPAIN

During the thirteenth and fourteenth centuries, written agreements between kings and nobles were common throughout Europe. These agreements could be thought of as medieval constitutions insofar as kings or other similar regional rulers (often referred to as barons or dukes in English) acknowledged limits in taxation and law enforcement. To assure those limits were adhered to, representative councils or parliaments of major taxpayers were often established. For English readers, the Magna Carta will be the most familiar of the documents, but similar documents were negotiated in present-day Sweden, Denmark, the Netherlands, France, and Spain. These documents often described legal rights for nobles and commoners that included court trials, fiscal restrictions on the executive authority (relevant king, duke, count, etc.), and procedures for adopting new taxes. These were not simply copies of English innovations, but reflected older norms and institutions throughout medieval Europe. The cortes – the usual name for Spanish parliaments – of the Kingdom of Leon was founded in 1188, several decades before the Magna Carta and about a century before the British parliament.

The early European parliaments nearly all had veto power over new taxes, which played a role in the development of political institutions throughout the late Middle Ages and early modern period. Rulers had a variety of standing sources of revenues, but were restricted from adopting new taxes without majority support in their parliament. These included revenues from royal lands, sales of monopoly privileges, customary tariffs, and colonial enterprises. Majorities for new revenues were difficult to obtain except during times of crisis; so rulers called their parliaments into session only during fiscal crises. These were sufficiently common that kings would normally call parliaments into session every two or three years, at which time the parliaments would often temporarily increase taxes, often in exchange for changes in royal policies of interest. This was also true of the Spanish kingdoms during the sixteenth and seventeenth centuries (Livermore 1958: 268). Although new royal revenues from the New World reduced the need for cortes-approved taxes, the cost of continental battles and colonization exceeded even those revenues.

On other matters, the medieval parliaments of Europe had relatively limited authority. They were not 'self-calling'. They met when called by their respective 'kings' and only as long as the kings required. They did not have significant legislative authority, although their veto authority over new taxes often allowed them to trade new taxes (normally granted for a short period) for policy shifts desired by parliamentary majorities and occasionally for additional policymaking authority.

Medieval parliaments were multicameral, often with separate chambers for nobles, commoners, and the Catholic clergy. In some cases, there were four chambers, as in Aragon where high and low nobles each had their own chamber, or two, as in England where the clergy were included in the noble chamber. Members of the commoner chamber were often elected through a wealth or tax-restricted suffrage, in which 5–10 per cent of male voters were eligible to cast votes for representatives. In other cases, members of the commoner assembly were appointed by local governments (who were themselves often partly elected).

Seats in parliaments were normally held by members of privileged families, who were often from noble families, although they did not all personally hold noble titles. These elite families largely controlled government and commerce, except in those areas controlled by the king or church.[2] In practice, they also had considerable influence over the areas of royal and church control, because most senior bureaucrats and military officers came from those same families.

For day-to-day governance at the level of kingdoms, the king's royal council (or cabinet of ministers) and his bureaucracy were far more important than parliaments, because kings delegated a good deal of authority for making day-to-day policy decisions to their ministers. The members of the council were appointed by the king and served at his pleasure. They were often nobles and/or clergy who were also members of parliament, but this was not usually a requirement of office.

In 1400, there were many independent polities in Spain and most had their own 'kings' and 'parliaments' (the latter were called cortes in most Spanish polities). Except for the odd independent city, these independent polities were essentially family territories and were passed on to children through inheritance and amalgamated through marriage. Marriage did not automatically cause two polities to become one, but did mean that the same noble would rule several territories, although each territory would have its own cortes and councils. Marriages were thus normally arranged with such shifts of property and policymaking authority in mind (Livermore 1958: chs 6–7).

During the fifteenth century, most of the territories of Spain were brought into a single family by the marriage of Isabella I of Castile and Ferdinand II of Aragon. As Catholic king and queen (both sovereign in their own territories) they continued the long war to drive the Moors (Muslims) out of Spain. They also funded the Italian Christopher Columbus on his famous trip to find a shortcut across the Atlantic to the spices of the 'Far East'. His distance calculations proved incorrect, but fortunately for Spain and his place in history, Columbus found an enormous, previously unknown, body of land about a third of the way to China and India. He and other explorers claimed most of the new lands for Spain.

Family politics continued. Isabella's second daughter, Juana, was married to Philip the Handsome, of the powerful Austrian Hapsburg family. In this manner, the Hapsburg family obtained control of the royal office for Spain. Their son, Charles I (Carlos I), inherited both the Castile and Aragon titles and other properties associated with his grandmother's titles, including the Netherlands. Through his grandfather, he was elected to the throne of the Holy Roman Empire (as Charles V).[3] In this manner, Charles became ruler of one of the largest territories ever assembled, through well-planned parentage, rather than wars or conquest.[4] He was the first sovereign of essentially all of Spain, having inherited both Isabella and Ferdinand's titles.

It bears keeping in mind that geopolitics during this period were familial, rather than national. Although the Kingdom of Spain was the largest and most important property ruled by the Hapsburgs, it was only one of many of their territories. For most purposes, Carlos I should be thought of as the leading Hapsburg of his era, rather than as the king of Spain. Carlos I was not simply a 'Spanish' king and, indeed, did not initially speak Spanish. He moved from his native Belgium (then a Hapsburg-Burgundian territory) to Spain as a very young man in 1517.

Carlos I and his son Philip II invested much of their time, attention, and money in other parts of Europe, including opposing French efforts to annex territories in Italy, countering Ottoman efforts in Eastern Europe, resisting Dutch efforts at succession, and suppressing the Protestant Reformation in their German territories. Gold from the new Spanish South American colonies helped finance these European military and political efforts. It did so in a manner that did not require consulting dozens of regional parliaments throughout Europe to raise new taxes. The Hapsburg properties were split after Charles's retirement in 1555; the central European properties went to his younger brother (Ferdinand) and his Spanish and Burgundy properties went to his son Philip II. This reduced 'Spanish' influence in Europe, but did not end it.

Hapsburgs ruled Spain for about a century, but the line died out with the absence of a clear Spanish successor in 1700. The last Spanish Hapsburg left his title to a member of the Bourbon family, which had long ruled France. This produced a geopolitical crisis in Europe, because the Austrian Hapsburgs and the English were concerned that the French and Spanish crowns would sit on the same head and produce an extremely powerful state. After a bit of negotiation, warfare, and more negotiation, a compromise was found: the Bourbon Philip (the Duke of Anjou) obtained the Spanish crown, but renounced all claims to the French crown and ceded some territories in Italy to the Austrian Hapsburgs.

3. SPANISH GOVERNANCE AND LIBERALISM IN THE EIGHTEENTH CENTURY

At the beginning of the eighteenth century, Hapsburg governance was somewhat more centralized in Spain than elsewhere, because of revenues from the American colonies; however, a good deal of political authority remained vested in the historic kingdoms of Spain, which continued to have their own parliaments (cortes), laws, and special privileges. Cortes (or corts) included ones in Aragon, Castile, Catalonia, Valencia, Navarre, and the Basque country. To the extent there was a Spanish government in 1700, it had emerged as a consequence of the practical requirements that a single sovereign faced when dealing with many regional and local parliaments.

National policymaking, especially foreign policy, had gradually become centered in Castile, but the regions had their own laws, court systems, and privileges.

3.1 Bourbon Spain and Centralization

Philip's (Felipe V's) claim to the throne was ultimately settled through international warfare and treaties in 1714, rather than the usual Spanish legal practices (acceptance by the various royal cortes and the church). As a consequence, the custom of bargaining with parliaments was weakened and the importance of the Spanish army increased, which tended to increase royal authority.

Felipe V, unlike the Hapsburgs, was not used to dealing with a variety of parliaments and territories, each with its own laws and privileges. After his claim to the throne was buttressed by international treaties, Felipe V attempted to create a more unified government in Spain. For example, he took revenge on the regions that had supported the Hapsburg (Austrian) claims to the throne during the war over the Bourbon (French) ones. In 1707 the Nueva Planta Decrees eliminated most of the privileges and independence of Aragon (Aragon, Catalonia, and Valencia), which had sided with the Hapsburgs. The territories of Aragon would henceforth be subject to the laws of Castile. Castilian Spanish also became the official language of legal proceedings in Spain at that time.[5]

Local government autonomy was also greatly reduced, because noble privileges were somewhat diminished and pivotal seats in local governments would be appointed by the central government. In practice this made the Castilian bureaucracy, councils, and cortes the central government of Spain, although regional interests could not be entirely ignored.

Royal authority became more independent of the parliament(s), because of tax and military reforms adopted early in Felipe V's long rule. As a consequence, even the Castilian councils and cortes were less often called and consulted by the Bourbon rulers than by the Hapsburgs (Livermore 1958: ch. 10; Payne 1973: ch. 16).

3.2 Eighteenth-century Economic Liberalism in Spain

Europe was connected by networks of trade, travel, and religion. These international connections brought books to the hands and ideas to the minds of educated men and women throughout Europe. In the eighteenth century, this common knowledge base included an increasing number of secular works. For example, Spinoza, Bacon, Hobbes, Locke, and Montesquieu were well known and fairly widely read, although several of their books were banned by the Catholic Church. Much of the literature of the Enlightenment was originally published in or translated into Latin, which made it readily accessible to literate Spaniards. The use of French at the Bourbon court also made contemporary French contributions to philosophy, economics, and politics more accessible, because persons seeking favor at the Bourbon court benefited from knowing French customs, language, and literature.

Together, expanded trade, early industrialization, government finance, and the ideas of scholars caused economic theory to become more sophisticated in Spain and elsewhere. New theories of taxation, finance, and economic development attracted broad attention, because policies that could increase economic growth and/or raise additional government revenues were of interest inside and outside government. Early liberal ideas about property, commerce, and free trade were also somewhat more evident in Spain than political liberalism, because economic ideas were less subject to censorship.

In the second half of the eighteenth century, a number of economic clubs were established in Spain, and many of these evidently lobbied for economic reforms at both the local and national levels of government. The fiscal system was also analyzed, for example by Leon de Arroyal, who proposed an idea that anticipated Lindahl's notion of an ideal tax system in the 1770s: the ideal state was one in which 'each partner contributes to the common expenses in proportion to the benefits from the common fund' (Stein and Stein 2003: 346). Spanish economists such as Campomanes and Jovellanos argued that modernizing property law (e.g., creating freer markets in land) was the key to revitalizing Spanish agriculture (Ringrose 1998: 169–70).

Partly as a consequence of such arguments, there was a substantial shift of ownership from medieval forms to 'freehold' ownership, under which property could be more freely bought and sold. These liberal land reforms were reinforced by pragmatic interests in additional government revenues. Fiscal pressures and constitutional constraints induced the king to sell royal properties and former Jesuit holdings that became available after the Jesuits were expelled from Spain in 1767 (Ringrose 1998: 384).

Similarly, free trade arguments began to be heard in Spain. For example, in 1765, several years before Adam Smith completed his most famous book, Pablo de Olivide, the superintendant of Seville, wrote that 'The [wheat] supply of Madrid would be assured, since the bakers cannot run short of grain as long as any is available in Spain. It might be expensive, but this would attract more to market, and thus its very expensiveness, attracting competition will produce cheapness' (quoted in Ringrose 1998: 171). Supply would follow demand, without the need for government rationing. With such ideas in mind, the internal grain market was liberalized the same year (Payne 1973: ch. 16).

A few years later, Carlos III formed a relatively liberal cabinet headed by José Moñino (the Count of Floridablanca).[6] That cabinet adopted a number of economic reforms, including the free trade law of 1778, which substantially reduced barriers to trade within the Spanish empire, and induced a rapid expansion of trade in the next decades. In Fisher's (1985) words:

> Free trade promoted a massive expansion in the value of exports from Spain to America. The rise was uneven, but in the period 1782–96 as a whole their average annual value was 400% higher than in the base year of 1778 . . . The share of Spanish products in total exports from Spain to America rose from 38% in 1778 to an average of 52% in 1782–96.

All this is not to suggest that Spain was filled with liberal reformers, even in the economic sphere, but simply to indicate that early forms of economic liberalism had relatively broad and active support in Spain's government and literate society – before the American and French Revolutions took place and before Adam Smith's influential book on economics was published. Liberal economic reforms were often in the interest of otherwise conservative governments.

3.3 Political Liberalism in Eighteenth-century Spain

Political liberalism was less evident during the eighteenth century than economic liberalism, because suggestions for major political reforms were often subject to censorship and treason laws, and subjected to tough penalties. In the seventeenth and eighteenth centuries, a good deal of European political theory was published anonymously or at Dutch presses where censorship was far less stringent and threatening than elsewhere in Europe. Spain's censorship was somewhat broader and more threatening than most: the Inquisition was still a possibility until it was formally abolished in 1834, and the Bourbons had long attempted to suppress political dissent in France.

As a consequence, Spain's political liberals published little during the late Hapsburg and Bourbon periods. Indeed, the *Encyclopedia of Philosophy* (1972, Vol. 7: 514) includes no entries for Spanish philosophy between Francisco Suarez (1548–1617) and Jaime Balmes (1810–48), who is credited with attempting to reintroduce philosophical discussion in Spain. It bears noting that Spanish scholars had written about political constraints before the arrival of the Hapsburg and Bourbon dynasties. For example, Mariana had explored issues concerning the scope of legitimate authority in his *De Rege et Regis Institutione* (1599) – perhaps influenced by the Dutch experience in the late sixteenth century (Braun 2007).

Censorship is rarely complete, however: private discussions can take place and smuggled books can be read, even when censorship is rigorous. Eighteenth-century philosophical work by Spanish and neighboring Portuguese scholars also had a significant impact in Spain, for example, the work of Benito Jeronimo Feijoo and Luis Antonio Verney, who were both influential among Spanish intellectuals. Although these intellectuals were not explicitly political, they raised questions about the appropriate methodology for understanding the world, which indirectly directed attention to the constitutional experiments taking place elsewhere in the world, as in the North American colonies, the Netherlands, and England (Israel 2002: 534). It may also be presumed that Spanish political reform was discussed at the various economic clubs established throughout Spain during the second half of the eighteenth century. Economic reforms could often be accomplished indirectly by first adopting political reforms, although this did not occur in Spain.

The political ideas of Spanish liberals became apparent during and after the French Revolution. During the French Revolution, moderate Spanish liberals, as elsewhere, were shocked by the excesses of the Committee of Public Safety and the use of the guillotine. Others who were more sympathetic to the idea of revolutionary reform and confident that Spain could avoid French excesses called for a new constitutional convention:

> Spaniards: The time has come to offer the truth to all peoples; tyranny tries in vain to smother their cries. The country of liberty [France], where the people are king, offers asylum to philosophers and the defenders of humanity, who are safe from any worry in the heart of France . . . This sublime revolution, which has solemnly toppled superstition and tyranny from their golden throne in order to place equality and reason on it . . . You have but one means remaining, Spaniards, of destroying religious despotism and that is to convoke a meeting of your Cortes . . . Your Cortes are well known [for their rules and rigid limits]. France needed a revolution; Spain needs only rejuvenation. (Excerpt from Jose Marchena's *To the Spanish Nation* (1792), translation from Cowans (2003: 261–3))

Marchena's thoughts were a minority opinion even among Spain's liberals, and Spain, perhaps naturally because of its Bourbon rulers, joined the alliance against the French Republic. This, nonetheless, accelerated land reforms, as the monarchy sold its land and church land to help finance the war effort. (Evidently, freehold claims could be sold at higher prices than more encumbered claims.) Napoleon's armies proved too effective for Spanish forces, just as they were for most other armies in Europe.

Spain's king, Carlos IV, and his son Ferdinand VII were 'persuaded' to abdicate in June 1808. They were taken to France where they were held in isolation, and rule of the kingdom of Spain was turned over to Napoleon's brother Joseph. However, Joseph did not have an easy time governing, because of Spanish resistance (supported by British troops) throughout most of Spain.

That those resisting French rule were mainstream opponents of Napoleonic rule, rather than revolutionaries, is indicated by the steps that they took. In the absence of the proper king, a national parliament (central junta) was organized, which asked the elderly José Moñino, the former prime minister for Carlos III three decades earlier, to head the government in exile in 1808. He accepted, although the rigors of travel at his age led to his demise.

4. THE CÁDIZ CORTES AND THE CONSTITUTION OF 1812 AS A WINDOW INTO SPANISH POLITICAL LIBERALISM

Although not all opponents of Napoleon and his brother were liberals, the constitutional efforts undertaken suggest that Spanish liberals, rather than conservatives (traditionalists), played major roles. This became clear when the resistance formed a central administration in the absence of the king. The various regional groups organized a national umbrella organization, the Supreme Central and Governmental Council (Junta) of Spain. It met in Aranjuez in September 1808 with José Moñino as president.[7] It called for a cortes of the Spanish Nation that would write a new constitution for the nation as a whole.

The members of the Constitutional Cortes were to be elected representatives from both Spain proper and Spanish territories in the New World, rather than Spanish nobles or members of the clergy. One representative for every 50,000 freemen was to be (indirectly) elected from Spain and one from every 100,000 freemen from Spanish territories in the New World.

As the provisional government retreated before French forces, the resistance found itself meeting in Cádiz, an important, easily defended, port city with a major Spanish naval base, about as far away from France as it is possible to get without leaving Spain.[8] The Constitutional Cortes assembled there in 1810 and included representatives from both new and old Spain. Not all communities could send representatives, because of the French occupation. Replacements were appointed by the conference organizers, who were somewhat more liberal than the typical Spaniard (or local representative) would be; indeed they could be considered radical liberals by the standards of 1800.

The result of two years of deliberations was a document that was the most liberal of its kind in Europe. The constitution was grounded on popular sovereignty and it characterized a government with a dominant, unicameral, parliament to be elected by very broad suffrage. Its provisions substantially increased civic equality by reducing aristocratic and monopoly privileges. It was briefly implemented in 1812–14, which made it an actual constitutional document, rather than an entirely theoretical exercise, as might be said of Germany's Frankfurt constitution of 1848.

In many respects, the document of 1812 was similar to that of the Frankfurt convention 36 years later. It characterized a constitutional monarchy, rather than a republic. It called for a parliament elected on the basis of essentially universal male suffrage. It was also a product of negotiations among liberals, rather than the result of constitutional bargaining among persons in government with the authority to adopt constitutional reforms.

That neither the king nor conservative officeholders participated in the negotiations allowed the document to take a very liberal form. Because it represented the consensus in Spanish liberalism at that time, it became an important symbol for liberal reformers throughout the Spanish world for many decades.[9] However, the absence of constitutional bargaining with conservatives and the king, also made it likely that the document would have a short life as a true constitution after the war with Napoleon and his brother was won.

The specifics of the negotiation process are neglected here in order to focus on the results. The 1812 constitution is of interest, both as a clear window into Spanish political liberalism of the time and as a response to the constitutional experiences of America and France in the late eighteenth century. It should be kept in mind that eighteenth-century liberals generally agreed about the proper direction for reform, rather than the specifics of reform or a particular vision of the 'good society'. Areas of both consensus and disagreement among liberals are evident in the document that emerged from the cortes at Cádiz.

Eighteenth-century liberals generally agreed that constitutions should be written, rather than unwritten, and that parliaments should be more broadly elected than they were at that time. They also believed that royal authority should be subject to the rule of law and that parliamentary authority should be increased. Most believed that legitimate governments were grounded on popular sovereignty and had a duty to advance the interests of all members of their polities, rather than just the interests of the well born. These areas of agreement are all advanced by the constitution of 1812.

Some moderate liberals, following Montesquieu and Burke, favored royal systems with bicameral parliaments, as in England. They believed that such systems balanced competing interests fairly well and had proven to be fairly stable. Republics were evidently less so, given the experience of France in the 1790s. Other more radical liberals favored republican systems, both because they opposed familial privileges and because they thought that it was essentially impossible for parliaments to constrain a king. Most believed that cabinets should be appointed by, or at least responsible to, the parliament.

The Cádiz Constitution was clearly a product of negotiation and compromise. In areas where liberals agreed on principles, they were able to find words acceptable to a majority of liberals. Chapter I states that 'sovereignty belongs to the nation' and that 'the nation is obliged, by wise and just laws, to protect the liberty, property, and all other legitimate rights, of every individual which composes it.' The document describes rights to education in chapter IX (which tends to equalize opportunity) and rights to due process before the law in courts staffed by judges that serve for life (unless they violate the law) in chapter V.

Fiscal matters were to be decided by the parliament (cortes) and 'every Spaniard, without exception, is obliged to contribute, in proportion to his means, to the finances of the State.'

The government was to have a king, but a weak king, relative to other European kings of the time. The constitutional language is clear and detailed on royal powers; it includes enumerated powers, prohibitions, and titles. Article 14 states that 'the Government of the Spanish nation is a moderate, hereditary monarchy' and 'the King shall be styled, his Catholic Majesty.' Chapter IV describes the extent and limits of royal authority. Article 170 states that 'the exclusive power of enforcing and rendering the laws effective resides in the King, whose authority extends to whatever may be conducive to the interior regulation, and exterior security and defense of the State, consistently with the laws and the Constitution.' Article 171 lists royal authorities, including the following:

(3) To declare war and make and ratify peace; laying, afterwards, authentic documents of the same before the Cortes;

(4) To nominate, by and with the assistance of the council of State, all civil and criminal magistrates;
(5) To appoint all civil and military officers;
(6) To present, by and with the advice of the council of State, to all bishoprics, ecclesiastical benefices and dignities . . .
(8) To command the navy and army, and appoint the generals . . .
(11) To regulate the coinage of money, on which shall be impressed his image and name.

These were normal authorities of European kings at the time. However, the document places many restrictions on the king's authority, some of which were new for Europe and most of which had been absent from Spain for many decades, indeed centuries.

Article 172 lists policy areas in which kings could not act without the consent of the cortes. Many of these were policy areas affecting property rights and civil liberties:

(5) The king cannot make any offensive or defensive alliance, or special treaty of alliance or commerce, with any foreign power, without the consent of the Cortes . . .
(7) He cannot cede or make over the national property without consent of the Cortes;
(8) He cannot, without a previous decree of the Cortes, directly or indirectly, impose contributions, or make loans, under any name or for any object whatsoever;
(9) Neither can he grant any exclusive privilege to any person or corporation;
(10) He cannot dispossess any corporation or individual of their property; neither can he disturb them in the enjoyment or direction and profit of it; and if, in case of necessity, for the general advantage of the public good, it should be required to convert that of an individual for a particular object, it cannot be done without a full indemnification, by just valuation of respectable persons;
(11) The King cannot punish, in any manner whatsoever, or deprive any individual of his liberty, under any pretense; the secretary of State who signs and the judge who executes the order shall be responsible to the nation; and, in such case, punished as criminals against civil liberty.

Chapter III describes the authority and composition of the reformed and strengthened parliament. As developed above, Spain had long had parliaments at the regional level and had a national parliament for much of the eighteenth century. However, the authority of these parliaments was quite limited: they were not self-calling; all of their proposed laws were subject to a royal veto; and in the eighteenth century their veto power over new taxes was narrowly interpreted. The cortes had largely been ignored during the Bourbon period. In contrast, the reformed parliament would have power to adopt and repeal laws, and broader authority over revenues, succession, and military deployments.

The authorities of parliament listed in article 131 include the following:

(1) To propose and decree the laws and interpret and repeal them, when it shall be necessary;
(2) To administer the oath to the King, and Prince of Asturias and to the Regency, according to the forms directed in their proper places . . .
(7) To approve, *before their ratification* [author's emphasis], the treaties of offense, alliance, subsidy, and particularly those of commerce . . .
(8) To grant or deny the admission of foreign troops into the kingdom . . .
(10) To fix, by proposals from the King, the proportion of sea and land forces for the year; determining the standing force in time of peace and augmentation in war;
(11) To issue codes of established instructions to the army, navy, and national militia, for their direction, under all circumstances;
(12) To fix the expenses of the public service;
(13) To establish the annual contributions and imposts;
(14) To borrow money, in cases of emergency, on the credit of the nation;
(15) To approve the division of the proportion of contributions to be levied on each province . . .
(17) To establish customhouses and the rates of duties;
(18) To make the necessary dispositions for the administration, preservation and expenditure of the public funds;
(19) To determine the value, weight, standard, impression and denomination of the circulating medium;
(20) To adopt the system of weights and measures, which may appear to them most just and convenient;
(21) To promote and encourage all descriptions of industry and remove the obstacles which may check them;
(22) To establish a general plan of public education throughout the whole monarchy and approve that which is pursued for the instruction of the Prince of Asturias;
(23) To approve the regulations for the general health and police of the kingdom;
(24) To protect the political liberty of the press;
(25) To make the responsibility of the secretary of State and other public officers, effective;
(26) Lastly, it belongs to the Cortes to give or refuse its consent to all those acts and circumstances, in which, according to the Constitution, it may be necessary.

The list includes many authorities that no other European parliaments possessed in 1812, although most were held by the US Congress and (implicitly) by the British parliament. Authorities 12–18 provide the cortes with a stronger power of the purse than the British parliament formally had at this time. Authority 21 encouraged the cortes to remove internal and external barriers to trade.

The cortes also oversaw the activities of the secretary of state (prime minister) to assure that he, rather than the king, was responsible for his actions (e.g., that they were lawful) and determined the limits of censorship. It also had obligations to oversee education reform and public health in the kingdom, both of which were policy concerns of liberals of the day. (Contemporaries who claim to be 'classical liberals' often forget that such policy concerns were part of the classic liberal reform agenda, although it bears noting that the early proposals were very modest ones by the standards of a twenty-first century welfare state.)

All seats in the cortes were to be elected, although elections to the parliament were to be indirect. Representation was to be uniform, with a representative (deputy) for each 70,000 citizens in the worldwide Spanish nation-state. (The colonies were to elect their own representatives (deputies) to the parliament.) Elections were to be held every two years (Article 108). The electorate was to comprise the entire citizenry. Citizens, described in chapter I, were to be free-born men (of Spanish parents or born within Spanish territory), immigrants who had lived in a particular village for 10 years, freed slaves, and others naturalized by law. Only citizens were eligible to hold government jobs.

The elections for seats in the cortes took place in three stages. First, the citizenry was divided into groups of 200, each of which elected a representative. Those representatives gathered in the major towns of their respective regions and elected an 'elector' who then met in their regions' major cities to elect their deputies to the cortes. Such three-part elections would tend to generate moderate, relatively well-qualified members of the cortes.

The Cádiz Constitution also included innovative procedures for the adoption and repeal of legislation. The king could delay, but could not permanently block legislation adopted by the cortes. If parliament passed a law once each year for three years, it became law. If, however, it was passed once or twice, but vetoed by the king on those occasions, it would not.

Although a relatively complete constitution, some issues evidently could not be resolved by compromises among the participants. For example, article 91 states that: 'to be a member of the Cortes, it is also necessary to possess a sufficient real and personal property,' but makes no effort to describe how much property would be necessary. In many constitutional compromises reached in other countries later in the century, relatively high wealth requirements were often adopted to obtain noble support for other liberal constitutional reforms.

More important, as a constitutional matter, the document repeatedly mentions the council of state (cabinet) and its members (secretaries of state), but characterizes neither its duties nor its membership. In the mid-to-late nineteenth century, control over such councils of state (cabinets) was a significant area of constitutional negotiation. In other European countries at the time (toward the end of the Napoleonic period), the king appointed cabinets, which served at his pleasure; they, like the king, were above the law. In the Cádiz Constitution, cabinet members were clearly to be 'responsible' (Article 130, part 25) and the king was to coordinate his policies with or through them. However, the king was not responsible in this sense. Article 168 states that 'neither is he [the king] responsible for any thing.'

These clauses implicitly suggest that the king would appoint the cabinet, which would serve as the main channel of executive authority. Cabinet ministers (secretaries of state) could be held responsible for violating the laws adopted by parliament, rather than the king. However, the constitution does not state this explicitly, which contrasts with the broad range of other procedural issues and authorities that are clearly stated. This ambiguity suggests that moderate and radical liberals could not reach agreement on this important constitutional point, possibly because they hoped that the king would accept the new constitution and believed that the power to appoint the cabinet was necessary to obtain his support.

Other issues were also left unresolved. For example, the constitution mentions slavery, but does not explicitly support, criticize, or eliminate it. Nonetheless, with its very broad electorate, expanded parliamentary authority, and provisions for the protection of property and due process, the Cádiz Constitution would have been the most liberal constitution in Europe in 1812.

5. CONCLUSIONS AND POSTSCRIPT

Ferdinand VII was 'restored' in March 1814 following the defeat of Napoleon (by the alliance of Russia, England, Prussia and Austria). He initially accepted the Cádiz Constitution, but after the voices of conservative defenders of the long-standing medieval system of government were heard, which included both nobles and rural farmers, he revoked the constitution and ruled under the pre-Napoleonic Bourbon constitution (which was largely unwritten).

The 1812 constitution nevertheless continued to influence politics in Spain and in the New World. It was a rallying point for constitutional liberals, who managed to reinstate the constitution twice in the next two decades. It also served as a model and inspiration for reformers in the New World, many of whom had participated in the constitutional deliberations in Cádiz. Among these were Miguel Ramos Arizpe of Mexico, Joaquín

Fernández de Leiva of Chile, Vicente Morales Duárez of Peru, and José Mejía Lequerica of Ecuador, who subsequently played significant roles in politics in the New World countries, many of which seceded from Spain in the decades that followed. The elections undertaken in 1813 under the 1812 constitution were the first national elections in Spain or Spanish America (Rodríguez 1998).

That other well-organized groups, such as the clergy and the nobility, did not accept the new document is not surprising. Relatively few persons from these groups participated in the constitutional deliberations, their interests were not represented, and no constitutional bargains between liberals and conservatives were agreed. For the purposes of this chapter, however, the imbalanced representation of Cádiz has clear practical advantages. The document, as a product of negotiations among liberals, provides an especially clear window into Spanish political liberalism in the early nineteenth century. The 1812 constitution demonstrates that, although Spanish scholars produced relatively little written liberal political theory, Spanish political liberals and theories did exist, and were well organized and influential.

After the war with France was over, the old regime was restored and constitutional bargaining began again. The subsequent process of constitutional negotiation and exchange, however, did not fully deliver on its potential in nineteenth-century Spain, as it did elsewhere in Europe (Congleton 2011), although some progress was made. The bargaining failure in Spain may have been a consequence of circumstances in Spain, where political liberals may have been more doctrinaire and less willing to compromise than elsewhere – in part, because they already had a specific constitutional design in mind. It may also have been partly a consequence of the constitution of 1812 itself, which provided a natural 'all or nothing' offer for liberal proponents. In other places, liberals lacked a clear vision of what they wanted to achieve, which made bargaining incremental and also easier for liberals and conservatives to accept. Bargaining failure in Spain also reflected the breakdown in traditional quasi-constitutional governance during the Napoleonic period, which increased the size and political importance of the Spanish army in a manner that made negotiations and compromise by conservatives more difficult.

What is important for the present analysis is not the failure of the 1812 constitution to become the law of the land, but that it represented a sophisticated synthesis of liberal thought about constitutional design. There was a long history of constitutional experiments in Spain, and many lessons from that history were obvious to Spain's political reformers. They could recall, for example, the value that the cortes had added in pre-Bourbon Spain. They could also observe the effects of liberal political and economic reforms in the United States, England, France, and the Netherlands.

Their efforts to design a liberal constitutional monarchy produced a very plausible result, one that was in many ways similar to those that would emerge in the late nineteenth and early twentieth centuries in Belgium, Denmark, the Netherlands, Norway, and Sweden. The Cádiz Constitution was not a document written by radical revolutionaries who explicitly aimed to end the monarchy, Catholic Church, and nobility; these were all preserved. It contained no grand statement of the rights of man. It was a compromise worked out by serious men, who deliberated in the midst of a war of resistance, while the site of their negotiations was under siege by the enemy.

The result makes it clear that constitutional political economy and political liberalism were well advanced in Spain at the beginning of the nineteenth century. Had the king accepted his greatly reduced authority under the Cádiz Constitution and foreign powers not intervened as they had in France, Spanish history for the next two centuries might have been very different.

It is beyond the scope of the present analysis to explore those possibilities in any detail, but it seems clear that the 1812 constitution might have produced stable governance, not only for Spain, but for Spanish America as well. After a few decades, the constitution's liberal political and economic provisions would have become the norm and been taken for granted in Spanish politics. With civil and economic liberties guaranteed and broad representation, there would have been less reason for the various Spanish territories to secede.

It is also likely that the Cádiz Constitution would have been gradually revised through the nineteenth century. Given its early start, it also seems likely that the reforms would have been at the forefront of other constitutional liberalizations in Europe. Women would presumably have been made eligible for suffrage and slavery eliminated.

In the long run, it seems likely that that result would have been better for Spain, for South America, and for the king and nobility than the turbulent constitutional and political history that actually followed. This too suggests that constitutional political economy was well advanced in Spain in 1812. Indeed, it may have been more so at that time than at any other point, until relatively late in the twentieth century.

NOTES

1. This chapter is written for a Festschrift honoring José Casas Pardo, whose nickname, like that of the constitution analyzed below, is Pepe.

2. There were a surprising number of noble families in Spain. About 10 per cent of the population had noble privileges, although wealth and power were concentrated in the upper strata of the nobility (Payne 1973: ch. 15).
3. The position of emperor of the Holy Roman Empire was formally an elective office determined by nine electors, but the electors routinely selected Hapsburgs for the office and normally the next male child in line for the office.
4. Charles had one name, but many titles, and his name has many translations. The number associated with his name varies with the title and territory. He was Carlos I (Charles I) in Spain, Charles II in the Netherlands, and Charles V (or Karl V) in the Holy Roman Empire. 'Carlos I' is used in this chapter, since it is about Spain. I have used 'II' and 'V' elsewhere as appropriate for other papers and book chapters.
5. Centralization was partly a matter of convenience and partly to punish those in Aragon who had resisted Philip V's accession to the throne. 'Considering that the kingdoms of Aragon and Valencia and all their inhabitants have through their rebellion completely broken the oath of fidelity they swore to me and lost all the fueros, privileges, exemptions, and liberties that they enjoyed and that they had been so liberally granted to them . . .' Cowans (2003: 203). The Navarre and Basque territories remained separate, at this point. Excerpts in Spanish from the *Decretos de Nueva Planta* are available at http://es.wikisource.org/wiki/Decretos_de_Nueva_Planta.
6. The word 'relatively' is important here, as Carlos III was certainly not a liberal himself. Moreover, liberals, then as now, often disagreed about the nature of 'ideal' reforms, although they might agree about the proper direction for reform. Compromises and bargains were always necessary. So, along with some important reductions in monopoly privileges and education reform came stronger dress codes and some rent control (Payne 1973: ch. 16).
7. José Moñino was by that time 80 years old and in poor health. He died in November 1808.
8. The constitutional negotiations within the cortes took place while Cádiz was under siege by the French army. The siege was finally lifted in 1812 after the Spanish victory at the battle of Salamanca.
9. The Frankfurt constitution was intended to become a constitution for Germany, rather than a symbolic document. The crown created by that constitution was offered to the King of Prussia, who rejected it, as Ferdinand VII would later reject the Cádiz Constitution.

BIBLIOGRAPHY

Barbier, J.A. and H.S. Klein (1981), 'Revolutionary wars and public finances: the Madrid Treasury, 1784–1807', *Journal of Economic History*, **41**, 315–39.

Braun, H.E. (2007), *Juan de Mariana and Early Modern Spanish Political Thought*, Aldershot, UK: Ashgate.

Brennan, G. and J.C. Pardo (1991), 'A reading of the Spanish Constitution of 1978', *Constitutional Political Economy*, **2**, 53–79.

Casey, J. (2002), *Early Modern Spain, A Social History*, London: Routledge.

Cervantes, M. (1620), *De Don Quixote*, Volume II (translated by J. Ormsby), Project Gutenberg E-Book 996 (2004).

Congleton, R.D. (2011), *Perfecting Parliament: Constitutional Reform, Liberalism, and the Rise of Western Democracy*, Cambridge, UK: Cambridge University Press.

Congleton, R.D. (2008), 'America's neglected debt to the Dutch, an institutional perspective', *Constitutional Political Economy*, **19**, 35–60.

Cowans, J. (2003), *Early Modern Spain: A Documentary History*, Philadelphia, PA: University of Pennsylvania Press.
Fisher, J. (1985), 'The Imperial response to "free trade": Spanish imports from Spanish America', *Journal of Latin American Studies*, **17**, 35–78.
Israel, J.I. (2002), *Radical Enlightenment: Philosophy and the Making of Modernity 1650–1750*, Oxford: Oxford University Press.
Livermore, H. (1958), *A History of Spain*, London: George Allen & Unwin.
Marichal, C. and M.S. Mantecón (1994), 'Silver and Situados: New Spain and the financing of the Spanish Empire in the Caribbean in the eighteenth century', *Hispanic American Historical Review*, **74**, 587–613.
Payne, S.G. (1984), *Spanish Catholicism: An Historical Overview*, Madison: University of Wisconsin Press.
Payne, S.G. (1973), *A History of Spain and Portugal*, Madison: University of Wisconsin Press.
Ringrose, D. (1998), *Spain, Europe, and the Spanish Miracle, 1700–1900*, Cambridge, UK: Cambridge University Press.
Rodríguez, J.E.O. (1998), *The Independence of Spanish America*, Cambridge, UK: Cambridge University Press.
Stein, S.J. and B.H. Stein (2003), *Apogee of Empire: Spain and New Spain in the Age of Charles III, 1759–1789*, Baltimore, MD: Johns Hopkins University Press.
The Political Constitution of the Spanish Monarchy, Biblioteca Virtual 'Miguel de Cervantes', online version of a partial translation originally published in Cobbett's Political Register, Vol. 16 (July–December 1814).

5. Reforms and decentralization: friends or foes?*

Pierre Salmon

1. INTRODUCTION

Systemic concerns about markets, capitalism and the role of the state in the economy are salient again. Relatively large-scale reforms of economic and/or social arrangements are seriously considered and some (in the financial sector in particular) are undertaken or may be imminent. Historical experience suggests that reforms of that kind are sometimes associated with changes in the 'architecture of government' – to borrow the title of a recent book on political decentralization (Treisman 2007). Inspired in part by historical experience, discussions about economic systems or about 'national models' of economic governance now often give a role to the relationship between national and sub-national governments. A case in point is the political economy literature on China. In that literature, an influential view is that the economic performance of China is related to the way it has organized the relations between central and regional and local authorities, both in its official institutions and within its ruling party. Decentralization is also an object of attention in discussions about the economic conditions of countries such as Argentina, Brazil, India, Nigeria and Russia. From the perspective of an international organization such as the World Bank, two positive worldwide evolutions occurred over the last decades, liberalization of markets and political decentralization, and a relation between the two seemed plausible even if difficult to establish empirically.

In the case of Europe, the relation between the governmental and the economic systems is relevant mainly at the level of the European Union (EU). The policy-making capacity left to the member states interacts in a somewhat conflicting way with the ambitiously strict features adopted as a binding norm or ideal for the 'internal' market. There is a parallel between the way that interaction is evolving and the experience of the United States, more precisely the way in which, in that country, entrenched political convictions about state autonomy and the role of the federal government interacted with the mainly economic concerns embodied in the Commerce Clause.

If it is difficult to deny the possibility of an important link between economic systems and the 'architecture of government', or between reforms of the first and changes in the second, it must be acknowledged that the literature explicitly addressing that question in general terms is limited – Weingast (e.g 1995, 2009) being one of the exceptions, albeit from a particular standpoint. It must be stressed also that the relation is far from being unambiguous. To fight the Great Depression, the New Deal led to an increased centralization of the American governmental system. Conversely, but under the same logic, to preserve or foster markets, Ronald Reagan in the United States and the Communist Party in China favoured decentralization. However, for the same purpose, the Conservative government in Britain under Margaret Thatcher and her successor favoured centralization both in Britain and, ironically, at the level of the EU. And, in France, François Mitterrand was elected in 1981 on the basis of a platform focussed on large-scale economic and social reforms, increasing considerably the involvement of government in the economy. Yet, a major legacy of his presidency was the relatively extensive political decentralization enacted in 1982.

To account for these differences and to explore the relationship between economic reforms and political decentralization, the chapter argues that a reform has two dimensions, at least potentially. It is a process and it is a design. This is true whether the reform concerns the economic system or is about decentralization (or centralization). The organization of the chapter is inspired by this distinction. For economists, it seems natural to reason in terms of design – that is, to perceive reform as the replacement of one state by another, presumably better in some sense, at least better in the eyes of the promoters of the reform. This is in agreement with the method of comparative statics, in which one compares an equilibrium position or situation with another. Given our focus on the interaction between reforms of the economic system and political decentralization, this approach suggests a discussion in terms of complementarities – that is, a discussion of how a set of characteristics of the economic system and some features of the relationship between levels of government do or do not match up. Regarding reforms, should the present combination be replaced by another? To return to the cases mentioned above, should a more market-friendly type of economic system be associated with a more decentralized system of government, and, conversely a more interventionist and redistributive economic system with more political centralization? The New Deal, the platform of Reagan and perhaps the contemporary Chinese experience suggest this kind of association. But other experiences – Thatcher's, or possibly Mitterrand's – suggest opposite complementarities. The first part of the chapter is based on the design perspective, which, although it is dominant in the literature, proves in the end somewhat disappointing. The second part is devoted to the process perspective, which has also inspired a relatively large body of work on economic reforms, albeit most of it unconcerned with decentralization. We argue in the second part that integrating decentralization in an analysis of reforms as processes seems promising. But only an exploration of some of the possibilities will be attempted.

2. THE INSTITUTIONAL DESIGN PERSPECTIVE

In this section, we remain on a broad level and concentrate on the question of how views on the relations between economic systems and economic performance, on the one hand, and political decentralization or centralization, on the other, have been associated with views about government and about competitive markets. This will allow us to address the puzzle created by the fact that Reaganism and Thatcherism, two apparently close ideologies, have adopted contrasting positions regarding political decentralization.

2.1 Decentralization and Views on Government

Even among liberal (i.e., pro-market) economists, journalists and politicians, the views held on the state are not identical on the two sides of the Atlantic. The difference is reflected at the intellectual level in the observation that Public Choice, as a subfield of economics and of political science, has not had in the United Kingdom the success it has had in the United States.[1] The difference also explains in part the opposite approaches to decentralization adopted by Reaganism and Thatcherism.

Distrust of the state in general and of its bureaucracy in particular was one of the sources of inspiration of Public Choice. Welfare economics and, to a lesser extent, public economics used to focus on market failures and to discuss the policies a government, supposedly benevolent if not also omniscient, should adopt to deal with them. The field now known as Public Choice flourished in part as an elaborate critique of that approach. Throwing analytical light on governmental or public sector failures succeeded in undermining many cases made too hastily for public intervention or in showing the naivety of many economists' specifications of intervention tools. By performing this critical task, Public Choice certainly contributed to improving the quality of the debate among economists on policy issues.

Some authors have gone further and discussed the implications of a more encompassing perspective of governments. They portray them as predatory, at least potentially, or likely to become the prey of interest groups, including their own bureaucracies. As a consequence, it is urgent in their opinion to investigate, and if need be promote, mechanisms that can constrain government – that can 'tame the Leviathan' (Brennan and Buchanan 1980). The two main classes of mechanisms stressed in this literature are, on the one hand, constitutional constraints, which *inter alia* protect individual rights and limit the power of a simple majority to exploit the minority, and, on the other hand, federalism or decentralization, which allows interjurisdictional competition for mobile individuals and capital to limit over-regulation and the exploitation of tax payers (yardstick competition, an effect of federalism or decentralization which is emerging intellectually as a second channel of competition, will be discussed later). To have a sufficient impact, it may be advisable that both kinds of constraints operate together.

This is the case in the system advocated by Barry Weingast (1993, 1995) under the name of 'market-preserving federalism'. In it, 'the authority to regulate markets is not vested with the highest political government in the hierarchy' and 'the lower governments are prevented from using their regulatory authority to erect trade barriers against the goods and services from other political units.' According to him, this was more or less the system adopted in the United States in the nineteenth century and, in that case, it was constitutionally entrenched and enforced by the Supreme Court. The basic underlying mechanism, in Weingast's contributions of that period, is that of mobility-based competition, more or less as in Brennan and Buchanan (1980). Its virtues were presented as follows by Yingyi Qian and Weingast in an article published in 1997 (cited by Daniel Treisman 2007, p. 74):

> Just as market competition pressures firm managers to reflect the interests of shareholders, competition among local governments helps to limit government's predatory behaviour. Mobile resources can quickly leave jurisdictions with inappropriate behaviour. Competition for mobile sources of revenue prevents local political leaders from imposing debilitating taxes or regulation.[2]

The relationship between assessments of what would be the best system of economic governance and attitudes toward reform depends on whether or not the institutional status quo is deemed satisfactory. If it is, there will be a tendency to oppose reforms implying institutional changes. If it is not, the link with reforms as designs will be direct. Moving from the status quo toward the new system will be advocated by economists and others and may be undertaken by politicians. Distrust of 'big government' was a major inspiration of the Reagan administration, which also held the view that decentralization would be a good way to curb government's size, powers and financial resources. The widely cited assertion that government 'is not the solution to our problems, . . . government is the problem' was pronounced in 1981 by Reagan in his Inauguration Address. Then (in his State of the Union address), Reagan announced a New Federalism scheme. In particular, a number of programmes would be transferred by the federal government to the states (see Pierson 1994). It seemed clear to all observers that the programmes would then be downsized as a result of mobility-based competition among the states.[3]

The Conservatives in Britain shared with the Republicans in the United States a desire to privatize a number of organizations and programmes, implying some downsizing of government. But the British government did not hesitate to increase taxes, at least those collected by the central government, and to reduce the powers and autonomy of the subcentral authorities. The difference is often ascribed to partisan considerations, local governments and other authorities (those in charge of housing in particular) being in their majority strongholds of the Labour Party. It is also often explained by the fact that the concentration of powers in the hands of the central government normally facilitates the implementation of the decisions of that government. If the United States had not been a federal country with many powers and competencies of the states entrenched in the Constitution and protected by the Senate and the Supreme Court, it is conceivable that the central government could have obtained a reduction of the financial capacity of the subcentral governments by the use of authority, as happened in Britain, rather than by relying on the erosion effects of mobility-based competition, as it planned to do. But that avenue was not constitutionally open to the Reagan administration. Finally, the authoritarian personality of Thatcher may also have played a role.[4] Without denying the relevance of these reasons, I think that a cause that I have already alluded to goes deeper. Whereas economic conservatism in the United States includes many views also held in Public Choice, in particular the centrality of distrust of government, this is not the case of economic conservatism or liberalism in Britain, which is more traditional and more narrowly economic. It stresses free trade, competitive markets, sound public finance and sound monetary policy. Downsizing government and reducing its revenues may be the consequence of the pursuit of other objectives but they have no priority. If the pursuit of these other objectives requires political centralization rather than decentralization – and (to reduce the public deficit, for instance) increases rather than decreases in taxation – this is more acceptable for economic conservatives or liberals in Britain than it would be for their counterparts in the American context.

The foregoing comparison between Reaganism and Thatcherism is logically incomplete. With regard to the British Conservatives, what has been argued so far is only that their views on government *allowed* – that is, were no obstacle to – political centralization. It was different on the other side of the Atlantic, where, in themselves, the views held on government by the Republicans were not only an obstacle to centralization but constituted even an *inducement* to promote decentralization. We turn now to differences in the views of what is required for a market to be truly competitive. We will see that the conception held by Thatcherism provided a positive inducement to increase centralization whereas the conception held by the Republicans allowed – that is, was no obstacle to – a decentralization to be pursued for other reasons.

2.2 Decentralization and Views on Competitive Markets

The starting point of the discussion must be the too often unheeded fact that genuine political decentralization fragments markets and distorts competition among firms (Breton and Salmon 2001). This is necessarily so whenever subcentral governments, whether regional or local, are given significant powers and autonomy, and in particular are encouraged to undertake innovative policies. Some differences in regulation among regions are a consequence, at any point in time, of the freedom to innovate. Others are related to local conditions, including the nature of the political equilibrium. Whatever their causes, many regional differences regarding regulation will generate non-tariff impediments to the exchange of goods and especially services across regional borders. Competition among subcentral governments to attract people or investments takes the form of state aids, tax holidays and various forms of in kind support. All have in common the consequence, at least as a side effect, of distorting competition among firms – and thus of precluding the maintenance or establishment of a perfectly 'level playing field'. The observation of decentralized federations such as Canada and Switzerland confirms these facts.[5] And so does, to a lesser degree, the observation of the United States.

Of course, there are limits to the tolerance of impediments to exchange and of distortions of competition. The three countries just mentioned have policies that aim at keeping them under control. In Canada and Switzerland procedures exist whose explicit aim is to complete the 'common' or 'internal' market. These procedures rely in part on federal institutions, including the courts, but also, interestingly, on negotiations among sub-national governments akin to international negotiations among sovereign states.[6] In the United States, where no such inter-regional negotiation takes place, the federal institutions – i.e., the Congress, the President, the Supreme

Court, and some federal agencies – act to safeguard what is considered in that country as a healthy competitive internal market. Under Reagan, the result was not very different from what it was under other administrations: a combination of tolerance of many impediments or distortions (for instance, state aids) and the ruling out of others, thus limiting but not suppressing the discretion enjoyed by state governments. It must also be noted that, in practice, contrarily to its electoral platform and proclaimed ideology, the Reagan administration did increase centralization in many domains (Rodden and Rose-Ackerman 1997). However, this may only reflect the constraints to which platforms and ideologies must adjust in the real world. From a doctrinal point of view, which is what counts for our purpose in this section, the essential point is that the ideology underlying Reaganism had no problem in favouring political decentralization because it included a conception of competitive markets that was flexible or broad enough to accommodate the side effects of that decentralization.

Many economists and, perhaps inspired by them, many politicians and journalists have a conception of market competition which is far more demanding. Their support for free trade is uncompromising and entails a demand for eliminating all impediments to exchange, whether based on border tariffs or on regulations, and whether truly inspired by protectionism or only consequent on the side effects of unrelated policies. Similarly, they have no patience with the distortions of competition generated by state aids, tax holidays, etc. and are thus defending the enactment and enforcement of rules that will ban these instruments typically used by subcentral authorities.[7] This, in a sense traditional, conception of competitive markets implies that very little leeway may be left to politically decentralized government.

Thatcherism displayed this logic within the United Kingdom. It increased the political centralization of an already centralized country. But the logic is illustrated more strikingly at the level of the EU. Although highly suspicious of any step toward more integration, their conception of a competitive market led Thatcher herself and her successor, John Major, to accept and even favour, as far as the internal market was concerned, increased powers at the Brussels level. Because most policies have a bearing on the internal market, this has allowed more centralization at the Brussels level than one would have expected from the position of Thatcherism on European integration in general (Salmon 2003).

2.3 Discussion

Over time, it turns out that the New Federalism of Reagan brought no major change. In a sense, it achieved less than the initially less ambitious

New Federalism of Richard Nixon (Pierson 1994). Similarly, political centralization in Britain under Thatcher was only a modest accentuation of a system of government already centralized. Some substantial retrenchment of the state did obtain in the United States but this had little to do with decentralization. The most durable consequences of the views of British Conservatives on the question of markets were observed in Europe, where, especially with the Single Act, they contributed to increased centralization in Brussels.

Weingast illustrated 'market-preserving federalism' with the experience of the United States in the nineteenth century but also with the system currently in place in Communist China. But it is interesting to note that, later, there has been a shift in his arguments. In his more recent writings (e.g., Jin et al. 2005; Weingast 2009), pro-market policies are no more in the fore. They are subsumed under pro-growth policies. Decentralization is claimed to be an essential component in the economic success of the Chinese system because, in that system, subcentral governments are given a large share of the surplus generated by growth. Given the observed growth, this distribution of the surplus may be claimed to provide sub-central governments with a financial incentive to adopt pro-market policies if one thinks that pro-market policies are mainly responsible for economic growth. If one has a more qualified or hesitant opinion, the incentives given to these governments by the distribution of the growth surplus may still be deemed important by inducing them to adopt the policies that they think best for growth, whether or not these policies are pro-market.[8] The argument does, however, reflect a continuing distrust of central government. As noted by Treisman (2007), the implication of a larger share of the surplus given to the subcentral jurisdictions is a smaller share retained by the central government, whose incentives to adopt pro-growth policies are, following the logic, diminished as a consequence.[9]

The literature relating the degree of political decentralization or centralization to economic systems and their performance, in particular economic growth, is not limited to the authors cited. There is a significant volume of empirical work, whose conclusions are not, however, very illuminating. A question which has recently emerged, with a tribute to the early contribution of William Riker (1964), is the possibility that the political party system – in particular whether it is itself centralized, as in China, or decentralized, as in Russia before but not since Putin – may play a role in the comparative performance of institutionally decentralized systems (Blanchard and Shleifer 2001; Enikolopov and Zhuravskaya 2007). This could be related to the distinction, central in Treisman (2007), between administrative decentralization and political decentralization. But the meaning of political decentralization or centralization under dictatorships or authoritarian regimes needs more thought than it has been given so far.

The literature stressing the benefits of mobility-based competition may be called *a-democratic* in the sense that, in most of it, votes – or, more generally, consent (Breton 1996) – do not play a very significant or very explicit role. The question of whether governments at the different levels are democratic is implicitly treated as secondary. Glossing over the distinction between democracies and dictatorships may be convenient inasmuch as it increases the scope or applicability of the analysis, especially when its main concern is development. But, in particular with regard to the effects of decentralization in the rich, industrialized countries, the neglect of democratic mechanisms constitutes a weakness of the approach – a serious one in the case of the earlier literature, a more easily rectifiable one in the more recent work. As has been often noted, not only 'bad' policies may be eroded by mobility-based competition, but also 'good' ones (the 'race to the bottom' possibility). But this is a normative or prescriptive argument. From a positive economics standpoint, what counts is that, in democracies, mobility-based competition may potentially erode or endanger policies to which the population is strongly attached – and this whether we, as observers, choose to deem these policies 'good' or 'bad'. As a consequence, some forms of decentralization may be politically unsustainable. The a-democratic characteristic just noted leads to the neglect of this essential point.[10]

In the developed countries, democratic mechanisms interact with the necessity, less constraining in the American context than in the British one but operative nonetheless, of limiting the magnitude of non-tariff barriers and spatial distortions of competition. The democratic setting implies that, if they are given the power to do so, subcentral governments will respond to the demands of the population by adopting policies whose side effects may cause such impediments and distortions. Admittedly, mobility-based competition will make some of these policies impossible or costly, or will limit their magnitude. The courts may also restrict some policies. But other policies, demanded by the population or a segment thereof, will remain legally accessible to the subcentral governments and will be implemented by them in disregard of the side effects. To respond to the public's demand and at the same time avoid the side effects, the only solution will be the adoption of the policies by the central government itself.[11]

There is no incompatibility between taking into account the democratic dimension of governance and sharing the view – essential to Public Choice – that voters are at a disadvantage because of information asymmetry. To assess many kinds of public policies, voters do not have all the information that office-holders hold and they cannot rely completely on what they are told (not only by incumbents and other candidates, but also by interest groups). In a world exposed to rapid historical change and various kinds of shocks, the obstacles voters encounter in many policy areas to assess the performance of government are substantial. The fact that some information is available to voters from outside the jurisdiction makes a difference, however. No such possibility is taken into account in the world implicitly assumed by much of the Public Choice literature. This is one of the two major reasons why that literature displays such scepticism with regard to the democratic dimension (the other reason being the logic of voters' rational ignorance, whose significance in practice tends to be exaggerated). In a political universe supposed closed to information from outside, office-holders transact with interest groups and/or keep some resources for their own discretionary uses. General interest objectives such as economic growth are sacrificed. Once informational openness is acknowledged, things change. As argued in Salmon (1987), comparisons by voters between what obtains in their jurisdiction and what happens in others may reduce information asymmetry. In turn, the fact that office-holders are aware of the existence or possibility of these comparisons affects their decisions. If pressed by electoral competition, they want to be judged as performing comparatively well. This is the basis of what has been called 'yardstick competition' among governments, which, under favourable circumstances, may strengthen the right kind of incentives in governments (not only the politicians in office, but also, indirectly, the bureaucracy, the legislature, the courts, the political parties, etc.). For these comparisons to be at all possible, the simultaneous existence of several governments is necessary. Federalism and political decentralization imply such simultaneous existence and consequently offer a way to make office-holders more accountable.

If, because of yardstick competition in particular, voters are better informed and office-holders are more accountable to voters, there will be less possibility of discretionary behaviour, and thus less governmental or bureaucratic slack and more alignment of public policies with what voters want. Do such effects of yardstick competition when it works well (not always the case) have a bearing on economic governance or systems? The fact that distrust in government is less justified does not by itself means that markets must be less trusted. Only if distrust of government was an essential ingredient in the case for markets would the improvement in accountability of government have an effect on the economic system in the direction of less reliance on markets. On the whole we can consider analyses based on competition among governments of the yardstick competition variety as neutral with regard to the economic system. Decentralization, by allowing yardstick competition, may improve governance but this can affect the degree of reliance on markets in any direction.

What complicates the matter is that yardstick competition among governments may also play a role at the international level. The comparative performance involved in the mechanism may concern countries rather than sub-national jurisdictions. Suppose for a moment that accountability concerns only one variable or dimension. Inasmuch as international yardstick competition improves the accountability of office-holders and thus the quality of economic governance in a country, this makes it less likely that decentralization in that country and the yardstick competition among subcentral governments that ensues will be as accountability-enhancing as it would have been if the country had been closed to international flows of information. This means, in this single dimension case, that yardstick competition processes at the different levels are largely substitutes. As already argued in Salmon (1991), a small informationally open economy will typically not gain very much in terms of accountability of its office-holders by adopting a federal and decentralized political system. In a large, relatively closed economy with regard to information from outside, such adoption may improve accountability more significantly. If, more realistically, we assume that the governmental performance is assessed along many dimensions, there is a role for yardstick competition to play in a complementary way on several governmental tiers as well as internationally. This may in particular mitigate the consequences of the problems of measurement raised by multi-tasking. Urban policies are likely to be central in the comparative assessment of local authorities by voters, whereas economic growth performance is a particularly suitable object of international comparisons. Comparisons of growth rates or income per head will give central governments an incentive to ensure that the national economy does not fall behind, whether or not the governmental system is decentralized.

To conclude this section, the design perspective, although it is adopted by many scholars, does not seem particularly fruitful for the purpose of relating degrees or forms of political centralization or decentralization, on the one hand, and economic systems or systems of economic governance, on the other. There is a temptation to elevate the Chinese experience of decentralization-cum-centralization into a model or blueprint which could be provided to all developing countries. The large differences between the choices made by Reaganism and Thatcherism, or by India and China (Singh and Srinivasan 2006; Singh 2007), suggest that no model or experience endowed with some generality is available. The variables considered so far stand in relations of complementarity with many particular characteristics of countries, many of them of a non-economic kind. Does this mean that nothing a little general can be said, and that in each country the idea of some inspiration stemming from the observation or analysis of arrangements adopted abroad is meaningless? The process perspective, to which I now turn, may offer a relatively less discomforting answer to these questions.

3. THE PROCESS PERSPECTIVE

After some general remarks on the process approach to reforms, and then on how decentralization may be integrated into it, I explore in a third subsection the possibility of explaining variations in decentralization as open-ended reform processes.

3.1 General Remarks on Reforms as Processes

The process dimension of economic reforms has been an object of serious study in economics for a long time now.[12] Although political processes are discussed as central elements in most of the contributions, the authors of these contributions are seldom Public Choice scholars in a strict sense. Their interest in reform typically stemmed from an interest in economic development, international economics or the conversion to capitalism and market economy of the former Communist countries. Whatever its merits, the work done by these economists over the last decades is no substitute for the contributions made, over a longer period of time, by political scientists, sociologists and historians. The remarks that follow concern the whole literature, not only the part that can be ascribed to economists.

A first remark is that the degree to which the process perspective departs from the design one is variable. In the case of many contributions, the reasoning supposes that the end-state of the process is well known. The question studied may concern the mechanisms which delay or prevent the passage from the status quo to a state deemed preferable. Or it may be about how to organize the transition from one state to another. In particular, should the transition take the form of one big, encompassing 'jump', or should it consist of a sequence of piecemeal reforms? The design perspective may be relevant also to characterize the process itself, for instance to specify the sequence of decisions which will ultimately lead to the end-state. However, with some authors – e.g. Gérard Roland (2000) – transition is understood in a way that gives less room to design and a greater role to uncertainty and experimentation.

A second remark is that economic systems are always evolving. Thus many reforms are relatively small-sized, with a limited scope, concerning only a segment or single characteristic of the overall economic and social system.[13] They often prove more successful and durable in the end than more visible and ambitious ones. The New Deal, the reforms undertaken by Reagan and Thatcher, or by Mitterrand in 1981 are large-scale reforms (if obviously less large-scale than the reforms implemented in the former collectivist systems). In democratic settings, this type of reforms usually requires an 'authorization' by voters (Keeler 1993). Some typical characteristics of these authorizations are worth noting:

- they are conceded to national governments rather than to regional or local ones;
- they follow a sentiment of crisis, a growing awareness of serious underperformance and/or general acquiescence to the inevitability of yielding to external constraints (e.g to obtain financial support);
- they are particularly powerful when reforms are expected to follow rapidly a clear-cut electoral victory and have been properly announced before the election.

Franklin Roosevelt, Thatcher, Reagan and Mitterrand clearly got authorizations of that kind. A counter-example is Jacques Chirac in 1995. Once elected, he attempted reforms that were almost the exact opposite of what he had announced and he lost the legislative election of 1997 largely as a consequence.

3.2 Introducing Decentralization

Decentralization and federalism occupy a relatively secondary place in the literature on reforms as processes. A question which has not lacked attention, however, is: does existing decentralization, or do federalist features, of the political system make the process of reform slower and more difficult? The immediate answer to the question is that they do (Treisman 2007). In the language of Tsebelis (2002), decentralization and *a fortiori* federalism increase the number of 'veto players'. This may occur at the level of the subcentral governments if their acquiescence or cooperation is needed, either to enact the reform or to implement it once enacted. It may also occur at the central level inasmuch as the subcentral governments are represented there. This representation may be official as is the case with the Bundesrat in Germany (as was also the case of the Senate of the United States until 1909) and, if we extend our reasoning to the EU, with the Economic Council and the Council of Ministers in Brussels. But the representation and veto powers may also be *de facto*, as is the case with the senates in many countries (the United States after 1909, Switzerland or

France, for instance). A particular mechanism is the 'cumul des mandats' in France: most members of the two houses of parliament and many ministers are also elected officials in subcentral governments (mayors of large cities or presidents of regional or 'general' councils, in particular). This gives these governments a *de facto* representation in the central institutions and a degree of veto power, particularly likely to be employed whenever they are concerned in one way or another by a planned reform.

The blocking powers of veto players should not be exaggerated, however. Their main effect is to impose negotiation, side payments and compromise. Some politicians are better than others at dealing with veto players. According to Pierson (1994), Nixon and his own brand of 'New Federalism' were more successful than Reagan and his scheme because Nixon found ways to gain the acquiescence of the states. Veto powers, like the rule of unanimity where it applies, are likely to slow down decision-making, change and reforms processes but seldom to block them (see Salmon 2004 for an elaboration of that argument in the EU context). The likelihood that veto players will be unable (or unwilling) to block reform is greater when the authorizations and mandates given by the electorate are particularly clear and strong. According to Bruce Ackerman (1993, 2000), 'We the People' mandates occurred rarely in the history of the United States but when they did occur their strength proved overwhelming, including over veto powers related to federalism.

An additional remark is that decentralization may weaken the blocking capacity of players situated at the centre of the system, in particular the central bureaucracy and the national lobbies (we return to that in the next subsection). And another remark is that slowing change and imposing negotiation and compromise may make reforms more durable and their reversal more difficult (see Salmon 2004 in the EU context).

A second question raised by the introduction of decentralization in the discussion of reforms as processes is the role that decentralization or centralization programmes play in these processes. A distinction between the course initially planned and how things turn out may be useful at this stage. With regard to intentions and endeavours, it seems clear that centralization was instrumental to the New Deal programme, particularly in its spending and regulatory dimensions. As we saw, decentralization and centralization were also instrumental in Reagan's and Thatcher's programmes. In the former, decentralization seemed a good way to deregulate, reduce spending and, most importantly, curb the bureaucracy in Washington. For Thatcher, centralization was meant to facilitate privatization, especially given the local positions held by the Labour Party, and to promote a competitive market economy. In the platform put forward by Nicolas Sarkozy in 2007, it seems that the modest attention given to the matter of decentralization was inspired mainly by the central objective of reducing public spending. In these different cases, albeit to a varying degree, changing the degree or the form of decentralization is clearly an instrument to facilitate the main reforms, which have other objectives.

In other instances, the association of decentralization or centralization with economic reforms is dictated by considerations of coalition building or of getting voters' 'authorization'. The question of centralization or decentralization is, so to say, 'orthogonal' to the reforms themselves. This is the case of the Mitterrand reform of 1981. Decentralization was necessary not to implement or facilitate the main programme but to get the support of fractions of the Socialist Party led by Gaston Deferre and by Michel Rocard. In a similar way, with some differences related to the political setting, the reform programme announced by Silvio Berlusconi in 2008 had a decentralization dimension that reflected the necessity of getting the support of the federalists of the League. The matter is more subtle in the case of the centralization process at work in the EU. Centralization is required both by the logic of the change in the economic system (establishing a unified regulatory space to 'complete' the internal market, especially with regard to services) and by the necessities of coalition building (Salmon 2004). Finally, decentralization may become necessary for coalition building outside any context of large-scale economic reform. Canada and Spain illustrate that possibility, which lies outside the scope of our discussion.[14]

When it is instrumental, has the variation in decentralization helped achieve the main objective? A brief answer is: 'yes' in the case of the New Deal, notably because centralization has benefited from a 'We the People' authorization; 'yes' again in the case of Thatcher, because the centralization has crushed the opposition to reform of the Labour-held local authorities; and 'not really' in the case of Reagan, the substantial deregulation which was achieved owing little to decentralization. Mitterrand's overall reforms collapsed rapidly independently of the decentralization which was implemented concurrently and which did prove durable.

3.3 Variations in Decentralization as Open-ended Reform Processes: A Tentative Hypothesis

Treisman (2007) concludes as follows the chapter of his book in which he reviews the empirical work published on the effects of political decentralization: 'To those convinced that theory in this area implies almost no general effects, the weak, partial, and inconclusive flavor of the empirical literature is not puzzling at all. It is what one would expect.' At some level of generality, I think that we may agree with that assessment. There is no compelling reason to predict that countries that are more decentralized – or, for that matter, centralized – will be found to have a better economic system or a higher rate of economic growth. It will all depend on many idiosyncratic characteristics of the country. In some cases decentralization will be complementary with the way the market functions, and the association of both will be efficient or growth enhancing. In other cases, centralized governance will prove more appropriate. The combination which works best in France or Japan, given the traditions of the countries, the way their elites are educated, the mentality of their citizens, etc. may be different from the combination which works best, say, in Canada or Switzerland. Consequently, it is not surprising that empirical work does not uncover robust relations between these two sets of variables (economic performance and the state of political decentralization).

The matter is somewhat similar to the question of whether we can derive robust results from theorizing about the organization of business firms. In spite of a huge literature and much work of the highest quality, little can be said with real confidence about what structure of the firm or of organization of its management will prove, in a general way, most efficient or most favourable to profits, growth, survival, or the welfare of its various stakeholders. A conjecture may be formed, however, that a given business firm, in a competitive environment, will have some incentive to adopt the form of management and control which is the most appropriate to its particular circumstances, or at least that it will have an incentive to change the arrangements in force if they turn out to be seriously deficient or unsatisfactory along some dimension deemed essential. This will necessarily follow a trial and error pattern – or, in the language of Karl Popper, a conjecture and refutation pattern. Of course, many *caveats* come to mind: irrationality, intellectual fads, personal interests opposed to 'the interest of the firm', path dependency, and so on.

In a similar vein, if we can assume that, as an effect of yardstick competition at the international level or for some other reason, national governments are not wholly inefficient, we may form the conjecture that, if they can, these governments will vary the degree or the scope of decentralization to improve the country's performance when it is found particularly deficient. They may do that in particular domains (health, education, culture, etc.) or more broadly. Again, this will follow a trial and error, or conjecture and refutation, pattern; and many *caveats* should be introduced (influence of fads, the World Bank, selfish calculations, and so on).[15] Instead of the usual cross-section analysis relating states of decentralization and performance, our reasoning suggests focussing on the relation between *changes* in decentralization and either *levels* of performance or *changes* in these levels, these variables being measured in absolute or preferably comparative terms by experts. To make the suggestion somewhat more precise (at the cost of making it even more tentative), let me formulate the following hypotheses:

H_1 Some of the observed positive or negative variations in the degree of decentralization in country *j* are explained by observed (comparative) underperformance;

H_2 Some of the observed positive or negative variations in the degree of decentralization in country *j* are followed by an improvement in observed (comparative) performance.

The hypotheses could concern macroeconomic variables like the rate of economic growth or sectional ones like education or health. All this is clearly in need of much elaboration (see Salmon 2010 for a small step in that direction). For the time being, I will limit myself to three remarks.

First, the same empirical hypotheses could be derived from a different but related mechanism, even more distant than the foregoing from any notion of design. Many years ago, Mancur Olson (1982) stressed the negative effect on economic performance of a slow process in which collective decisions are progressively captured by the increasing number of interest categories which manage (in spite of the logic of free riding) to mobilize themselves into organized pressure groups. If unchecked, this process tends to generate over time a sclerosis of the economic system. Ronald Wintrobe and Albert Breton (1986) proposed a mechanism based on the accumulation of trust that may lead to a comparable result. According to Olson, a positive side effect of major disruptions such as revolutions and wars is that of destroying the mobilization underlying the organization of the pressure groups and thus the basis of capture itself. Thanks to the disruptive events, the economy is liberated and can grow again or more rapidly. Drawing some inspiration from the story, we may form the hypothesis that governments can change the decentralization arrangements just for the sake of disaggregating networks that are a cause of persistent underperformance. For instance, if decision-making on education is concentrated at the level of the central government and is captured by a coalition of education officials located at this level and unions, transferring competencies in that area to a lower level of government may be a way to destroy the network and improve performance in education – and as a consequence, if that area is deemed important, performance of the economy as a whole. Or it may be the other way around – that is, transferring the competencies from the lower tiers of government to the higher tiers may do the job. A strategy of this kind may underlie in some cases the empirical hypotheses mentioned above. And its repetition could also account for a more extended sequence in which decentralization and recentralization are observed to alternate – although such observation might simply reflect the trial and error pattern mentioned earlier.

A second remark is that the scepticism expressed in the last section about analytical systemic 'models' of the relationship between governance and decentralization does not extend to the role of models of the same relationship in the perceptions and decisions of office-holders and voters. The Chinese experience is certainly a source of inspiration to many other countries, but the way it is interpreted and transposed to the setting of any one of these countries should be seen as part of the trial and error process mentioned above. Under a Popperian or quasi-Popperian perspective, the way conjectures are formed does not matter as much as the way they are tested and rejected if necessary. Voters and office-holders seek and find their inspiration as they want (or can), and come to their own conclusions about what works and does not. This explains that countries may remain faithful to solutions that seem initially unorthodox but prove efficient with hindsight. *Mutatis mutandis* (because it is not a democracy) a case in point is China itself.

As a last remark, I must note that the same variations in decentralization and the same relations between them and performance could be the consequence, not of a deliberate policy by the central government responding alone to underperformance, but the effect of a dynamic version of the efficiency-enhancing vertical competition among governments analyzed by Breton (e.g. 1996, 2006). For instance, the underperformance of the overall governmental system in some policy area, might, in a context of competition for consent, trigger a response from the regional governments, or some of them, rather than from the central government, and this may eventually bring about a durable change in the degree of decentralization in that policy area or more broadly. The federal or unitary nature of the governmental system certainly has a bearing on the relative importance of processes of that kind and on the way they are to be specified.

4. CONCLUDING REMARKS

Large-scale reforms of the economic system typically occur in political contexts in which the central governments are authorized to reshape institutional arrangements concerning their relationship with subcentral governments. Actually, in democratic and rich countries at least, large-scale reforms of the economic system do not seem to have been accompanied by durable changes in these arrangements, the main exception being the

New Deal. This might be somewhat surprising given the emphasis that the recent work on fiscal federalism puts on the effects on the economy of features of the institutional and political system related to centralization or decentralization. The problem seems to be that most of the literature addresses the relation between the economy and the institutions as a matter of design, subject to the usual treatment in comparative statics. Under that perspective, not much that is general has been established (except, perhaps, the proposition that there is no general significant effect of decentralization on the economy). A perspective in which changes in the economic system and/or in the state of decentralization are treated as processes seems more promising. Even though the state of political centralization and decentralization is very dependent on idiosyncratic characteristics of the countries, most of them of a non-economic kind, under that second perspective some hypotheses may be tentatively formulated about the relationship between the performance over time of an economy, or a subset thereof, and variations in decentralization.

NOTES

* The chapter has been prepared for a volume of essays in honour of Professor José Casas Pardo. It draws in part on a presentation at the conference *Modello Piemonte: sistemi ed economie territoriali a confronto*, organized by *IRES Piemonte* for its 50th anniversary, Turin (Italy), 12–13 February 2009.

1. The case of Public Choice in Britain is relatively straightforward. Few economists or political scientists associate themselves with Public Choice or political economy in that country, and they were even fewer at the time of Thatcher, which is the time period relevant for the claim formulated in the text. Consequently, to support that claim, it is unnecessary, in the case of Britain, to discuss the nature of the association of individual scholars with Public Choice. Extending the comparison to other European countries (Germany, Italy and Switzerland in particular), in which Public Choice seems to have been more successful, would require taking into account not only the number of scholars associated in some sense with Public Choice but also the content of their work.
2. This comparison turns out to be a little unhappy in the light of what we have discovered recently about financial markets and the remuneration of managers.
3. An estimate of the diminution that could result was provided by Gramlich (1982).
4. Cf. Judt (2005), pp. 540–41: 'What Thatcherism stood for more than anything else was "the smack of firm government" Indeed, and for all her talk of the individual and the market, Margaret Thatcher presided over a remarkable and somewhat disconcerting revival of the British state. In administration she was an instinctive centralizer. To ensure that her writ carried throughout the land, she reduced the powers and budgets of local government (the 1986 Local Government Act dismantled Britain's metropolitan authorities, taking their powers back to London, just as the rest of Europe was engaged in a large-scale decentralization of power). The direction of educational policy and regional economic planning reverted to central government departments under direct political control.'
5. Richard Bird and François Vaillancourt (2005, p. 36) note: 'It should be understood that Canada is not, and never has been, a full internal common market. There has been a long tradition of accepting that provinces not only may have their own economic poli-

cies but can and do sometimes implement them in ways that reduce national economic efficiency.' And (p. 37): 'Regulatory federalism in Canada . . . does not easily fit the Weingast (1995) conception of "market-preserving federalism". The "competitive" subnational governments envisaged in that framework may have a substantial regulatory role, but they are assumed to exercise that role within a common market enforced by the federal government to ensure nation-wide free markets and full mobility of factors, goods and services. In many fields Canada's federal government either cannot exercise such a role or has chosen not to do so.'

6. In Canada, negotiations of that kind, addressing only a subset of impediments to trade and distortions of competition, led to the 'Internal Agreement on Trade' signed by the provinces and territories in 1995.
7. See Mueller (2000) for a more sympathetic political economy analysis of state aids.
8. As Weingast (2009) writes: 'Whatever the goals of subnational officials, greater revenue relaxes their budget constraint, allowing them to further their goals.'
9. If there is no reason to distrust the central government more than the subcentral ones, one may interpret Weingast's financial incentives approach as relevant not for the justification of political decentralization but for the way financial resources should be shared in an already existing decentralized system.
10. The point is relevant also, to some extent, to non-democratic settings (provided they are not of an extreme variety as is the case currently of North Korea). In all political regimes, office-holders typically seek some consent from the population. Consequently, if decentralization in China is considered to have played a large role in the performance of that country this may be, in part at least, because the way it has been implemented has ensured that governments or authorities at all levels have received some consent on the part of the population. This argument is not incompatible with the stress put on the distribution of the growth surplus because it is possible that part of this surplus is used to gain the consent of the local population – which may compensate for some popular policies being eroded by mobility-based competition. For this to be investigated, an explicit acknowledgement of the relevance of democratic or quasi-democratic mechanisms would be needed however.
11. As Susan Rose-Ackerman wrote in a book published in 1991 (cited in Breton and Salmon 2001), the response of the Reagan administration 'to the growth of state regulatory activity was to propose preemptive regulations in such areas as nuclear power, trucking, state workfare, drug labeling, products liability, coastal zone management, taxicab licensing, affirmative action, the minimum drinking age, and the transport of hazardous waste.' She adds: 'According to one study, ninety-one explicit federal preemption statutes were enacted during the two Reagan administrations. These statutes represented 25 percent of all federal preemption laws enacted since the founding of the republic. This seems an odd outcome to emerge from an administration supposedly committed to the "new federalism" of increased state authority.'
12. A volume including many seminal contributions is Sturzenegger and Tommasi (1998). See also Rodrik (1996).
13. An interesting collection of case studies of such reforms and a convincing systematization inspired by them are offered in the volume produced by Boeri et al. (2006) for the Rodolfo Debenedetti Foundation.
14. On the political decentralization associated with the Spanish transition to democracy and the way it was reflected in the Constitution of 1978, see Brennan and Casas Pardo (1991).
15. Although they do not refer to yardstick competition and do not focus on economic growth or performance, a fallibilist perspective in the spirit of Popper apparently underlies Bird and Vaillancourt's analysis of the vagaries of intergovernmental arrangements in Canada when they write: '"Muddling through" may not only describe how Canadian federalism has to date dealt with changing times: it may also . . . describe the best way in which fallible people – let alone fallible politicians – have yet developed to cope with the complex reality of managing a multi-ethnic federal country in a globalizing world' (2005, p. 39).

REFERENCES

Ackerman, Bruce (1993, 2000), *We the People*, Volumes 1 and 2, Cambridge, MA: Harvard University Press.

Bird, Richard M. and François Vaillancourt (2005), 'Changing with the times: success, failure and inertia in Canadian federal arrangements, 1945–2002', MS.

Blanchard, Olivier and Andrei Shleifer (2001), 'Federalism with and without political centralization: China versus Russia', *IMF Staff Papers*, **48** (4 Special Issue), 171–9.

Boeri, Tito, Micael Castanheira, Riccardo Faini and Vincenzo Galasso (eds) (2006), *Structural Reforms Without Prejudice*, Oxford and New York: Oxford University Press.

Brennan, Geoffrey and James M. Buchanan (1980), *The Power to Tax: Analytical Foundations of a Fiscal Constitution*, Cambridge and New York: Cambridge University Press.

Brennan, Geoffrey and José Casas Pardo (1991), 'A reading of the Spanish Constitution (1978)', *Constitutional Political Economy*, **2** (1), 53–79.

Breton, Albert (1996), *Competitive Governments. An Economic Theory of Politics and Public Finance*, Cambridge and New York: Cambridge University Press.

Breton, Albert (2006), 'Modelling vertical competition', in E. Ahmad and G. Brosio (eds), *Handbook of Fiscal Federalism*, Cheltenham, UK and Northampton, MA, USA: Edward Elgar, pp. 86–105.

Breton, Albert and Pierre Salmon (2001), 'External effects of domestic regulations: comparing internal and international barriers to trade', *International Review of Law and Economics*, **21** (2), 135–55.

Enikolopov, Ruben and Ekatarina V. Zhuravskaya (2007), 'Decentralization and political institutions', *Journal of Public Economics*, **91** (11–12), 2261–90.

Gramlich, Edward M. (1982), 'An econometric examination of the New Federalism', *Brookings Papers on Economic Activity*, **2**, 327–60.

Jin, J., Y. Qian and B.R. Weingast (2005), 'Regional decentralization and fiscal incentives: federalism, Chinese style', *Journal of Public Economics*, **89**, 1719–42.

Judt, Tony (2005), *Postwar: A History of Europe Since 1945*, London: Pimlico Edition, 2007.

Keeler, John T.S. (1993), 'Opening the window for reform: mandates, crises, and extraordinary policy-making', *Comparative Political Studies*, **25** (4), 433–86.

Mueller, Dennis C. (2000), 'Public subsidies for private firms in a federalist democracy', in Gianluigi Galeotti, Pierre Salmon and Ronald Wintrobe (eds), *Competition and Structure: The Political Economy of Collective Decisions: Essays in Honor of Albert Breton*, Cambridge and New York: Cambridge University Press, pp. 339–63.

Olson, Mancur (1982), *The Rise and Decline of Nations*, New Haven, CT: Yale University Press.

Pierson, Paul (1994), *Dismantling the Welfare State? Reagan, Thatcher, and the Politics of Retrenchment*, Cambridge and New York: Cambridge University Press.

Riker, William H. (1964), *Federalism: Origins, Operation, Significance*, Boston: Little, Brown, and Co.

Rodden, Jonathan and Susan Rose-Ackerman (1997), 'Does federalism preserve markets?', *Virginia Law Review*, **83** (7), 1521–72.

Rodrik, D. (1996), 'Understanding economic policy reform', *Journal of Economic Literature*, **34** (1), 9–41.
Roland, Gérard (2000), *Transition and Economics: Politics, Markets, and Firms*, Cambridge, MA: The MIT Press.
Salmon, Pierre (1987), 'Decentralisation as an incentive scheme', *Oxford Review of Economic Policy*, **3** (2), 24–43.
Salmon, Pierre (1991), 'Checks and balances and international openness', in Albert Breton, Gianluigi Galeotti, Pierre Salmon and Ronald Wintrobe (eds), *The Competitive State*, Dordrecht: Kluwer, pp. 169–84.
Salmon, Pierre (2003), 'Accounting for centralisation in the European Union: Niskanen, Monnet or Thatcher?', in Jean-Michel Josselin and Alain Marciano (eds), *From Economic to Legal Competition: New Perspectives on Law and Institutions in Europe*, Cheltenham, UK and Northampton, MA, USA: Edward Elgar, pp. 165–91.
Salmon, Pierre (2004), 'The assignment of powers in an open-ended European Union', in Charles B. Blankart and Dennis C. Mueller (eds), *A Constitution for the European Union*, Cambridge, MA: The MIT Press, pp. 37–60.
Salmon, Pierre (2010), 'Improving performance by political decentralization (or centralization)?', MS.
Singh, Nirvikar (2007), 'Fiscal decentralization in China and India: competitive, cooperative or market preserving federalism?', MS.
Singh, Nirvikar and T.N. Srinivasan (2006), 'Federalism and economic development in India: an assessment', MS.
Sturzenegger, Federico and Mariano Tommasi (eds) (1998), *The Political Economy of Reform*, Cambridge, MA: The MIT Press.
Treisman, Daniel (2007), *The Architecture of Government: Rethinking Political Decentralization*, Cambridge and New York: Cambridge University Press.
Tsebelis, George (2002), *Veto Players: How Political Institutions Work*, Princeton: Princeton University Press.
Weingast, Barry R. (1993), 'Constitutions as governance structures: the political foundations of secure markets', *Journal of Institutional and Theoretical Economics*, **149** (1), 286–311.
Weingast, Barry R. (1995), 'The economic role of political institutions: market-preserving federalism and economic development', *Journal of Law, Economics, and Organization*, **11** (1), 1–31.
Weingast, Barry R. (2009), 'Second generation fiscal federalism: the implications of fiscal incentives, *Journal of Urban Economics*, **65**, 279–93.
Wintrobe, Ronald and Albert Breton (1986), 'Organizational structure and productivity', *American Economic Review*, **76** (3), 530–38.

6. Democracy-preserving institutions: the quasi-federal system of South Africa

Giorgio Brosio

INTRODUCTION

Since Montesquieu, de Tocqueville and the Federalists, federal and decentralized systems are considered as a political/constitutional medicine for introducing/preserving/enhancing democratic rule. This argument has been recently used for recommending federal/decentralized arrangements – as a starter of democracy – in a number of countries, including Iraq, Afghanistan, Somalia and Sudan, and all with no tradition of democratic institutions. It has also been, and is still, used – as a preserving/enhancing mechanism – for countries with democratic institutions that have been, or could be, put at risk by potentially democracy-undermining practices, such as sustained single party rule, as in the case of Mexico, or as at present in South Africa.

The present chapter intends to contribute to this debate by illustrating and debating the case of South Africa, one of the most interesting cases of current decentralization processes. This interest stems not only from the peculiarities of the fiscal institutions that have been introduced and/or transformed, but also from the peculiar socio-political framework in which the transformation is taking place.

The territorial system of government of South Africa is torn between two distinct, wrenching and pulling apart pressures, namely, centralization and decentralization. A central priority of post-apartheid governments in South Africa has been to provide basic services to its entire people as soon as possible and to eliminate the legacy of the previous regime on the distribution of income and wealth. The urgency to fill the most blatant gaps would have called, according to a widely held view, for a centralized system. However, most public services have been decentralized through the creation, under the constitution of 1996, of a three-layered quasi-federal system.

This constitution is the result of the negotiation between all political movements that took place during the transition from apartheid to democracy (Lodge, 1994, 1999; Schlemmer, 1999; Shapiro, 1993; Sparks, 1995). Constitutional provisions, however, have been implemented to date with a view to strengthening the powers of the central government. Its present policy is to promote a substantial equalization of public services, and is based on a strong belief that centralization is indispensable for reaching an equitable provision of services.

In principle, there is no opposition between decentralization and equitable provision of services. The international experience shows that highly decentralized systems are capable of implementing a far-reaching equalization of public services. At the same time, a decentralized or federal system is a fundamental checks and balances mechanism. This is particularly true for a country, such as South Africa, that still shows deep racial divisions, where wealth is distributed extremely unequally, where the electoral gap between the governing party, the ANC, and the opposition is extremely wide and where the former has high chances of remaining unchallenged in power at the central level for the next few decades. At the provincial level, however, the ANC is less monolithic, allowing some competition into the public sector. A well designed decentralized system is thus essential for enhancing democracy in a country with the socio-economic and political characteristics of present South Africa and for equitable and efficient provision of services.

The chapter is structured into five sections, plus the conclusion. The first section illustrates the political framework of present-day South Africa. The second section is mostly theoretical and deals with democracy-preserving institutions for highly divided societies. The third section illustrates briefly the territorial system of government under apartheid. The fourth section details the new decentralized institutions as they emerge from the constitutional provisions. The fifth section illustrates the evolution of the system and its actual working. It is followed by the conclusions.

1. THE POLITICAL FRAMEWORK OF SOUTH AFRICA

A few basic facts characterize present-day politics in South Africa.

The first of these is the existence of a predominant party – the African National Congress (ANC) – which has collected almost two-thirds of total votes (and seats, given the pure proportional representation system) at all post-apartheid parliamentary elections (1994, 1999, 2004 and 2009). Even the recent split (2008) of the ANC caused by the creation from its ranks of

COPE (Congress of the People) did not scratch the predominance of the ANC. Its share of the total votes in 2009, 65.9 per cent, was only barely lower than that received in 2004 (69 per cent), despite the party split.

The ANC is still reaping the fruits of its long-standing struggle against apartheid. The ANC is able to hugely distance itself from its closest competitor, now the Democratic Alliance (DA), which in 2009 got 16.66 per cent of the vote, with an increase of about 4 percentage point since the previous election of 2004.

The third political movement is, traditionally, the Inkatha Freedom Party (IFP), whose constituency is mostly restricted to the Zulu-speaking areas. The results of the elections are shown in Table 6A.1 of Appendix 1.

The second fact that characterizes South African politics is the clear racial alignment of voters. Although the main political movements have made substantial efforts to expand their constituency beyond racial borders by including in their election lists candidates from other ethnic groups, they are still failing to overcome the legacy of the past. The ANC receives the support of about 90 per cent of blacks and of most of the better-educated Indian voters, as well. The ANC is able to capture the votes of only 2 to 3 per cent of the white constituency, despite the recent merge with the old National Party, which was in power continuously from 1948 and negotiated the transition to democracy. The DA has mainly a white and colored constituency. The same incapacity to attract votes in all ethnic groups also characterizes the electoral record of the Inkatha Freedom Party. (See Deegan, 1999; Reynolds, 1994.)

The third fact worth mentioning is the adoption, by the constitution of 1996, of a Westminster system of representative government. The Westminster model is characterized by the unity of the legislative and the executive. This model makes for parties strictly controlled by their leadership and produces a strong central government with few checks and balances operating at the same level of government. In fact, in this system the main check on the governing party comes from the contestability of government; that is, from the possibility that the party in power will be effectively challenged and defeated, at elections, by the opposition. However, given South Africa's ethnic demographics and the strong racial alignment of voters, the chances of any alternation in power look quite slim.

The combination of these three facts has raised fears – both at home and abroad – that a single party dominant system, with a winner-takes-all politics, has been established for a long time in South Africa. This could endanger the survival prospects of the newly born democratic system. These fears are based on different grounds. Some of these are largely theoretical. Some refer to present-day politics in South Africa.

The main theoretical argument mirrors Schumpeter's view of procedural democracy. According to this view, the selection of rulers through a fully competitive struggle for the people's vote characterizes a democratic system. If this is the essence of democracy – the argument goes – its survival in South Africa could be endangered by the impact on competition of the racial alignment of voters. This is because, when it prevails, voters' choices are not dictated by the evaluation of the performance of the governing party, but rather by loyalty factors, thus reducing competition.

As Lodge (2002, p. 154, quoted by Matshiqi, 2009) has written,

> if that party is a nationalist movement that broadly represents a racial majority in a society which has a history of racial conflict and racial oppression, and if it represents the formerly oppressed group most closely, it might be argued that its supporters will be fairly uncritical or undemanding and that this leaves its leadership scope for plenty of misbehavior.

A second argument combines theoretical issues and real world problems. Democracy, it is advanced, is a fragile, self-enforcing mechanism. It relies on the participation of all the relevant political groups, although the democratic process may produce outcomes that severely hurt some of these groups. Thus, democratic institutions have to be devised in such a way as to offer the relevant political forces 'a prospect of eventually advancing their interests that is sufficient to incite them to comply with immediately unfavorable outcomes' (Przeworski, 1991, p. 19; the reference he makes is to transition to democracy in Latin America). In South Africa, the group that is facing the prospect of unfavorable outcomes is presently the white minority. White voters still dominate the economy and the income distribution still shows still a clear racial alignment.

South Africa had, and still has, one of the most unequal distributions of income anywhere across the world. From 1996 to 2008 there has actually been no reduction in inequality in South Africa as a whole; the Gini coefficient has a value of 0.66 in 2008. Obviously, there is a huge inequality not only between races, but also within race groups. Table 6.1 gives a succinct description of both inequalities, by reporting (in the middle column) the median and mean income per capita of different racial groups, and the ratio of median to mean, in the last column. The higher this ratio, the larger is inequality.

The average per capita income of the white people is in 2008 approximately 9.5 times higher than that of the black people. Asians fare much better than black and colored people, but much worse than whites. The income inequality within the races is very pronounced and higher for black and Asian peoples than for whites. It is also connected mostly to the location of income earners. For example, blacks living in large metropolitan areas have a per capita income much higher than that of blacks living in the rural areas.

Table 6.1 South Africa: mean and median per capita income by racial component, 2008 (Rands)

	per capita income	% of median to mean
African: mean	845	
African: median	453	53.61
Colored: mean	1495	
Colored: median	712	47.6
Asian: mean	2986	
Asian: median	713	23.8
White: mean	8141	
White: median	5667	69.6
Total: mean	1631	
Total: median	537	32.9

Source: Presidency of South Africa, *Development Indicators 2009*.

Table 6.2 Infant mortality rate (per 1000 live births) in 2009

Black	48.2
Colored	38.8
Asian	28.7
White	19.5
South Africa	45.7

Source: The Presidency of South Africa, *Development Indicators 2009*.

The same gap, or an even higher one, appears in the provision of public, especially urban, services that impact directly on the well-being of citizens. The infant mortality rate (reported in Table 6.2) summarizes both socio-economic conditions of households and their access to basic services such as health and education.

Inequalities, combined with the racial alignment of voters, constrain the range of options for redistribution policies. The most obvious – and the one that has actually been chosen – is to concentrate redistribution mostly on the racial divide. In addition to taxes and transfers, a racially oriented policy requires the redistribution of property rights and affirmative action, such as the empowerment of blacks. These latter policies, while redressing the secular and hideous discrimination against non-white citizens, are potentially highly divisive, especially if implemented by a party in power enjoying a predominant and undisturbed political support.

On the other hand, the ANC government has been under pressure to proceed as fast as possible with the redistribution. In fact, threats to the unity of the party are coming from its left wing and from trade union-supported organizations. This puts the ANC on quite a knife edge.

2. DEMOCRACY-PRESERVING DEVICES

Democracy may be preserved in highly divided societies by a number of institutional devices that can be grouped into two distinct categories. The first is made up of checks and balances mechanisms, while the second includes systems of power sharing – also referred to as consociationalist provisions – between the parties that represent distinct communities.

Before entering this field, mention has to be made of the possibility that, even in a system with a predominant political party, democracy may be protected by competition within the field, that is, by competing forces operating inside the predominant party. According to some commentators (see, in particular, Horowitz, 1991, and Koelble, 1997), competition within the field is likely to play an important role in South Africa. They argue that the ANC is far from being a monolithic party. It is, rather, an umbrella of ideologically, ethnically and even historically diverse forces held together by the struggle against apartheid. However, these comments understate the importance of organization issues, as shown by the secession from the ANC and the creation in 2008 of COPE, which has only slightly reduced the electoral strength of the ANC. In any case, despite the present democratic credentials of the ANC, nobody can predict how this party will evolve as a consequence of its staying in power. Thus appropriate institutional devices are still needed.

Consociationalist provisions are widely used across the world (Bogdanov, 1997; Lijphart, 1969, 1977). They may be either formal or, as in the Swiss case, informal. In any case, they require the concurrence of all groups in all major decisions and the delegation of decisions involving only the interests of particular groups to the groups in question. These provisions may refer to the election system, or they can impact on the government, that is, on the executive level. An example of sharing of power at the election level was provided by India until 1985, where 15 per cent of the seats in the federal Lower House were reserved for the so-called Scheduled tribes and Scheduled castes.

The South African constitution does not make use of this instrument. The proportional system of closed party lists introduced for the selection of legislators gives minorities a representation that perfectly matches the number of their voters. An example of sharing of power at the executive level is provided by Belgium, where the new constitution requires that, 'with the possible exception of the Prime Minister, the cabinet comprises an equal number of French-speaking and Dutch-speaking ministers'. This provides an over representation to the French-speaking segment of the population.

Consociationalism, while protecting minorities, enhances the role of the elites and favors the political status quo. It is consequently considered a poor instrument for protecting the rights of the poorest segments of the population and for fostering equality.

Consociationalist devices were hotly debated in South Africa during the transition phase, without finally finding a fertile soil. The apartheid history made the idea of giving specific rights to the various ethnic groups – the targeted group being in reality the white minority – taboo, and all the proposals made by the ANC had thus to be abandoned. Consociationalist devices were used only temporarily during the Government of National Unity, which assumed office in 1994 and included representatives from all the main political parties. The agreement was that it should last for no more than five years, but it came to an early anticipated end in 1996 after the NNP decided to withdraw. No similar provision was introduced in the final constitution.

The constitution of 1996 includes a number of checks and balances. There is a Constitutional Court and an extensive list of basic rights whose infringement may be brought to the Court. However, the most effective check on the dominance of central government by the actual occupier is potentially the quasi-federal system; that is, the sharing of power between different levels of government, as is done in federal or highly politically decentralized systems.

Decentralization and federalism mean fundamentally vertical separation of powers. They are competition-promoting institutions, as was clearly illustrated in the *Federalist Papers* more than two centuries ago. In a federal or decentralized system there are two different kinds of competition: namely, vertical and horizontal.

Vertical competition is competition for power between different layers of government. It derives from the quest for power by politicians (and bureaucrats). It plays, among layers of government, the same role played – within the same layer – by horizontal competition, that is, by horizontal separation of powers. When citizens are dissatisfied with their central government, they can address their local government, and vice versa. Vertical competition can take place even where responsibilities are completely separated between different layers of government. This is because vertical competition does not derive from the overlapping of functions, but rather from the intersection of the effects of separate functions.

Horizontal competition takes place between governments situated within the same layer. There are many models of horizontal competition. Tiebout's model is the most famous, but it requires mobility and other equally unrealistic assumptions. Pierre Salmon (1987a, 1987b), has suggested an alternative and much more realistic model. Salmon postulates that citizens assess their government performance by comparing, in the field of their interest, this performance to that of governments in other jurisdictions. Because of this performance comparison, each government has an incentive to do better than governments in other jurisdictions in terms of levels and quality of services, levels of taxes, or more general economic and social indicators. The strength of this incentive depends on the possibility and willingness of citizens to make assessments of comparative performance, and on the impact these assessments will have on politicians.

The Salmon mechanism appears to be fairly realistic, especially in the present era of rapidly circulating information. Moreover, it requires neither mobility nor homogeneity of preferences within jurisdictions and non-homogeneity of preferences between jurisdictions, as other famous models, such as Oates's, do. Instead, performance comparisons are more likely to take place when preferences are non-homogeneous within and homogeneous between jurisdictions, as is likely to be the case of present-day South Africa.

In the South African context, where sub-national government units were not created along racial divides, federalism not only mitigates the extremes of winner-takes-all politics, but it can also promote some intra-ethnic political fragmentation – that is, a non-racial but policy-oriented alignment of voters. This looks still very slow to emerge, although at the provincial level electoral competition does not completely reflect the national pattern. To be more precise, in the Western Cape Province, the coloreds and not the Africans are the majority of electors. Here the ANC has never won an absolute majority of votes and in the 2009 election the DA won the majority of seats in the provincial council. Thus, out of nine provinces, one is now not governed by the ANC. In addition, in the KwaZulu-Natal province the vote is split significantly between the ANC and Inkatha Freedom Party (IFP). In other words, the single-party dominance of the ANC is a national phenomenon that is not completely mirrored in all of the nine provincial electoral contests.

In a recent paper, Myerson (2006) has developed an argument in favor of federal/decentralized government even in situations – like the South African one – where a limited discrepancy between national and provincial government coalitions is not likely to evolve enough to produce alternation in power at the central government level, but where it still may provide a check on the predominant, or single, party in power. His argument runs as follows.

In countries emerging from one or more generations of authoritarian rule, political leaders and parties that have established reputations for using political power within constitutional limits, are by necessity lacking. To win high office in authoritarian regimes, officials need to cultivate reputations for using power to serve their superiors and to reward their supporters in the political hierarchy. As a consequence, voters in a new democracy would naturally expect that the winner of the first election for control of the national government will use power only for personal benefit and to benefit the inner circle of active supporters. They would also expect that any other politician would behave the same way, if that politician came to power. 'With such low expectations, voters are unlikely to support democratic challengers to the ruling party, and they might see little reason to protest if the government suppressed its political opposition' (Myerson, 2006, p. 4). A solution to this problem may derive from giving to more politicians independent opportunities to cultivate such reputations. This is the case of federal/decentralized systems, where the division of powers creates a layer of independent provincial leaders who have motivation and opportunities to start cultivating reputations for good democratic government. The key, according to Myerson, is that provincial leaders exercise real governmental power, and they have incentives to use this power to challenge the national leadership. Thus, in a federal system, the forces of democratic competition may be sharpened by the national ambitions of local leaders.

To complete the picture the party in power at the national level could also be aware of this potential challenge and could be tempted to reduce the risk by reducing the powers of decentralized governments and leaders. This is more than a possibility. On the other hand, provincial leaders and parties could use their reputation to build secessionist threats.

In both cases federalism and decentralization – and their potential impact – could be imperiled by the behavior of political parties and leaders, as explained by Bednar et al. (1999) and Filippov et al. (2004).

The remainder of this chapter concentrates on the South African solution, starting with an account of how things were before the start of the transition.

3. THE OLD SYSTEM OF TERRITORIAL GOVERNMENT

Let us begin with the territorial implications of the apartheid regime (see Ahmad, 1998; Cameron, 1995; Cloete, 1982). Apartheid was a system of racial separation, or, more precisely, of racially based exploitation.

Exploitation started with land ownership. In fact, territory, or rather sheer discrimination in the distribution of rights to use territory, was the embodiment of the apartheid regime (Mamdani, 1996). Apartheid reserved 87 per cent of the land for whites, whose percentage in the total population has shrunk in the last two decades from 20 to little more than 10 per cent. The black population was herded into the 'homelands' that contained some of the most barren land in the country. Apartheid also shaped the urban landscape of South Africa. At the peak of apartheid, only whites were allowed to live in city centers and the surrounding areas. Urban blacks, Indians and coloreds were forced to live almost exclusively in the *townships*, that is, in dormitories that were created at a substantial distance from the centers of the cities and their white suburbs. They were, however, not allowed to buy properties in the townships, but had to rent publicly provided accommodation. Moreover, manufacturing and services were located exclusively in the white areas.

The territorial system of government strictly paralleled these land-use discriminatory policies. That is, it was fragmented along racial lines, totally inequitable in the distribution of resources and highly centralized. It comprised three different layers: the central government, the regional government and the local government. At the central level there were three separate administrations, covering whites, Indians and coloreds under a tricameral system.

The regional layer included three different types of government units: (a) four provincial administrations referring directly to the White House of Assembly; (b) four independent states, and (c) six self-governing territories. Both the independent states and the self-governing territories – the adjectives are clearly misleading, these being mostly puppet states – had a legislative assembly and a very few sources of autonomous revenue, which were supplemented by centrally provided transfers. Lacking democratic legitimacy, both types of regional government indulged in clientelistic and corrupt practices that produced bloated bureaucracies and abysmally low levels of service provision. Moreover, there was no threat of political change and the appointed leaders of the homelands governments had no incentive to improve their performance by better serving their community (Ahmad, 1998). The four provinces – which were the heirs of the corresponding historical four republics that were merged into the Union of South Africa in 1911 – were in charge of health, education and welfare. At the end of the apartheid system, the provinces had been reduced to mostly deconcentrated administrations. They were, however, entitled to receive generous transfers from the central government. As a consequence, their level of services was generally quite high.

Local government was built around two main types of units, namely the

White Local Authorities (WLAs) and the Black Local Authorities (BLAs). Furthermore, a very few local authorities were created for the colored and Indian populations. The WLAs were responsible for the provision of urban services to white residential and commercial areas. The BLAs were responsible for the provision of services to residents of the townships.

Property tax and some minor local taxes, such as the tax on liquor sales, were used to finance both types of local government units. But while WLAs were self-sufficient for revenue matters, given the concentration of wealth within their borders, BLAs and Indian and colored local authorities had to rely on central government transfers, since ownership of property and formal economic activities were forbidden in the townships, thus reducing to zero their actual tax bases. This asymmetry in revenue capacity was obviously paralleled by huge gaps in the level of service provision. While WLAs had standards typical of highly industrialized countries, the standards of BLAs were close to those of less developed countries. It has been estimated (World Bank, 1995) that over half of the black community in urban areas lived in informal settlements without access to basic services, such as electricity, water and sanitation.

In 1987, a higher tier of local government was created, namely the Regional Services Councils (called Joint Services Boards in the province of Natal). Their jurisdictions included both WLAs and BLAs and their councils were responsible for the financing of infrastructure and the provision of some basic services outside the urban areas. They raised their own revenue through the establishment of two taxes, known as the regional services levy, based on wage bills, and the regional establishment levy, based on turnover. The clear purpose of these new units was the reduction of the existing gaps by redistributing some money from WLAs to BLAs. In other words, their creation represented a small, initial blow to territorial apartheid.

4. THE CONSTITUTIONAL FRAMEWORK OF THE NEW SYSTEM

South Africa's intergovernmental system that emerged from the provisional constitution of 1994 and from the final constitution of 1996 represents a substantial transformation. A formerly highly centralized system has been turned into a quasi-federal one, by radically restructuring provincial government through the creation of nine units that have both legislative and executive powers. A three-layered system has emerged, based on the central, the provincial and the local government. The constitution calls for the existence of three distinct and autonomous spheres.

This implies, among other things, that there is no hierarchical relationship between provinces and local governments. The South African constitution diverges in this respect from classical federations and introduces potential competition between layers of government.

However, the constitution also calls for a cooperative system of intergovernmental relations concerning in particular the sharing of resources between the three levels of governments. A special body, the Financial and Fiscal Commission, has been set up by the Constitution (Section 220) to make recommendations to Parliament on the distribution of fiscal and financial resources between the three spheres of government and all issues that may concern sub-national levels of government, such as: (a) grants to sub-national governments; (b) taxes which provinces intend to impose; (c) borrowing by local and provincial governments; (d) criteria to be used for allocating grants. Potentially, the Commission's role could ensure the working of an effective, equitable and sustainable system of intergovernmental fiscal relations.

However, over time a dense network of intergovernmental cooperation bodies – that is, a system of federalism of the executive – has been created. This reduces inevitably the actual role of the Financial and Fiscal Commission, as we will see.

4.1 Provincial Government: Legislative Power and Expenditure Responsibilities

The legislative power of the provinces is closely intertwined with that of the national government. In fact, the constitution of 1996 establishes a bicameral structure, closely reminiscent of the German model. There is a first chamber, the House of Representatives, whose members are popularly elected according to a pure proportional system, and a second chamber, the National Council of Provinces (NCOP), which is composed of delegates from the provinces (ten from each, including six on a permanent basis and four on an ad hoc basis). Only the head of each delegation has the right to vote. This means that unanimity is expected from provinces, even if their legislatures include representatives from rival parties. All questions before the NCOP are agreed when at least five provinces vote in favor of the question.

NCOP's assent (with the supporting vote of at least six provinces) is needed for constitutional amendments. This is clearly a federal characteristic. NCOP's assent is also needed for all bills referring to matters of provincial interest. In other words, provinces take part in the process of passing the legislation that fixes the principles with which their own subsequent legislation will have to be consistent. Bills referring to matters that are not of direct provincial interest also have to be submitted to NCOP, but it has no veto power over them.

Coming to the direct legislative power of provinces, their councils – which are popularly elected with a proportional system – may pass both concurrent and exclusive legislation (as in the German federal model). The main areas of concurrent legislation are provincial planning, roads and transport, economic affairs, social services, health and education. Concurrent legislation means that provincial laws have to be consistent with the general principles set up by the national parliament for the same areas. Bear in mind that these very general principles need the assent of a majority of provinces, via the NCOP. In other words, the legislative power of provinces, considered as a whole, is quite substantial, according to the letter of the constitution.

Exclusive legislation – where provinces have autonomous decision power – refers mostly to culture, sports and recreation; that is, to areas that are much less important in terms of expenditure. (See Appendix 2, for a more inclusive list of provincial responsibilities.)

4.2 Provincial Government: Revenues

The constitution stipulates, as a general principle, that: (a) nationally raised revenue must be distributed equitably between the three spheres of government following the recommendations of the Financial and Fiscal Commission and (b) the provincial share must be divided equitably between the nine provinces. Moreover, the constitution (Section 228(1)) allows provinces to impose taxes, levies and duties other than income tax, VAT, sales tax, rates on property and customs duties. Provinces may also levy a flat-rate surcharge on the tax bases of any tax, levy or duty imposed by national legislation, except for corporate income tax, VAT, rates on property and customs duties. Such taxes must be regulated in terms of national legislation.

Finally, the Constitution (Section 230) allows provinces – as well as municipalities – to borrow capital and bridging finance, subject to national regulation.

While the constitution confers significant autonomy on provincial governments, it creates a coordinating and monitoring role for national government to ensure macroeconomic stability, achievement of national policy goals and obligations, and a consistent standard of services, so that citizens are not prejudiced based on their place of residence. The government achieves this through framework legislation, or setting norms and standards.

Summing up, there is clearly an asymmetry between the powers assigned to the central government and those assigned to the provinces. The national executive has a strong control power *vis-à-vis* the provinces. This asymmetry explains the qualified definition, in this chapter, of South Africa as a quasi-federal country. More precisely, while the central government's assent is needed for all decisions concerning the provinces, the contrary does not hold. Equality of status between the two spheres – which is typical of federal states – does not exist in South Africa.

4.3 Local Government: Structure

The 1996 Constitution mandated a complete transformation of the local government system through the consolidation of the previously existing municipalities into a small number of larger units. There are now three categories of municipalities: metropolitan, district and local (referred to in the constitution as categories A, B and C). Metropolitan (or category A) municipalities (presently six in number) represent large regions that encompass some urbanized areas. In areas that are primarily rural, the local government is divided into district municipalities and local municipalities.

District (or category C) municipalities are the main divisions of provinces. Their present number is 46 and they are subdivided into local (or category B) municipalities. Local municipalities share authority with the district municipality under which they fall. Metropolitan municipalities have no official subdivisions, except in one case, the Johannesburg Metropolitan Municipality.

4.4 Local Government: Missions and Responsibilities

The constitution makes local authorities in South Africa responsible for the promotion of social and economic development and of a safe and healthy environment within their jurisdiction. However, the list of the functions assigned specifically to them is rather short, at least according to international standards, and is concentrated on the provision of urban infrastructure and basic services, such as water, sanitation, transport, and roads. In fact, a peculiarity of the territorial system of government in South Africa is that it assigns a distinct role to the two layers of government *vis-à-vis* capital formation. While provinces are responsible for the provision of social services and thus have to attend to the development of human capital, local governments are responsible for the development of public physical capital and its related services.

4.5 Local Government: Revenue

The Constitution specifies that local authorities may levy rates on property and fees for services. Moreover, if authorized by national legislation, they can also collect other taxes, levies and duties appropriate to local government, with the exclusion of income tax, value-added tax, general sales tax, or customs duties. They are also entitled to an equitable share of national revenue. This provision implies that revenue from municipal own sources may be supplemented by transfers provided by the central government and/or by provinces.

5. THE NEW SYSTEM: HOW IT WORKS

The system has evolved rapidly over the past four years. Being superimposed on existing structures, it has created a number of problems. Tensions have appeared between the national and the sub-national governments.

5.1 Provincial Government: Unevenness of Structure

The process of provincial demarcation took place in 1993; that is, before the promulgation of the new constitution. All political forces took part in the process. Supporters of a decentralized system strongly advocated the creation of provinces with equal fiscal capacity. In their view, this would have narrowed the role of the central government, by reducing the need for equalization and arbitrage between provinces. However, provinces with equally strong fiscal capacity did not make a lot of sense, either in market or in public services terms. It would have implied cutting across metropolitan and/or industrial areas, for example (Muthien and Meshack, 1998).

Demarcation was based mainly on the Development Regions established in the National Development Plan. Obviously, political criteria were not discarded. At the end of the process, nine new provinces came out of the merging of the previous provincial administrations, the independent states and self-governing territories. Provinces vary widely in terms of area, population, urban/rural characteristics and especially in terms of socio-economic development. A few provinces, such as the Western Cape and Gauteng, have a large urban population and are close, in terms of economic and social development, to industrialized countries such as Canada and Singapore. Most of the other provinces are mainly rural and underdeveloped, with a huge proportion of poor households.

Although not created from scratch, but by merging already existing

Table 6.3 Total provincial expenditure, 1996–97 and 2007–08

	1996–97	2007–08	% of total
Education	36 606	88 377	41.4
Health	20 640	62 582	29.3
Welfare	15 938	6 181	2.9
Other expenditure	18 626	56 292	26.4
Total expenditure	91 810	213 432	100.0

Source: Department of Finance, *Intergovernmental Fiscal Review 1999 and 2009*.

institutions, provincial governments had quite difficult beginnings. In most cases, the previous administrative units had to be split into two distinct provinces. The difficulties of merging hugely different institutions were compounded by the general lack of administrative skills. In addition to this, provinces were flooded with personnel coming from the previous 'homelands', who were reabsorbed into the new provinces. As of the end of 1999, provinces accounted for 70 per cent of total public sector employment. Personnel still accounts for a large share of total expenditure. Another substantial share is absorbed by pension payments, thus leaving very little room for other expenditure, such as the purchase of supplies and the building of infrastructure. In other words, the discretionary power of provinces is small.

Huge expenditure commitments, insufficient financial resources and financial mismanagement have brought many provinces to the verge of financial collapse. Some of them have had to be rescued by central government intervention.

Provinces are clearly an important component of the South African public sector. Currently they absorb 43.5 per cent of total national revenue. Their expenditure (Table 6.3) is concentrated into two main categories, namely education (41.4 per cent of the total) and health (29.3 per cent).

5.2 Legislation

As mentioned before, provinces take part in the national legislation process through the National Council of Provinces. At least two basic conditions have to be satisfied if provinces want to play a non-marginal role in legislation. The first one is that provinces are able to send to the NCOP skilled legislators, who are willing to play their institutional role. The second condition is that provincial councils should not be a perfect replica of the political alignment prevailing at the national level. In other words, if the same party or party coalition prevails at both the central and the provincial level, there must be some difference on policy issues between the central government and the provinces.

It is very difficult to check how far the first condition can be fulfilled. The NCOP was introduced in February 1997 and it is generally accepted that, due to its short existence, its members have yet to develop their role fully. Coming to the second condition, both the 1996 and 1999 provincial elections ended up with only two out of nine provinces, Western Cape and KwaZulu-Natal, having a governing coalition different from the national one. In the 2004 provincial elections only KwaZulu-Natal maintained a different coalition, while after the 2009 election both Western Cape and KwaZulu-Natal have a different government coalition. Two are clearly quite short of the six provincial votes that are needed to validate a NCOP decision. To put together these six provincial votes, a cross-party majority needs to be formed. In other words, four out of the seven provinces presently governed by the ANC should deflect from party discipline and align themselves with the other two on specific issues of provincial concern. Otherwise, if these provinces have views that differ from both those of the central government and those of the two non-ANC governed provinces, they should push these views through the parliamentary process. This has not taken place yet, allowing the ANC to enforce its uniform policy platform across the country.

5.3 The Fiscal Dimension of the Transformation

The central government share of total expenditure decreased between 1989 and 2008 from more than 80 per cent to about 50. The main beneficiaries have been the provinces. However, the sheer magnitude of the expenditure does not tell the truth about the effective degree of decentralization that has taken place. In fact, things have changed much less on the revenue side. Intergovernmental fiscal relations are characterized by a huge vertical imbalance: the share of total revenue accruing to the central government is still overwhelming, almost 90 per cent. This is mostly because provinces have been denied any significant source of own revenue.

5.4 Equitable Sharing

'Equitable Share' is a fundamental principle of the new constitution with regard to the division of the national resources between the three spheres of government. Its implementation requires an act of parliament. Interpretation of the principle has been widely debated and a broad agree-

Table 6.4 Division of revenue between levels of governments, 2008–09

	Million Rand	%
Central government	291 205	50.1
Provincial governments	245 646	42.2
of which: Equitable Share	204 010	
Conditional grants	41 636	
Local governments	44 689	7.7
of which: Equitable Share	25 560	
Conditional grants	19 129	
Total	581 540	100.0

ment has been reached on the recognition that distribution has to be performed according to national standards and costing factors. Obviously, the division is essentially a bargaining process between distinct layers of government and between sectoral interests. It is actually made through a two-step process. First, an allocation is made for expenditures of national interest without any sectoral identification, such as debt service costs, contingency reserve or special funds. Then, the remaining resources are divided between the three spheres. Allocations for the 2008–09 fiscal year are shown in Table 6.4.

5.5 Provincial Government: Minimal Tax Autonomy

The central government stress on equalization in service provision helps to explain, in part, the revenue policy it has pursued. In fact, despite the quite generous constitutional provisions in terms of revenue, provinces have been denied access to own sources of revenue and have had to rely almost entirely on centrally provided grants. At the same time, new cooperative governance mechanisms concerning the revenue policy have been introduced by ordinary legislation. Again, they are reminiscent of the German federal system.

Provincial revenues are represented by fees on hospital services, motor vehicle licenses and gambling taxes. They account for only 4 per cent of total revenue. Own revenues have declined by about 20 per cent in the past few years, partly reflecting a policy decision in health to provide free care. In part, this reduction also reflects a reluctance by provinces to use their own revenue instruments when massive grants are provided by the center. A proposal to substantially increase the tax autonomy of provinces by allowing them to introduce a flat-rate surcharge on the personal income tax base was forwarded by the Financial and Fiscal Commission

(1995a, 1995b, 1996 and 1999). More precisely, the FFC recommended as a starting point the introduction of a 5 per cent surcharge, with the possibility for distinct provinces to increase it up to a maximum of 7 points in a period of six years. Correspondingly, the central government should have reduced its tax rates to make room for the provincial surcharge without increasing the total national tax pressure. The proposal would certainly have increased the fiscal capacity and accountability of provinces and, at the same time, it would have strengthened their role within the territorial system of government.

However, the surcharge was rejected by the central government with the argument that the personal income tax base is still too small and highly unequally distributed across provinces, and that administrative costs would be high despite the low number of taxpayers. More in general, it was argued that this solution would not be adequate to a developing country such as South Africa. The present policy of the central government is to leave the range of taxes devolved to provincial governments as small as possible and to have them rely mostly on transfers from the central purse. This reluctance to extend provincial tax powers is partly due to the macroeconomic strategy of South Africa, which includes maintaining tax revenue at 25 per cent of GDP in order to promote both national and foreign investments.

5.6 Provincial Government: General Transfers

Grants were provided by the central government until 1998 in an absolutely discretionary way, that is, according to the Ministry of Finance estimates of the needs of each distinct province. Each province was thus at the mercy of the central government.

Since fiscal year 1998–99, central government discretion has been considerably reduced – with a parallel improvement of the grants system through the introduction of a formula-based system of allocation. This system, illustrated in Box 6.1, is in fact a collection of six separate components, with a different weight given to each.

The weights of the components are neither indicative budgets, nor guidelines as to how much should be spent on those functions in each province or by provinces collectively. The grant is thus perfectly unconditional. This means that provinces have discretion regarding the determination of departmental allocations for each function, taking into account the priorities that underpin the division of revenue.

However, evidence suggests that budgetary allocations across provinces, especially in education and health, tend to mimic the weights in the formula.

BOX 6.1 THE GRANTS SYSTEM FOR PROVINCES

The system includes six different components (the weight given to each is shown in parentheses).

- An **institutional share** (5 per cent) divided equally among the provinces. That is, it is a lump sum grant to take into account the indivisibility elements in the provision of public services.
- An **education share** (51 per cent) allocated on the average size of the school-age population (ages 6–17) and the number of students enrolled in ordinary public schools.
- A **health share** (26 per cent) allocated according to the differential use of the public health system by people with and without medical aid or health insurance.
- A **basic share** (14 per cent) based on each province's share of the total population of the country.
- An **economic activity share** (1 per cent) based on the distribution among provinces of GDP.
- A **poverty share** (3 per cent) introduces a redistributive element within the formula. It is based on the share of the poor population on total population.

Overall, the present distribution of transfers shows an equalizing pattern, because they are allocated on the basis of needs. The equalization of expenditure levels is, however, modest, although total grants represent 95 per cent of total provincial revenue. Per capita levels of expenditure in health and education remain uneven, because own provincial revenues are hugely concentrated in the rich provinces, although they account for a mere 5 per cent of total revenue.

Table 6.5 reports the actual working of the formula. To understand it, one has to look at the component that is based on population. If with another component a province receives more than its population share, this means that the province gains from distribution. For example, Gauteng, the richest province, gets less than its population share for education, health and poverty, while Mpumalanga, one of the poorest provinces, shows the opposite pattern. All in all the formula redistributes national resources from the richest to the poorest provinces.

Table 6.5 Equitable share to provinces: allocations for 2009 (%)

	Education 51	Health 26	Basic 14	Poverty 3	Economic activity 1	Institutional 5	Weighted average 100
Eastern Cape	16.8	13.8	13.5	16.7	7.8	11.1	15.2
Free State	5.7	5.8	5.9	6.1	5.4	11.1	6.0
Gauteng	15.1	20.5	21.5	15.0	33.6	11.1	17.4
KwaZulu-Natal	23.0	21.2	20.8	22.2	16.3	11.1	21.5
Limpopo	14.2	11.4	10.8	14.2	6.8	11.1	12.8
Mpumalanga	8.5	7.5	7.4	8.7	6.8	11.1	8.2
Northern Cape	2.2	2.3	2.3	2.6	2.2	11.1	2.7
North West	6.5	7.2	7.0	8.2	6.4	11.1	7.1
Western Cape	8.2	10.2	10.8	6.2	14.6	11.1	9.2
Total	100.0	100.0	100.0	100.0	100.0	100.0	100.0

Source: Ministry of Finance.

5.7 Provincial Government as a Checks and Balances Mechanism

Two main issues are at stake here. The first one refers to the role of provinces in the legislative process; that is, to their capacity to devise and to implement their own policies. Up to the present time, it has been practically non-existent. It could, however, become more effective, paralleling the increased skill of provincial legislators and their willingness to play their role fully: that is, to compare national priorities and standards set up by the central government with the preferences of their own constituents, and to make proposals for change if national and local preferences do not correspond.

The second issue refers to accountability of provincial legislators and administrators. It could clearly be enhanced by the introduction of more autonomy on the revenue side. However, the central government is firmly resisting this change.

In the medium term, the tax capacity has to be substantially expanded to avoid the problems usually associated with fiscal dependence on centrally provided grants. The wide tax base of the rich provinces would make grants redundant for them, allowing the central government to concentrate its allocation on the neediest provinces. Thus efficiency could be added to equity. However, the central government seems inclined to avoid increasing the political power of the richest provinces, which usually grows with tax autonomy.

Finally, the present borrowing discipline for provinces, which is clearly inspired by the need to enforce fiscal discipline for the entire public sector, is not entirely consonant with a federal state. This is because the Ministry of Finance retains an exclusive regulating power based on its own evaluations. In federal systems, states are usually free to determine their borrowing policy, or borrowing takes place within a legal framework worked out by all jointly with the federal government. If strictly enforced, this latter solution may combine provincial autonomy with sound macroeconomic management.

5.8 Local Government: Structural Reform and Mission

One of the most visible results of the consolidation process is the marked reduction in the number of local authorities. The central government's clear preference has been for large local government units. The main impulse has been redistribution. At a certain point, the central government realized that the simple merging of adjacent WLAs and BLAs would not solve the problem. This was because some fiscally strong WLAs were not close enough to BLAs to justify the merger. The large units allow a high degree of redistribution, at the expense, to some extent, of fiscal and political accountability, since the latter are usually associated with smaller dimensions (Masuko, 1996; Reschovsky and Smoke, 1999; Solomon, 1998).

Local government share of total public expenditure is far from negligible, standing at around 7 per cent of GDP. This is a high level even according to the standards of developed countries. However, around 50 per cent of local budgets in South Africa are absorbed by the delivery of electricity and water. In most countries, these services are provided by public or private companies with separate budgets. In other words, accounting practices in South Africa tend to inflate the role of local government in the consolidated budget of the public sector.

The role of local government is centered on the provision of basic urban and infrastructural services, such as water, sanitation, roads and, in addition, electricity distribution. However, local governments show a clear aspiration to be involved in the provision of social services. The urban ones are more involved in them.

Finally, despite the consolidation, glaring differences still exist between distinct areas, both rural and urban, concerning their financial viability and their capacity to provide services. For example, a high proportion of local authorities have been and still are close to bankruptcy, while data on the provision of basic services, such as access to water and sanitation, show huge gaps. Big metropolitan cities have higher own revenue and a

Table 6.6 Economic and social status of different categories of municipalities

	Overall budget (million Rands)	% of own revenue	Reliance on transfers (%)	N. of households	% of poor households	Average income (Rands)
Johannesburg	21.151	83	17	543063	32	1973
Nelson Mandela	4.525	82	18	225912	41	1256
Rustenburg	1.699	58	42	116665	46	1130
Stellenbosch	562	81	19	35124	17	1987
Moshaweng	78	27	73	20281	74	190
Ntambanana	14	0	100	13844	57	286

Source: Financial Fiscal Commission, *Technical Report, 2009.*

lower poverty rate, and are able to provide satisfactory services to most of their population, while smaller, poor and rural municipalities have no revenue of their own and are forced to rely on central government money, as shown in Table 6.6.

5.9 Local Government: A Largely Autonomous Revenue System

South African local government has – it is widely held – a high degree of fiscal autonomy. More specifically, local own revenues – i.e. user charges, fees and taxes – cover a predominant share of total operating revenue. This view needs at least two qualifications. The first one refers to the direct inclusion in municipal budgets of electricity, water and related services. This inclusion clearly inflates the degree of fiscal autonomy. If the usual accounting practices were used – where revenues from trading services are not included in local revenue and only trading surpluses are included in local budgets – the role of user charges and fees would appear much smaller. Taxes would show a higher share, but also transfers from other levels of government would show a higher share. The second qualification refers, again, to the huge disparities between distinct areas to which I refer below.

The revenue system has been based on three main pillars: namely, user charges, property rates and the Regional Levy.

User charges and fees

Approximately 60 per cent of total revenue derives from this source. However, only trading surpluses (and losses) really impact on the fiscal capacity of local governments. More specifically, trading surpluses – which amount to an implicit fee on the consumption of electricity and water – allow local governments to expand their service provision in the same or in other sectors, while losses imply that consumers are subsidized by taxpayers and that service delivery has to be curtailed in other sectors. Recent information shows that there are cases of substantial surpluses, but also of worrying losses, resulting from the difficulty of recovering payments from users. In general, large cities succeed in earning a significant surplus from the sale of their services, while the majority of smaller ones do not, or else incur losses.

Property rates

As in most countries, the property tax is the single most important source of revenue for local governments, representing 20 per cent of the total. There are of course wide disparities across the country, some of which are attributable to inefficiency in collection. But many of the differences derive also from structural characteristics. Basically, the tax is collected only in the urban areas and its revenue is especially important in the largest cities. Its legal framework is fragmented and uncertain. There are differences in the tax base and in rate-setting autonomy across the various areas. This is because, in the past, the tax was determined mostly by old provincial ordinances rather than national legislation.

Regional Services Council (RSC) levy

The levy has been recently eliminated for both metropolitan municipalities and district municipalities and replaced with a share of the general fuel levy. Thus there has been a curtailment of the local tax autonomy. These levies were taxes on business activities that are widely used, in different versions, around the world for financing sub-national governments. The South African version of this tax was based on a combination of payroll and turnover taxes. The tax has a huge potential base. However, the extremely low tax rate – approximately 0.25 per cent on payroll and 0.1 percent on turnover – and its widespread non-exploitation resulted in modest collections: less than 5 per cent of total recurrent revenue of local governments, but with very large differences among individual units.

5.10 Transfers: Clear Residual Role

Until the 1998–99 fiscal year, most of the transfers for recurrent purposes to local governments were channeled through provinces. Some of these transfers were paid on a pure agency basis; that is, to cover the cost of provision of services on behalf of provinces. Some had a gap filling function and were allocated mostly on the basis of ad hoc unpredictable and/or negotiating criteria. Implicit transfers from the national government supplemented the provincial ones. Local governments also received funds for capital expenditure through a vast array of central government infrastructure financing programs.

Starting from fiscal year 1998–99, a new system of transfers has been devised. This system is partly based on the recommendations made by the Financial and Fiscal Commission. It includes distinct formula-based categories of transfers. The first one is the Equitable Share transfer that is unconditional. The formula includes five components:

$$\textit{Equitable Share grant for municipalities} = BS + D + I - R +/- C$$

- BS basic services (water, sanitation, electricity, refuse collection and environmental health)
- D development (not introduced)
- I institutional support
- R revenue raising capacity correction
- C correction and stabilization factor

A second important transfer is that for municipal infrastructure, with the following formula:

$$\textit{Municipal infrastructure grant for municipalities} = B + P + E + N + M$$

- B basic residential infrastructure for backlogs in water supply, roads and other (streetlighting and solid waste removal) – 75% of total MIG allocation
- P public municipal service infrastructure – 15% of total MIG allocation
- E other institutions and micro-enterprises – 5% of total MIG allocation
- N nodal municipalities in urban renewal and rural development programs – 5% of total MIG allocation
- M performance related adjustments – not yet activated

There are also a number of specific transfers, mainly for investment purposes, whose number has increased over the years. The same proliferation of specific grants can also be observed for provinces. This shows more attention to decentralized provision of services but also an expanding grip of the central government on sub-national units.

5.11 Cooperation Between Levels of Government: The Executive Federalism

A basic principle mandated by the South African constitution with regard to intergovernmental relations is the cooperation among levels of government. Cooperation refers to revenues – the above mentioned Equitable Share – and to design and implementation of policies. In fact, the South African model of decentralization is largely informed by the German one, which is a typical model of cooperative federalism.

At the legislative level the National Council of Provinces provides – like the German *Bundesrat* – a forum of interaction and cooperation between levels of government. This house should ensure that provincial interests are represented and made compatible with the national ones in the legislative process.

Much more structured is institutional cooperation on the executive side (Malan, 2005). It starts with the President's Coordinating Council. This consists of the president, deputy president, Minister in the Presidency, the Minister of Provincial and Local Government, the Minister of Finance, Minister of Public Service and Administration, the Premiers of the nine provinces and the Chairperson of the South African Local Government Association. The mission of the President's Coordinating Council is to address issues pertaining to provincial government while acting as a consultative forum for the president. The president convenes the meetings and determines the agenda of the Council, which must meet at least twice a year.

More relevant for the design and implementation of actual policies are the various intergovernmental forums labeled as the Committees of Ministers and Members of Executive Councils (MINMEC). Some examples of such committees are the MINMEC for Social Development, the MINMEC for Local Government and the Department of Environmental Affairs and Tourism MINMEC. A typical Committee of Ministers and Members of Executive Councils consists of the national line function minister, of national deputy ministers and of the provincial members of the Executive Council responsible for a similar functional area in their respective provinces. These national intergovernmental forums are established to discuss matters of national interest within a specific functional area with provinces and, if appropriate, with local governments.

The current MINMEC structures are faced with numerous challenges. Some of the challenges are that these committees are informal, advisory and executive structures and therefore do not have real decision-making powers.

The most relevant MINMEC structure is the Budget Council

(established and regulated by the Intergovernmental Fiscal Relations Act of 1997). The Budget Council is the most relevant cooperation body because it can make binding decisions and differs from other committees of MINMECs in this respect. Its relevance also derives from the extreme centralization of revenue sources in South Africa. The power of the purse gives to the Ministry of Finance a predominant role in intergovernmental relations. The Budget Council consists of the Minister of Finance as well as of the various members of executive councils concerned with finance of each province.

The functions of the Budget Council include consultation on any fiscal, budgetary or financial matter and the evaluation of proposed legislation or policy pertaining to finance. Issues concerning financial management, or the monitoring of finances of the provinces, may also be discussed in the meeting of the Budget Council twice every financial year.

Various provincial coordinating structures also exist and their establishment is provided for in the Intergovernmental Relations Framework Act, 2005.[1]

The premier of a province may establish a formal provincial intergovernmental forum to promote and facilitate effective and efficient intergovernmental relations between the province and local governments in the province with respect to a functional area. The Intergovernmental Relations Framework Act, 2005, also determines that the premier of a province must establish a premier's intergovernmental forum, which should consist of the premier, the member of the executive council responsible for local government in the province, at least the mayors of district and metropolitan municipalities and a representative of organized local government in the province.

It is quite difficult to evaluate the effective working of this dense network of cooperative bodies. Most of them, particularly the Budget Council, are dominated by the Ministry of Finance, and in many cases the participation of the provinces in intergovernmental forums is partial and erratic. Clearly, the development of executive federalism has downsized the role of the Financial and Fiscal Commission. This body is still producing very informative and accurate analyses of South African intergovernmental relations, but its recommendations are less authoritative than they were presumed to be at the inception of the new system.

6. CONCLUSIONS

The interpretation and implementation of the constitutional provisions by the central government of South Africa has been mostly centropedic. The provincial units that have been created are uneven in terms of socio-economic characteristics and have not been assigned with own revenue sources. The central government is using this dependency to equalize provision and to enforce national standards and policy guidelines. These are sound objectives, especially considering blatant disparities in service provision and in capacity. In the long run, however, fiscal dependency may create unaccountable and institutionally weak governments. While provincial weakness may be (and presently is) a central government goal, lack of accountability is clearly not.

On the one hand, the weakness of provinces impacts negatively on the potential role that this intermediate tier of sub-national government could play as a checks and balances mechanism. On the other hand, a possible scenario is that South African provinces will continue to build their capacity during the next few years and will afterwards ask for fiscal autonomous powers. The empowerment of provinces will also depend on the degree of political competition. It is unlikely that the predominance at the national level of the ANC will be reduced in the near future. However, good governance by alternative political coalitions in some provinces, such as the Eastern Cape after 2009, could enhance competition, even within the ANC. The evolution of regional governments in Italy and Spain shows that these factors – fiscal autonomy and political competition – are important factors for increasing the strength of sub-national government. For more than 20 years, regional governments in Italy and their Spanish equivalent, the autonomous communities, were devoid of fiscal powers. They then slowly built up their capacity and started to ask, and to receive, autonomous sources of revenue, becoming more active players within the intergovernmental relations system. This has been helped by the frequent discrepancy between the political coalition governing at the national level and political coalition governing in some regions.

In South Africa increasing attention has been paid to local government in recent years. The central government has completed a process of structural reform that has increased substantially the average size of local government units. However, their fiscal instruments have been reduced. The view of the national government is that to improve the level of service provision in the most distressed areas, transfers have to be increased.

Redistribution, fiscal and political control of sub-national governments are the guidelines of the policy of intergovernmental relations followed by the central government, which is proceeding on a very fine line between a strong demand for the equalization of service levels and the need to keep the macroeconomic financial equilibrium constraint, and to avoid sharp political opposition by the well-to-do part of its non-black population.

NOTE

1. Examples of such provincial intergovernmental relations structures are the Eastern Cape Provincial Political Intergovernmental Forum, Free State Provincial and Local Government Coordinating Committee, Gauteng Intergovernmental Forum, Gauteng Premier's Coordinating Committee, KwaZulu-Natal Provincial Cabinet Clusters, Mpumalanga Intergovernmental Relations Forum, North West Intergovernmental Forum and the Western Cape Provincial Advisory Forum.

REFERENCES

Ahmad, Junaid (1998), 'South Africa: an intergovernmental fiscal system in transition', in R. Bird and F. Vaillancourt (eds), *Fiscal Decentralization in Developing Countries*, Cambridge University Press.

Bednar Jenna, William N. Eskridge and John Ferejohn (1999), *A Political Theory of Federalism*, June, mimeo.

Bogdanov, Vernon (1997), 'Forms of autonomy and the protection of minorities', *Daedalus*, **126** (2), pp 65–86.

Cameron, Robert (1995), 'The history of devolution of powers to local authorities in South Africa: the shifting sands of state control', *Local Government Studies*, **21** (3), 396–417.

Cloete, J.J.N (1982), *Central, Provincial and Municipal Institutions of South Africa*, Pretoria: J.L. van Schaik.

Deegan, Heather (1999), 'Good governance and accountability', in J.E. Spence (ed.), *After Mandela. The 1999 South African Elections*, London: The Royal Institute of International Affairs.

Filippov, Mikhail, Peter C. Ordeshook and Olga Shvetsova (2004), *Designing Federalism: A Theory of Self-Sustainable Federal Institutions*, Cambridge University Press.

Financial and Fiscal Commission (1995a), *The Allocation of Financial Resources Between the National and Provincial Governments, Recommendations for the Fiscal Year 1996/7*, Midrand, September.

Financial and Fiscal Commission (1995b), *Framework Document for Intergovernmental Fiscal Relations in South Africa*, Midrand, July.

Financial and Fiscal Commission (1996), *The Allocation of Financial Resources Between the National and Provincial Governments, Recommendations for the Fiscal Year 1997/8*, Midrand, May.

Financial and Fiscal Commission (1999), *Project 2001 Report*, Midrand, November, mimeo.

Horowitz, Donald, L. (1991), *A Democracy for South Africa? Constitutional Engineering in a Divided Society*, Berkeley and Los Angeles: University of California Press.

Koelble, Thomas (1997), *The Global Economy and Democracy in South Africa*, Rutgers, New Jersey University Press.
Lijphart, Arend (1969), 'Consociational democracy', *World Politics*, **21**, 219–15.
Lijphart, Arend (1977), *Democracy in Plural Societies*, New Haven: Yale University Press.
Lodge, Tom (1994), 'The African Congress and its allies', in Andrew Reynolds (ed.), *Elections 1994: South Africa*, New York: St Martin's Press.
Lodge, Tom (1999), *South African Politics since l994*, Capetown: David Philip Publisher.
Lodge, Tom (2002), *Politics in South Africa (From Mandela to Mbeki)*, Kenilworth, Cape Town: David Philip.
Malan, L. (2005), 'Intergovernmental relations and co-operative government in South Africa: the ten-year review', *Politeia*, **24** (2).
Mamdani, Mahmood (1996), *Citizen and Subject: Contemporary Africa and the Legacy of Late Colonialism*, Princeton University Press.
Masuko, Louis (1996), 'Zimbabwe', in Patricia McCarney (ed.), *The Changing Nature of Local Governments in Developing Countries*, Toronto University Press.
Matshiqi, Aubrey (2009), 'Democratic consolidation, substantive uncertainty and institutional certainty: prospects for the re-alignment of opposition politics in South Africa', Centre for Policy Studies, Johannesburg.
Muthien, Yvonne and Meshack Khosa (1998), 'Demarcating the New Provinces: a critical reflection on the process', in Muthien and Khosa (eds), *Regionalism in the New South Africa*, Aldershot, UK: Ashgate.
Myerson, Roger B. (2006), 'Federalism and incentives for success of democracy', *Quarterly Journal of Political Science*, **1**, 3–232.
Przeworski, Adam (1991), *Democracy and the Market*, Cambridge University Press.
Reschovsky, Andrew, and Paul Smoke (1999), 'Reforming local government in South Africa', mimeo.
Reynolds, Andrew (1994), *Elections 1994: South Africa*, New York: St. Martin's Press.
Salmon, Pierre (1987a), 'The logic of pressure groups and the structure of the public sector', *European Journal of Political Economy*, 55–86.
Salmon, Pierre (1987b), 'Decentralization as an incentive scheme', *Oxford Review of Economic Policy*, **24**.
Schlemmer, Lawrence (1999), 'Democracy or democratic hegemony: the future of political pluralism in South Africa', in H. Giliomee and Charles Simkins (eds), *The Awkward Embrace. One Party-Domination and Democracy*, Cape Town: Tafelberg Publishers.
Shapiro, Ian (1993), 'Democratic innovation, South Africa in a comparative context', *World Politics*, 120–50.
Solomon, David (1998), *Local Government in South Africa: Challenges and Solutions*, Pretoria: Idasa.
Sparks, Alistair (1995), *Tomorrow is Another Country. The Inside Story of South Africa's Road to Change*, The University of Chicago Press.
World Bank (1995), 'South Africa. Economic performance and policies', Discussion Paper.

APPENDIX 1

Table 6A.1 Allocation of seats at the National Assembly after the elections of 1994, 1999 and 2009

	1994	1999	2009
African National Congress	252	266	264
Democratic Alliance			67
New National Party	82	28	–
Inkatha Freedom Party	34	34	18
COPE			30
Democratic Party*	7	38	–
Others	25	34	21
Total	400	400	400

Note: * With Democratic Alliance in 2009.

Source: Statistics S.A.

APPENDIX 2

Policy Responsibilities of the Provinces

Primary concurrent functions

- Education
- Health services
- Welfare services
- Agriculture
- Public transport
- Road traffic regulation
- Tourism
- Casinos, racing, lotteries
- Property transfer fees
- Vehicle licensing
- Housing

Exclusive functions

- Abattoirs
- Ambulance

- Archives and libraries other than national
- Liquor licenses
- Museums other than national
- Provincial planning
- Provincial cultural matters
- Provincial recreation and amenities
- Provincial sport
- Provincial roads and traffic
- Veterinary services, excluding regulation of the profession

PART III

Political Competition and Voting

7. On Machiavelli's conspiracy paradoxes

Manfred J. Holler*

Secret de Deux,
Secret de Dieu,
Secret de Trois,
Secret de Tous.[1]

1. SOME PARADOXES

In his *Discorsi*, Machiavelli dedicated a full chapter to the discussion of conspiracy. This does not seem to come as a surprise if we share the common, but rather questionable (and unjustified) view that ranks Machiavelli as master of cruelties and betrayals.[2] However, the analytical and historical depth of his discussion seems remarkable and might trigger second thoughts.

In this chapter, I will mainly draw from the material of Chapter VI of Book III of Machiavelli's *Discourses*, entitled 'Of Conspiracies'. This chapter summarizes most of what can be found on conspiracies in *The Prince* and the *History of Florence*, although Chapter XIX of the former and the Eighth Book of the latter contain treasures. Some of the material will be quoted below.

Machiavelli (*Discourses*, p. 329) starts his lecture on conspiracy with a somewhat paradoxical observation: On the one hand, 'history teaches us that many more princes have lost their lives and their states by conspiracies than by open war', and, on the other hand, conspiracies, 'though so often attempted, yet they so rarely attain the desired object'. The answer to this riddle is that conspiracies are ubiquitous but very often fail because preparation and execution were inadequate, the executors were incompetent or unlucky, and the situation was not what it was supposed to be. Economists would call these failures a social waste.

Machiavelli (*Discourses*, p. 329) promises that he will 'treat the subject at length, and endeavor not to omit any point that may be useful to the one or the other . . . so that princes may learn to guard against such dangers, and that subjects may less rashly engage in them, and learn rather to live contentedly under such a government as Fate may have assigned to them.'

Is it to reduce the social waste of unsuccessful conspiracy or to reduce the inclination of the people to revolt if they were unhappy with their prince? It seems that Machiavelli is especially concerned about such conspirators who 'almost himself a king . . . blinded by the ambition of dominion, they are equally blind in the conduct of the conspiracy, for if their villainy were directed by prudence, they could not possibly fail of success' (*Discourses*, p. 333). Social waste again!

It seems quite paradoxical that Machiavelli's analysis sharpens the tools of either side of the conspiracy game. Potential conspirators will learn when there is a chance of success and how to increase this chance. The princes are told how to reduce this chance. In the equilibrium we would see successful conspiracy only, triggered in situations that the princes could not avoid. The chance to face such situations can be minimized, and this might be Machiavelli's message, if the prince is 'loved by the people', he installs good laws and submits himself to these laws.

Given this interpretation, however, it seems rather paradoxical to assume that Machiavelli was interested in the social waste of unsuccessful conspiracy and therefore tries to implement 'economic rationality' into the agents of both sides, which he did. He developed a rational theory of conspiracy that follows the pattern of a cost-benefit analysis – with the qualification that expected benefits are likely to be zero, if benefits are standardized such that zero is the minimum, and costs 'converge to infinity', in case that the conspiracy is expected to fail. Of course, the value of infinity is ill defined.

There is still another puzzle involved: ' . . . conspiracies have generally been set on foot by the great, or the friends of the prince; and of these, as many have been prompted to it by an excess of benefits as by an excess of wrongs' (*Discourses*, p. 333). Plots are generally organized by 'great men of the state, or those on terms of familiar intercourse with the prince' (*Discourses*, p. 332).

There are strong arguments why only those agents can stage a successful conspiracy that are close to the prince, and why, as history shows, those conspire who enjoy generous benefits from this closeness. 'A prince, then, who wishes to guard against conspiracies should fear those on whom he has heaped benefits quite as much, and even more, than those whom he has wronged; for the latter lack the convenient opportunities which the former have in abundance' (*Discourses*, p. 333).

It appears that princely benefits to close friends do not prevent conspiracies as expectations about success seem most promising to this group of people. However, probabilities that capture expectations are not given, but subject to the interaction of the agents involved. To some extent the forming of expectation boils down to a game theoretical problem but, as we will see, this does not guarantee that there is a satisfactory solution to it. Non-uniqueness of equilibria is ubiquitous and a source of uncertainty even for rational agents. Moreover, the set of agents, those who participate in the conspiracy and those who counteract it, is often subject to the course of the game itself.

Why did Machiavelli develop such a theory if not for demonstrating that the prince can avoid conspiracies if potential conspirators are rational enough to accept the benefits which a rational prince offers to them, given the risks involved? Was this another step towards his demystification of power and politics or did he want to demonstrate to the reader how skilled and capable he was in political reasoning?[3] We will come back to this issue in the concluding Section 5 of this chapter. Section 2 deals with Machiavelli's treatment of strategies of the conspirators while Section 3 contains advice to the prince on how to counteract conspiracies. Section 4 is dedicated to the conspiracy of the prince for power.

2. THE CONSPIRATOR'S STRATEGIES

Machiavelli identifies three phases of danger for the conspirators: the plotting, the execution of the plot, and the period after the plot has been carried out. If the plot is formed by a single person, then, of course, the 'first of the dangers' is avoided. In addition, the project can be postponed or put to rest without major costs or risks. This could be a great advantage when its success does not look very promising, especially since the situation has changed. Many such plots never leave the state of planning and rejection: they are a secret and remain secret. Machiavelli notes that 'it is not uncommon to find men who form such projects (the mere purpose involving neither danger nor punishment), but few carry them into effect; and of those who do, very few or none escape being killed in the execution of their designs, and therefore but few are willing to incur such certain death' (*Discourses*, p. 332). As the latter lack support to structure the minutes after the execution in a constructive way, single assassins are likely to lose their lives even when they successfully kill a tyrant.

One-person plots are somewhat degenerated conspiracies. They lack the elements of communication, coordination and trust that characterize non-degenerate conspiracies and often cause their failures. However, as Machiavelli demonstrates, successful multi-person conspiracies are often designed such that they simulate one-person plots. The one-person plot is therefore a model case. But only plots that involve a number of persons necessitate a conspiracy proper implying problems of coordination and perhaps communication.

Machiavelli distinguishes between two arrangements of conspiracy proper: the two-person plot and the multi-person plot. The two-person plot has the disadvantage that possible actions are still constrained by numerical capacity. However, compared to a plot that involves more than two persons, it offers a series of advantages, as we will see. In fact, if there are more than two persons involved then, according to Machiavelli, most successful strategies either reduce the situation to a two-person plot or, if possible, even to a one-person plot. In case of more than one agent, most conspiracies fail because of denunciation and not because of lack of means or occasions. Machiavelli states:

> Denunciation is the consequence of treachery or of want of prudence on the part of those to whom you confide your designs; and treachery is so common that you cannot safely impart your project to any but such of your most trusted friends as are willing to risk their lives for your sake, or to such other malcontents as are equally desirous of the prince's ruin.

However,

> men are very apt to deceive themselves as to the degree of attachment and devotion which others have for them, and there are no means of ascertaining this except by actual experience; but experience in such matters is of the utmost danger. And even if you should have tested the fidelity of your friends on other occasions of danger, yet you cannot conclude from that that they will be equally true to you on an occasion that presents infinitely greater dangers than any other. (*Discourses*, p. 334)

In other words, there is no adequate test for conspirators; the only test is the conspiracy itself. But is this a test?

Alternatively, a potential conspirator could collect information, but, of course, the willingness and competence of others to conspire is secret and information is lacking or likely to be biased. Indirect evidence can be deceptive and change the situation to the disadvantage of the conspirator. As Machiavelli observed:

> If you attempt to measure a man's good faith by the discontent which he manifests towards the prince, you will be easily deceived, for by the very fact of communicating to him your designs, you give him the means of putting an end to his discontent [by passing on valuable information to the prince.[4]] It is thus that so many conspiracies have been revealed and crushed in their incipient stage; so that it may be regarded almost as a miracle when so important a secret

> is preserved by a number of conspirators for any length of time. (*Discourses*, p. 334)

Needless to say, a discovery from a lack of prudence increases with the number of conspirators involved and with the time of preparation that elapses. There can be imprudence that invites discovery by conjecture. Machiavelli reports the following incidence:

> The day before he was to have killed Nero, Scevinus, one of the conspirators, made his testament; he ordered his freedman Melichius to sharpen an old, rusty poniard, enfranchised all his slaves and distributed money amongst them, and had bandages made for tying up wounds. Melichius surmised from these various acts what was going on, and denounced it to Nero. Scevinus was arrested, and with him Natales, another conspirator, with whom he had been seen to converse secretly for a length of time. As their depositions respecting that conversation did not agree, they were forced to confess the truth, and thus the conspiracy was discovered to the ruin of all that were implicated. (*Discourses*, p. 335)

Of course, Scevinus' preparations were of utmost imprudence; however, if Natales, the second conspirator, had not been identified, Scevinus still could have made up a story and finding out the truth would have been impossible. In fact, it was in Scevinus' interest to make up a story which explains his preparations conclusively without any reference to a conspiracy. Competent conspirators should prepare an alternative story. These elements are reflected in the case of a conspiracy against Hieronymus, King of Syracuse:

> Theodorus, one of the conspirators, having been arrested, concealed with the utmost firmness the names of the other conspirators, and charged the matter upon the friends of the king; and, on the other hand, all the other conspirators had such confidence in the courage of Theodorus, that not one of them left Syracuse, or betrayed the least sign of fear. (*Discourses*, p. 335; with reference to Titus Livius)

A theory of rational decision making could reveal to us that for Theodorus it does not take much courage but rather requires the insight that if he confesses or names a conspirator who knows about the plot, the book is slapped on him. (Those books can be very painful.) As long as none of the other conspirators was identified the situation had the structure of a one-man plot in its planning stage.

It is a most promising strategy to keep a multi-person conspiracy in this stage until its execution. Machiavelli illustrates the implementation of such a policy by the example of Nelematus, who,

> unable to bear the tyranny of Aristotimus, tyrant of Epirus, assembled in his house a number of friends and relatives, and urged them to liberate their country from the yoke of the tyrant. Some of them asked for time to consider the matter, whereupon Nelematus made his slaves close the door of his house, and then said to those he had called together, 'You must either go now and carry this plot into execution, or I shall hand you all over as prisoners to Aristotimus'. Moved by these words, they took the oath demanded of them, and immediately went and carried the plot of Nelematus successfully into execution. (*Discourses*, p. 336)

The example demonstrates that Nelematus did not rely only on the speed of execution but also on the double-binding power of treachery. Those who can betray can often also be betrayed. Often it is only a question who is the first mover; Nelematus has grabbed the first-mover advantage.

However, if possible, a conspirator should confide his secret project to one man only even when it involves a larger number of conspirators. One man,

> whose fidelity he has thoroughly tested for a long time, and who is animated by the same desire as himself . . . is much more easily found than many . . . and then, even if he were to attempt to betray you, there is some chance of your being able to defend yourself, which you cannot when there are many conspirators. I have heard many wise men say that you may talk freely with one man about everything, for unless you have committed yourself in writing the 'yes' of one man is worth as much as the 'no' of another; and therefore one should guard most carefully against writing, as against a dangerous rock, for nothing will convict you quicker than your own handwriting. (*Discourses*, p. 337)

A handwritten message can transgress the individuality or the communication between two persons and make it public. What could be one word against another is no longer confined to such a degree of 'privacy' when it is written down.

In summary, Machiavelli identifies two risks

> in communicating a plot to any one individual: the first, lest he should denounce you voluntarily; the second, lest he should denounce you, being himself arrested on suspicion, or from some indications, and being convicted and forced to it by the torture. But there are means of escaping both these dangers: the first, by denial and by alleging personal hatred to have prompted the accusation; and the other, by denying the charge, and alleging that your accuser was constrained by the force of torture to tell lies. But the most prudent course is not to communicate the plot to any one, and to act in accordance with the above-cited examples; and if you cannot avoid drawing some one into your confidence, then to let it be not more than one, for in that case the danger is much less than if you confide in many. (*Discourses*, p. 338)

3. THE COUNTER-PLOT OF THE PRINCE

There are numerous examples that the glory and the pomp of the prince but also his royal or divine position and reputation stopped conspirators from putting their daggers in his breast. Sometimes the kindness or the beauty of the prince also prevents a successful execution.[5] However, history shows that this pattern, appealing to sheer properties of personality and position, does not always work and the prince is well advised to develop an ex-ante strategy. In Machiavelli's writings, we find substantial material that could help the prince discourage conspirators if he feels that glory, pomp, reputation, and divinity may not be sufficient to protect his life and position. Of course, thinking about on-the-spot solutions, the corresponding strategies of the prince to counter a plot are generally defined by the action the conspirators take. Typically, conspiracy is a sequential game that sees the prince as a second mover when it comes to the *execution*. Often, however, conspiracies are triggered off by the prince himself and, in fact, he is the first mover in this game. Of course, poor policy could invite conspiracy, but sometimes the princely invitation to plot is even more specific. In the extreme, a conspiracy can be suggested by a threat to take away the fortune or the life of persons close to him. The deadly plot against Emperor Commodus, reported in the *Discourses* (p. 339), illustrates the second case. He

> . . . had amongst his nearest friends and intimates Letus and Electus, two captains of the Prætorian soldiers; he also had Marcia as his favorite concubine. As these three had on several occasions reproved him for the excesses with which he had stained his own dignity and that of the Empire, he resolved to have them killed, and wrote a list of the names of Marcia, Letus, and Electus, and of some other persons, whom he wanted killed the following night. Having placed this list under his pillow, he went to the bath; a favorite child of his, who was playing in the chamber and on the bed, found this list, and on going out with it in his hand was met by Marcia, who took the list from the child. Having read it, she immediately sent for Letus and Electus, and when these three had thus become aware of the danger that threatened them, they resolved to forestall the Emperor, and without losing any time they killed Commodus the following night.

This case demonstrates that 'the necessity which admits of no delay produces the same effect as the means employed by Nelematus' described above (*Discourses*, p. 339). It also reveals how a prince can provoke a conspiracy. This could be a profitable strategy, if the prince is aware of it, but it can be a deadly one otherwise. Of course, if a prince wants to avoid a conspiracy then he should never design a situation in which the agent has only two alternatives: to perish or to fight.

However, this can only be a necessary condition, but not a sufficient one if conspiracy should be avoided. The sequential structure of the execution of a conspiracy suggests that a high degree of unsteadiness in the daily routine of the prince might be a good protection. Given the constraints of secret communications, conspirators have in general great difficulties to adapt to changing conditions or even to revise their plans. The standard example is the conspiracy of the Pazzi against Lorenzo and Giuliano de' Medici.[6] Plans were made that, in April 1478, the two should be killed at a dinner with Cardinal San Giorgio. While the two Medici and the Cardinal attended mass in the cathedral the rumor spread that Giuliano would not come to the dinner. Plans had to be changed and it was decided to commit the murder in the church. Not only did this alienate Giovan Battista, a competent conspirator who was assigned to kill Lorenzo, such that the roles had to be redistributed, but it led to a series of mistakes. Giuliano was killed by Francesco Pazzi as planned, but, because of the incompetence of Antonio da Volterra who was supposed to kill him, Lorenzo was able to defend himself and got away slightly wounded. Not only did he become Lorenzo Magnifico, to govern Florence with almost dictatorial power until his death in 1492, but he also had the means to go ruthlessly after those conspirators who were not killed on the spot – like Franceso Salviati, the Archbishop of Pisa – and to erase the Pazzi from the Florence scenery.

In fact, when the conspirators tried to gain control over the government, to some rather unexpectedly, the people of Florence rallied to the Medici. This proves that investing in the love of the people, as Machiavelli repeatedly pointed out, can be a very efficient means to counter conspiracy. '. . . of all the perils that follow the execution of a conspiracy, none is more certain and none more to be feared than the attachment of the people to the prince that has been killed. There is no remedy against this, for the conspirators can never secure themselves against a whole people' (*Discourses*, p. 345).

As the Pazzi conspiracy was supported by Pope Sixtus IV, a two-year war with the papacy followed, placing a very heavy burden on the City of Florence. But Florence survived and had a brilliant future, and so had the Medici. Perhaps it should be noted that Lorenzo's son Giovanni ended as Pope Leo X, and Giulio, the natural son of Lorenzo's murdered brother Giuliano, followed him in the papacy as Pope Clement VII,[7] not to mention the fact that members of the Medici family became Grand Dukes of Tuscany and mothers to French kings. However, we should emphasize that the support of the people of Florence on the day of the Pazzi conspiracy was decisive for the career of the Medici. Not only did Lorenzo survive, but his position was immensely strengthened by the unsuccessful conspiracy. Machiavelli concludes '... conspiracies rarely succeed, and often cause the ruin of those who set them on foot, whilst those against whom they were aimed are only the more aggrandized thereby' (*History*, p. 368). The latter effect was definitively true in the case of Lorenzo and the Medici.

It seems that a prince who has the love of the people is relatively well protected if conspirators are rational and think about their lives and fate after execution.

> ... on the side of the conspirator there is nothing but fear, jealousy, and apprehension of punishment; whilst the prince has on his side the majesty of sovereignty, the laws, the support of his friends and of the government, which protect him. And if to all this be added the popular good will, it seems impossible that any one should be rash enough to attempt a conspiracy against him. For ordinarily a conspirator has cause for apprehension only before the execution of his evil purpose; but in this case, having the people for his enemies, he has also to fear the consequences after the commission of the crime, and can look nowhere for a refuge. (*The Prince*, p. 61)

To gain the love of the people can, however, be very costly and reduce the resources of the prince considerably, and there can be trade-offs which do not allow full use of this potential. This was the problem most of the Roman Emperors faced:

> where in other principalities the prince had to contend only with the ambition of the nobles and the insolence of the people, the Roman Emperors had to meet a third difficulty, in having to bear with the cruelty and cupidity of the soldiers, which were so great that they caused the ruin of many, because of the difficulty of satisfying at the same time both the soldiers and the people; for the people love quiet, and for that reason they revere princes who are modest, whilst the soldiers love a prince of military spirit, and who is cruel, haughty, and rapacious. And these qualities the prince must practise upon the people, so as to enable him to increase the pay of the soldiers, and to satisfy their avarice and cruelty. (*Prince*, p. 63)

Many Roman Emperors were installed, exploited and, in the end, even murdered by the soldiers that were meant to protect them. They did not, contrary to the Medici, succeed in activating the love of the people for protection.

The Medici case also demonstrates the difficulties of conspiring against a multitude of people. As noticed by Machiavelli,

> to strike two blows of this kind at the same instant and in different places is impracticable, and to attempt to do so at different moments of time would certainly result in the one's preventing the other. So that, if it is imprudent, rash,

> and doubtful to conspire against a single prince, it amounts to folly to do so against two at the same time. (*Discourses*, p. 342)

As a consequence, sharing power looks like a very promising device to decrease the potential of conspiracy. From here, it seems straightforward to argue in favor of the republic, or at least for the creation of a parliament.[8] However, as Machiavelli observed, conspiracies

> against the state are less dangerous for those engaged in them than plots against the life of the sovereign . . . . In the conduct of the plot the danger is very slight, for a citizen may aspire to supreme power without manifesting his intentions to any one; and if nothing interferes with his plans, he may carry them through successfully, or if they are thwarted by some law, he may await a more favorable moment, and attempt it by another way.

This applies to a republic that is already partially corrupted, 'for in one not yet tainted by corruption such thoughts could never enter the mind of any citizen' (*Discourses*, p. 345).

If a successful conspiracy is obstructed by a multitude of people to be conspired against, the multitude and anonymity of potential conspirators can also be a good protection for the prince, especially if the prince can avoid putting too much pressure on a single individual or a smaller group.

> For if the great men of a state, who are in familiar intercourse with the prince, succumb under the many difficulties of which we have spoken, it is natural that these difficulties should be infinitely increased for the others. And therefore those who know themselves to be weak avoid them, for where men's lives and fortunes are at stake they are not all insane; and when they have cause for hating a prince, they content themselves with cursing and vilifying him, and wait until some one more powerful and of higher position than themselves shall avenge them. (*Discourses*, pp. 332f).

Indeed 'those who know themselves to be weak . . . are not all insane', on the contrary, they might be called 'rational'. They view themselves as members of a large group as defined in Mancur Olson's seminal book *The Logic of Collective Action* (1965). The group does not contain a member whose potential and interest are strong enough to organize a conspiracy, irrespective of what the other members do, given the difficulties of execution and the draconic punishment in case of failure. In principle, the prince can feel safe, even if there are many enemies, as long as there is no pioneer conspirator strong and interested enough to take the lead as they will '. . . wait until some one more powerful and of higher position than themselves shall avenge them', as observed above. Large groups are generally not self-organizing and membership remains dormant if the group does not offer selective incentives that cover membership costs. Membership costs can be extremely high in conspiracy.

There is an additional element that may prevent actions against the prince even when the group of potential conspirators is small and they know of each other. Each of them might hope that the other will do the dangerous job, to avoid risk of failure, on the one hand, and to qualify for the time after if the conspiracy is successful, on the other.[9] Those who have killed a tyrant are hardly ever invited to become his successor.

As a consequence, the prince should choose a policy that does not polarize the opposition such that it forms small groups. However, if he cannot avoid polarization then it can be safer to have several opponents which compete with each other, rather than a single rival who is strong and motivated enough to organize a conspiracy. If a prince cannot crush such a rival then he had better create a second one.

But as Machiavelli notes, 'princes cannot always escape assassination when prompted by a resolute and determinate spirit; for any man who himself despises death can always inflict it upon others' (*The Prince*, p. 66). However, he also demonstrates that the prince has the means to reduce the odds of conspirators and to get them interested in other more promising targets.

4. WHAT IF A PRINCE CONSPIRES?

Of course, the prince can also use conspiracy as a means to strengthen his position. This is the general experience we observe in the relationship of one prince to another; it is epitomized in the idea and practice of secret diplomacy.[10] Cases are abundant and many are household knowledge. Perhaps less prominent are cases that show a prince who conspires against one of his ministers or generals, following Machiavelli's advice that 'princes should devolve all matters of responsibility upon others, and take upon themselves only those of grace' (*Prince*, p. 62). The range of this strategy reaches from the obfuscation policy of democratic governments, which thereby hope to be re-elected,[11] to the prince sacrificing a confidant to gain the support of the people. 'Having conquered the Romagna', Cesare Borgia, called the Duke,

> found it under the control of a number of impotent petty tyrants, who had devoted themselves more to plundering their subjects than to governing them properly, and encouraging discord and disorder amongst them rather than peace and union; so that this province was infested by brigands, torn by quarrels, and given over to every sort of violence. He saw at once that, to restore order amongst the inhabitants and obedience to the sovereign, it was necessary

> to establish a good and vigorous government there. And for this purpose he appointed as governor of that province Don Ramiro d'Orco, a man of cruelty, but at the same time of great energy, to whom he gave plenary power. In a very short time D'Orco reduced the province to peace and order, thereby gaining for him the highest reputation. After a while the Duke found such excessive exercise of authority no longer necessary or expedient, for he feared that it might render himself odious. He therefore established a civil tribunal in the heart of the province, under an excellent president, where every city should have its own advocate. And having observed that the past rigor of Ramiro had engendered some hatred, he wished to show to the people, for the purpose of removing that feeling from their minds, and to win their entire confidence, that, if any cruelties had been practised, they had not originated with him, but had resulted altogether from the harsh nature of his minister. He therefore took occasion to have Messer Ramiro put to death, and his body, cut into two parts, exposed in the market-place of Cesena one morning, with a block of wood and a bloody cutlass left beside him. The horror of this spectacle caused the people to remain for a time stupefied and satisfied. (*Prince*, p. 25)

This story not only tells us how a prince may establish the law and bring order, and to get rid of a possible rival and potential conspirator, but also how to satisfy the people who had to suffer in this process of transformation. Staging a conspiracy, however, is not always without risk even for the prince, especially if it should serve as a litmus test for the support of confidants. 'Dion of Syracuse . . . by way of testing the fidelity of some one whom he suspected ordered Callippus, in whom he had entire confidence, to pretend to be conspiring against him . . . Callippus, being able to conspire with impunity against Dion, plotted so well that he deprived him of his state and his life' (*Discourses*, p. 349).

It seems safer for a prince just to pretend that there is a plot, assign the responsibility to some people he wants to get rid of, and then let justice prevail. It might be difficult to prove that the suspect is a conspirator, but more often it is impossible for a suspect to prove that he is not. The veil of secrecy is asymmetric and in the end it favors the powerful. There are numerous examples that testify this fact, and the powerful often make use of it. No wonder, that if a prince discovers a plot, ' . . . and he punishes the conspirators with death, it will always be believed that it was an invention of the prince to satisfy his cruelty and avarice with the blood and possessions of those whom he had put to death' (*Discourses*, p. 347). Machiavelli offers

> an advice to princes or republics against whom conspiracies may have been formed. If they discover that a conspiracy exists against them, they must, before punishing its authors, endeavor carefully to know its nature and extent, – to weigh and measure well the means of the conspirators, and their own strength. And if they find it powerful and alarming, they must not expose it until they

> have provided themselves with sufficient force to crush it, as otherwise they will only hasten their own destruction. (*Discourses*, p. 347)

This quote is of interest in many ways. First, it mentions republics, and second it is explicitly meant as advice. This brings us back to the question of what motivated Machiavelli to present a 'rational theory of conspiracy'.

5. THE MACHIAVELLI CONSPIRACY

From Machiavelli's analysis, it follows that four categories are close neighbors: successful conspiracy, unsuccessful conspiracy, staged conspiracy, and pretended conspiracy. They are characterized by an *active* proposition of conspiracy. But there are also *passive* and counterfactual versions of conspiracy: the possible victim imagines that there is a conspiracy and even reacts to it, although it is imaginary. There was, for instance, the belief of the English in a 'fifth column', local civilians, mainly French or Belgian, who were eager to help the Germans drive the English to Dunkirk to leave the continent. This made a soldier of the London Regiment (Queen Victoria's Rifles) gun down a manifestly innocent old lady in Calais 'in the belief that the Germans must be masters of disguise as well as of mobile warfare', and a group of Belgian farm laborers was shot on the field. They 'were accused of mowing grass "in the formation of an arrow" to guide Stuka pilots to British troop formations' (Ferguson, 2006, p. 28). Every British soldier knew of the fifth column, however, to the Germans it was unknown.[12]

Machiavelli did not elaborate on the passive version of conspiracy. If his analysis was meant to advise the conspirators and the prince then this omission is plausible. There is hardly anything to learn from it for 'people of action'. At the outset of this chapter we raised the question of why Machiavelli wrote so extensively on conspiracy. Was it for the purpose of teaching the prince and his rivals to behave efficiently? Did he want to make sure that those who were virtuous, whether conspirators or princes, were successful and thereby improve the 'selection of the fittest' and thus contribute to the general welfare of mankind? Or is *Il Principe* simply a 'handbook for those who would acquire or increase their political power' (Gauss, 1952, p. 8) and the extensive treatment of conspiracy in the *Discorsi* just a concomitant paper that demonstrates the competence of its author?

The extended Appendix to this chapter tries to derive answers to some of these questions by means of game theory. Of course, game theory assumes that agents are rational. But perhaps Machiavelli was intoxicated by the pleasure of thinking and writing, delving into his own experience as high ranking Secretary to the Second Chancery of the Republic of Florence and special envoy to the King of France, to Rome and even to Emperor Maximilian, on the one hand, and victim of conspiracy, on the other. During his lifetime Machiavelli was repeatedly accused of conspiracy. When, in 1512, the conspiracy of Pietropaolo Boscoli and Agostino Capponi against the lives of Giuliano and Lorenzo de' Medici was discovered, Machiavelli was

> suspected of participation in this conspiracy, he was shut up in the prison of the Bargello, and had there to suffer the torture, the executioner having subjected him six times to the strappado. He was also kept for some days shackled, as we must presume from his writing that he had 'jesses' on his legs; it being well known that that word signifies the leather straps that hold one of the claws of the falcons. (Detmold, 1882, p. xxviii)[13]

Obviously, Machiavelli was not involved in this conspiracy. Detmold (1882, p. xxviii) concludes that

> the firm denial of Machiavelli under the pangs of torture ought certainly, with so honest and fearless a mind as his, to be taken for the truth, and should acquit him, not only of an unpatriotic act, but also of an act of folly in being one of a numerous body of conspirators, which folly no writer has ever exposed with greater clearness and more conclusive force of argument than himself.

But there is a certain spiritual conspiracy in Machiavelli's writing. The language is very plain, but people over the centuries, again and again, have been seduced into making the most controversial interpretations, not always in favor of Machiavelli's reputation. A careful reader of his work will find that Machiavelli was a moral person. To him a murder is a murder even if the murderer is Romulus, the founding hero of Rome. He does not subscribe to an ethics which postulates 'that the reason of state cannot be reduced to ordinary moral deliberation' (Bok, 1982, p. 173).[14] However, he proposes all kinds of cruel policies for those who want to gain power and keep it, including conspiracy. He convincingly argues that in most cases these cruelties are necessary and cannot be avoided. Because they cannot be avoided they might be justified by their success; however, in Machiavelli's view this does not imply that they are inherently good.

NOTES

* The author would like to thank Leonidas Donskis and Barbara Klose-Ullmann for helpful comments. An earlier version of this paper has been published as Holler, Manfred J. (2011), 'On Machiavelli's conspiracy paradoxes', *Homo Oeconomicus*, **28** (4), 549–69.

1. Found in the men's room of the Isabella Stuart Gardener Museum, Boston.
2. In a series of papers I tried to contribute to the qualification of this view. See Holler (2007a, b). Some of this material is used in the text that follows.
3. Note, unlike the *Il Principe*, the *Discorsi*, the main arena of Machiavelli's discussion of conspiracy, is not dedicated to a prince but to two friends: Zanobi Buondelmonti and Cosimo Rucellai. Machiavelli is very explicit about this dedication and explains: 'I give some proof of gratitude, although I may seem to have departed from the ordinary usage of writers, who generally dedicate their works to some prince; and, blinded by ambition or avarice, praise him for all the virtuous qualities he has not, instead of censuring him for his real vices, whilst I, to avoid this fault, do not address myself to such as are princes, but to those who by their infinite good qualities are worthy to be such; not to those who could load me with honors, rank, and wealth, but rather to those who have the desire to do so, but have not the power. For to judge rightly, men should esteem rather those who are, and not those who can be generous; and those who would know how to govern states, rather than those who have the right to govern, but lack the knowledge' (*Discourses*, pp. 91f). In 1522, Buondelmonti participated in the conspiracy against the Medici which, however, failed. He fled to France and served King François I until he could return after the expulsion of the Medici in 1527.
4. Machiavelli is more explicit about the problem of betrayal in his *Il Principe*: 'for he who conspires cannot act alone, nor can he take any associates except such as he believes to be malcontents; and so soon as you divulge your plans to a malcontent, you furnish him the means wherewith to procure satisfaction. For by denouncing it he may hope to derive great advantages for himself, seeing that such a course will insure him those advantages, whilst the other is full of doubts and dangers. He must indeed be a very rare friend of yours, or an inveterate enemy of the prince, to observe good faith and not to betray you' (*Prince*, p. 61).
5. Giovan Battista, the designated murderer of Lorenzo de' Medici in what became the conspiracy of the Pazzi, 'was filled with admiration for Lorenzo, having found him to all appearances quite a different man from what had been presented to him; and he judged him to be gentle and wise' (*History*, p. 372).
6. The Eighth Book of Machiavelli's *History of Florence* is dedicated to the description of this plot (see *History*, pp. 371ff). The *Discourses* (pp. 340f) contain a summary.
7. In fact, Leo X was followed by a 'German Pope' with the name of Hadrian VI. However, the latter managed to survive this difficult situation for hardly a year.
8. Machiavelli observes: 'Amongst the well-organized and well-governed kingdoms of our time is that of France, which has a great many excellent institutions that secure the liberty and safety of the king. The most important of these is the Parliament, and its authority' (*Prince*, p. 62).
9. The strategic problem can be represented as Volunteer's Dilemma; 'non-volunteering' is a likely outcome. See Diekmann (1985).
10. In his *Secret Diplomatic History of the Eighteenth Century*, Karl Marx (1969 [1856/57]) colorfully describes how England, from 1700, the date of the Anglo-Swedish Defensive Treaty, to 1719, was continually 'assisting Russia and waging war against Sweden, either by secret intrigue or open force, although the treaty was never rescinded nor war ever declared' (Marx, p. 86). England betrayed her allies to serve the interests of Imperial Russia and her own hopes for large benefits out of a flourishing Russian trade.
11. This is the theme of a recent volume edited by Breton et al. (2007), *The Economics of Transparency in Politics*.
12. For further details, see Glyn Prysor's (2005) 'The "Fifth Column" and the British experience of retreat, 1940'.

13. 'There is no mention of his torture in the public documents, nor in the resolutions of the Eight, where the condemnation of the other conspirators is recorded. But there can be no doubt about it, as he mentions it himself in a letter written to his friend Francesco Vettori on the 13th of March. Machiavelli was doubtless innocent of being a party to this conspiracy, which originated with Paolo Boscoli, a young man of one of the old and distinguished families of Florence, who had drawn Agostino Capponi into the plot. The latter committed the imprudence of letting fall a list of the conspirators, in going into the house of the Pucci; this list was picked up, and immediately communicated to the magistracy. Many of the most distinguished citizens were implicated, and Machiavelli amongst the rest. It is quite possible, however, that the list dropped by Capponi may have been merely a memorandum of those whom the originators of the conspiracy proposed amongst themselves to draw into the plot . . . . Whilst this process was going on, Pope Julius II died, and the Cardinal Giovanni de' Medici was chosen as his successor, and assumed the title of Leo X. So soon as he heard of Machiavelli's imprisonment, he ordered his fetters to be struck off, and had him set free, as well as all the others who had been charged with being implicated in the Boscoli conspiracy' (Detmold, 1882, pp. xxviiif). The reaction of the newly elected Pope suggests that the conspiracy, at least to some extent, was staged by the Medici themselves. 'Unhappily Boscoli and Capponi, having been found guilty, were executed before the Pope's pardon arrived' (Detmold, 1882, pp. xxix).
14. To Sissela Bok (1982, p. 173), the 'reason of the state' concept implies that ' . . . rulers may be justified when they lie, cheat, break promises, or even torture in order to further their state's welfare. And secrecy regarding such acts was often thought to be of the highest importance in furthering the designs of the state'. It is the 'reason of state' that '. . . legitimates action on behalf of a state that would be immoral for private individuals. It holds that the reason of state cannot be reduced to ordinary moral deliberation'.

REFERENCES

Andreozzi, L. (2002), 'Oscillations in the enforcement of law: an evolutionary analysis', *Homo Oeconomicus*, **18**, 403–28.

Andreozzi, L. (2004), 'Rewarding policemen increases crime. Another surprising result from the inspection game', *Public Choice*, **121**, 69–82.

Baake, P. and R. Borck (eds) (2007), *Public Economics and Public Choice: Contributions in Honour of Charles B. Blankart*, Berlin: Springer.

Bok, S. (1982), *Secrets: On the Ethics of Concealment and Revelation*, New York: Pantheon Press.

Breton, A., G. Galeotti, P. Salmon and R. Wintrobe (eds) (2007), *The Economics of Transparency in Politics (Villa Colombella Papers)*, Aldershot: Ashgate.

Detmold, C.E. (1882), 'The Life of Machiavelli', in C.E. Detmold (trans.) (1882), *The Historical, Political, and Diplomatic Writings of Niccolò Machiavelli*, Vol. 1, Boston, MA: J.R. Osgood and Company, pp. XV–XLI.

Diekmann, A. (1985), 'Volunteer's dilemma', *Journal of Conflict Resolution*, **29**, 605–10.

Ferguson, N. (2006), 'A "miracle of deliverance"?', *The New York Review of Books*, **53**, 26–9.

Gauss, C. (1952), 'Introduction to the MENTOR Edition of Niccolò Machiavelli', *The Prince*, New York: Mentor Books.

Holler, M.J. (1990), 'The unprofitability of mixed-strategy equilibria in two-person games: a second folk-theorem', *Economics Letters*, **32**, 319–23.

Holler, M.J. (2007a), 'Niccolò Machiavelli on power', in L. Donskis (ed.), *Niccolo Machiavelli: History, Power, and Virtue*, Vilnius: Versus Aureus (in English and Lithuanian). Republished in M. Baurmann and B. Lahno (eds), *Perspectives in Moral Science. Contributions from Philosophy, Economics, and Politics in Honour of Hartmut Kliemt*, Frankfurt: Frankfurt School Verlag and in L. Donskis (ed.), *Niccolò Machiavelli: History, Power, and Virtue*, Amsterdam and New York: Rodopi.

Holler, M.J. (2007b), 'The Machiavelli program and the dirty hands problem', in P. Baake and R. Borck (eds), *Public Economics And Public Choice: Contributions in Honour of Charles B. Blankart*, Berlin: Springer, pp. 39–62.

Machiavelli, N. (1531), *Discourses on the First Ten Books of Titus Livius*, in C.E. Detmold (trans.) (1882), *The Historical, Political, and Diplomatic Writings of Niccolò Machiavelli*, Vol. 2, Boston, MA: J.R. Osgood and Company, pp. 93–431.

Machiavelli, N. (1532), *The Prince*, in C.E. Detmold (trans.) (1882), *The Historical, Political, and Diplomatic Writings of Niccolò Machiavelli*, Vol. 2, Boston, MA: J.R. Osgood and Company, pp. 1–88.

Machiavelli, N. (1532), *History of Florence*, in C. E. Detmold (trans.) (1882), *The Historical, Political, and Diplomatic Writings of Niccolò Machiavelli*, Vol. 1, Boston, MA: J.R. Osgood and Company, pp. 3–420.

Marx, K. (1969 [1856/57]), *Secret Diplomatic History of the Eighteenth Century* and *The Story of the Life of Lord Palmerston*, London: Lawrence & Wishart.

Nash, J.F. (1951), 'Non-cooperative games', *Annals of Mathematics*, **54**, 286–95.

Olson, M., Jr. (1965), *The Logic of Collective Action*, Cambridge, MA: Harvard University Press.

Prysor, G. (2005), 'The "Fifth Column" and the British experience of retreat, 1940', *War in History*, **12**, 418–47.

APPENDIX

A rational conspirator i will initiate a plot if the expected utility from plotting is at least as large as the expected utility from not plotting.

$$ru_i(\text{successful plotting}) + (1-r)\, u_i(\text{plot and fail}) \geq u_i(\text{not plotting}) \quad (7.1)$$

Since r is the probability that i's plot is successful, condition (7.1) assumes that the expected utility hypothesis works. In general, a plot falls into one of the two categories: successful plot with a possibility to take the prince's position or to install an arrangement which comes close to it; and failure, which can imply all kinds of cruel punishment or related losses. It seems plausible to assume that i's preference order will be such that he prefers the outcome 'successful plotting' to 'not plotting' and 'not plotting' to 'plot and fail'. Thus condition (7.1) contains a decision problem.

Let's assume conspirator i can evaluate the utilities (payoffs) such that they can be expressed as cardinal measures so that the multiplication assumed in (7.1) can work. But does the conspirator know r? Probability r could be given by 'nature', or depend on the policy of the prince, on the behavior, number and competence of fellow conspirators. Machiavelli gives a series of factors that could influence r and proposes a set of tools to reduce it. The probability r may even depend on i's payoff.

We can illustrate such a possible relationship by the two-person game in Figure 7A.1. Here i is the conspirator and j is the prince. It is assumed that neither can i observe the strategy choice of j nor can j observe the strategy choice of i, i.e. the game is a case of imperfect information. This assumption seems quite plausible when it comes to conspiracy.

For the payoffs of the two players we assume that conditions $b > a$, $b > d$, $c > a$, and $c > d$ and $\alpha > \beta$, $\alpha > \gamma$, $\delta > \beta$, $\delta > \gamma$ hold.[1] We assume that both players know their payoffs but also the payoff of the other party.

		Prince j	
	Strategies	control	not control
Conspirator i	plot	(a,α)	(b,β)
	not plot	(c,γ)	(d,δ)

Figure 7A.1 Prince–conspirator game

This looks like a heroic assumption but Machiavelli convincingly argues that conspirators are close to the prince. Moreover, when it comes to prominent issues, such as power and death, then at least the ordinal values should be common knowledge. The following analysis, however, assumes that the expected utility hypothesis applies, which allows for multiplying utilities and probabilities, and thus presupposes that utilities are cardinal. However, we abstain from the assumption that utilities are interpersonally comparable. We cannot tell whether the prince is happier than the conspirator, or whether the reverse holds, although in some situations a conclusion seems to be straightforward.

Given these specifications, Figure 7A.1 represents the payoff matrix of a two-by-two game of complete, but imperfect information. Neither of the two players has a dominant strategy. Thus, what is good choice for player i depends on the strategy choice of j, and vice versa, i.e. Figure 7A.1 represents a non-degenerated strategic situation. Should a game theorist describe the expected outcome then he falls back on choices that imply a Nash equilibrium, i.e. a pair of strategies such that none of the two players can get a higher payoff by choosing an alternative strategy, given the strategy of the other player.[2] Obviously, no such pair of pure strategies exists in the game of Figure 7A.1 (which describes an 'inspection game'[3]). However, if we assume that i and j choose strategies 'plot' and 'control' with probabilities p and q, respectively, then the (p^*,q^*) defines a Nash equilibrium if p^* and q^* satisfy the following conditions:

$$p^* = \frac{\delta - \gamma}{\alpha - \beta - \gamma + \delta} \tag{7.2}$$

$$q^* = \frac{d - b}{a - b - c + d} \tag{7.3}$$

If conspirator i chooses p^* then the prince j is indifferent between 'control' and 'not control' and, of course, any p that mixes the two. The corresponding property applies to q^*. Thus, neither i nor j is motivated to deviate from p^* and q^*. The trouble with this equilibrium is that, given q^*, why should i select p^*, and why should j select q^* if i chooses p^*, or if j *assumes* that i chooses p^*?

The Nash equilibrium (p^*,q^*) is weak, i.e. if the conspirator deviates from p^*, then, of course, his payoffs will not increase, given q^*, as (p^*,q^*) is an equilibrium, but neither will his payoffs decrease. The same applies if the prince deviates from q^*, given the conspirator chooses p^*. Why should a player choose a Nash equilibrium strategy if he expects the other player to choose a Nash equilibrium strategy?

There are still other incentive problems with the Nash equilibrium. For instance, if the benefits of a successful plot increase (i.e. such that payoff b increases), equation (7.2) implies that this has no impact on the equilibrium behavior, p^*, of the conspirator (although it seems plausible to expect that plotting becomes more likely). Although the conspirator will not change his behavior, equation (7.3) tells us that the prince will increase, q^*, the probability of control that characterizes the Nash equilibrium. If q^* remained the same, then the conspirator would clearly prefer 'plot' to 'not plot'. This is not consistent with an equilibrium, because $q^* < 1$ is not the best reply to 'plot'. As we have argued, there is no equilibrium in pure strategies in the game in Figure 7A.1.

Similar, perhaps somewhat paradoxical, results can be derived for each cell of the matrix in Figure 7A.1. For instance, does an increase of punishment, i.e. a decrease of a, reduce the probability of 'plotting'? This seems to be a highly relevant question with respect to condition (7.1). Obviously, it has no impact on p^*. Thus, in the equilibrium, the probability of 'plotting' does not react on punishment. However, since $\partial q^*/\partial a > 0$, the probability of control will decrease if a decreases. This should reduce $1 - r$ the probability of 'plot and fail'. It seems there is a trade-off between $1 - r$ and ui(plot and fail) which is not captured by condition (7.1).

There are perhaps doubts about whether the mixed-strategy Nash equilibrium is an adequate instrument to analyze the game in Figure 7A.1. For a game-theoretically trained reader it is straightforward that the maximin solution of this game implies the probabilities

$$p^\circ = \frac{d - c}{a - b - c + d} \tag{7.4}$$

$$q^\circ = \frac{\delta - \beta}{\alpha - \beta - \gamma + \delta} \tag{7.5}$$

Moreover, the reader can check that the payoffs of the players that concur with the maximin solution and the Nash equilibrium are identical, i.e. the game is 'unprofitable'.[4] Since $\partial p^\circ/\partial a > 0$, an increase of punishment (i.e. a decrease of a) will result in a reduction of p° so that 'plotting' becomes less likely. This seems to be a plausible reaction. However, if we apply maximin to the prince then we see that an increase of the benefits of detecting a plot, α, will decrease his inclination to control. Note that $\partial q^\circ/\partial \alpha < 0$. This appears to be less likely if we follow Machiavelli's reasoning.

Notes

1. These conditions guarantee that both Nash equilibrium and maximin solution are in mixed strategies (see Holler, 1990).
2. This is the definition of a Nash equilibrium. In his doctoral thesis, John Nash (1951) has given the proof that for every finite game such an equilibrium exists: either in pure or in mixed strategies.
3. See Andreozzi (2002, 2004) for literature and further analysis.
4. See Holler (1990) for these results and their interpretation.

8. A general measure of the 'effective' number of parties in a political system

Vani K. Borooah

1. INTRODUCTION

An important aspect of the analysis of electoral outcomes is the evaluation of the distribution of votes and/or seats across political parties. For example, assessing the proportionality of an electoral system requires a comparison of the distribution of seats with the distribution of votes (Gallagher, 1991; Lijphart, 1995). Another example is provided by measures of the 'effective' number of parties in a system. As Lijphart (1995) notes, the problem here is how to count parties of different size and the assumption in the comparative politics literature is that some kind of weighting is required to solve this problem.

In essence, calculating the effective number of parties in a system involves assigning a scalar value to a vector of inter-party distribution of seats or votes. At one extreme, this scalar value will (should) equal the number of parties that actually contest the election. This will occur when votes (or seats) are distributed equally among the parties. At the other extreme, this scalar value will (should) equal unity. This will be the case when all votes (or seats) accrue to just one party. In between these extremes, the effective number of parties will be greater than one, but less than the number of parties contesting.

The general theme that underpins both examples is that of inequality analysis. Indeed, some of the well-known measures of both proportionality and effective number of parties are based on inequality indices. For example, the Lassko–Taagepera (L–T) measure of the effective number of parties (Lassko and Taagepera, 1979) – which is regarded as the 'widely accepted formula' for such calculations[1] – is based explicitly on the Herfindahl (1950) index. However, one of the drawbacks of existing analysis of such problems is that it does not do more than scratch the rich vein of methodology that the study of inequality provides. To use the language of Cowell (1995), many of the measures that are currently widely used, came about more or less by accident with concepts borrowed from statistics being pressed into service as tools of proportionality measurement.

Against this background, this chapter proposes a general measure of the effective number of parties, based on the family of *generalized entropy* inequality indices. This measure encompasses existing measures in the sense that these can be derived, through an appropriate configuration of parameter values, from this general measure. The proposed measure has attractive properties both in terms of interpretation and in terms of aggregation. In terms of interpretation, this measure always yields a value between 1 and N (N=the number of parties contesting) and takes one, or the other, extreme value depending on whether votes (or seats) are monopolized by a party or shared equally. In terms of aggregation, it is always the case that the effective numbers of parties at sub-national levels can be aggregated to yield a national figure. The aggregation is effected through weights which, themselves, have an appealing interpretation in terms of the different sub-national contributions to overall inequality in the distribution of votes (or seats). The use of this general measure is illustrated by applying it to the results of the 1997 and 2001 Parliamentary (Westminster) elections in Northern Ireland.

2. GENERALIZED ENTROPY INEQUALITY INDICES

There are N parties contesting an election. Let $v_i \geq 0$ represent the vote share[2] of party i where $\sum_{i=1}^{N} v_i = 1$. If the function $h(.)$ is defined, for $z \geq 0$, as:

$$h(z) = \frac{1 - z^{\beta}}{\beta} \text{ if } \beta \neq 0 \text{ and } h(z) = -\log(z) \text{ if } \beta = 0 \tag{8.1}$$

then the family of *Generalized Entropy (GE)* Inequality Measures, $G(\beta)$, is obtained in any of the following *equivalent* ways (Cowell, 1995):

$$G(\beta) = \frac{1}{1+\beta}\left[\sum_{i=1}^{N} \frac{1}{N} h\left(\frac{1}{N}\right) - \sum_{i=1}^{N} v_i h(v_i)\right] \tag{8.2a}$$

$$G(\beta) = \frac{1}{1+\beta}\sum_{i=1}^{N} v_i\left[h\left(\frac{1}{N}\right) - h(v_i)\right] \tag{8.2b}$$

$$G(\beta) = \frac{1}{\beta + \beta^2}\sum_{i=1}^{N} v_i[v_i^{\beta} - N^{-\beta}] = \frac{1}{\beta + \beta^2}\left(\sum_{i=1}^{N} v_i^{1+\beta} - N^{-\beta}\right) \quad (8.2c)$$

The logic of this class of measures is as follows. Suppose a random variable x can take values $x_1 \ldots x_N$ with probabilities $p_1 \ldots p_N$, $0 \leq p_i \leq 1$ $\sum p_i = 1$. Hence the information content h_i of observing x take the value x_i can be regarded as a decreasing function of p_i: if p_i is large/small, then it would not/would be a surprise if $x = x_i$ and so the 'information content', h_i, of the observation would be small/large (Renyi, 1965). A measure of the 'expected amount of information' or *entropy* conveyed by the observations, $x_1 \ldots x_N$ is $e = \sum p_i h(p_i)$ and equation (8.1), above, represents a formulation of the 'information content' function, $h(.)$ in terms of a parameter β.

The measure of inequality $G(\beta)$, in equation (8.2a), is obtained by subtracting the actual entropy of the distribution of votes across the N parties, $v_1 \ldots v_N$, from the maximum possible value of this entropy which obtains when every party gets an equal share of votes ($v_i = 1/N\ \forall i$). The expressions for $G(\beta)$ in equations (8.2b) and (8.2c) are derived from that in equation (8.2a), using – in the case of equation (8.2c) – the expression for $h(.)$ from equation (8.1).

When $\beta = 0$, from equation (8.2b) we have:

$$G(0) = \sum_{i=1}^{N} v_i\left[\log(v_i) - \log\left(\frac{1}{N}\right)\right] = \sum_{i=1}^{N} v_i \log(v_i) - \log\left(\frac{1}{N}\right)$$

$$= \frac{1}{N}\sum_{i=1}^{N}\frac{V_i}{\overline{V}}\log\left(\frac{V_i}{\overline{V}}\right) \quad (8.3)$$

where: V_i is the number of votes received by party i and $\overline{V} = N^{-1}\sum_i V_i$ is the mean of the votes received by the parties. The expression for $G(0)$ in equation (8.3) is Theil's inequality index (Theil, 1967).

For $\beta \neq 0$, under perfect equality ($v_i = 1/N\ \forall i$), $G(\beta) = 0$ and, under perfect inequality ($v_i = 1$ for some i), $G(\beta) = \frac{1}{\beta + \beta^2}[\frac{N^{\beta} - 1}{N^{\beta}}]$; for $\beta = 0$, the corresponding values are $G(0) = 0$ under perfect equality, and $G(0) = \log(N)$ under perfect inequality.

3. GENERALIZED ENTROPY MEASURES OF THE EFFECTIVE NUMBER OF PARTIES

Now consider the linear transformation:

$$H(\beta) = a + bG(\beta) \quad (8.4)$$

such that: $H(\beta) = 1/N$ if $v_i = 1/N \; \forall i$ (that is, there is perfect equality); and $H(\beta) = 1$ if $v_i = 1$ for some i (that is, there is perfect inequality). If one could effect such a transformation then a good measure of the *effective number of parties* (in constituency j) would be:

$$\Omega(\beta) = \frac{1}{H(\beta)} \tag{8.5}$$

Such a measure would have the following appealing properties:

1. Under perfect equality, with all parties getting an equal number of votes, $H(\beta) = 1/N \Rightarrow \Omega(\beta) = N$: the effective number of parties would be equal to the actual number of parties.
2. Under perfect inequality, with all votes accruing to a single party, $H(\beta) = 1 \Rightarrow \Omega(\beta) = 1$: the effective number of parties would be 1.
3. As inequality increased/decreased (the value of $G(\beta)$ and, therefore, of $H(\beta)$ rose/fell), the effective number of parties would fall/rise: $d\Omega(\beta)/dH(\beta) < 0$.
4. Properties 1–3, above, would be valid for all values of β.

In order to realize the transformation of equation (8.4), with its attendant properties, set $v_i = 1/N \; \forall i$ to obtain:

$$H(\beta) = a + \frac{b}{\beta + \beta^2} \sum_{i=1}^{N} v_i [N^{-\beta} - N^{-\beta}] = 1/N$$

$$\Leftrightarrow a = 1/N \tag{8.6}$$

and, then, set $v_i = 1$ for some i to obtain:

$$H(\beta) = \frac{b}{\beta + \beta^2}(1 - N^{-\beta}) + N^{-1} = 1$$

$$\Leftrightarrow b = \left[\frac{N-1}{N^{\beta} - 1} \frac{N^{\beta}}{N} \right] (\beta + \beta^2) \tag{8.7}$$

If $\beta = 1$ then $b = 2$ and so, from equations (8.2c), (8.4) and (8.5):

$$G(1) = \frac{1}{2}\left[\sum_{i=1}^{N} v_i^2 - \frac{1}{N} \right], \; H(1) = \sum_{i=1}^{N} v_i^2 \text{ and } \Omega(1) = \frac{1}{\sum_{i=1}^{N} v_i^2} \tag{8.8}$$

where: $H(1)$ is the Herfindahl index (Herfindahl, 1950); and $\Omega(1)$ is the Lassko–Taagepera (L–T) measure of the effective number of parties (Lassko and Taagepera, 1979). It is important to emphasize that the L–T measure is a special case of the general measure proposed, obtained by setting $\beta = 1$ in equation (8.5).[3] The significance of this restriction is discussed in the following subsection.

For $\beta = 0$, the linear transformation:

$$H(0) = a + bG(0) \text{ where: } a = \frac{1}{N} \text{ and } b = \frac{N-1}{N}\frac{1}{\log(N)}$$

ensures that, under perfect equality, $H(0) = 1/N$ and, under perfect inequality, $H(0) = 1$. Consequently, the effective number of parties when $\beta = 0$ is:

$$\Omega(0) = \frac{1}{H(0)} = \left[\frac{1}{N}\left(1 + \frac{1}{\log(N)}\frac{N-1}{N}\sum_{i=1}^{N}\frac{V_i}{\bar{V}}\log\left(\frac{V_i}{\bar{V}}\right)\right)\right]^{-1}$$

where Properties 1–3, above, also hold for $\Omega(0)$.

4. THE INTERPRETATION OF THE β PARAMETER

All inequality indices should embody the *weak principle of transfers*. In the case under discussion, this principle (also known as the Pigou–Dalton property: Dalton, 1920) requires that a transfer of votes from a 'larger' to a 'smaller' party should cause the value of the inequality index $H(\beta)$ to fall. More precisely, consider two parties, one with V votes and the other with $V + \delta$ votes. Then, by the weak principle of transfers, a transfer from the second ('larger') to the first ('smaller') party of ΔV votes, $\Delta V < \frac{1}{2}\delta$, will cause inequality to fall and, as a consequence, the effective number of parties to rise. Since $G(\beta)$, as a *bona fide* inequality index, satisfies this principle, so does its linear transform, $H(\beta)$.

But by *how much* the value of the inequality index will fall – and, therefore, by *how many* the effective number of parties will rise – following this 'egalitarian' vote transfer, will depend upon the value of the parameter, β. The value of β, therefore, measures the 'transfer sensitivity' of the inequality index: the larger the value of β, the greater will be the fall in inequality – and the rise in the effective number of parties – following a transfer of votes from a larger to a smaller party. In the context of the 'social welfare' approach to inequality measurement (Atkinson, 1970), the value of β represents society's degree of 'inequality aversion'.

More formally, as a consequence of a transfer of Δv of vote share from a 'larger' party ($i = 2$) to a 'smaller' party ($i = 1$), the inequality indices $G(\beta)$ and $H(\beta)$ will fall by:

$$\Delta G = \frac{1+\beta}{\beta(1+\beta)}(v_1^\beta - v_2^\beta)\Delta v = \frac{1}{\beta}(v_1^\beta - v_2^\beta)\Delta s$$

$$= \frac{1}{\beta}[(1 - v_2^\beta) - (1 - v_1^\beta)]\Delta s = [h(v_2) - h(v_1)]\Delta v \qquad (8.9a)$$

$$\Delta H = b[h(v_2) - h(v_1)]\Delta v \qquad (8.9b)$$

If one defines a *distance measure*:

$$\lambda(\beta, v_1, v_2) = h(v_1) - h(v_2) = \frac{v_2^\beta}{\beta} - \frac{v_1^\beta}{\beta} \geq 0$$

then the *strong principle of transfers* requires that the reduction in inequality, following an egalitarian transfer of Δv (that is, a transfer from a larger to a smaller party), depends *only* upon the distance between two shares, *regardless* of the parties between which the transfer is made. An egalitarian transfer of Δv from party 4 to party 3 will have the same effect on reducing inequality as an egalitarian transfer from party 2 to party 1 if, and only if, the 'distance' between v_4 and v_3 is the same as the 'distance' between v_2 and v_1 or, more formally, if and only if: $\lambda(\beta, v_4, v_3) = \lambda(\beta, v_1, v_2)$. The *greater* the distance between two vote shares the *larger* will be the fall in inequality following an egalitarian transfer of Δv.

The family of GE inequality indices – discussed above – satisfies the strong principle of transfers. For the purposes of this discussion, the relevant point is that, given the vote shares of four parties, $v_1 < v_2 < v_3 < v_4$, such that $v_4 - v_3 = v_2 - v_1$:

$$\lambda(\beta, v_1, v_2) > \lambda(\beta, v_2, v_4) \text{ if } \beta < 1$$

$$\lambda(\beta, v_1, v_2) = \lambda(\beta, v_2, v_4) \text{ if } \beta = 1$$

$$\lambda(\beta, v_1, v_2) < \lambda(\beta, v_2, v_4) \text{ if } \beta > 1$$

so that, if $\beta < 1 / \beta = 1 / \beta > 1$, a transfer of Δv from party 2 to party 1 will cause inequality to fall (and, therefore, the effective number of parties to rise) by an amount greater/equal/smaller than the amount by which it would fall if the same transfer was effected between parties 4 and 3.

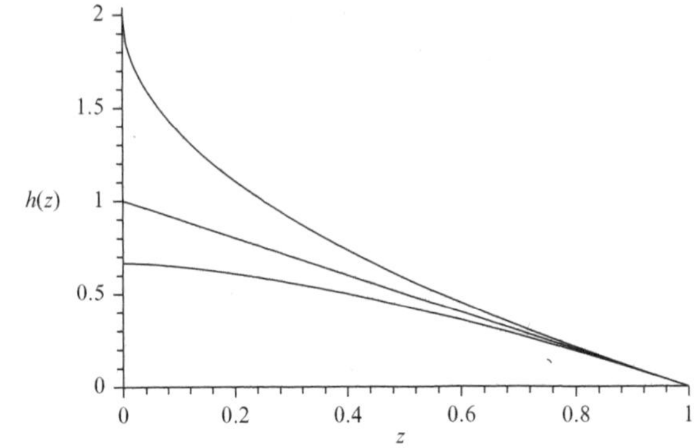

Figure 8.1 Distance and values of β

This follows because, from equation (8.1):

$$\frac{dh}{dz} = -z^{\beta-1} < 0 \text{ and } \frac{d^2h}{dz^2} = -(\beta - 1)z^{\beta-2}$$

so that $h(.)$ curve is: linear if $\beta = 1$ ($d^2h/dz^2 = 0$); convex to the origin if $\beta < 1$ ($d^2h/dz^2 > 0$); and concave to the origin if $\beta > 1$ ($d^2h/dz^2 < 0$). These outcomes are shown in Figure 8.1. The top curve relates to $\beta = 0.5$ and it is convex to the origin; the curve below it – the middle curve – relates to $\beta = 1$ and it is linear; the bottom curve relates to $\beta = 1.5$ and it is concave to the origin.

Figure 8.1 shows that the distance between the shares 0.6 and 0.8 is the same as/less than/more than the distance between the shares 0.2 and 0.4 when $\beta = 1/\beta < 1/\beta > 1$. Moreover, as the value of β decreases from $\beta = 1$, the curves will become more convex, and as the value of β increases from $\beta = 1$ they will become more concave. Therefore, the gap between the distances will increase with higher (absolute) values of β : as β increases (from $\beta = 1$) through negative[4]/positive values, we become increasingly more approving of egalitarian transfers at the lower/upper end of the distribution. It is in this sense that β may be thought of as a 'transfer sensitivity' (or, equivalently, the 'inequality aversion') parameter.

When $\beta = 1$, $\lambda(\beta) = h(v_1) - h(v_2) = v_2 - v_1$. Therefore, the implication of $\beta = 1$ is that the distance between a party with a 40 per cent share of the vote and another with a 35 per cent share is the same as the distance between a party with a 7 per cent share of the vote and another with a 2 per cent share of the vote. Consequently, an implication of the L–T measure of the effective number of parties is that a given change in vote shares, regardless of whether it occurred between a pair of mainstream parties or between a pair of fringe parties, would cause the effective number of parties to change by the same amount, provided the difference in vote shares was the same between the two sets of pairs.

However, if $\beta < 1$, then, using the preceding example, the distance between the mainstream parties would be smaller than the distance between the fringe parties and if $\beta > 1$, it would be greater. Consequently, if $\beta < 1/\beta > 1$, a given change in vote shares would cause the effective number of parties to change by more/less if the change occurred between a pair of fringe parties than if it occurred between a pair of mainstream parties. This is the point made by Wildgen (1971) when he proposed a 'hyperfractionalization' measure of the effective number of parties which accorded a higher weight to smaller parties. In the context of the above analytical framework, he was simply proposing a $\beta < 1$. On the other hand, Molinar (1991), who wanted a higher weight to be assigned to the largest party, was arguing for a $\beta > 1$.

The restriction implied by $\beta = 1$ is not always appealing. For example, if, in Britain, the Conservative share of the vote increased by 2 percentage points and the Labour party's share fell by a corresponding amount then it would be hard to argue that the effective number of parties had changed. On the other hand, if the British National Party – a right-wing, anti-immigrant party – increased its vote share by 2 percentage points, at the expense of, say, the Green Party, then that would be likely to increase the effective number of parties in Britain in the sense that the voice of both the British National Party and the Green Party would be heard in the nation's political debate. The general measure of the effective number of parties proposed in this chapter – offering, as it does, a menu of choices between different degrees of transfer sensitivity – is free of such restriction.[5]

5. AGGREGATION ISSUES

The effective number of parties in a political system can refer to a variety of geographical areas, ranging from a country, to regions within a country representing a conglomeration of constituencies, down to the individual constituencies themselves (Chhibber and Kollman, 1996; Chhibber and Nooruddin, 1999). This section draws out the relationship between the effective number of parties in, say, a country and the effective number of parties in the regions of that country.

There are M ($j = 1 \ldots M$) regions in the country with N_j parties contesting the elections in region j. Let $v_{ij} \geq 0$ represent the vote share of party i in region j. The effective number of parties in the country, $\Omega(\beta)$ can be written as a weighted sum of $\Omega_j(\beta)$, the effective numbers of parties in the regions, as follows:

$$\Omega(\beta) = \frac{1}{H(\beta)} = \sum_{j=1}^{M} \frac{1}{H_j(\beta)} \frac{H_j(\beta)}{H(\beta)} \frac{1}{M} = \sum_{j=1}^{M} \Omega_j(\beta) w_j(\beta) \qquad (8.10)$$

where:

$$H_j(\beta) = a_j + b_j G_j(\beta)$$

$$G_j(\beta) = \frac{1}{\beta + \beta^2} \left(\sum_{i=1}^{N_j} v_{ij}^{1+\beta} - N_j^{-\beta} \right)$$

$$a_j = \frac{1}{N_j},\ b_j = \left[\frac{N_j - 1}{N_j^{\beta} - 1} \frac{N_j^{\beta}}{N_j} \right] (\beta + \beta^2)$$

$$\Omega_j(\beta) = \frac{1}{H_j(\beta)} \text{ and } w_j = \frac{H_j(\beta)}{H(\beta)} \frac{1}{M}$$

The weights w_j in equation (8.10) may be interpreted as the 'scaled' contribution of inter-party vote-share inequality in a region to overall inter-party vote-share inequality. The scaling factor is the inverse of M, the number of regions: when $M = 1$, $w_j = 1$ and $\Omega(\beta) = \Omega_j(\beta)$. In the special case, when $\beta = 1$,

$$w_j = \frac{\sum_{i=1}^{N_j} v_{ij}^2}{\sum_{i=1}^{N} v_i^2} \frac{1}{M}$$

which is the ratio of the value of the regional and national Herfindahl indices, scaled by the number of regions.

6. TWO MEASURES OF ELECTORAL DISPROPORTIONALITY

Electoral disproportionality measures the degree of discord between the proportion of votes received by the various parties relative to the proportion of parliamentary seats obtained by them. If s_i represents the proportion of seats obtained by party i, then a popular measure of disproportionality, due to Gallagher (1991), is defined as:

$$\rho = \sqrt{\frac{1}{2}\sum(v_i - s_i)^2} = \sqrt{\frac{1}{2}\left(\sum_{i=1}^{N} v_i^2 + \sum_{i=1}^{N} s_i^2 - 2\sum_{i=1}^{N} v_i s_i\right)} \quad (8.11)$$

which is, essentially, the sum of the values of Herfindahl indices calculated on, respectively, vote and seat shares less the covariance between the seat and vote shares.

Alternatively, one may define the degree of disproportionality in an electoral system as the ratio of the effective number of parties calculated on *vote* shares (denoted $\Omega_v(\beta)$) to the effective number of parties calculated on *seat* shares (denoted $\Omega_s(\beta)$). On this definition, the degree of disproportionality is:

$$\sigma_\beta = \frac{\Omega_v(\beta)}{\Omega_s(\beta)} \quad (8.12)$$

such that the system is perfectly proportional when $\sigma = 1$ and 'disproportional' when $\sigma > 1$, with higher values of σ being associated with greater degrees of disproportionality.[6] When $\beta = 1$, the effective number of parties is defined by the L–T measure and the degree of disproportionality is simply the ratio of the Herfindahl indices calculated, respectively, on seat and on vote shares:

$$\sigma_1 = \frac{\Omega_v(1)}{\Omega_s(1)} = \frac{\sum s_i^2}{\sum v_i^2} \quad (8.13)$$

7. A NUMERICAL EXAMPLE

Results from the 1997 and 2001 elections in Northern Ireland to the British Parliament (Westminster) were used to put empirical flesh on the above analysis. These elections, which sent a member of parliament from each of 18 constituencies in Northern Ireland to Westminster, were contested on a first-past-the-post basis. Table 8.1 shows, for the 1997 election, the number of parties that contested the elections from each of the 18 parliamentary constituencies of Northern Ireland (column headed 'N') and also the effective number of parties, $\Omega(\beta)$, when, respectively: $\beta = 1$; $\beta = 0.5$; $\beta = 1.5$. Table 8.2 does the same for the 2001 parliamentary elections.

The effective number of parties when $\beta = 1$ is the reciprocal of the Herfindahl index calculated on the constituency vote shares and thus corresponds to the L–T measure. The effective number of parties was highest when $\beta = 1.5$ and lowest when $\beta = 0.5$. This was because, given a distribution of vote shares across the parties contesting an election in a constituency, higher values of β result in lower values of the inequality index H.

Table 8.1 Effective number of parties in Northern Ireland Westminster elections, 1997

Constituency	β=1	β=0.5	β=1.5	N
East Antrim	4.2	3.5	5.1	9
East Belfast	3.3	2.7	4.1	9
East Londonderry	4.0	3.3	4.8	8
Fermanagh & South Tyrone	2.7	2.4	3.0	5
Foyle	2.6	2.4	2.9	5
Lagan Valley	2.8	2.4	3.2	8
Mid-Ulster	2.9	2.5	3.5	6
Newry & Armagh	2.9	2.6	3.3	5
North Antrim	3.3	2.9	3.8	7
North Belfast	2.8	2.5	3.3	7
North Down	3.7	3.1	4.6	8
South Antrim	2.6	2.5	2.9	6
South Belfast	4.3	3.5	5.4	10
South Down	2.5	2.3	2.8	5
Strangford	3.2	2.8	3.8	7
Upper Bann	3.6	3.0	4.2	8
West Belfast	2.2	1.9	2.5	6
West Tyrone	3.1	2.6	3.7	6
Average over constituencies	3.2	2.7	3.5	7.1
Northern Ireland	4.6	3.7	5.8	10

Note: N = number of parties contesting election.

As Figure 8.1 shows, values of $\beta > 1$ compress the distance between two vote shares, $v_1 < v_2$ so that $\lambda(\beta, v_1, v_2) < v_2 - v_1$; however, these distances are inflated for $\beta < 1$ so that $\lambda(\beta, v_1, v_2) > v_2 - v_1$; lastly, when $\beta = 1$, $\lambda(\beta, v_1, v_2) = v_2 - v_1$. Since the effective number of parties is the reciprocal of the value of the inequality index, H, the result follows.

The penultimate rows of Tables 8.1 and 8.2 show, for the 1997 and 2001 elections respectively, the mean of the effective number of parties in the constituencies. These mean values are not the same as the effective number of parties in Northern Ireland. This number – shown in the last row of Tables 8.1 and Table 8.2 – is obtained from the effective number of parties in the constituencies as a weighted sum (see equation (8.10)) not as an arithmetic mean.

Northern Ireland has four major parties. Of these, the Democratic Unionist Party (DUP) and the Ulster Unionist Party (UUP) are the unionist parties and Sinn Fein (SF) and the Social Democratic Labour Party (SDLP) are the nationalist parties. Between them they won all the

Table 8.2 Effective number of parties in Northern Ireland Westminster elections, 2001

Constituency	β=1	β=0.5	β=1.5	N
East Antrim	3.5	3.0	4.1	7
East Belfast	3.7	3.0	4.5	9
East Londonderry	4.0	3.8	4.3	5
Fermanagh & South Tyrone	3.5	3.5	3.6	4
Foyle	2.9	2.6	3.1	5
Lagan Valley	2.7	2.6	2.9	5
Mid-Ulster	2.6	2.4	2.8	4
Newry & Armagh	3.5	3.4	3.6	4
North Antrim	3.0	2.8	3.3	5
North Belfast	3.5	3.0	4.0	6
North Down	2.2	2.0	2.6	6
South Antrim	3.5	3.2	4.0	6
South Belfast	3.2	2.7	3.9	8
South Down	3.3	3.0	3.5	5
Strangford	2.8	2.5	3.3	6
Upper Bann	3.8	3.4	4.1	5
West Belfast	2.1	1.9	2.3	7
West Tyrone	2.9	2.9	2.9	3
Average over constituencies	3.1	2.9	3.5	5.7
Northern Ireland	4.7	3.7	5.8	9

Note: N = number of parties contesting election.

18 parliamentary seats in Northern Ireland in 2001 and all but one in 1997. Collectively, they received 87 per cent of the vote in 1997 and 92 per cent of the vote in 2001. When $\beta = 1$, the effective number of parties was calculated as 4.6 in 1997 and 4.7 in 2001; with $\beta = 0.5$, the higher value of the inequality index reduced the effective number of parties to 3.7; and with $\beta = 1.5$, the lower value of the inequality index raised the effective number of parties to 5.8. These results illustrate that the choice of a value for β, the transfer sensitivity parameter, can significantly affect calculations of the effective number of parties in a system.

8. CONCLUSIONS

The central message of this chapter is that the construction of indices or measures which purport to give scalar representation to vectors of distributive outcomes cannot be wholly based on 'objective' considerations.

While there may be unanimity about the desirability of the value of an index falling, consequent upon an egalitarian transfer (the weak principle of transfers), there will inevitably be disagreement about the amount by which it should fall. The strong principle of transfers says that this amount should depend only upon the distance between two distributive positions but, as this chapter has shown, the distance between two positions depends critically upon the analyst's preferences about where in the income distribution he/she would most like to see redistribution effected. In short, it depends upon the analyst's 'transfer sensitivity' or, equivalently 'aversion to inequality'.

These remarks apply in full to the measurement of the effective number of parties in a political system. This measure, as has been shown, can be generated by taking the reciprocal of an index drawn from the family of generalized entropy inequality indices. But the family member chosen will determine the value of the inequality index and, hence, influence the calculation of the effective number of parties. Choosing a member from the family reduces to choosing a value of β the 'transfer sensitivity' parameter. If the choice, as with the L–T measure of the effective number of parties, is $\beta = 1$ then (perhaps without even being aware of it) the analyst is placing equal weight on transfers at all levels. On the other hand, the analyst who chooses $\beta < 1$ places more weight on transfers between smaller parties while the analyst who chooses $\beta > 1$ places more weight on transfers between larger parties. The point is that the answer to the question 'what is the effective number of parties?' depends partly upon the facts of electoral data, which will frame the answer, but it also depends upon what is in the heart of the person to whom the question is addressed.

NOTES

1. Chhibber and Nooruddin (1999), p. 54.
2. Though the analysis works equally well for seat shares.
3. In turn, the L–T measure encompasses Rae's (1971) index of 'party system fractionalisation', $F = 1 - \Sigma_i v_i$ since $\Omega(1) = 1/(1-F)$.
4. 1, 0.5, 0, −.5, −1 etc.
5. Which is not say that one may not, if it is deemed appropriate, wish to adopt such a restriction.
6. When $\sigma < 1$ the effect of the electoral system is to protect smaller parties. This is sometimes used to protect geographical minorities. For example, elections to the US Senate award two seats to every state, regardless of their respective sizes.

REFERENCES

Atkinson, A.B. (1970), 'On the measurement of inequality', *Journal of Economic Theory*, **2**, 244–63.

Chhibber, P. and K. Kollman (1996), 'Party aggregation and the number of parties in India and the United States', *American Political Science Review*, **92**, 329–42.

Chhibber, P. and I. Nooruddin (1999), 'Party competition and fragmentation in Indian national elections: 1957–1998', in R. Roy and P. Wallace (eds), *Indian Politics and the 1998 Election: Regionalism, Hindutva and State Politics*, New Delhi: Sage Publications.

Cowell, F.A. (1995), *Measuring Inequality*, London: Prentice Hall-Harvester Wheatsheaf, Second Edition.

Dalton, H. (1920), 'The measurement of the inequality of incomes', *Economic Journal*, **30**, 413–37.

Gallagher, M. (1991), 'Proportionality, disproportionality and electoral systems', *Electoral Studies*, **10**, 33–51.

Herfindahl, O.C. (1950), 'Concentration in the steel industry', PhD Dissertation, Columbia University.

Laasko, M. and R. Taagepera (1979), 'Effective number of parties: a measure with application to Western Europe', *Comparative Political Studies*, **12**, 3–27.

Lijphart, A. (1995), *Electoral Systems and Party Systems: A Study of Twenty-Seven Democracies, 1945–1990*, Oxford: Oxford University Press.

Molinar, J. (1991), 'Counting the number of political parties: an alternative index', *American Political Science Review*, **85**, 1383–91.

Rae, D.W. (1971), *The Political Consequences of Electoral Laws*, New Haven, CO: Yale University Press.

Renyi, A. (1965), 'On the foundations of information theory', *Review of the International Statistical Institute*, **33**, 1–14.

Theil, H. (1967), *Economics and Information Theory*, Amsterdam: North-Holland.

Wildgen, J. (1971), 'The measurement of hyperfractionalization', *Comparative Political Studies*, **4**, 233–43.

9. Party competition and electoral turnout: Downs's calculus in a multiparty system*

Juha Helin and Hannu Nurmi

1. INTRODUCTION

Democratic government presupposes a reasonable consonance between the governmental policies and the opinions of the electorate. In direct democracy the consonance is achieved through public debate and electoral involvement in decision making concerning policies to be adopted. In representative forms of government the electoral input is limited to electing representatives whose task is to make or control the policy decisions. Either way, a link is supposed to exist between popular opinion and government decisions.

In many Western democracies the link has been weakened over the past decades, not because of the governments' unwillingness to respond to popular opinions, but due to the apparent lack of interest of the electorate to express their opinions. The overall trend in electoral turnout has been declining in many countries of Western and Northern Europe. In fact exceptions to this are mainly to be found in countries where voting is compulsory.

In this chapter we shall focus on explanations of the act of voting, i.e. answers to the question of why people cast their vote. This question is rather fundamental in understanding politics and collective behavior in general. Indeed, it has often been seen as a crucial test of what is known as the rational choice theory (RCT, for brevity); if the theory is incapable of providing a plausible rational explanation for the act of voting, the theory based on rationality assumption has to be abandoned.

The task of explaining the decline in turnout is of course related to that of accounting for the fact that people participate in elections or, in fact, to explaining the decision to contribute to the provision of collective goods in general (Riker and Ordeshook 1973, 72; Uhlaner 1993, 68). If one finds a set of conditions or factors that explains why people vote in general, one might look for the explanation of the lowering turnout in those conditions or factors as well. Perhaps their presence has become less frequent over time or some new conditions have diminished their causal efficacy.

One of the considerations that is sometimes equated with the RCT account of the act of voting is the perceived impact one's vote would likely have on the electoral outcome. The more likely one's vote is to change the outcome, the stronger is the incentive to vote. Consider the well-known expression in voter calculus (Downs 1957; Tullock 1968):

$$R = PB - C \tag{9.1}$$

where R is the reward from the act of voting, P is the probability of the vote changing the outcome to the one favored by the voter, B is the benefit from the favored outcome and C is the cost of voting. The standard argument is that since P for any individual voter in any real world election is bound to be minuscule, no matter how much value B the voter attaches to his/her favored outcome, C is almost certain to exceed PB. Therefore, the reward is bound to be negative, whence the act of voting is not rational in the expected utility maximization sense. Consequently, the most fundamental political act cannot be explained by the descriptive rational choice theory. By the same token, the normative rational action theory would seem to yield an absurd prescription not to vote for the generic voter.

We shall evaluate this argument more fully in the penultimate section of this chapter, but for now we focus on some of its implications. To wit, if the argument is correct, then the following statements would hold:

- By voting the voter increases the probability of his/her favorite outcome from what it would have been had he/she (hereinafter she) not voted, ceteris paribus.
- The closer the election, the more likely the voter is to vote rather than abstain.

On closer inspection, it turns out that the former statement pertains to properties of voting schemes, while the latter is an empirical claim regarding voter behavior. We shall discuss these statements in turn.

2. VOTING PROCEDURES AND INCENTIVES

The very rationale of holding an election or 'going to the people' as the British are accustomed to saying, is that the more support a party, candidate or alternative receives from the voters, the more likely it or she is to win. From the voter's point of view, the more she cares about the outcome of the election, the stronger incentive she has to express her views by voting for her favorite. Thus, to the extent that people do not show up at the polls, it can be argued that they are not really interested in the electoral outcomes. Indeed, this explanation has often been heard. It has, however, a hollow ring to it if it turns out that the likelihood of a candidate, party or alternative winning does not always increase with the increase of her or its support among the electorate. Yet, many texts on voting systems reveal that there are systems in which the rationale of going to the people necessarily holds, and others in which it doesn't hold.

2.1 Systems That Encourage Voting

Fortunately, many commonly used voting systems are monotonic, i.e. satisfy the condition which says that whenever a candidate or alternative wins in an electorate, it should also win when its support is increased, provided that no other changes occur in the electorate. As an example of monotonic system, consider the first-past-the-post (FPTP) system: every voter has one vote and the candidate who receives the largest amount of votes is the winner. Surely, this system is monotonic.

Another monotonic system is the Borda Count. This system takes individual preference rankings as inputs and turns these into collective preference rankings. Given a profile over k alternatives $a_1,\ldots,a_k$, this is done by first encoding the preference ranking of voter i into vector with k components

$$v_i = (n_{1i},\ldots,n_{ki})$$

where n_{1i} denotes the number of alternatives ranked lower than a_1 in i's ranking, n_{2i} the number of alternatives ranked lower than a_2 in i's ranking etc. Summing over voters gives:

$$B = \sum_{i \in N} v_i = (B_1,\ldots B_k)$$

which is the vector of Borda scores of alternatives.

To see that the Borda Count is monotonic, consider a vector of Borda scores and see what happens to it if any voter or group of voters decides to rank the winner higher than they did originally. This would mean that the winner's score becomes now larger than it was since some voters now rank more alternatives below it than originally. In particular, no other alternative than the winner gets a higher score than originally. Hence, after the change the original winner remains the winner.

Table 9.1 Non-monotonicity of plurality runoff

34% of voters	35% of voters	31% of voters
a	b	c
c	c	b
b	a	a

Consider now another theoretical property that is directly pertinent to turnout, viz. the participation axiom. It states that in terms of electoral outcomes no voter group is ever better off by abstaining than by voting according to its preferences, ceteris paribus (i.e. other voters' behavior remaining the same). It is clear that FPTP system satisfies the axiom since by voting for its first ranked alternative a voter can never bring about a worse outcome (for herself) than by not voting at all. Of course, it may be the case that abstaining or voting is accompanied with no change in the outcome, but the point of the axiom is that abstaining will not result in a better outcome than voting from the abstainer's point of view.

Equally obvious is the conclusion with regard to the Borda Count. By voting according to one's preferences one cannot bring about a worse outcome than by abstaining. Thus, both FPTP and Borda Count satisfy the participation axiom and are monotonic. In this sense they both encourage voting.

2.2 Systems That Do Not Encourage Voting

There are, however, also systems that may respond in counterintuitive ways to preference modifications. Non-monotonic systems may, by definition, respond to an increased support of a winner by turning it into a non-winner. Consider the widely used plurality runoff system and the following profile over three alternatives $\{a, b, c\}$(Table 9.1) (Nurmi 1999, 57).

In plurality runoff system each voter votes for one alternative. If some alternative is voted for by more than 50 per cent of the voters, it is elected. Otherwise, there will be a second round of voting where two front runners are confronted with each other. Whichever of these two gets more votes, is elected.

In the profile of Table 9.1 – assuming that voters vote according to their preferences – a second round is needed since none of the alternatives is supported by more than half of the electorate. In the second round *a* and *b* are faced with each other, whereupon *b* will be elected since the 31 per cent of the voters whose most preferred alternative is not present will presumably vote for *b*. Hence, *b* is elected.

Table 9.2 No-show paradox

26% of voters	47% of voters	2% of voters	25% of voters
a	b	b	c
b	c	c	a
c	a	a	b

Suppose now that *b* had somewhat more support to start with so that 4 per cent of voters had the preference *bac* rather than *acb*. Hence the largest groups would be *bca* (35 per cent) and *cba* (31 per cent). Thus, *b* and *c* would be present in the second round, where *c* would win. This shows that additional support may turn winners into losers in plurality runoff. In other words, plurality runoff is non-monotonic.

It is also vulnerable to the no-show paradox (Fishburn and Brams 1983), i.e. does not satisfy the participation axiom. Table 9.2 illustrates this (Nurmi 2002, 95). Assuming again that the voters vote according to their preferences, the second round contestants will be *a* and *b*, whereupon *a* wins. This is the worst outcome for 49 per cent of the voters. By abstaining the group consisting of 47 per cent of the voters may bring about a runoff contest between *a* and *c*. This will, then, be won by *c*. Hence, the outcome is better for the abstainers than the one that results from their voting according to their preferences.

Plurality runoff is by no means the only system that violates monotonicity and the participation axiom. Another well-known example is the single transferable vote (STV) which in the context of single-winner elections is known as Hare's system. When the number of alternatives is three, the behavior of STV is identical with that of plurality runoff. Therefore, the above examples also demonstrate that Hare's system is nonmonotonic and vulnerable to the no-show paradox.

As was just seen, the no-show paradox occurs when a group of voters can improve upon the voting outcome (from their own viewpoint) by abstaining, from what it would be if they voted according to their preferences and everything else remained the same. A strong no-show paradox occurs when the abstainers not only improve upon the outcome but achieve their best outcome (i.e. first-ranked alternative) by abstaining (Pérez 2001; Saari 1989, 1995). The strong version of the paradox is obviously more dramatic than the earlier one. Fortunately, none of the systems commonly used in elections is vulnerable to the strong no-show paradox. However, the quite common parliamentary voting procedure known as amendment procedure may lead to a strong version of the paradox.

2.3 Some Results

Monotonicity and participation axiom are intuitively compelling requirements of voting systems. Indeed, one could go as far as to maintain that it is to be expected that in systems violating these requirements the turnout is lower than in those satisfying them, ceteris paribus. The problem in ascertaining this expectation is that ceteris are not paribus, i.e. a number of different factors enter into voter calculus, the electoral systems type being only one among them. Especially noteworthy is the fact that, in addition to monotonicity and the participation axiom, there are several other intuitively plausible requirements one could impose on a voting system. Unfortunately, some of these are incompatible with the two desiderata just mentioned.

Three incompatibility results are particularly worth mentioning. The first is Moulin's (1988). It states that all Condorcet completion systems are vulnerable to the no-show paradox whenever the number of alternatives exceeds three. Condorcet completions are systems that result in the choice of the Condorcet winner when one exists in a preference profile. If one deems a Condorcet winner a plausible choice – as many people do – then Moulin's result is a quite unpleasant incompatibility result on two desiderata.[1]

More recently, Pérez (2001) has been able to extend Moulin's incompatibility result to nearly all Condorcet completions and to the strong version of the no-show paradox. In other words, almost all Condorcet completions can lead to strong no-show paradoxes. The only exception is the maxmin method (Kramer 1977) which is not used in election settings.

Since a Condorcet winner is determined on the basis of pairwise comparisons with simple majority rule determining the winner in each comparison, it could be argued that resorting to higher than simple majorities might give a way to escape no-show paradoxes. Holzman's (1988–89) result, however, pretty much eliminates this possibility. It states that in order to avoid the no-show paradox one must insist on a very high majority threshold.

3. ANOTHER PUZZLE OF PARTICIPATION

In principle one could expect that in systems vulnerable to the no-show paradox the turnout is lower than in systems satisfying the participation axiom for the nearly tautological reason that the latter provide voters with the assurance that under no circumstances can they do harm to their own interests by voting instead of abstaining. Yet, even a cursory glance at

Table 9.3 Turnout percentages in recent Finnish elections

Year	Parliamentary elections	Municipal elections	Presidential elections
2003	69.7	–	–
2000	–	55.9	76.9 / 80.2
1999	68.3	–	–
1996	–	61.3	–
1995	68.5	–	–
1994	–	–	82.2 / 82.3
1992	–	70.9	–

empirical data suggests that systems vulnerable to the no-show paradox do not in general have lower turnout rates than systems invulnerable to it. If one compares, for example, turnout data from the Finnish presidential elections, which since 1994 have been conducted using the plurality runoff system, and from the Finnish parliamentary elections (PR), the former seem to be accompanied with higher rather than lower turnout rates than the latter. In Table 9.3 we present some turnout percentages in recent Finnish elections.

Clearly, the plurality runoff system seems to activate voters more than the plurality based PR systems of parliamentary and municipal elections. Thus, contrary to what one would expect, the system not satisfying the participation axiom is accompanied with higher turnouts than systems satisfying it. On the other hand, the voters seem 'rational' in the sense that the turnout on the second round of presidential elections is higher than on the first one. From the point of view of the no-show paradox this makes sense: on the second round there is no chance that the voter might regret voting for her higher ranked candidate, i.e. the second round is invulnerable to the no-show paradox.

Obviously, each electoral system has many other properties than the eventual vulnerability to the no-show paradox. FPTP is known to be accompanied with relatively small numbers of parties or candidates, while the plurality runoff system encourages candidates with relatively small support to enter the race (Wright and Riker 1989). After all, it is easier to be first or second than first in terms of electoral support. If FPTP leads to a two-party system, as according to Duverger's Law it does, then the candidates may be tempted to converge to the median in order to capture as large a share of votes as possible. This may, in turn, lead to a setting where voters have difficulty in finding meaningful differences between them. Consequently, the turnout may get low because of the perceived similarity of the candidates' policy stands.

The runoff system has been in use in the three most recent Finnish presidential elections. On the basis of this experience, one district-level observation is worth making. To wit, the turnout has been consistently higher in presidential elections than in the parliamentary ones in all electoral districts over the period in which the current plurality runoff system has been in use. This holds for both rounds of the presidential elections (Statistics Finland 2007). Indeed, the difference is typically of the order of 10 percentage points.

For example, in the largest district of Uusimaa, the difference in the turnout of the 1994 presidential (first round) and the 1995 parliamentary one was 12.3. For the 2000 presidential (first round) and 1999 parliamentary elections the corresponding difference was 10.2. Between the 2006 presidential and 2007 parliamentary elections this difference was 9.3 in Uusimaa district

As already pointed out, there seems to be a systematic difference between the first and second round turnouts in the Finnish presidential elections. In contrast to what has been observed in the US gubernatorial and senatorial primaries (Bullock et al. 2002), the turnout in the Finnish presidential elections has been consistently higher on the second than in the first round. With the exception of 3 districts out of 15 in one election – 1994 – the second round has attracted more voters to the polls than the first round.

To the extent the Finnish parliamentary elections resemble the FPTP elections, we may thus conclude that the system vulnerable to the no-show paradox attracts more voters than the system where this paradox cannot occur. From the RCT perspective this is certainly puzzling. In the US the lower turnout in the second has been explained by the fact that there are typically far fewer other offices to be voted on in the second round. In the Finnish elections, no other issues or offices are being voted on. Hence, the comparison between the first and second round turnouts is closer to the proverbial ceteris paribus condition.

4. DOES CLOSENESS COUNT?

What about the closeness of the election? In other words, does the difference in the variable *P* in equation (9.1) explain turnout differences? Perceived probability of making a difference in outcomes would provide a reasonable RCT explanation for the act of voting. We shall look at evidence from two very different political systems, the British and Finnish ones. The former is based on majoritarian principles, while the latter is a proportional representation system. We start with the latter.

Table 9.4 Turnout in Finnish elections

Support for the largest party (%)	Parliamentary elections 2003 (%)	Municipal elections 2000 (%)	Number of Municipalities
< 25	69.8	59.4	7
25 – 29.9	69.9	58.1	51
30 – 39.9	69.6	60.9	121
40 – 49.9	69.2	63.2	94
50 – 59.9	69.7	63.9	97
60 – 69.9	72.6	66.8	33
70 – 79.9	75.0	69.5	20
> 80	77.3	72.0	7

Source: Bengtsson (2004).

4.1 Finnish Municipal Elections

In an effort to find out factors accounting for variation in turnout in Finnish parliamentary elections of 2003 and municipal elections of 2000, Bengtsson (2004) compares two explanatory hypotheses, one emphasizing the contextual factors, i.e. the socio-economic circumstances under which the voters live, and the other looking at voting as an act of choice. Table 9.4 summarizes the turnout data from municipalities with various levels of support for the largest party (Bengtsson 2004, 9). The last column refers to the number of municipalities that belong to each largest party support category in the municipal elections of 2000.

The share of votes given to the largest party is certainly a fairly good indicator of the lack of political competition prevailing in a municipality. We shall present a somewhat more detailed indicator shortly, but before doing that let us observe that Bengtsson's table seems to suggest a nearly inverse relationship between the level of competition – as measured by the vote share of the largest party – and the electoral turnout in both parliamentary and municipal elections. Especially marked is the high turnout in municipalities where one party gets more than two-thirds of the votes. Rather than competition it seems that the lack thereof explains differences in turnout. This conclusion has also been made – with some qualifications –in Grönlund's (2004) comprehensive study.

The share of votes to the largest party is, however, a somewhat crude measure of political competition. In the following section we shall outline a somewhat more detailed descriptive methodology.

4.2 Clusters of Party Support

In determining the nature of political competition within a constituency, one crucial piece of information is the distribution of support over the parties within the constituency. It is often intuitively easy to discern similar distribution patterns in various constituencies. Some are characterized by strong and equal support of the main parties with relatively small support for the other parties. In other constituencies, there may be one dominant party with competitors trailing far behind. It would be nice to have a method that would recognize support distribution patterns so that one could classify constituencies into clusters of support distribution such that within each cluster the constituencies would be very similar, differing considerably from constituencies of other clusters.

Using the clustering methodology applied by Aleskerov and Alper (2000) to analyze the performance of branches of Turkish banks, Aleskerov and Nurmi (2003) analyze seven most recent municipal elections in Finland in order to find out distribution patterns that would best describe the competitive situation of each election and of each constituency. Of 400+ municipalities and seven elections, it turns out that 87 patterns are needed to classify the support distributions in clusters that are optimal in the sense of providing best classification of data (the ratio of within cluster variation to between cluster variation is minimal).

For the analysis of turnout data it seems relevant to consider clusters characterized by intensive competition, i.e. relatively small support difference between largest parties, on the one hand, and clusters dominated by one party, on the other. If closeness of competition is to have importance to voting decisions, it makes more sense to consider a lagged process so that one looks at how competition at election t affects turnout at election $t+1$ than to compare the closeness of the race and the turnout both at election t.

We singled out two support patterns which we think describe relatively tough competition setting. In both clusters of municipalities the average support difference between two largest parties is less than 10 per cent. The clusters differ mainly with regard to which parties are largest: in one of them it is the Social Democratic Party (SDP), and in the other it is the Center Party (KESK).

In 10 clusters characterized by small or nearly nonexistent competition, the average difference in support between the dominant party and the runner up is more than 20 per cent units and in each one of them the dominant party's vote share exceeds 50 per cent. Our preliminary findings are presented in Tables 9.5 and 9.6.

These data provide no support for the contention that the toughness of

Table 9.5 Turnout in Finnish clusters with tough competition

Cluster no.	Average turnout at t	Next election turnout (t + 1)
3	72.4	69.8
10	73.9	73.8

Table 9.6 Turnout in Finnish clusters with one-party dominance

Cluster no.	Average turnout at t	Next election turnout (t + 1)
1	75.8	74.6
4	74.9	74.7
9	77.1	75.5
11	77.2	76.8
31	77.1	78.9
32	76.4	76.3
33	72.7	73.1
40	77.3	77.4
58	76.9	78.2

competition at election t would increase the turnout in the following election. Differences are minor in both tables, but the overall turnout seems to suggest that the one-party dominance is accompanied with higher turnout level than the level prevailing in clusters of tough competition. In any event, toughness of competition does not seem to increase turnout in the Finnish municipal elections.

4.3 British Elections

The Finnish evidence of the possible influence of the competition situation on the turnout seems to contradict the Downsian voter calculus. In fact, it appears to support the idea that the larger the relative share of a homogeneous group of voters in a constituency, the larger the turnout among the group members and, ceteris paribus, the turnout in the constituency as a whole. This idea was suggested by Tingsten (1937) and has more recently been elaborated by Karvonen and Grönlund (1995) and Grönlund (1999).

But what about other countries? Does this observation extend to majoritarian systems as well? To provide some insight into the latter question we looked at the clusters of party competition in the three most recent British parliamentary elections preceding (Aleskerov and Nurmi 2003). We analyzed three clusters of tough party competition and compared

Table 9.7 Turnout in British clusters with tough competition

Cluster no.	Average turnout at t	Next election turnout (t + 1)
5	75.5	72.3
7	69.0	64.8
8	68.3	62.5

Table 9.8 Turnout in British clusters with one-party dominance

Cluster no.	Average turnout at t	Next election turnout (t + 1)
1	62.3	56.3
2	70.1	65.8
4	72.8	69.7

those clusters with three one-party dominant clusters. The results are in Table 9.7 and 9.8.

Three remarks are worth making.

- If the tightness of the electoral competition were to explain voter turnout, Table 9.7 should show an increase in turnout from 1992 to 1997 and from 1997 to 2001 elections. This is obviously not the case. Rather, the clusters exhibit decreasing turnout from one election to the next.
- On the same grounds one would expect decreasing turnout from one election to the next in one-party dominance clusters. This appears to be the case.
- Although high competition constituencies tend to be characterized by higher turnout than the one-party dominant ones, this does not hold in general. Especially, clusters 4 (characterized by average support for the Conservatives of more than 50 per cent) and 8 (characterized by a tough contest between the Conservatives and the Liberal Democrats, each receiving more than one-third of the votes on the average) contradict the general tendency.

So, the evidence from the three elections seems to partly contradict and partly support the hypothesis that the turnout increases with the probability of making a difference in the outcomes. The picture becomes more nuanced when we observe that the overall trend in the turnout in all constituencies over the span of the three elections is decreasing (Grönlund 2004, 512). In fact, this is not just in terms of overall turnout, but applies to practically all constituencies. The turnout dropped from 78.04 per cent in 1992 to 71.47 per cent in 1997 and from that to 59.12 per cent in 2001. In less than a decade one-fifth of the British electorate has lost interest in parliamentary elections, a dramatic trend, indeed.

If we compare the overall turnout rates to those in high competition and one-party dominance constituencies we notice that in the former the turnout, although decreasing from one election to the next, actually remained higher than the average. Also the drop in turnout in the high competition constituencies was less than the one in the overall turnout.

Somewhat surprisingly, similar observations can be made with regard to the one-party dominance constituencies and the overall turnout. Cluster 1 constituencies – the largest group – form an exception: the turnout is lower than the overall one and decreases from one election to the next. In one-party dominance constituencies the average turnout dropped pretty much at the same rate as the overall turnout.

The evidence from the British elections is, thus, ambivalent: the prediction that the prevalence of high competition at the time of an election increases the turnout in the next elections is clearly refuted in the span of the elections we focused upon. This is partly due to the fact that the overall trend in British elections has been one of declining turnout. Once the trend is omitted, the evidence lends some support to the hypothesis that high competition leads to high turnout.

Our results on British elections seem at least partly discordant with those obtained by Abramson et al. (2007) in their analysis of a much larger set of British election data. They found a negative correlation between decisiveness and turnout in constituency level data. The correlation was observed both in simultaneous and lagged measurements of decisiveness data. Moreover, the correlation between decisiveness values in two consecutive elections was observed to be strong and positive. The same is true of participation values in two consecutive elections. Abramson et al. also look at the contribution of participation to the correlation between consecutive decisiveness values. Overall, these results suggest that decisiveness tends to increase turnout. This was also suggested by Grönlund (2004). This is partly in contradistinction with our results.

There are several possible explanations of this discordance. Firstly, we may have an instance of Simpson's (1951) paradox at hand: an association is observed in all subsets of a population, but it vanishes when the total population is examined (see also Cohen and Nagel 1934, 449). In other words, the heterogeneity of the population under scrutiny may account for the discrepancy in inferences. Tables 9.7 and 9.8 suggest that there is considerable turnout variation among both one-party dominance constituencies, but also among tough competition ones. Secondly, the clusters identified take into account not only the share of the largest party in each constituency but also the overall support pattern of all parties. We find this plausible since although in the FPTP elections the second and third largest parties get no representation in a constituency, the competition for the second place may still activate voters more in the constituencies where the support shares are far apart. In PR systems the overall support pattern is the only reasonably reliable indicator of the intensity of competition. Our focus on the 'global' pattern of support rather than the share of the winning party may thus explain the difference in results. Thirdly, Abramson et al. resort to correlation analysis of decisiveness and competition, while our focus is on the variation of average support in constituencies belonging to various clusters of support distribution. This has the advantage of recognizing the dramatic downward trend in turnout over the three elections studied. On the face of it, it cannot be due to changes in the degrees of competition. Fourthly, the data analysis differs: Abramson et al. and Grönlund (2004) analyze a much larger set of British elections than we do. It is thus possible that what they have found is a long term invariance which, however, has been changing in the course of those elections we focused upon.

5. RATIONAL CHOICE THEORY UNDER ATTACK

In the preceding we have implicitly assumed that RCT predicts that tough competition increases turnout. This assumption can, however, be challenged. Grofman (1993) provides several plausible reasons to give a negative answer to this question. Perhaps most important is the following. Suppose that there are two front runners in a election and that they are nearly identical in their policies (e.g. due to the convergence to the median position). Then the probability of each voter casting a decisive vote is relatively high, but the utility difference between the candidates is small. Contrast this with an election where the two front runners are very different and where one is clearly ahead of the other in terms of popular support. Then an individual voter's P-value is small, but B is large. The value of PB in these two types of elections may be very similar, and yet the elections represent very different competition settings (Glazer and Grofman 1992).

The preceding observations can be viewed as evidence for Tingsten's hypothesis, i.e. for the contextual theory of voting and against the choice theoretic approach. One might even be tempted to say that the data we have discussed constitute a refutation of RCT. But what would be the RCT explanation for voting? Briefly the following: an individual votes if she prefers voting to not voting. Rationality in the thin sense is simply acting in accordance to one's preferences (Harsanyi 1977; Elster 1983). When certain conditions concerning preference relations are satisfied, the choice of the preferred alternatives can be seen as maximizing individual utility. Utility maximization does not, however, constitute an explanation, i.e. it does not make sense to say that rational people vote in order to maximize their utility. Rather, it can be said that they vote because they prefer voting to not voting and their preference can (under some conditions) be represented in terms of a utility function.

This, of course, begs the question of why people prefer voting to not voting. One possibility is that those who vote do so because they think that by so doing they contribute to the outcome they prefer to the one ensuing from their not voting. This is the common view of what the RCT explanation of the act of voting amounts to. As we have just pointed out, the view is incorrect insofar as it equates rationality with an instrumental view of voting.

Our view is that there is no incompatibility between the view that people are rational choosers and the assumption that they deem voting as something inherently valuable regardless of one's probability of casting a decisive vote. There is also no incompatibility between contextualistic interpretations and choice theoretic view. Even rational choosers may succumb to pressure towards uniformity in strongly homogeneous political environments. Indeed, the act of not voting might be directly utility decreasing because of various social sanctions inposed on non-voters.

In short we do not deem the above observations as tests of RCT. Indeed, it is not even conceptually clear what rationality would dictate in election systems that do not encourage voting. What our empirical observations show, in our opinion conclusively at least in PR systems, is that Downsian voter calculus is misleading: the probability of changing the outcome is not the only consideration in the voter calculus. Nor are the costs related to going to the polls solely relevant. Surely, for a vast majority of voters the costs involved have in relative terms decreased over the past decades. Yet, there is an almost universal downward trend in turnout.

6. CONCLUSION

The voter calculus attributed to Downs implies that, ceteris paribus, the voters should be voting more actively in closely contested elections than in decisive ones. Although Downs's interest was focused on FPTP elections, one would intuitively expect that the calculus applies to PR elections as well. In the latter, though, the tightness of competition may be seen not only in the vote share of the largest party but in the distribution of votes over all contestants. Also in single-member constituency systems, one would expect higher turnout in constituencies where the support shares of the second and third largest vote recipients are close to each other, than in those where the vote shares are far apart.

This suggests that in assessing the competitive situation prevailing in a constituency one should look at the overall distribution of support over parties or candidates. Using the cluster analysis technique devised by Aleskerov and Alper we have looked at the evidence on turnout in constituencies which belong to distribution clusters characterized by high competition and compared it with data on low competition clusters. In the Finnish PR system the evidence seems to contradict the voter calculus prediction. Here our analysis concurs with the study of Bengtsson. With regard to the British election data, our conclusions are less clear-cut. On the basis of three parliamentary elections, it seems that a clear downward trend in the overall turnout is prevalent. In general, it seems that the turnout is not in general higher in the high competition constituency clusters. Our evidence, thus, does not support the view that the competition situation would activate voters in the way suggested by the voter calculus.

NOTES

* The authors are grateful to Dan S. Felsenthal for comments on an earlier version. The work on this chapter was supported by the Academy of Finland

1. Dan S. Felsenthal (personal communication) has called our attention to the fact that it seems impossible to construct an example of the no-show paradox without assuming that the underlying profile (either before or after the abstention of a group of voters) contains a Condorcet cycle. In Felsenthal's opinion this essentially undermines the seriousness of the incompatibility results

REFERENCES

Abramson, P.R., A. Diskin and D.S. Felsenthal (2007), 'Nonvoting and the decisiveness of electoral outcomes', *Political Research Quarterly*, **60**, 500–515.

Aleskerov, F. and E. Alper (2000), 'A clustering approach to some monetary facts: a long-run analysis of cross-country data', *The Japanese Economic Review*, **51**, 555–67.

Aleskerov, F. and H. Nurmi (2003), 'Patterns of party competition in British general and Finnish municipal elections', Moscow University: High School of Economics, Preprint 7.

Bengtsson, A. (2004), 'Valdeltagande i Finland. Rationalitet eller social tryck?', *Politiikka*, **46**, 3–16.

Bullock, C.S., III, R.K. Gaddie and A. Ferrington (2002), 'System structure, campaign stimuli, and voter falloff in runoff primaries', *Journal of Politics*, **64**, 1210–24.

Cohen, M. and E. Nagel (1934), *An Introduction to Logic and Scientific Method*, London: Routledge and Kegan Paul.

Downs, A. (1957), *An Economic Theory of Democracy*, New York: Harper.

Elster, J. (1983), *Sour Grapes*, Cambridge: Cambridge University Press.

Fishburn, P.C. and S.J. Brams (1983), 'Paradoxes of preferential voting', *Mathematics Magazine*, **56**, 201–14.

Glazer, A. and B. Grofman (1992), 'A positive correlation between turnout and plurality does not refute the rational choice model', *Quality & Quantity*, **26**, 85–93.

Grofman, B. (1993), 'Is turnout the paradox that ate rational choice theory?', in B. Grofman (ed.), *Information, Participation & Choice*, Ann Arbor, MI: The University of Michigan Press.

Grönlund, K. (1999), *Kontext, valsystem och aktivitet*, Åbo: Åbo Akademis förlag.

Grönlund, K. (2004), 'Voter turnout in politically homogeneous and dichotomous contexts', *Electoral Studies*, **23**, 501–24.

Harsanyi, J.C. (1977), *Rational Behavior and Bargaining Equilibrium in Games and Social Situations*, Cambridge: Cambridge University Press.

Holzman, R. (1988/89), 'To vote or not to vote: what is the quota?', *Discrete Applied Mathematics*, **22**, 133–41.

Karvonen, L. and Grönlund, K. (1995), 'Tingsten's law of the social center of gravity', *Law and Structure*, 1.

Kramer, G.H. (1977), 'A dynamical model of political equilibrium', *Journal of Economic Theory*, **16**, 310–34.

Moulin, H. (1988), 'Condorcet's Principle implies the no show paradox', *Journal of Economic Theory*, **45**, 53–64.

Nurmi, H. (1999), *Voting Paradoxes and How to Deal with Them*, Berlin/Heidelberg/New York: Springer-Verlag.

Nurmi, H. (2002), *Voting Procedures under Uncertainty*, Berlin/Heidelberg/New York: Springer-Verlag.

Pérez, J. (2001), 'The strong no show paradoxes are common flaw in Condorcet voting correspondences', *Social Choice and Welfare*, **18**, 601–16.

Riker, W.H. and P.C. Ordeshook (1973), *An Introduction to Positive Political Theory*, Englewood Cliffs, NJ: Prentice-Hall.

Saari, D.G. (1989), 'A dictionary for voting paradoxes', *Journal of Economic Theory*, **48**, 443–75.

Saari, D.G. (1995), *Basic Geometry of Voting*, Berlin/Heidelberg/New York: Springer-Verlag.

Simpson, E. (1951), 'The interpretation of interaction in contingency tables', *Journal of Royal Statistical Society*, **B13**, 238–41.

Statistics Finland (Online), November 2007 http://www.stat.fi/.

Tingsten, H. (1937), *Political Behavior*, London: P.S. King & Son.

Tullock, G. (1968), *Toward a Mathematics of Politics*, Ann Arbor, MI: University of Michigan Press.

Uhlaner, C.J. (1993), 'What the Downsian voter weighs: a reassessment of the costs and benefits of action', in B. Grofman (ed.), *Information, Participation & Choice*, Ann Arbor, MI: The University of Michigan Press.

Wright, S.G. and W.H. Riker (1989), 'Plurality and runoff systems and numbers of candidates', *Public Choice*, **60**, 155–75.

PART IV

Public Choice and Public Policy

10. The political economy of Dutch Disease: a survey

Martin Paldam[1]

1. INTRODUCTION: THE ENCLAVE VERSION OF DUTCH DISEASE

It is well known that most resource-rich countries become wealthy in the short run, but grow less than other countries in the longer run, so that the long-run effect is ambiguous. This is illustrated in Section 3 which looks at OPEC countries. The standard explanation is that even though resource-rich countries get a high income, they come to suffer from Dutch Disease, which generates low and often erratic growth. The 'disease' element is defined as follows: *Dutch Disease is the resource induced revaluation of the real exchange rate.*

The best-known theory of Dutch Disease is found in a couple of unusually lucid papers by Max Corden,[2] who considers the resource sector as a booming sector in the economy. Like Corden, we take oil to be the archetypal resource. This chapter changes the theory to take the development in technology and scarcities into account: today, a resource sector (notably an oil sector) is a small international enclave in the economy. Sometimes it is even offshore. It is normally run by international firms using expatriate experts and specialized, highly capital-intensive technologies to extract the resource. They also process it and transport it to the world market, where it is sold. The production uses few domestic workers, and the firms involved finance their real capital by borrowing on the world capital market. Most of the value added is not really 'produced'. It is resource rent.

The government of the country can – and surely will – try to appropriate the resource rent. A full appropriation of the rent will happen when a perfect world market exists for the resource, and there is perfect competition between the international firms extracting, processing and transporting it to the market. There are always small imperfections on such markets, so the appropriation may only be almost full.

It is arguable from economic theory that the government should appropriate the resource. Normally, competition creates efficiency, but the competition to acquire and keep a resource rent is a waste for society, except so far as it ensures that firms search diligently for more. Compared to other taxes, a tax on resource rent is consequently a good tax.

The resource rent accrues almost fully in foreign currency. Thus, the effect of the resource is due to the foreign exchange inflow to the government. How the economy reacts, depends upon the political decision processes set into movement by the inflow. Such processes are known to have large endogenous elements which are affected by two factors:

(A) The resource find will be known to everybody and generate great expectations.
(B) The expectations will be only partly fulfilled, so expectations will be disappointed.

The key to the analysis is the enclave nature of the resource sector, the appropriation of the resource rent as a resource tax paid by the rest of the world, and the political nature of the reaction. These features bring the analysis close to the old analysis of the transfer problem, considering the effects of international transfers between governments.[3] The transfer problem is the key to understanding the dubious effect of development aid and of international borrowing on economic development.[4]

A closely related subject is dealt with in the *resource curse* body of literature, see e.g. Sachs and Warner (1995) and Gylfason et al. (1999). It is generated by various attempts to measure the amount of resources per capita in the countries of the world. Once such a measure has been made, it is interesting to study how it is related to the income and the growth rate of countries. It appears that these relations are very weak. If anything, the growth rate is negatively correlated to resource richness. Several explanations have been explored, and the Dutch Disease discussion pursued at present is one such explanation.

The discussion will proceed as follows: Section 2 presents the basics of the Dutch Disease model, while Section 3 looks briefly at the OPEC countries and concludes with a stylized picture of one resource find. Sections 4 and 5 discuss the policy reactions of people and the government to a resource find. Section 6 contains a few concluding remarks.

2. BASIC SUPPLY AND DEMAND: AN EQUILIBRIUM REVALUATION

A resource find is a windfall gain that typically lasts for half a century. Section 2.1 shows the national accounting. The resource find promises

Table 10.1 The national account bookkeeping for the new resource sector

GDP	Identities	Definition
Y^R	$Y^R = Y_f^R + Y_d^R + R$	Value added, GDP, in economy, divided in:
Y_f^R	$s_f = Y_f^R / Y^R$	Imported production costs – enter the economy only as a formality
Y_d^R	$s_d = Y_d^R / Y^R$	Domestic production costs – the *true* production increase
R	$s_r = R / Y^R$	Resource rent – not produced: We assume $s_r > s_d + s_f$
N^R	$N^R \approx a Y_d^R$	Domestic employment effect: assumed proportional to the share of domestic production costs. A linear production technology is used

everybody in the economy an income gain. However, things are not as good as they look. This follows from the simple quasistatic supply and demand analysis for foreign exchange of Section 2.2. It is followed by a few preliminary remarks on the adjustment process taking the economy from the old to the new equilibrium.

2.1 Accounting for the Rise in Value Added and in Production

Table 10.1 looks at the national accounting and defines three fractions, $s_r + s_d + s_f = 1$ of the value added $Y^R = Y_f^R + Y_d^R + R - (s_r + s_d + s_f)\, Y^R$ generated by the resource.

Only Y_d^R is truly produced in the economy, and it is only a small part of the total value added of the sector, $Y_d^R << Y^R$. The imported production costs, Y_f^R, go in as an import and are then deducted as a cost, so it is a formal post in the national accounts only. The largest part of value added is the resource rent, R, which is the share of the public treasury. Formally, one can say that R is 'produced', but it is more precise to say that R is a tax that is mainly paid by foreigners actually living abroad.

Also, it is worth distinguishing between the startup period and the production period. Even if it is an oil find, some installation costs will have to be made. Pipelines, roads, storage tanks etc. have to be constructed. Most of the investment activity will be done by international companies using their own technology and experts, but some local workers will be employed. However, once it is done and production gets going, activity decreases.

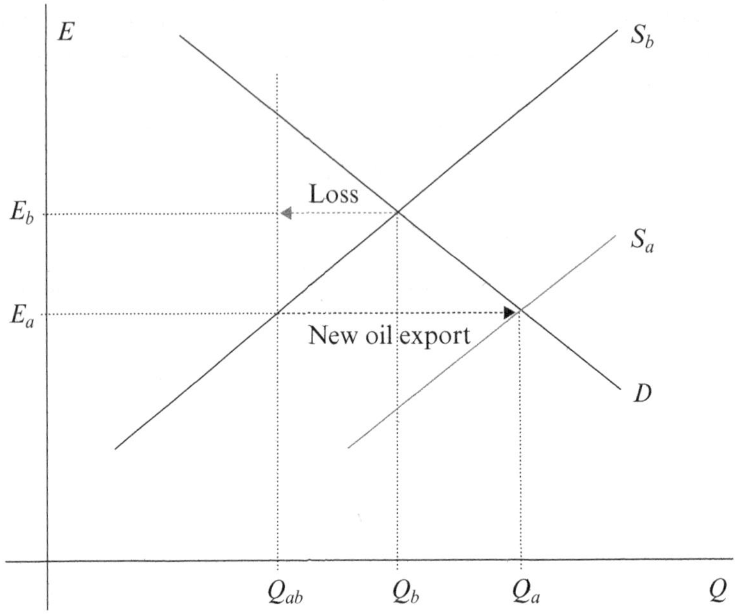

Note: The figure assumes that all foreign exchange trade is to finance international trade in goods and services.

Figure 10.1 Supply and demand for foreign exchange before and after an oil find

2.2 Supply and Demand for Foreign Exchange: Two Equilibriums

Figure 10.1 shows demand, D, and supply, S_b and S_a, for foreign exchange in real terms before (b) and after (a) the country has acquired a large and steady new supply of foreign exchange from the resource: the equilibrium moves from (E_b, Q_b) to (E_a, Q_a). The price of foreign exchange revalues (in real terms) from E_b to E_a.

The new resource export is $Q_{ab}Q_a \approx Y^R$. However, due to the revaluation the new equilibrium involves a reduction in the size of the old tradables sector. It is $Loss = Q_{ab}Q_b = Y^x$ on the figure. Thus, production does not rise with Y^R, but only with $Y^R - Y^x$. However, the true production in the resource sector rises only with $Y_d = s_d Y^R$ in the resource sector. It appears most likely that Y_d^R is smaller than Y^x, so that the employment effect of the new resource sector is negative. The effect on the private production sector is thus dubious. Some production capacity is moved to the resource sector from the rest of the tradables sector.

Contrary to the Corden model, it is not the resource sector that is the booming sector, but the public sector that receives *R*. If it does not expand, unemployment increases.

2.3 The Speed and Mechanics of Adjustment: The Assumption of a Fixed Exchange Rate

The quasistatic analysis says nothing about the speed of adjustment and the mechanisms whereby it happens. If the country has a freely floating exchange rate, one may imagine that the market will react quickly to the find and go to the new rate.

From now it is assumed that the exchange rate is fixed.[5] For a country with a fixed exchange rate, we know that balance-of-payments surpluses and deficits normally last several decades, so the period of adjustment from the old to the new equilibrium rate is long.

It is even possible to think of cases where there is no adjustment. The government may choose to place all the money on a special account abroad and keep it there, using only the real rate of return as the permanent income gain. Stories have even been told about dictators who have put a major part of the resource revenue on their personal account abroad.

2.4 Rising Expectations and the Pressures for Public Spending

Central to the political economy of the resource rent/tax story is the fact that the resource find cannot and will not be kept secret. It is a major event in the history of any country that oil (or some such resource) has been found. Everybody in the country will soon know that the country is rich. The news media will be full of figures with so many zeroes that few will know what they mean, except that they are huge. This will raise expectations dramatically.

The logic of the Dutch Disease is that wealth has increased, though not by as much as it seems at first. And as employment does not rise, there will be pressure on the government to spend more money. Thus, two consequences of the resource find will occur:

(A) The government is faced with a population that has *big expectations.*
(B) These expectations are *partly disappointed.*
(C) This generates *strong pressures on the government to spend.*

We shall return to the consequences of these points in Section 4, but first we shall look at the growth path of the oil countries, which illustrates the points made so far.

3. A LOOK AT THE GROWTH PATHS OF THE OPEC COUNTRIES

The purpose of this section is to look at the typical growth path of a resource-rich country, taken to be an oil country. The impressions gained are used in the stylized story of Section 4. Growth paths are drawn as the natural logarithm to *gdp*, which is GDP per capita. All data are from Maddison (2003) updated to 2006. The comparisons presented are defined in Table 10.2.

3.1 Pictures of the Growth Paths of OPEC vs non-OPEC Countries: 1950–2006

Figure 10.2 compares the development of the 13 OPEC countries and the 125 non-OPEC countries. This is *all* remaining countries with full data 1950–2006. Figure 10.3 makes the same comparison for Arab countries only.[6] The two figures tell the same story. I have tried to move some non-OPEC oil producers such as Brunei, Mexico and Norway into the oil group, but this has a marginal effect on the picture only.

The curves show that oil countries did become very wealthy relatively during the big oil-price boom 1973–80, but have developed rather poorly since then, while other countries caught up. Part of the poor development in 1980–2000 is due to falling oil prices, but it is still amazing to see the magnitude of the catch up by the non-oil countries.

Table 10.2 The country groups shown on Figures 10.2 to 10.4

Figure 10.2	OPEC [a]: Algeria, Angola, Ecuador, Indonesia, Iran, Iraq, Kuwait, Libya, Nigeria, Qatar, Saudi Arabia, UAE and Venezuela Non-OPEC: An unweighted average of the remaining 125 countries with full data
Figure 10.3	Arab OPEC: Algeria, Iraq, Kuwait, Libya, Qatar, Saudi Arabia and UAE Arab non-OPEC: Bahrain, Egypt, Jordan, Lebanon, Morocco, Oman, Syria, Tunisia and Yemen
Figure 10.4	Three main Latin American oil countries: Ecuador, Mexico and Venezuela compared with the USA

Note: a. Gabon used to be a member and Indonesia was suspended in 2009, but is included on Figure 10.2.

Source: Maddison homepage. The GDP per capita series, in natural logarithms.

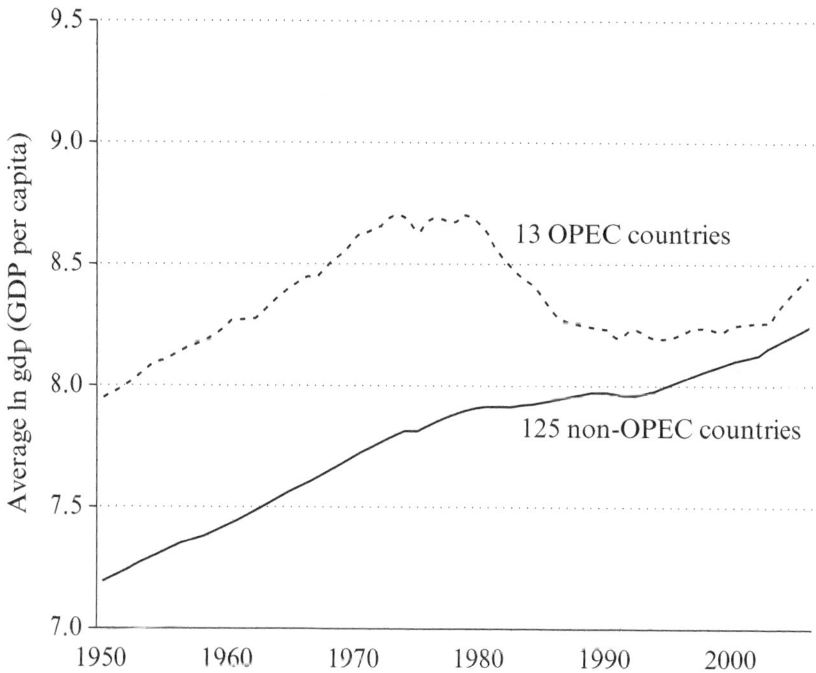

Figure 10.2 Development in OPEC vs non-OPEC countries (see Table 10.2)

3.2 The Three Main Latin American Oil Countries and the USA, 1900–2006

Figure 10.4 shows the paths of three oil countries where a longer time perspective is available. We have indicated major oil finds with four arrows. It is difficult to do this precisely as big finds are normally accompanied by many smaller ones. Fields get into production and new techniques allow much more oil to be extracted from old wells, etc. Figure 10.4 adds some flesh to Figures 10.2 and 10.3. It makes it clear that oil finds do increase income rather nicely in the country, but then cause low growth.

The development of Venezuela is an especially dramatic illustration. In 1950 to 1960 Venezuela had almost the same income as the USA, but since then income has stagnated. It is also important to note that the 60 years of low growth in Venezuela has made the country rather volatile politically, even by Latin American standards. Mexico has become more volatile both economically (with more inflation and currency crises) and politically since it became a major oil exporter.

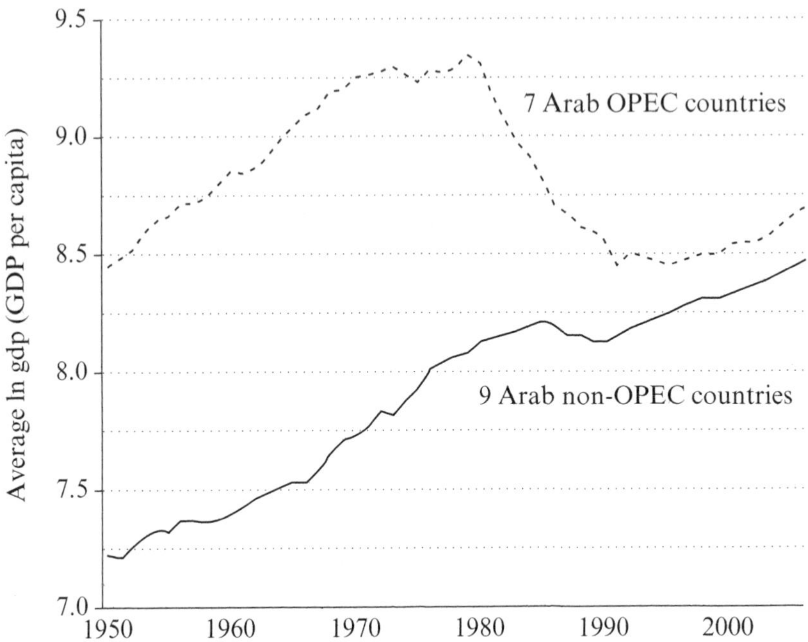

Figure 10.3 Development in Arab OPEC vs Arab non-OPEC countries (see Table 10.2)

The next section is an attempt to stylize the findings based on the graphs and other studies, and to make the link to the Dutch Disease theory.

4. AN INTERPRETATION

The actual cases have multiple finds, exogenous price movements, lags between finds and production, and so on. The stylized story is about one big resource find which is quickly put into production.

The steady state growth rate is a function of technological development relative to the level of GDP. The resource find causes the denominator to jump upward, so the rate of growth falls. It will be argued below that the resource causes people to choose more leisure, which also causes growth to taper off.

4.1 An Interpretation: The Good Story of a Gain

Figures 10.5a and 10.5b are two presentations of the stylized case. Before the find, the country grew around a steady growth path with normal fluc-

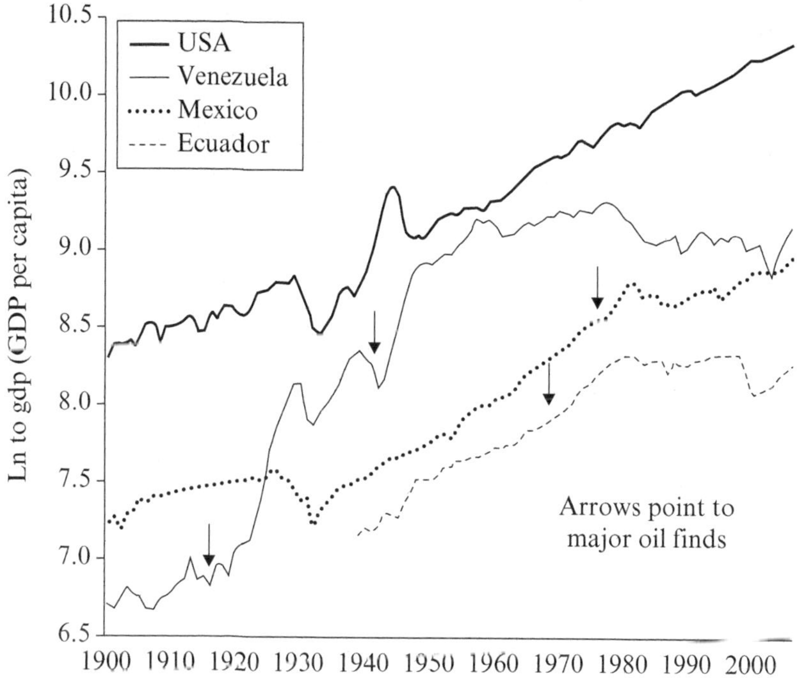

Figure 10.4 Three Latin American oil producing countries and the USA compared

tuations. After the resource find, the development has the following three features:

(f1) An initial upward jump to a new and higher growth path, due to the resource. It gives a *Gain* to the economy as shown on Figure 10.5a.
(f2) The natives expect *Gain* to be permanent, but the new growth path has a lower growth rate. This gives a *Loss*, relative to expectations, as shown on Figure 10.5b.
(f3) The jump causes *larger* fluctuations. They get smaller, but only slowly.

The Corden model covers (f1) and (f2), and parts of (f3), but gets the effects from the claim that the resource sector booms which attracts domestic resources. Below, we get it from the policy reactions. Figure 10.5a is the good story (f1) of the gain: incomes jump upward, and the old growth path is replaced by a new and higher one.

It is often noted that the resource does give a large *Gain*, which is the

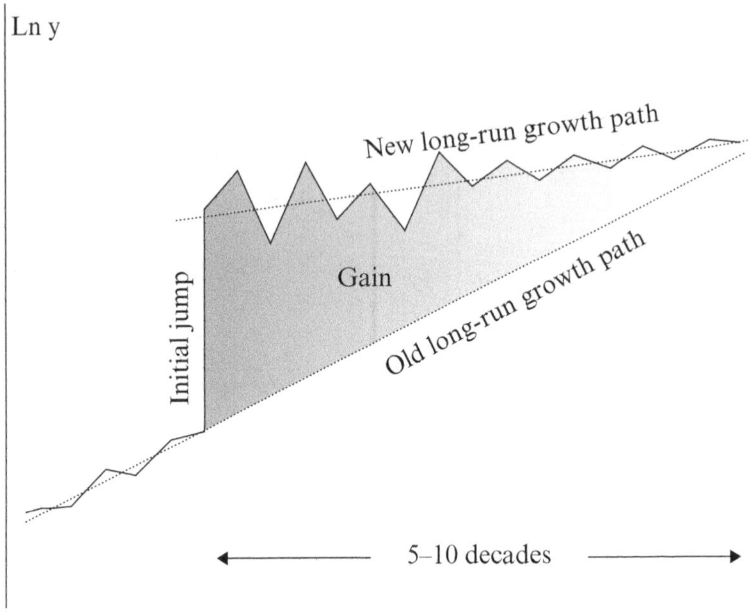

Figure 10.5a A country with one big resource find: the good story of a gain

light gray area on the graph, and that it hence gives a welfare increase. People may well *like* this disease.

4.2 The Corresponding Bad Story of the Loss

Figure 10.5b gives the corresponding bad story (f2). Many may expect that all that the resources find causes a onetime jump, and then a continuation of the old growth at the new level as shown by the expected path on the figures. They are disappointed and suffer the *Loss* shown on the figure.

The reason for the increased volatility (f3) after the upward jump is precisely that the processes whereby the unrealistically high expectations are gradually made realistic are likely to be associated with industrial conflict, inflationary waves, and political turmoil.

4.3 The Arithmetic of the Disease

We can calculate the net present value of both the gain, *NPG*, from Figure 10.5a, and the loss, *NPL*, from Figure 10.5b, at the time of the find, $t = F$:

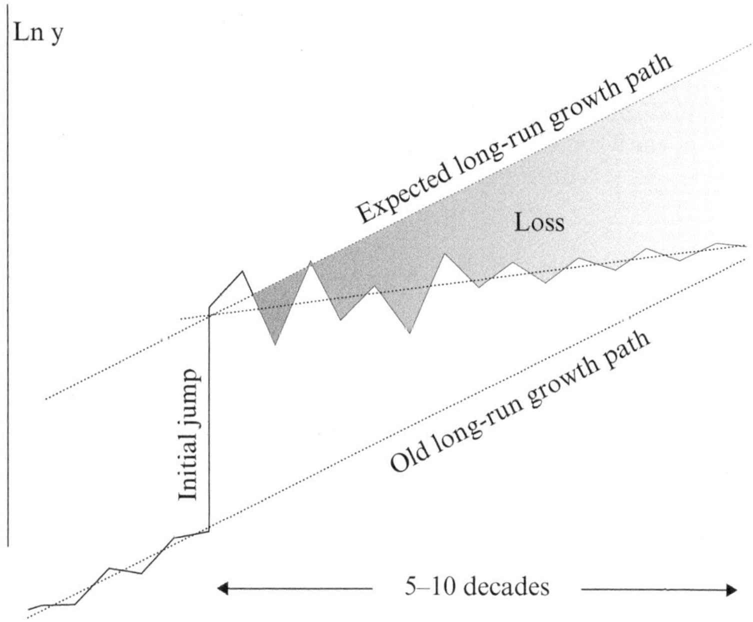

Figure 10.5b A country with one big resource find: the bad story of a loss

$$NPG = \int_F^{\infty} Gain \cdot e^{-\rho t}dt \text{ and } NPL = \int_F^{\infty} Loss \cdot e^{-\rho t}dt, \qquad (10.1)$$

We presume that the rate of discount ρ is so high that both NP-expressions are finite.

$$\text{The net gain is then } ENPG = NPG - NPL \qquad (10.2)$$

The Dutch Disease effect, δ, is:

$$\delta = NPL / ENPG, \text{ which is a ratio } 0 < \delta < 1.^7 \qquad (10.3)$$

Since we have argued that the Dutch Disease works through the actions/reaction of governments, we expect that competent and strong governments may manage to keep the δ-ratio low, while incompetent and weak governments cause the δ-ratio to become high.

The δ-ratio can be understood in one more way: it is a measure of the extent to which the expectations of the population are disappointed, and thus of the *frustrations* of the population – that is, item (B) from the introduction. People know that the country is rich, but somehow the actual gain becomes (much) smaller than expected. This is an important point to keep in mind when we turn to the political economy.

Finally, it should be mentioned that the discussion will not extend to what happens when the two trends intersect. This is typically so far into the future that it is futile to discuss it.

5. THE POLITICAL REACTIONS TO A LARGE INFLOW OF RENT

Consider the situation where a government from a certain day starts to receive a large long-run inflow of rent from abroad. This is well known to everybody in the country. The media and the rumor-exchange will be full of reports about the huge amounts of money that has fallen into the hands of the government.[8] The effects are likely to be somewhat different in a DC (developed country) and an LDC (less developed country).

5.1 Classifying the Effects

When everybody knows that the state is rich, this will change the political game in the country. In particular, it will greatly whet the appetite of every group in the country. This will lead to new spending for three reasons:

(a) The government is likely to choose to spend more for its own reasons. (a1) It may genuinely want to create more welfare, or (a2) it may spend to build support.
(b) It may be forced by voters and other powerful groups to spend more.
(c) The expectations of the population may lead to adjustments in the economy that force the government to spend.

The items (a) and (b) will often be difficult to distinguish in practice. So to span the possibilities, we consider three effects of the rent R:

(i) An increase in transfers to natives causing an upward shift in the labor supply and in the demand for labor due to the increased demand for goods.
(ii) An increase in public consumption causing an upward shift in the demand for labor.
(iii) A reaction in the market, giving an upward shift in the labor supply curve. People know that the country can afford to give them a higher income. Hence they demand it!

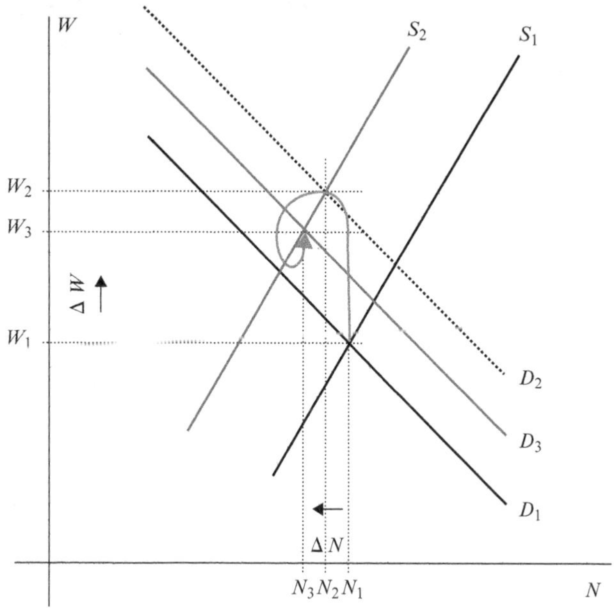

Figure 10.6a *Labor market effect of an increase in transfers: the DC case*

The three effects are analyzed using a basic framework of aggregate equilibrium on the labor market. It is simple indeed, and it catches the first round effects only. Note that the two effects in (ii) and (iii) are different from (i), but they reinforce (i). If we understand (i), it is easy to treat (ii) and (iii) by increasing the effect.

5.2 (i) An Increase in Transfers to Natives

Imagine that the outcome of the political process is a subsidy (or a set of subsidies) to the natives. For simplicity, imagine that the government gives all natives a state pension, ω, which is substantial relative to prior wages w_1. Figures 10.6a and 10.6b give the basic effects. We distinguish between the primary effects where the curves move from (S_1, D_1) to (S_2, D_2) and the secondary effects which are sketched only. Here, D_2 moves to D_3.

Primary effects The labor supply function shifts upwards, and the demand for labor goes up with the increase in domestic demand due to the income subsidy. Both of these effects give a *wage rise*, $\Delta w > 0$, but they affect employment both ways, so that the net effect on ΔN is ambiguous.

In the DC case, the labor supply curve,[9] S, is steep (the slope is large),

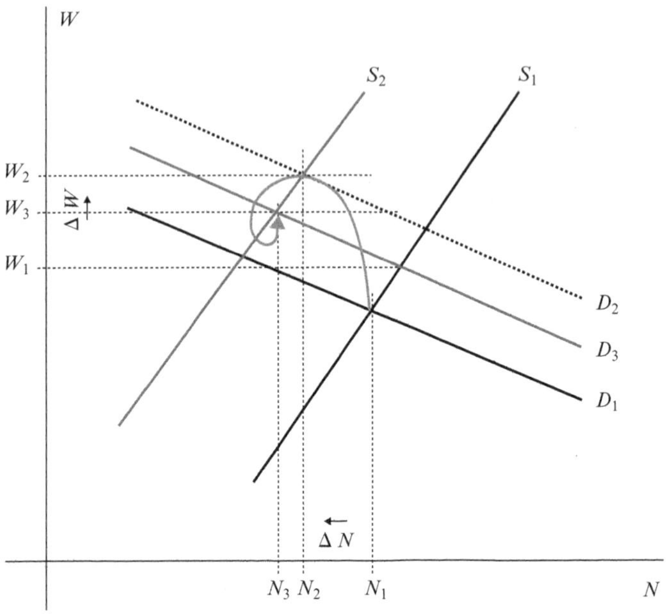

Figure 10.6b Labor market effect of an increase in transfers: the LDC case

and as the production structure is complex, we imagine that the tradables sector is large so that the labor demand curve, D, has a numerically smaller slope. Also, S is affected by the entire subsidy, and D is affected by the increase in demand for domestic goods only, so it is likely that the effect on Δw is a fairly large increase, and the net effect on ΔN is a small decrease.

In the LDC case, the labor supply curve is likely to be flatter, and as the production structure is concentrated on traditional goods with a low income elasticity, the D-curve is flatter and moves out less. The curves consequently look as shown on Figure 10.6b. Here, it is likely that the effect on Δw is a small increase, and the net effect on ΔN is a large decrease.

Secondary effects On both figures, wages rise by Δw, and the labor supply falls by ΔN. The effect is clearly that a larger part of the supply of goods on the domestic market has to be imported, as followed from the basic Dutch Disease model on Figure 10.1. Then with a higher wage, the competitiveness of firms in the tradables sector is reduced, and thus the production and the labor demand are reduced to D_3 which may, as drawn, be above D_2 or even below D_1 depending on the product mix of the tradables sector. Then things quickly become too complex to handle by the simple model,

Table 10.3 The effects summarized

	(i) Transfers to people			(ii) Public Consumption	(iii) Market reactions
	Sign	DC	LDC		
Primary effects	S and D up			D up	S up
Effect on *w*	Up	Larger	Smaller	Up	Up
Effect on *N*	Down	Smaller	Larger	Up	Down

but inevitably these further reactions are that the increase in Δw becomes smaller, and the fall in ΔN stabilizes.

5.3 (ii) An Increase in Public Consumption and (iii) A Reaction in the Market

An increase in public consumption can be drawn as a version of Figure 10.6, where labor supply stays unchanged, $S_1 = S_2$, while the labor demand rises (a lot). This has an unambiguous effect on both variables: Δw and ΔN are both positive. When we turn to the secondary effect it is likely that the outward movement of D_2 is so much larger than the latter inward movement of D_2 that some upward effect on ΔN remains. However, what is unambiguous is that employment moves from the tradables sector to the booming public sector.

Finally, (iii), imagine that people want to get a share of the new wealth. That may cause the labor supply function to shift upward. On Figure 10.6 this corresponds to a situation where $D_2 = D_1$, while S rises as shown. This has an unambiguous effect on both variables: Δw is positive, as it always is, and ΔN is negative. When we add the secondary effect Δw becomes less positive, and ΔN more negative. The effect on employment becomes rather negative.

Table 10.3 sums up the discussion. There is little doubt that the resource rent generates a wage increase, though the size is smaller in the longer run. Also, in most cases it generates falling employment, especially in the longer run. However, to the extent that it causes greater public consumption, the negative employment effect is reduced, and it might even turn positive.

5.4 Choosing Leisure

It is easy to supplement the above analysis with additional effects. Imagine that people behave as predicted by the economic textbooks and lose utility from working. A sufficiently high resource rent may thus liberate people from work. The natives, who receive the extra income, use it to employ foreigners to come and do the work. This reduces the rise in wages and generates a larger fall in native employment, but no increase in unemployment.

The result is a leisure economy with lots of guest workers – who will never become citizens – as can actually be observed in the oil countries on the Arabian Peninsula: Bahrain, Kuwait, Qatar, Saudi Arabia and UAE.[10] One may see a life of leisure as the ideal giving the highest welfare; however, the available measures of life satisfaction do not support this idea.[11]

6. CONCLUSIONS

The story of Dutch Disease is thus a story of a gain that becomes less favorable in practice. The key to understanding the way the story unrolls today is to recognize that a modern resource sector is an enclave which mainly affects the economy through the rent – and consequently the tax flow – it causes.

It is crucial that everybody recognizes that some of the expected gain will be lost due to Dutch Disease and that the economy is managed with the aim of reducing that loss. The most important issue probably is that the government makes sure that the population understands what the new public income means, and does all it can to reduce expectations. Also, it is important that some of the funds gained are used for public expenditures.

When it is taken into consideration that resources run out it appears essential that the spending programs are investments with a long economic life. Thus, it is possible to do a great deal to prevent the disease element from eating the gain.

In addition, it appears wise that a considerable amount of the resource rent is invested abroad with the aim of generating a permanent income stream instead of temporary resource rent.

NOTES

1. The chapter was inspired by the session on the origin of the Dutch Disease model and the contributions of Max Corden at the DEGIT conference in Melbourne, June 2007, where Corden was present. He made it clear that the booming sector he had in mind, was actually a new oil sector. The chapter is an attempt to introduce Public Choice into a subject where it has been sadly missing. The chapter is termed a survey, as it covers subjects that have often been discussed, but which seem not to have been put together in a simple way. The chapter was completed in 2008.

2. The main papers are from around 1980, see e.g. Corden (1982, 1984) and Corden and Neary (1982). It can be considered a special case of the Rybczynski theorem (from his 1955), see Feenstra (2004, p. 20). The roots are thus quite deep. The name 'Dutch Disease' came from newspaper articles about the natural gas discoveries in Northern Holland in the 1960s.
3. Here, the best-known analysis is probably the one of J.M. Keynes of the effects on Germany of the compensation it had to pay according to the Versailles Treaty after the First World War. A good survey of the old literature on the transfer problem is Iversen (1936).
4. However, the transfer problem is rarely mentioned in the aid effectiveness literature, as shown in the survey of the 105 papers of the literature in Doucouliagos and Paldam (2009). The only exceptions we found were Younger (1992), Paldam (1997) and Elbadawi (1999).
5. It is not clear what a fixed exchange rate means in a world where e.g. oil prices are quoted in US$ and the $ is floating. This will not be discussed at present. It is just assumed that the exchange rate is somehow fixed.
6. The transitory growth wave 1975 to 1990 in the non-oil Arab countries is commonly attributed to the Arab development aid program run by the oil countries to help their non-oil brother Arabs. The wave indicates that the aid-wave gave extra consumption, but not extra growth.
7. It is possible to think of cases where δ is outside the interval given, but such cases appear unreasonable.
8. The author worked as an economic advisor to one of the states of the Nigerian Federation during 1973 and 1974 when the oil revenue of the federation went up seven times. Nigeria had a military government and my state was quite far from the capital and had no newspapers and no television. Nevertheless, 'everybody' knew.
9. I presume that the complex labor market in a DC has a higher share of exciting jobs than the more simple labor market in a LDC. Hence, more people have fun working in a DC, and consequently labor supply curves are steeper.
10. The institutional arrangement in these countries, with Dubai as the main example, is sketched in Chand and Paldam (2006).
11. See Table 11 in Paldam (2009) for an analysis of the relevant questions in the World Values Survey.

REFERENCES

Chand, S. and M. Paldam (2006), 'Some economics of immigration from an LDC to a DC. Stressing the case of a Nordic welfare state', Chapter 6 in F. Foders and R.J. Langhammer (eds), *Labor Mobility and the World Economy*, Berlin and Heidelberg: Springer, pp. 145–73.

Corden, W.M. (1982), 'Booming sector and Dutch Disease economics: a survey', ANU, Faculty of Economics and Social Sciences, WP 079.

Corden, W.M. (1984), 'Booming sector and Dutch Disease economics: survey and consolidation', *Oxford Economic Paper*, **36**, 359–80.

Corden, W.M. and J.P. Neary (1982), 'Booming sector and de-industrialization in a small open economy', *The Economic Journal*, **92**, 825–48.

Doucouliagos, H. and M. Paldam (2009), 'The aid effectiveness literature: the sad results of 40 years of research', *Journal of Economic Surveys*, **23**, 433–61.

Elbadawi, I.A. (1999), 'External aid: help or hindrance to export orientation in Africa', *Journal of African Economics*, **8**, 578–616.

Feenstra, R.C. (2004), *Advanced International Trade, Theory and Evidence*, Princeton, NJ: Princeton University Press.
Gylfason, T., T.T. Herbertson and G. Zoega (1999), 'A mixed blessing: natural resources', *Macroeconomic Dynamics*, **3**, 204–25.
Iversen, C. (1936), *Aspects of the Theory of International Capital Movements*, London: Oxford University Press.
Maddison, A. (2003), *The World Economy: Historical Statistics*, Paris: OECD.
Paldam, M. (1997), 'Dutch disease and rent seeking: the Greenland model', *European Journal of Political Economy*, **13**, 591–614.
Paldam, M. (2009), 'An essay on the Muslim gap. Religiosity and the political system', in M. Ferrero and R. Wintrobe (eds), *The Political Economy of Theocracy*, London: Palgrave, Macmillan.
Rybczynski, T.M. (1955), 'Factor endowment and relative commodity prices', *Economica*, **22** (88), 336–41.
Sachs, J. and A.M. Warner (1995), 'Natural resource abundance and economic growth', NBER Working Paper 5398, published in several versions.
Younger, S.D. (1992), 'Aid and the Dutch Disease: macroeconomic management when everybody loves you', *World Development*, **20**, 1587–97.

11. Higher education as private good and as quasi public good: the case of Italy

Silvia Fedeli and Francesco Forte

1. INTRODUCTION

Human capital is central for economic development. An increase of the human capital may determine an increased rate of GDP growth (Lucas, 1988; Romer, 1986, 1990; Benhabib and Spiegel, 1994)[1] allowing higher per capita wages, even with a constant labour force. According to Galor and Weil (2000) the trend to a stationary or decreasing population is due to the tendency of parents to invest in the quality of children rather than in their number.[2] A virtuous circle may ensue that the increase in the quality of human capital replaces the demographic failure in sustaining economic growth. There is no assurance, however, that the virtuous circle is automatic.[3] If the market mechanism is not sufficient, public policy must be devoted to increasing the human capital level, as a quasi public good, where it gives the highest social returns.[4] Moreover, higher education *per se* may not be a sufficient condition to get the virtuous circle: scientific and technological research may be needed. To this end, qualified higher education is required. Thus, its character of quasi public good re-emerges.

The literature on human capital, overlooking the basic distinction between higher education as producing a market capital goods or as giving a quasi public capital good, maintains that in the developed countries there is an excess of expenditure for human capital because of the excess of net private return over the net social returns of education (Psacharopoulos and Patrinos, 2004).[5] The idea is simple: by investing in education, individuals become more productive in the market economy and so reap a reward in the form of higher lifetime earnings. Therefore, in a competitive economy, with an efficient labour market, individuals will invest in education up to the point where the internal rate of return on education equals the rate of return available on other investments, thereby following the 'eleventh commandment' by Mark Blaug (1970): 'thou shalt equalize rates of return in all directions'. According to this line of thought, however, the private net rate of return[6] tends to coincide with the social net rate of return on the revenue side but not on the cost side: benefits coming from the increased productivity, with some exceptions, are fully captured in the private earnings.[7] On the other hand, because governments provide (quasi) free education, private costs consist only of foregone earnings (or output), while social costs include also the full costs of these services. Thus, social rates of return appear lower than the private ones and in those areas in which education is not rationed there may be over-education.

The adopted concept of human capital, in this current stream of economics of education, appears too simplified. Human capital is conceived as a mere individual endowment, totally protected by individual property rights, which can be freely exchanged in the market. Nevertheless, this last proposition is not correct, as noted by Friedman (1955 and 1962) and by Schultz (1972a) many years ago. Furthermore, this notion of 'human capital' as fully protected by property rights appears contradictory to the very notion of 'knowledge', which is made of ideas. The property rights on ideas are, by definition, weak and their use, by definition, is often non rival. Because of these reasons, the human capital *of a nation* – i.e., its heritage of knowledge – has the nature of a stock of quasi public goods. This line of reasoning is that of the neoclassical theory on human capital, also tested with empirical research. Indeed, Becker (1964), on the basis of US data, showed that while people with higher education have differential incomes, social returns are higher than the private returns, sometime up to double. However, there is a great variance in the returns which are also lagged in time. Therefore, the private investment in education appears particularly risky. On the other hand, distributional consideration should not be overlooked. Schultz (1968), on the basis of empirical researches, argued that the investment in human capital is a powerful means to reduce the inequality of income distribution because it increases, as compared with other capital investments, the income from labour with respect to income from properties, with the latter having much more unequal distribution than the former. Therefore, Schultz (1972b) maintains that the market has to be developed by means of public financing in order to provide funds to students to invest in themselves. More recently, Johnes (2004) maintains that public funding can yield welfare gains, due to the tension between private optimality and social efficiency that arises when the impact of education on the income distribution is considered. Rauch (1993), arguing that workers receive higher wages and, most likely, are more productive, when they are in the vicinity of other more-educated workers, concludes that education gives great external effects. OECD (2001), approving the generally favorable picture of the impact of human capital provided by Temple (2001), concludes that the productivity effects of education are at least as large as those identified by labour economists. However, these results are not uncontroversial.[8] In a more articulate view Gemmell (1996) and Barro and Sala-i-Martin (1995) find that tertiary education is relatively more important for explaining growth in OECD countries, whereas primary and secondary schooling are more important in poor countries. As observed by Davies (2002), tertiary education has a special role in preparing workers for technological adoption or innovation. This seems consistent with growth's effects of education in the rich countries operating largely via 'ideas' rather than via physical goods.

This reasoning leads back to the analytical distinction by Tollison and Willett (1973) between general higher education and hard science studies and doctoral programmes, where important externalities exist and are not sub marginal. The externality argument relating to public human capital as distinct from private human capital leads to a diversified approach to the public financing of education. For example, Judson (1998) analysed two questions – 'does investment in education help growth?' and, 'does the allocation of investment in education matter?' – by a model where individual ability is heterogeneous and education both trains students and reveals their suitability for further training. UNESCO data on educational enrolments and spending were used to estimate the efficiency of existing educational allocations in a panel of countries. A cross-country growth decomposition regression showed that the correlation of human capital accumulation and GDP growth, while not significant in countries with poor allocations, is significant and positive in countries with better allocations. According to Romer (2000) innovation policy in the United States has erred by subsidizing the private sector demand for scientists and engineers without asking whether the educational system provides that supply response necessary for these subsidies to work. He therefore suggests those specific programmes that could increase the numbers of scientists and engineers available to the private sector.

In this chapter, we explore, for Italy, the issues related to higher education and formation of human capital. We distinguish between private human capital and public human capital as depending on the returns given, respectively, (mainly) to private individuals and (mainly) to society as a whole. Therefore, we analyse the relations between earnings (obtained (immediately) after graduation in various university courses, taken as a proxy of private productivity) and the socio-economic variables available (see below). We want to look at the incentives and distributional effects to private human capital formation from a market point of view. As for public human capital formation, we focus on the determinants of graduation in those curricula that may be assumed to be most important for the improvement of public human capital. In this respect, notice that singling out the post secondary education that increases the public human capital of a country is a ticklish and ambiguous task, as is the notion of human capital. Nevertheless, we need some guideline to distinguish the two. According to the Italian Ministry of University and Research (MIUR), the post secondary education that most increases public human capital in Italy is that from hard science faculties. In this respect the formation is considered not sufficient in Italy, where, over recent years, a 'vocation crisis for science research has emerged'. The MIUR's analyses show that the youngest generations perceive science as not so attractive and pleasant because the socio-economic system in Italy devotes scarce attention to science research.[9] Some formative routes such as chemistry, physics and mathematics have thus became the object of government programmes aiming at encouraging the approach of young generations to science and at increasing their enrolment in science faculties (Cammelli, 2007a).

Our analysis shows that, in Italy, two different types of unexpected inequalities emerge[10] and are likely to reproduce themselves in the future. It turns out that the highest paid graduates, not classifiable among those increasing the public human capital more than the private, are likely to belong to the richest families. Moreover, the graduates who mostly contribute to public human capital formation, according to the MIUR, are likely to belong to the highest educated families, although not necessarily the richest. On the other hand, while the flow of graduates in Italy is constantly increasing at an important rate, the share of those mostly contributing to public human capital is declining. Several policy implications may be drawn from our results. One would be that the existing policies of student subsidies – in the form of scholarships, free tuition and reduced costs or free lodging – should be increased, particularly for the area of hard science, independent of family income, although with some attention to territorial differences. Student loans should be preferred for those curricula allowing for high earnings. In such cases, for efficiency reasons, student loans may help to widen students' admittance, with grants given only to (low) family income students with high performance.

In Section 2, the determinants of productivity (as proxied by the earnings of new graduates) of private human capital and of public human capital *per se* are tested with data on Italian universities. Conclusions follow in Section 3.

2. THE ITALIAN CASE

2.1 Some Stylized Facts

In Italy, government and/or private institutions' policies towards education have been the object of a wide debate since the periods of student unrest at the end of the '60s. It is well known that education, mainly at a university level, has a fundamental importance for both economic growth and individual careers and incomes (CENSIS, 1969). Therefore, public expenditure for education has to be considered as a type of investment of clear economic value, and governments should pursue policies toward higher education, which instead has been neglected with respect to other educational purposes (OECD, 2006).[11] In this respect, note that Italy's percentage of population aged 25–34 years with tertiary education, is the second lowest of the countries reported in Figure 11.1. The Italian position among the OECD countries improves when considering tertiary-type A graduation rates without age limits: see Figure 11.2, which also shows that in Italy the graduation rate has almost doubled from 2000 to 2005.

However, when considering those faculties that are the focus of the

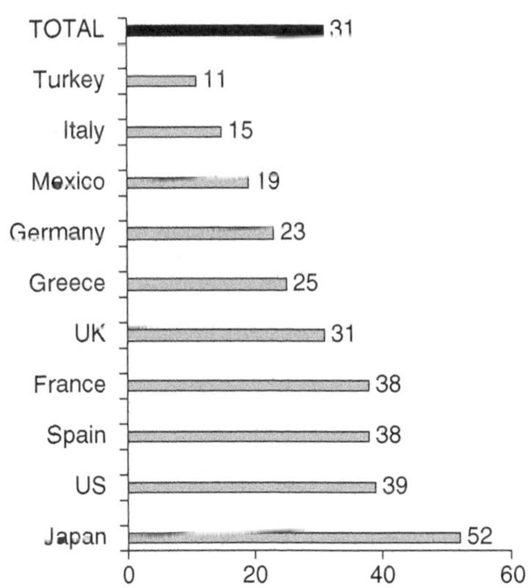

Note: Classification ISCED 1997.

Source: OECD (2006).

Figure 11.1 Percentage of population aged 25–34 with tertiary education in 2004

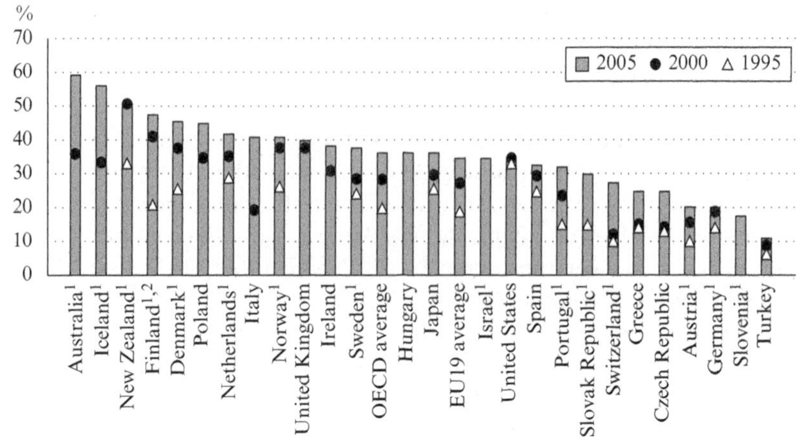

Notes:
1. Net graduation rate is calculated by summing the graduation rates by single year of age in 2005.
2. Year of reference 2004.

Countries are ranked in descending order of the graduation rates for tertiary-type A education in 2005.

Source: OECD. Table A3.2. See Annex 3 for notes (www.oecd.org/edu/eag2007).

Figure 11.2 Tertiary-type A graduation rates (number of students completing tertiary-type A programmes for the first time, in 1995, 2000 and 2005, as a percentage of the relevant group)

MIUR programmes – e.g., sciences (mathematics, physics, chemistry, including biotechnological science, bio-science, bio-technologies and IT) plus pharmacy and statistics – the situation worsens: the number of people registered in those faculties is the lowest of the European countries of roughly equivalent population (Figure 11.3).

The distinction between hard science faculties (mathematics, physics and chemistry) and technological faculties (the other focus of the MIUR programme, plus engineering) gives a (slightly) more negative picture, with a declining number of people registered in the hard science faculties more than compensated by the increases of registrations in technological-science faculties (Figure 11.4). In Italy in 2005, those graduating in science numbered 4593, which is only 1.5 per cent of total graduates.

On the basis of the above considerations, we now look at the profile of Italian graduates emerging from a recent survey (Cammelli, 2007b). Table 11.1 summarizes some features of the graduates in all the Italian universities belonging to Almalaurea Association in 2006. Full details are

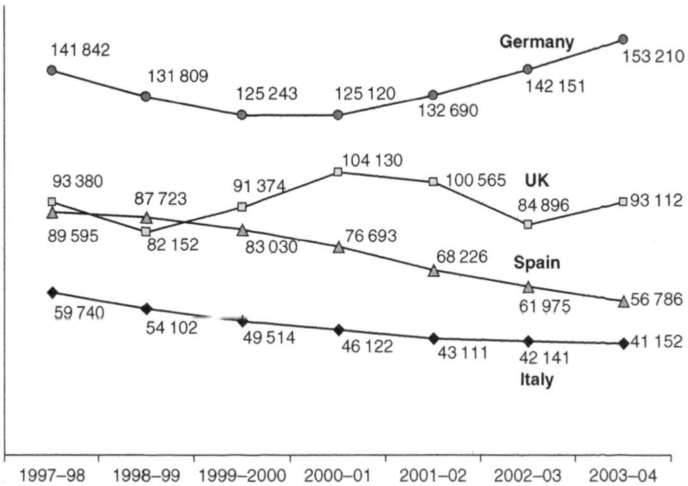

Note: Classification ISCED 1997.

Source: EUROSTAT.

Figure 11.3 *People registered in science and statistics faculties in Europe*

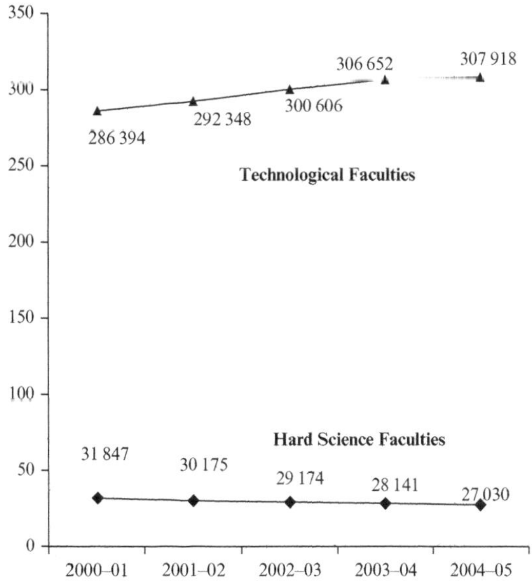

Figure 11.4 *Students registered in hard science faculties and in technological faculties*

Table 11.1 Graduate profile 2006

Number of graduates 185 361 (Number of graduates surveyed 159 287)		%
Gender	Male	40.2
	Female	59.8
Age at graduation	less than 23 years	17.6
	23–24 years	28.7
	25–26 years	21.0
	27 years and more	32.8
	Average age at graduation	27.1
Parents' education	Both graduates	9.4
	Only one graduate	15.7
	Secondary education	42.7
	Primary education or nothing	29.8
Social class of origin	Upper class	23.2
	Middle class	31.0
	Lower class	20.1
	Working class	21.8
Regular attendance	More than 75% of courses	63.2
	50–75%	20.6
	25–50%	8.6
	Less than 25%	6.5
Awarded scholarship		24.5
With job experience		75.1

Source: Consorzio Interuniversitario AlmaLaurea (22/05/2007).

in Cammelli (2007b). In the survey, the observations are the individual faculties and inter-faculty courses. Thus, for the 42 Italian universities included in the survey, we have 371 observations of which we know the number and the profile of all graduates (Appendix Table 11A.1). It is notable that about 60 per cent of Italian graduates are women. The social class of origin is, for more than half of graduates, the middle or lower class.[12] More than 70 per cent of graduates have parents without a university degree. Only 24.5 per cent of graduates have been awarded a scholarship, whereas about 75 per cent had a job and about 10 per cent studied abroad during their university course.

Cammelli (2007a) analyses the employment situation of new graduates.[13] This is based on a survey sample of about 89 000 graduates of 40 universities. It investigates graduates' job experience in the five years after graduation. Figure 11.5 shows the ranking of the monthly net earnings of the graduates grouped by faculties. The groups[14] (in decreasing order of net average earnings after the degree) are: medical sciences; engineering;

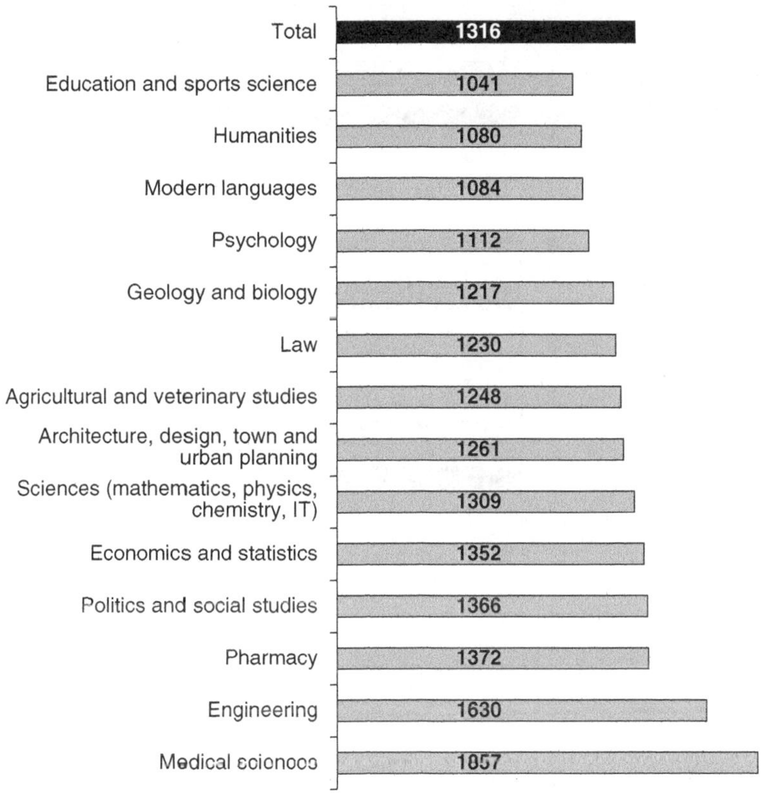

Source: Cammelli (2007a).

Figure 11.5 Graduate net monthly average earnings in euros (ordered by groups of faculties)

pharmacy; politics and social studies; economics and statistics; sciences (mathematics, physics, chemistry, IT); architecture, design, town and urban planning; agricultural and veterinary studies; law; geology and biology; psychology; modern languages, humanities, education and sports science.[15]

Notice that hard sciences are among those studies giving net earnings much lower than, say, medical science and engineering, which are the most market-profitable professions. Figure 11.6 shows how the situation has changed for graduates' earnings respectively one, three and five years after graduation, and the earnings differential between hard science graduates and graduates in technological faculties.

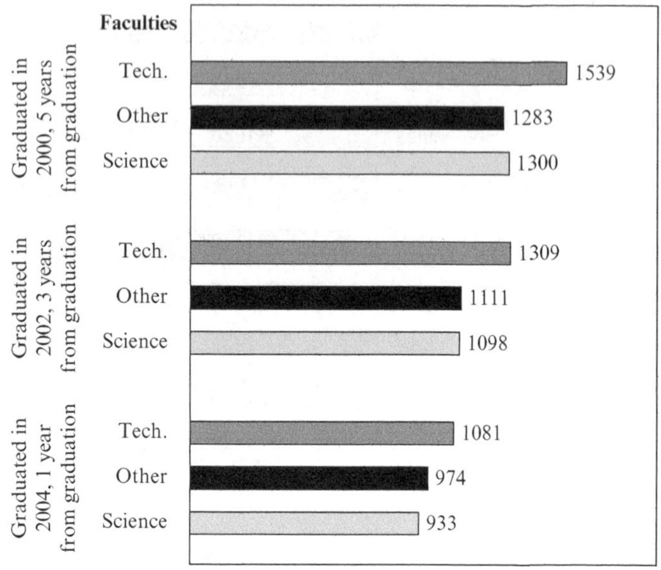

Source: Cammelli (2007a).

Figure 11.6 Graduate net monthly average earnings in euros, by groups of faculties

In the next sections, we empirically analyse: (i) relations between earnings obtained after graduation (depending on the type of university education) and all the socio-economic variables available; (ii) the determinants of public human capital formation.[16]

2.2 The Determinants of New-graduate Earnings

We assess the relation between earnings immediately after graduation in different faculties and the main social-economic features of Italian graduates, by estimating an ordered probit model based on the following assumptions. We know the earnings immediately after the university degree. We assume that they are the result of a process not directly observable, called 'latent process'. These earnings – e.g., the dependent variable, retr_lev* – can be logically ordered by groups of faculties on the basis of the information obtained by the graduates of the previous five years (see Figure 11.5). Moreover, for each faculty, we know the variables depicting the profile of its graduates as surveyed by Almalaurea in 2007. These variables are: number of graduates for each faculty, gender, age of graduation, social class of origin and parents' education, university skills, outcomes and educational conditions, such as residence, scholarships, foreign studies, job experiences, languages and ICT knowledge (see Appendix Table 11A.1). The universities to which each faculty belongs are known and grouped into North, Centre and South Italy.[17] On these bases, through econometric analysis by means of an ordered probit model (Greene, 2003), we can infer the statistically relevant factors affecting the probability that graduates enter into a given class of earnings, and disentangle the impact of each of them.

For the class of latent variable models of the ordered probit type (Greene, 2003), the dependent variable is categorical and ordered as follows

$$\text{retr\_lev}_i^* = X_i\beta+\varepsilon_i,\ \text{retr\_lev}_i^* = j,$$
$$\text{if } \mu_j < \text{retr\_lev}_i^* \leq \mu_{j+1}\ j = 0,\ldots m-1\ (\text{m} = 5),$$

where $\mu_j\,\mu_{j+1}$ are the estimated thresholds and $\mu_0 = -\infty$, $\mu_j \leq \mu_{j+1,}\ \mu_{m-1}=\infty$. In this model, retr_lev_i^* is the observed categorical variable; the μs are the estimated threshold parameters which determine the length of each class increase category; X_i is the set of independent variables that affect the probability of being in the interval of variation of the earning class, $\varepsilon_i \sim N$ (0,1) is the error component of the model. The probability of observing a specified category of earning (under the assumption of a normally distributed error) is

$$Pr(\text{retr\_lev}_i = j) = \Phi\,(\mu_{j+1} - X_i\beta) - \Phi\,(\mu_j - X_i\beta),$$

where Φ(.) is the normal cumulative distribution function. The threshold values μ are estimated along with β coefficients by maximizing the log-likelihood function

$$\ell(\beta,\mu) = \sum_{i=0}^{N}\sum_{i=0}^{M}\log(Pr(\text{retr\_lev}_i = j|x_i,\beta,\mu)) \cdot 1(\text{retr\_lev}_i = j),$$

where 1(.) is an indicator function taking the value of 1 if the argument is true and 0 if the argument is false.

On the basis of the available information also given in Figure 11.5, we have shaped the dependent variable Retr_level. It is depicted in Table 11.2, where retr_lev defines five levels of earnings from the lowest (Retr_level=0, including sports science and all inter-faculty degrees; education; humanities; psychology; modern languages; geology and biology; law) to the highest, Retr_level=4 (medical sciences only). As

Table 11.2 The dependent variable: faculties are aggregated and ordered by earnings of their graduates from the lowest to the highest level of income

retr_level	Groups of faculties	Freq.	%	Cum.
Retr_level = 0	Sports science and all inter-faculty degrees; education; humanities; psychology; modern languages; law; geology and biology	144	38.81	38.81
Retr_level = 1	Agricultural and veterinary studies; architecture, design, town and urban planning	46	12.4	51.21
Retr_level = 2	Sciences (mathematics, physics, chemistry, IT) ; economics and statistics	97	26.15	77.36
Retr_level = 3	Politics and social studies; pharmacy; engineering	59	15.9	93.26
Retr_level = 4	Medical sciences	25	6.74	100
Total		371	100	

for the independent variables, we have tested all the variables reported in Appendix Table 11A.1.

Table 11.3 shows the main results of the regression.[18] In particular, it reports the estimates of the ordered probit model and the marginal effects of the independent variables showing significance. As for the social origins of graduates, neither parents' education nor a lower or middle class origin is significant. Only the upper class (including entrepreneurs with at least 15 employees, professionals and top managers) is significant. Amongst the features related to university skills and outcomes and educational conditions, those regarding the distance from home to the university, the regular attendance of university courses, languages and computer skills have never been significant. The variables specifying whether the students have been regular attenders, had a scholarship, studied abroad, had job experience, and intended to go on with studies after the degree are significant.

The sign of the coefficients changes at cut1, which means that the two lowest levels of earnings go together. Marginal effects are reported in the last five columns of Table 11.3. The probability of getting lower earnings is inversely related to male gender, upper class, regular studies, and benefiting from scholarships. It is positively related to younger age (less than 23 years old), overseas study before the graduation, having a job while studying, and wishing to continue to study. Notice, however, that the relation between age and earnings can be partially explained by the fact that the

Table 11.3 *Results from ordered probit estimates (robust standard errors) and marginal effects for each class of the graduate earnings*

Dependent variable: retr_level Number of observations = 371 Wald chi2(10) = 92.12; Prob > chi20 Log pseudo-likelihood = −444.137 Pseudo R2 = 0.175				Retr_level = 0 0.349	Retr_level = 1 0.150	Retr_level = 2 0.331	Retr_level = 3 0.154	Retr_level = 4 0.016
Variable	Coef.	Robust Std.Err	Z	dy/dx	dy/dx	dy/dx	dy/dx	dy/dx
Male	0.0023	0.00064	3.51	−0.00084	−6.5E-05	0.00033	0.00048	9.08E-05
Less than 23 years old	−0.0102	0.00218	−4.7	0.00379	0.000295	−0.0015	−0.00218	−0.00041
Upper class	0.0035	0.00165	2.11	−0.00129	−0.0001	0.00051	0.000741	0.00014
Regular	0.0077	0.00101	7.64	−0.00285	−0.00022	0.001125	0.001636	0.00031
With awarded scholarship	0.0057	0.00214	2.67	−0.00212	−0.00016	0.000836	0.001215	0.00023
With study-experience abroad	−0.0059	0.00177	−3.33	0.00218	0.00017	−0.00086	−0.00125	−0.00024
With job experience	−0.0083	0.00194	−4.29	0.00309	0.00024	−0.00122	−0.00177	−0.00034
With prospects of further studies	−0.0041	0.00112	−3.68	0.00152	0.000118	−0.0006	−0.00087	−0.00017
Centre Italy	0.2026	0.15323	1.32	−0.07417	−0.00649	0.028279	0.04375	0.008634
South Italy	0.1215	0.18042	0.67	−0.04459	−0.00384	0.017121	0.026187	0.005116
cut1	−0.3428	0.13789	ANCIL-					
cut2	0.0433	0.14398	LARY					
cut3	0.9994	0.15213	PARA-					
cut4	2.1861	0.18342	METERS					

degree in medical sciences, which gives the highest earnings, lasts for six years whereas lower income degrees last four years.

The clear direct relation between high earnings and (male) gender is related to persisting gender discrimination and to the fact that some of the less well-paid jobs, such as teaching, may require shorter working hours, allowing more time for family care. The discussion of the gender issues in higher education, however, is beyond the purpose of the present chapter. The inverse relation between low earnings and upper class social origin may be explained both by the better opportunities of access to the best paid careers available to sons and daughters belonging to high income families, and by their desire to achieve an income that maintains them in the upper class. Working students obtain lower earnings once they graduate. Finally, studying abroad does not lead to better paid jobs. This may help to prove that there is not necessarily a relationship between the income earned and the full product of the human capital accumulated by individuals, through their higher education curricula.

2.3 Public Human Capital Formation

We now analyse the determinants of public human capital formation (in particular, the determinants of the science degrees in Italian universities) by means of a count model. An event count is the realization of a nonnegative integer-valued random variable. The ordinary least squares (OLS) method for event count data might result in biased, inefficient, and inconsistent estimates (Long, 1997). Various nonlinear models have been developed to analyse these cases, some of them based on Poisson distribution and negative binomial distribution, which we shall refer to for our analysis (see Long, 1997; Maddala, 1983; Cameron and Trivedi, 1990, 1998).[19]

Our dataset contains the count of the number of graduates in science faculties (the focus of programmes by the MIUR), which is our dependent variable Sc_Graduates. The faculties are: sciences (mathematics, physics, chemistry,[20] IT), pharmacy and statistics. Among the Italian universities considered in the dataset, only 60 faculties out of 371 are the focus of incentives from the MIUR. Table 11.4 shows the dependent variable, grouping universities in the North, Centre and South of Italy.

Table 11.5 shows the results from the negative binomial regression model and the marginal effects of the independent variables to show statistical significance. The three log-likelihood statistics for the Poisson regression model, restricted negative binomial regression model (constant-only model) and unrestricted negative binomial regression model (full model) are also reported.[21] The variables showing significance (Table 11.5) are the

Table 11.4 The dependent variable: science graduates in the Italian faculties

	Observations (no. of faculties)	No. of scientific faculties	No. of graduates in science faculties	Min.	Max.
Sc_Graduates	371	60	17558	0	1379
Universities in South of Italy	123	22	5782	0	904
Universities in Centre of Italy	141	23	7115	0	1379
Universities in North of Italy	107	15	4661	0	927

following: 'both parents graduates' (note that none of the variables of the groups related to parents' education was significant in the previous model of Section 2.2); one social class of origin (the upper class); studies abroad whilst attending Italian university; and the prospect of continuing one's studies with a doctoral programme if financed by a scholarship. Gender variables are not significant. The last columns of Table 11.5 report the marginal effects at the mean of the independent variables and for a change from 0 to 1 of dichotomous variables (the relevant effects are in bold).

Looking at the direction of the effects, it emerges that the dependent variable (graduates from science faculties) is positively related to parent's education (both parents graduates), and to the aim of continuing studies with a doctoral programme, but only if financed by a scholarship. Universities in the North and Centre of Italy, both significant, get a positive sign. Periods of study abroad during university education, and upper class origin, are inversely related to the dependent variable. The positive relation emerging for the North and Centre universities may be explained by their average high quality level in these science areas. As for the residence of students in the area where these faculties are located, it could be argued that in the Centre and North of Italy there is a higher propensity for science studies because of the higher industrial-economic development, and hence greater possibilities of finding interesting jobs with these qualifications. As for the fact that the variable 'studies abroad' is inversely related to the choice of science degrees, the possible explanation is that students of science prefer to follow the curriculum of their own faculty, rather than interrupt it with temporary periods abroad in different universities, leaving the option of studying abroad to subsequent periods. Another explanation may be that they feel that the preparation offered by these faculties is adequate. From the negative relation with the variable 'upper class', one may infer that the average earnings from science degrees

Table 11.5 Negative binomial regression model estimates and marginal effects for the variable Sc_Graduates

Dependent variable: Sc_Graduates
Number of observations = 371
LR chi2(7) = 120.21
Prob > chi2 = 0
Log likelihood = −552.937
PseudoR2 = 0.098
Poisson model: log-likelihood = −18079.2
Constant-only model: log-likelihood = −613.042

	Coef.	StdErr.	Z	Marginal effect from the change from 0 to 1 of independent variables	:+−1/2	:−+sd/2	Marginal effect at the mean x of the independent variables	X	sd(x)
Both parents graduates	0.159	0.039	4.08	0	0.0004	0.2552	**0.0004**	46.950	57.91
Upper class	−0.148	0.027	−5.43	−9.20E+03	−0.0004	−30.077	**−0.0004**	115.28	126.54
Studies abroad	−0.124	0.033	−3.79	−0.1609	−0.0003	−0.1535	**−0.0003**	50.856	66.235
With prospects of doctoral programme	0.156	0.036	4.37	0	0.0004	0.0195	**0.0004**	20.543	26.41
Further studies if financed by scholarship	0.352	0.156	2.26	0.0002	0.0009	0.007	**0.0009**	4.8949	6.38
Centre Italy	2.841	0.754	3.77	**0.0181**	0.0099	0.0035	0.0072	0.2884	0.4536
North Italy	1.882	0.702	2.68	**0.0069**	0.0055	0.0024	0.0048	0.3801	0.486
Constant	3.486	0.511	6.82						
/lnalpha	2.628	0.146							
Alpha	13.85	2.029							
Likelihood-ratio test of alpha = 0				exp(xb):0.0025					
Chibar2(01) = 3.50E+04 Prob > = chibar2 = 0									

are not considered high enough to meet the aspirations of junior members of upper class families. On the other hand, they may have an incentive to continue the economic activities of their families, whose earnings are not necessarily related with a particularly high level of parents' education. The cultural environment of the family appears to have an important role in the choice of the type of higher education. This seems to be confirmed by the sign of the variable related to level of the parents' education. There is a positive relation between the science degree and the variable 'both parents graduates'. On the other hand, the negative sign of the variable 'upper class' (if considered with the positive sign of the parents' education, showing a preference for degrees that do not imply *per se* the highest earnings) can be explained by a search for cultural satisfaction rather than for income. This seems to support the thesis that cultural variables may be more important than the motivation of income maximization in the choice of scientific careers. In the Italian environment, at least, they do not lead to particularly high incomes, but have a social return markedly higher than the private return because of positive externalities regarding national economic growth. On the other hand, the students from high income families, whose education is generally higher than that of low income families, are attracted by the income maximizing professions. The consequence is that a generalized quasi free higher education system, while not offering enough incentive to study for careers with the highest social return, gives a rent to the persons belonging to families who already have high education with a high private rate of return, and who have more means to pursue studies than the members of low income families. Therefore, this system does not reduce economic inequality and is not efficient for the objective of sustaining economic growth by public expenditure on human capital as a public good.

It is interesting that the intention of continuing to study with a doctoral programme gets the same sign as the intention of continuing with a scholarship awarded. The reason is that the parents are likely to belong to the middle/low income classes. The relation between higher level of parents' education and Centre/North Universities suggests that cultural and geographic variables are more relevant than the economic incentives related to the private revenue from higher education.

Given that science courses do not give high private returns and are chosen on the basis of cultural motivations, one might argue that, in order to increase the numbers choosing these courses student loans are not effective, unless they have a big gift component. The need to pay back the loan might dissuade the low and middle income class borrowers from science in favor of other more profitable curricula. Generalized grants might be a better choice for these curricula, because this education has important elements of quasi public goods and it does not seem to originate new income inequalities. The positive sign of the Centre-North universities, on the other hand, poses a question about the regional distribution of the public subsidies. Either more public expenditure should be devoted to promote scientific research centres in the South, or the subsidies to science students in the Centre/North Universities should be shaped so as to avoid discrimination against Southern students. Or perhaps both policies should be pursued.

3. CONCLUSIONS

We have argued that increasing the endowment of human capital may be one of the ways to sustain economic development. We have focused on higher education as the main way to increase human capital, distinguishing private human capital, whose returns are mostly in the market economy, and public human capital, which has larger non market returns and hence has the character of a quasi public good. In this respect, the thesis that in developed countries there is generally an excess of higher education is not warranted for Italy. The number of persons with a higher education degree, whose returns are in the market, has greatly increased, whereas those with sciences degrees, which give largely non market returns, have decreased as share of the total graduate population. Our econometric research shows that the highest paid graduates, not considered by the MIUR among those of critical importance for public human capital, tend to belong to the upper class families. On the other hand, the probability of getting a science degree – which MIUR considers paramount for the formation of public human capital – has no relation with the graduates' belonging to the upper class or to any other socio-economic class. It is instead related with the (high) education of the family.

If the highest earnings after graduation can be taken as a proxy of the private human capital contributions to the market sector, an increased provision of student loans, organized according to some of the various existing schemes (Blaug, 1965, 1980; Barr, 1989; Woodhall, 1984; Creedy, 1993) might be useful to widen student admittance to these courses. On the other hand, it seems clear that, to increase the number of students attending science courses, student aids in form of scholarships and free goods aids should be increased and more resources should be provided to universities, also to reduce the regional disparities. Further research may be needed to explore regional hindrances to access to various degrees for students from the South. The aspects related to existing gender discrimination may also require research.

It clearly emerges, however, that the pre-school formation acquired by children in the family of origin is of the utmost importance in determining the educational formation relevant for public human capital. In this respect, incentives given to adults might not seem sufficient to remedy the basic human capital deficit. On this basis, the thesis, also widely held in Europe, that public policy should give increased attention to the education of children of poor and less educated families, seems justified (Commission of the European Community, 2006; Wobmann and Schutz, 2006). However this extra attention needs to be accompanied by additional higher education assistance with loans and subsidies.

NOTES

1. The new growth theories (Mankiw et al., 1992; Nelson and Phelps, 1966) generally give human capital a preeminent place. The theoretical work in this area was given empirical support by Levine and Renelt (1992). While early work focused on the quantity of schooling, more recent analyses have considered issues such as schooling quality (Hanushek and Kimko, 2000) and the distribution of educational opportunities (Castelló and Doménech, 2002).
2. On some of these problems, see Lagerlöf (2006).
3. Many studies in developed countries indicate that high school completion and increased years of schooling reduce the probability that teenage females will give birth. McMahon (1999) finds that there is a strong negative effect of education on fertility in cross-national data. In his 40-year simulations of the effects of raising education expenditures by 2 percentage points as a fraction of GNP or raising secondary enrolment by 20 percentage points, McMahon (1999) finds that the increased expenditures would reduce fertility by about 10% in 2035 in the US. In the UK the effect is about 15%. The impact of the enrolment policy is about half as great as that of the expenditure policy in the UK, and about two-thirds as great in the US.
4. The human capital model of income determination has its origins in the work of Adam Smith (1776), but in the modern era is associated with Schultz (1961), Becker (1964) and Mincer (1974).
5. Johnes (2007) warns that, since the seminal contributions of Arrow (1973) and Spence (1973), it has been well understood that education might act as a screening device or a signal of an individual's innate ability, and that it might be this innate ability rather than education itself that allows productivity, and hence earnings, to be augmented (Brown and Sessions, 2004). As Lazear (1977) argued, it is particularly difficult to disentangle the effects of human capital accumulation from those of signalling and screening because they are observationally equivalent – or nearly so.
6. The rate of return to education may be calculated using a variety of methods (Psacharopoulos and Patrinos, 2004). The full method involves gathering information about the (smoothed) income streams of individuals of different education levels over the life cycle, and about the costs of education. The rate of return that equates the costs to the present discounted value of the benefits of education is then found by solving a high-order polynomial equation. See Johnes (2007).
7. Johnes (2007) notes 'the social return to education, somewhat perversely, is not usually defined to include well-established positive externalities such as better health, lower crime, or responsible attitudes to the environment.' A variety of beneficial non-market effects of education is found by Behrman and Stacey (1997), McMahon (1999), and Wolfe and Haveman (2001). These two authors conclude that the non-market benefits

of education are likely similar quantitatively to the market benefits. These non-market effects increase the individual and aggregate welfare but not necessarily the income of individuals. Indeed it turns out that education is associated with greater health and with better health behaviour. Witte (1997) and McMahon (1999) found that, other factors constant, the propensity of those who have completed schooling to commit crime is weak. There is some evidence that individuals with greater education are more likely to vote in elections. Probably they vote in a more informed and rational manner. McMahon (1999, 2001) finds significant effects of secondary education rates on indexes of democratization, human rights, and political stability. Higher schooling is also associated with greater charitable giving and more volunteerism (Dye, 1980; Hodgkinson and Weitzman, 1988; Freeman, 1997). On the basis of international data, it is found that higher education has a positive effect on democratization and political stability.

8. See for instance Acemoglu and Angrist (2000).
9. See Cammelli (2006, 2007a) and Ghiselli (2006) and also the law (D.M. 23-10-2003, *Fondo per il sostegno dei giovani e per favorire la mobilità degli studenti* and *Progetto lauree scientifiche* available on www.progettolaureescientifiche.it.
10. In addition to those related to North-South divisions and gender discrimination, which are beyond the scope of the present research.
11. The economics of post secondary education financing in Italy began to emerge only during the '70s. For a survey of the basic/classical literature on students' aids see Fedeli and Forte (2007).
12. Social classes are as follows: upper class (including entrepreneurs with at least 15 employees, professionals and top managers); middle class (including clerical workers; clerks; employees); lower class (including entrepreneurs with less than 15 employees, autonomous workers); working class. Where only one parent is working, class is defined by the class of the working parent (Cammelli, 2007b, p.65).
13. The graduates of 2005 involved in the survey are two-thirds of all Italian graduates, thus reflecting the composition by faculties and gender of total Italian graduates. On the basis of the Italian universities involved with Almalaurea, the North is over-represented with respect to the Centre in 2005 (see Cammelli, 2007a). Nevertheless, the survey's results are quite close to those by ISTAT 2004.
14. The classification of groups is in Appendix 2.
15. The survey mentioned points out that, with respect to the previous survey of 2005, the share of employment is reduced by more than 9%, with a corresponding increase (about 8%) of those continuing to study with a specialist degree. One year after the degree, the share of employed with respect to 2005 is reduced by about 1.2%, whereas the share of graduates in search of a job increases. Job stability is reduced by more than 8%, mainly due to the introduction of fixed term contracts. Notable differentials in earnings, emerging for all the different types of degree, are related to gender. They emerge the first year after the degree and increase in time. Gender differences in income are present for both the public and the private sector, with men always earning more than women (Cammelli, 2007a).
16. Our analysis is limited to 2006 (the last year of the survey), because the number of universities surveyed has changed over the last years with the biggest universities included only since 2006. Moreover, a number of questions, such as that on student aids, have been added only since 2006.
17. The universities are: North Italy, Bolzano, Milano IULM, Padova, Piemonte Orientale, Torino (statale e politecnico), Genova, Trento Trieste, Udine, Venezia Ca'Foscari, Venezia IUAV, Verona; Centre Italy: Bologna, Camerino, Ferrara, Firenze, Modena, Parma, Perugia, Roma Biotecnologia, Roma Lumsa, Roma Tre, Roma La Sapienza, Siena, La Tuscia; South Italy: Bari, Basilicata, Cagliari, Calabria, Cassino, Chieti-Pescara, Catania, Catanzaro, Foggia, Lecce, Messina, Molise, Reggio Calabria, Salerno, Sassari.
18. The matrix of correlation of the estimated coefficients of each model is available on request.

19. The Poisson probability distribution, $P(y|\mu) = e^{-\mu}\mu^y/y!$, assumes the same mean and variance (equidispersion) and that events are independent. Therefore, this distribution does not fit well in the presence of heterogeneity. The Poisson regression model incorporates observed heterogeneity into the Poisson distribution function, $\mathrm{Var}(y_i|x_i)=E(y_i|x_i)=\mu_i=\exp(x_i\beta)$. As μ increases, the conditional variance of y increases, the proportion of predicted zeros decreases, and the distribution around the expected value becomes approximately normal (Long, 1997). The conditional mean of the errors is zero, but the variance of the errors is a function of independent variables, $\mathrm{var}(\varepsilon|x) = \exp(x\beta)$. The errors are heteroscedastic. Thus, the Poisson regression model rarely fits due to overdispersion (Long, 1997; Maddala, 1983). The negative binomial probability distribution is

$$P(y_i|x_i) = \frac{\Gamma(y_i + v_i)}{y_i!\Gamma(v_i)}\left(\frac{v_i}{v_i + \mu_i}\right)^{v_i}\left(\frac{\mu_i}{v_i + \mu_i}\right)^{y_i},$$

where $1/v_i = \alpha$ determines the degree of dispersion and the Γ is the Γ probability distribution. As the dispersion parameter α increases, the variance of the negative binomial distribution also increases, $\mathrm{Var}\ (y_i|x_i)=\mu_i(1 + \mu_i/v_i)$. The negative binomial regression model incorporates observed and unobserved heterogeneity into the conditional mean, $\mu_i = \exp(x_i\beta + \varepsilon_i)$ (Long, 1997). Thus, the conditional variance of y becomes larger than its conditional mean, $E(y_i|x_i)=\mu_i$, which remains unchanged. When $\mathrm{Var}(y_i|x_i)>E(y_i|x_i)$, there is overdispersion.

Estimates of a Poisson regression model for overdispersed data are unbiased, but inefficient with standard errors biased downward (Cameron and Trivedi, 1998; Long, 1997). The likelihood ratio test for overdispersion examines the null hypothesis of $\alpha = 0$ (no overdispersion). The LR statistic follows the chi-squared distribution with one degree of freedom. If the null hypothesis is rejected, the negative binomial regression model is preferred to the Poisson regression model.

20. Including also biotechnological science, bio-science, and bio-technologies.
21. The likelihood ratio test for overdispersion rejects the null hypothesis of alpha=0. The statistically significant evidence of overdispersion indicates that negative binomial regression model is preferred to the Poisson regression model.

BIBLIOGRAPHY

Acemoglu, D. and J. Angrist (2000), 'How large are human capital externalities? Evidence from compulsory schooling laws', *NBER MacroeconomicsAnnual*, **15**, 9–58.

Arrow, K.J. (1973), 'Higher education as a filter', *Journal of Public Economics*, **2** (3), 193–216.

Barr, N. (1989), 'Student loans: the next steps', Hume Paper, no. 15, Aberdeen, UK: Pergamon, Aberdeen University Press.

Barro, R.J. and X. Sala-i-Martin (1995), *Economic Growth*, New York: McGraw-Hill.

Becker, G. (1964), *Human Capital*, Columbia University Press, 1964; 2nd edn, 1975; 3rd edn, 1993, University of Chicago Press.

Behrman, J.R. and Nevzer Stacey (eds) (1997), *The Social Benefits of Education*, Ann Arbor, MI: University of Michigan Press.

Benhabib, J. and M.M. Spiegel (1994), 'The role of human capital in economic development: evidence from aggregate cross-country data', *Journal of Monetary Economics*, **34** (2), 143–73.

Blaug, M. (1965), 'The rate of return on investment in education in Britain', *The Manchester School*, **33** (3), 205–51, republished in M. Blaug (ed.), *Economics of Education 1, Selected Readings*, with the title 'The rate of return on investment in education', Baltimore, MD: Penguin Books.
Blaug, M. (1970), *An Introduction to the Economics of Education*, Harmondsworth: Penguin.
Blaug M. (1980), 'Student loans and the NUs', *Economic Affairs*, October.
Brown, S. and J. Sessions, (2004), 'Signalling and screening', in G. Johnes and J. Johnes, (eds), *International Handbook on the Econonomics of Education*, Cheltenham, UK and Northampton, MA, USA: Edward Elgar, pp. 58–100.
Cameron, C. and P. Trivedi (1990), 'Regression based test for overdispersion in the Poisson model', *Journal of Applied Econometrics*, **46**, 347–64.
Cameron, C. and P. Trivedi (1998), *Regression Analysis of Count Data*, New York: Cambridge University Press.
Cammelli, A. (2006), 'Le lauree scientifiche e tecnologiche: dall'accesso all'Università alla prova del mercato del lavoro', Available at http://www.almalaurea.it/universita/altro/laureescientifiche.
Cammelli, A. (2007a), 'Condizione occupazionale dei laureati', IX survey 2006, available at http://www.almalaurea.it.
Cammelli, A. (2007b), 'I laureati dell'università riformata: profilo dei laureati 2006', available at http://www.almalaurea.it/universita/profilo/profilo2006/premessa/pdf-file/totale.pdf.
Castelló, A. and R. Doménech (2002), 'Human capital inequality and economic growth: some new evidence', *Economic Journal*, **112** (3), C187–C200.
CENSIS (1969), *Costi e ricavi dell'istruzione*, Note e Commenti, numero speciale 91–92, April, Rome.
Commission of the European Community (2006), *Employment in Europe Report 2006*, Brussels.
Creedy, J. (1993), *The Economics of Higher Education*, Aldershot, UK and Brookfield, VT, USA: Edward Elgar.
Davies, S. (2002), 'Marketing in higher education: matching promises and reality to expectations', in *Responding to Student Expectations*, Paris: OECD, pp. 103–14.
Dye, R.F. (1980), 'Contributions to volunteer time: some evidence on income tax effects', *National Tax Journal*, **33** (1), 89–93.
Englander, A.S. and A. Gurney (1994b), 'OECD productivity growth: medium term trends', *OECD Economic Studies*, **22**, 111–29.
Fedeli, S. and F. Forte (2007), 'Il dibattito teorico sugli aiuti agli studenti nell'istruzione superiore: una verifica empirica per l'Italia' (scritto con Francesco Forte), paper presented to the 2007 conference of the Società Italiana di Economia Pubblica, Pavia, 13 September.
Freeman, R.B. (1997), 'Working for nothing: the supply of volunteer labor', *Journal of Labor Economics*, **15** (1), Part 2, S140–S166.
Friedman, M. (1955), 'The role of government in education', in R.D. Solo (ed.), *Economics and the Public Interest*, New Brunswick, NJ: Rutgers University Press.
Friedman, M. (1962), *Capitalism and Freedom*, Chicago: The University of Chicago Press.
Galor, O. and D.N. Weil (2000), 'Population, technology and growth: from the

Malthusian regime to the demographic transition', *American Economic Review*, **90** (4), September, 806–28.
Gemmell, N. (1996), 'Evaluating the impacts of human capital stocks and accumulation on economic growth: some new evidence', *Oxford Bulletin of Economics and Statistics*, **58** (1), 9–28.
Ghiselli, S. (2006), 'I laureati nel settore chimico: caratteristiche ed esiti occupazionali', available at http://www.almalaurea.it/universita/altro/chimica2006.
Greene, W.H. (2003), *Econometric Analysis*, 5th edn, New York: Prentice Hall.
Hanushek, E.A. and D.D. Kimko (2000), 'Schooling, labor force quality, and the growth of nations', *American Economic Review*, **90** (5), 1184–208.
Hodgkinson, V. and M. Weitzman (1988), *Giving and Volunteering in the United States: Findings from a National Survey, 1988 Edition*, Washington, DC: Independent Sector.
Johnes, G. (2004), 'The evaluation of welfare under alternative models of higher education finance', in P. Teixerira, B. Jongbloed, D. Dill and A. Amaral (eds), *Markets in Higher Education: Rhetoric or Reality?*, London: Kluwer.
Johnes, G. (2007), 'Cherry-picking in the economics of education orchard: a selective survey of recent developments', Keynote address to the 2007 conference of the Società Italiana di Economia Pubblica, Pavia, 13 September.
Judson, R. (1998), 'Economic growth and investment in education: how allocation matters', *Journal of Economic Growth*, **3**, 337–59.
Lagerlöf, Nils-Petter (2006), 'The Galor–Weil model revisited: a quantitative exercise', *Review of Economic Dynamics*, **9** (1), 116–42.
Lazear, Edward (1977), 'Academic achievement and job performance: a note', *American Economic Review*, **67**, 252–4.
Levine, Ross and David Renelt (1992), 'A sensitivity analysis of cross-country growth regressions', *American Economic Review*, **82** (4), 942–63.
Long, S. (1997), *Regression Model for Categorical and Limited Dependent Variables*, Thousand Oaks, CA: Sage.
Lucas R.E. (1988), 'On the mechanics of economic development', *Journal of Monetary Economics*, **22**, 3–42.
Maddala, G. (1983), *Limited Dependent and Qualitative Variables in Econometrics*, New York: Cambridge University Press.
Mankiw, N. Gregory, D. Romer and D. Weil (1992), 'A contribution to the empirics of economic growth', *Quarterly Journal of Economics*, **107** (2), 407–37.
McMahon, W.W. (1999), *Education and Development, Measuring the Social Benefits*, Oxford: Oxford University Press.
McMahon, W.W. (2001), 'The impact of human capital on non-market outcomes and feedbacks on economic development', available at http://www.oecd.org/edu/educationeconomyandsociety/1825143.pdf.
Mincer, J. (1974), *Schooling, Experience and Earnings*, New York: Columbia University Press.
Nelson, R. and E. Phelps (1966), 'Investment in humans, technological diffusion, and economic growth', *American Economic Review*; *Papers and Proceedings*, **61**, 69–75.
OECD (1998), *Human Capital Investment: An International Comparison*, Paris: Centre for Educational Research and Innovation, OECD.
OECD (2000), *Education at a Glance*, Paris: OECD.
OECD (2001), *The Well-Being of Nations, The Role of Human and Social Capital*, Centre for Education Research and Innovation, OECD.

OECD (2002), *Education at a Glance, OECD indicators*, Paris: OECD.
OECD (2006), *Education at a Glance*, Paris: OECD.
Peacock, A.T. and J. Wiseman (1964), *Education for Democrats*, London: Institute of Economics Affairs.
Psacharopoulos, G. and H.A. Patrinos (2004). 'Human capital and rates of return', in G. Johnes and J. Johnes (eds), *International Handbook on the Economics of Education*, Cheltenham, UK and Northampton, MA, USA: Edward Elgar, pp. 1–57.
Rauch, J. (1993), 'Productivity gains from geographic concentration of human capital: evidence from the cities', *Journal of Urban Economics*, **34** (3), 380–400.
Romer, P. (1986), 'Increasing returns and long-run growth', *Journal of Political Economy*, **94**, 1002–37.
Romer, P. (1990), 'Endogenous technological change', *Journal of Political Economy*, **98**, part 2, 71–102.
Romer, P. (2000), 'Should the government subsidize supply or demand in the market for scientists and engineers?', NBER Working Paper No. 7723.
Schultz, T.W. (1961), 'Investment in human capital', *American Economic Review*, **51**, 1–17.
Schultz, T.W. (1968), 'Resources for higher education', *Journal of Political Economy*, **76**, 327–47.
Schultz, T.W. (1972a), *Human Capital: Policy Issues and Research Opportunities*, introduction by G.S. Becker, New York: National Bureau of Economic Research.
Schultz, T.W. (1972b), 'The optimal investment in college instruction: equity and efficiency', *Journal of Political Economy*, Supplement, May–June.
Smith, A. (1776), *The Wealth of Nations*, available at http://www.econlib.org/LIBRARY/Smith/smWN.html.
Spence, M. (1973), 'Job market signaling', *Quarterly Journal of Economics*, **87** (3), 355–74.
Temple, J. (2001), 'Growth effects of education and social capital in the OECD', in J.F. Helliwell (ed.), *The Contribution of Human and Social Capital to Sustained Economic Growth and Well-being: International Symposium Report*, Ottawa: Human Resources Development Canada and OECD.
Tollison, R.D. and T. D. Willett (1973), 'The university and the price system', *Journal of Economics and Business*, Spring–Summer **25** (3), 191–7.
Topel, R. (1997), 'Factor proportions and relative wages: the supply-side determinants of wage inequality', *Journal of Economic Perspectives*, **11** (2), 55–74.
Witte, A.D. (1997), 'Social benefits of education: crime', in J.R. Behrman and N. Stacey (eds), *The Social Benefits of Education*, Ann Arbor, MI: University of Michigan Press, pp. 219–46.
Wobmann, L. and G. Schutz (2006), 'Efficiency and equity in European education and training systems', Analytical Report for the European Commission.
Wolfe, B. and R. Haveman (2001), 'Accounting for the social and non-market benefits of education', in J.F. Helliwell (ed.), *The Contribution of Human and Social Capital to Sustained Economic Growth and Well-being: International Symposium Report*, Ottawa: Human Resources Development Canada and OECD.
Woodhall, M. (1984), 'Student loans', in G. Psacharopoulos (ed.), *Economics of Education Research and Studies*, Oxford, New York: Pergamon Press, 1987.

APPENDIX 1

Table 11A.1 Graduate profile 2006

Personal data		%
Gender	Male	40.2
	Female	59.8
Age at graduation	less than 23 years	17.6
	23–24 years	28.7
	25–26 years	21.0
	27 years and more	32.8
	Average age at graduation	27.1
Foreign students		2.3
Place of residence	Same province as the university	51.7
	Different province, same region as the university	25.2
	Different region as the university	22.6
	Abroad	0.5
Social origin		
Parents' education	Both graduates	9.4
	Only one graduate	15.7
	Secondary education	42.7
	Primary education or nothing	29.8
Social class of origin	Upper class	23.2
	Middle class	31.0
	Lower class	20.1
	Working class	21.8
High school		
High school	Science liceo	36.4
	Technical high school	26.6
	Classics liceo	17.0
	Other high schools	7.5
	Languages	5.5
	Professionals	2.9
	Arts	1.7
	Foreign degree	1.7
Average high school score (out of 100)		81.8
University outcomes		
With previous univ.		18.6
experiences	Ended with degree	9.9
	Not finished	8.7

Table 11A.1 (continued)

Personal data		%
Reason for choice of faculty	Both cultural and professional	52.1
	Mainly cultural	30.1
	Mainly professional	8.2
	Neither cultural nor professional	7.8
Enrolment	Regular or 1 year late	81.8
	2 years late	18.2
Average score at university exams (out of 30)		26.2
Average graduation score (out of 110)		102.8
Period of study	As prescribed	34.3
	1 extra year	22.4
	2 extra years	15.0
	3 extra years	8.2
	4 extra years	5.5
	5 extra years	14.6
Average years of duration		5.7
Average delay in study (years)		1.9
Educational condition		
Living close to the faculty (less than one hour)	More than 50% duration of the univ. courses or always	70.9
	Less than 50% duration of the univ. courses or never	27.7
	More than 75% of courses	63.2
Regular attendance	50%–75%	20.6
	25%–50%	8.6
	Less than 25%	6.5
Awarded scholarship		24.5
Studies abroad whilst attending Italian university		10.3
	Erasmus or other EU programme	6.4
	Other recognized programmes	1.2
	Personal	2.6
	Always in Italy	87.9
Work during studies		
With job experience		75.1
	Working students	8.8
	Other job experiences: full time	4.5
	Job experiences: part-time	21.5
	Seasonal job	40.3
	No job	23.9
	Job consistent with studies	19.8

Table 11A.1 (continued)

Personal data		%
Language and ICT skills		
'Good' knowledge of foreign languages	Written English	59.8
	Spoken English	52.0
	Written French	21.0
	Spoken French	20.5
	Written Spanish	10.0
	Spoken Spanish	10.2
	Written German	4.4
	Spoken German	4.1
'Good' knowledge of ICT	Internet	83.4
	Word Processing	70.6
	Operating systems	50.7
	Excel	50.3
	Multimedia	31.0
	Databases (Oracle, SQL server, Access, . . .)	20.7
	Programming	19.6
	CAD/CAM/CAE	15.0
	Web design	14.4
	Data networks	13.9
Prospects of studies		
Aim to continue studies		66.4
	Specialist degree	35.6
	Master	7.3
	Specialist school	6.1
	Doctoral programme	4.2
	Apprenticeship; training	3.9
	Other	3.6
	New different degree	1.2
	Further studies – only if financed by scholarship	1.0
	Other professional experiences	3.2
	None	32.9

Notes: Number of graduates 185 361; number of graduates surveyed 159 287.

Source: Consorzio Interuniversitario AlmaLaurea (22/05/2007).

APPENDIX 2 CLASSIFICATION OF FACULTIES

For the classification of faculties used in ranking graduate earnings we refer to Cammelli (2007b, p. 65). The faculties are grouped by types of study as follows: agricultural and veterinary studies; architecture, design, town and urban planning; pharmacy; economics and statistics; sports science; geology and biology; law; engineering; education; humanities; modern languages, medical sciences; politics and social studies; psychology; sciences (mathematics, physics, chemistry, IT).

12. The actual role of government intervention for the recovery of the Italian economy

Gian Cesare Romagnoli

1. INTRODUCTION

The decline of public intervention, which began in the UK and spread to the United States and to most European countries in the early 1980s, started in Italy, as in China, about twelve years later. As neutral finance saw its end with the Great Depression of the 1930s, likewise the Keynesian model of economic policy, which had been unable to deal with the stagflation of the 1970s, gave way to the pure cycle economic model which offered a rationale for it. After almost 40 years, the global financial crisis, originated by the subprime mortgages in the United States, and still running in Europe, has again raised serious questions about the markets' self equilibrating capability. The bailing out of financial institutions has given rise to the reappraisal of the economic debate on State intervention delivered into the economy not only through market regulation but also through the public production of goods and services.

In an oft-quoted passage, John Maynard Keynes said (Keynes, 1936):

> Speculators may do no harm as bubbles on a steady stream of enterprise. But the position is serious when enterprise becomes the bubble on a whirlpool of speculation. When the capital development of a country becomes a by-product of the activities of a casino, the job is likely to be ill-done.

The Italian public firms experience, in particular, has recently been recalled and re-proposed in the United States and in Europe in spite of its sad sunset in Italy in the mid 1980s. In contrast, Robert Shiller sees the public bailing out of privately owned banks and firms as a form of hypocrisy.[1] During the actual crisis, the principle according to which capital losses, in case of insolvency, are born by the shareholders has been disregarded and taxpayers have been charged for the private losses paid off by the State.

The aim of this chapter is to indicate some proposals of government intervention for the recovery of the Italian economy. After this introduction, the chapter is divided into three sections. The first deals with some ill-functionings of the State in Italy, the second reports the contrasting results obtained by the Italian public firms, and the third deals with structural reforms which may lead to the recovery of the Italian economy. Notes on the importance of public institutions conclude the chapter.

2. SOME ILL-FUNCTIONINGS OF THE STATE IN ITALY

Besides the Montesquieu triad, the political function of the State in Italy, as in many other countries, is to govern the community and to exercise, in a coercive way, economic activities such as the production or the distribution of public goods for which private initiative is supposed to be inadequate, together with coordination, control and regulation of the market activities. In order to exercise its functions the State disposes of financial resources stemming from taxes, rents of its own property, *seigniorage* and public debt.

In the market system decisions are taken by the agents, but the political allocation mechanism is based on the centralization of decision power and its coerciveness. Neither of these two institutions can carry on well, by itself, the allocation of economic resources since both of them are prone to failures due to the externalities produced by market activities and the internalities produced by bureaucracy (Wolf, 1979). If the State maintains a *laissez faire* attitude, the market fails because of the natural monopolistic inclination of economic agents. Nevertheless, a revival of economic liberalism has been experienced, after the 1970s, as the legacy of a serious debate on the foundations of public economics. Even the actual crisis may be seen as the outcome of a State failure due to its incapability, or to its unwillingness motivated by capture, to prevent a number of market failures, the opacity of the structured financial products, and the interest conflicts which have biased the management of firms and of financial institutions, including the rating agencies.

The actual crisis originated from the myopia – the short term view – of the agents and eventually of the policy makers. This has brought back the need for long term structural policies in the market economies and even the nationalization of several financial institutions. Italy has suffered from the crisis more than its European partners because of the long lasting decline of its productivity growth and of its export shares.

The indication of the competences that the State should keep in Italy today in order to favour the recovery of the Italian economy benefits from an overview of ill-workings of the State in the last four decades (Reviglio, 1994). By and large the main references are to:

1. The irresponsible use of financial illusion[2] which has allowed governments, eager to earn popular consensus, to accumulate excessive public debt since the early 1970s and to drive its ratio to GDP progressively away from the European average;[3]
2. A wide structural public deficit which originated neither from a low tax pressure, nor from excessive public expenditure, *vis-à-vis* other industrial countries, on items like general services, defence, education and health, but rather from excessive social security expenses[4] and interest payments on public debt. A complicated, heavy and unfair fiscal system has increased the tax pressure, since the 1970s, more than in any other industrial country, and its actual level is higher than the European average;
3. A cumbersome and slow public administration whose inefficiency (Niskanen, 1971) is still well represented by the length of judicial proceedings and administrative procedures (e.g. public payments, completion of public competitions);
4. Extensive public property combined with diffused inefficiencies of public firms. Management since the 1970s outside any economic principle brought, in the early 1990s, a strong quest for privatization, but only part of the ambitious program drawn up then has been realized;
5. Inadequate protection of savers and consumers which shows that the constitutional revision, introduced in 2001, is not a substitute for good ordinary laws. A clear example has been given by the recent law intended to protect savers[5] where some interest conflicts have been eliminated though leaving untouched interwoven holdings, voting trusts, and a medley of audit agencies' tasks.
6. The fiscal drag has not been given back.

Economic crises bring with them changes in mainstream economics. The pro-cyclical use of Keynes's anti-cyclical policy was a serious mistake. It was welcomed by several politicians and theoretically legitimized by the Keynesian economists whose imperative was to fill output gaps which persisted even when economic activity was increasing. In Italy, partisan politics had a big role in shaping public expenditure schemes that were finalized to support coalition governments with the agreement of the major opposition party. This was done through a model of consent aggregation associated to a distribution of benefits to various categories of people. The persistently growing deficit spending produced, in the period 1972–92, a strong distributive distortion against Italian future generations and has severely threatened the country's financial stability. After a few years of declining public expenditure to GDP ratio in the 1990s, a high and growing level of public expenditure combined with inefficient distribution and supply of poor quality public services has started again in the last decade. Italian public administration, confronted by the social problems connected with exclusion from economic life, i.e. from participation in the labour and goods market, has adhered to a view of social protection, publicly supplied on a citizenship basis, in the fields of health, education, communications and transport. On the contrary, it is obvious that if a society wants to provide effectively for the old and new needs of truly marginal people deserving help, it should prevent public administration from giving cash or in-kind transfers to all citizens. This policy, in fact, is either too expensive or insufficient for those who are really in need. An inadequate amount of infrastructure *vis-à-vis* other European countries and expensive, poor quality public investments are the result of their small and decreasing volume in public administration expenditure. The most severe suffering from this situation is in the Mezzogiorno. Public resources should not be used to guarantee a 'minimum income' to whoever lacks it, as has been suggested, but rather to provide income or tailor-made services to people who are in need. Income redistribution should be pursued through the tax system, rather than through costly social policy interventions, like imposing lower selling prices utterly unrelated to the unit cost of goods and services. This is the real revolution which has to take place in the various sectors of Italian public expenditure.

3. CONTRASTING RESULTS OF PUBLIC FIRMS IN ITALY

In the last century we find two periods when the Italian economy grew more than the European average and more than the United States economy: these were the years before World War I and after the end of World War II. In both these periods we see a positive interaction between public and private firms. Up to the 1970s, public firms operated in various sectors of the Italian economy, achieving productive expansion and price reductions, supporting the government economic policy in its effort to correct regional imbalances, and most of all jumpstarting the development process in territories like the Mezzogiorno, where private enterprise was scarce. The ENI (National Holding for Hydrocarbons), for example, broke up sectors previously characterized by a monopolistic structure, bringing along an effective price control that a public company could use to the benefit of the community instead of exchanging it for private profit.

The same can be said for other State participated companies like the IRI (Institute for Industrial Reconstruction) controlled Italcable.

Since 1974, according to Guido Carli,[6] the flaws of Italian public industry and the hothouse climate of private industry were exacerbated by the corruption of the politico-economic system and the anti-system and anti-development behavior of the Italian trade unions. Montedison is an emblematic case of these faults. The merger of Montecatini and Edison companies, which was expected to improve the efficiency of the Italian chemical industry through economies of scale, optimal size, and better financing opportunities, became instead an illustration of the basic vices which were on the way to taint the Italian economic structure (Carli, 1976). Even the rather successful policy aimed at industrializing the Mezzogiorno, where per capita income had converged to the national average for twenty years, came to an end in the 1970s before giving rise to a new divergence which is still increasing. Credit facilities ended up with the deviation and deformation of the country's industrial system, large amounts of financial resources were spent to create a productive structure which was relatively useless and associated with very low productivity, and low employment, income and export effects. In order to obtain credit facilities from the government, the industrial lobbies changed more and more into political and pressure groups. In brief, a collusive political mechanism had become the main reason for the degeneration of the Italian political system which reached its peak in the early 1990s. Unfortunately, the so-called passage from the First to the Second Republic which was expected to stop and revert this trend failed, and even the literature on public firms dried up in Italy. Increasing public debt, extended public property and inefficient management of public firms and public utilities eventually led, in the 1990s, to a strong quest for privatization in Italy. For several years, the citizens had suffered the inefficiency of public firms through the poor quality of the services supplied in transport, communications, post, education, and health care, most of all in the Mezzogiorno. The administration of public firms had substantially taken away their control from the market and brought it into the political arena. Only a part of the ambitious privatization program proposed was realized in the subsequent years. The big hit to public firms in Italy was not delivered by public awareness that the firms had been considered by politicians, for many years, a property which could be used for personal aims different from social utility, but by the financial crisis of central government and by the contemporaneous veto on publicly subsidizing them imposed by the European economic constitution. The Italian Antitrust Authority was often confronted with private monopolies which had a public interest, but the Authority could not do anything about them but ask the State itself to give ground, to do its job, and not to protect private interests in the utilities, in commercial distribution and in other sectors where innovation was needed.

Even the privatizations in Italy were not designed in the taxpayers' interest, but in that of the merchant banks (Romagnoli, 1997). In order to realize a serious program of dismantling of State owned firms it is necessary to meet some conditions which were mostly missing in the country: a private industry capable of intervening into the privatization process, a capital market able to control the managers of the firms to be sold, and a regulatory framework independent from politics and not prone to capture. Hence the difficulties and the delusions of the privatization process in Italy, which missed the chance to initiate a sound reform of the country's economic institutions. In the near future, the alternative will be between public or foreign business property because on the one hand Italian entrepreneurs either do not own the necessary financial resources or prefer offshoring their production activity if they do, and on the other hand the pension funds do not exist, or after the present crisis will not do so for long.

The well known distinction between production and provision has been proposed in the literature of public finance in the case of privatization of public utilities because it is credited with joining the minimization of production costs and the regulation of provision. In fact the plain privatization of public firms and utilities combines private profit maximization and consumer surplus minimization via the adoption of monopoly prices. This emblematic market failure is the base of private firms' regulation through Ramsey-Boiteux prices for goods and services which are not exposed to competition (Romagnoli, 1997).

After twenty years of privatization, decentralization and liberalization, the world financial and economic crisis once again turns this intellectual fashion inside out. The State ceases to be the problem and in many cases is called back as a solution, even though the bailing out of the financial institutions makes this reversal shortlived. The point is that the market has to keep its role in resources allocation and the State, though exposed to capture, has to regulate it in order to defend the consumer surplus.

4. STRUCTURAL REFORMS

There is a general convergence among economists on the causes of the long lasting Italian stagnation (small businesses do not grow and tend to populate the underground economy even in a globalized market, and the relationships between industrial and financial capital, capital markets and banking off-brokerage are difficult), but politicians still hesitate to adopt the economic measures which could give a new start to the recovery (Romagnoli et al., 2008). For many years it has been widely held that the solution is to be found in the design of structural policies which should eventually become the main focus for the government (Romagnoli, 1999).

The economic crisis may offer the opportunity to take the structural actions to keep Italy in the group of most advanced countries in spite of the difficulties faced by its political system, which are due more to the strength of vested interests than to cultural hostility. There are several measures that can be aimed at either microeconomic targets, like the productivity of different sectors, including public administration, or macroeconomic targets like the domestic demand for goods and services through tax and expenditure policies.

Among the microeconomic measures, the following are particularly relevant:

- incentives to increase working hours;
- revision of labour market contracts, which should be related to productivity changes;
- liberalization of goods and services markets, following the privatization of public monopolies, and completion of the reform of the labour market;
- a reconsideration of the negative effects (with special reference to the loss of know-how), associated with the static and dynamic gains of productive specialization in this period characterized by international trade contraction.

Among the macroeconomic measures concerning tax inlays, the following ones are particularly relevant:

- the redistribution of the tax burden through family income splitting;
- the restitution of fiscal drag which has mainly hit workers and retired people;
- the extension of fiscal federalism though the Berlusconi government has cancelled the property tax on the first non luxury houses in order to keep the Premier's electoral pledge;
- measures against tax evasion.

Finally, among the macroeconomic policies concerning public expenditure, the following are particularly relevant:

- replacement of the universal provision approach with one aimed at specific needs in order to concentrate the available resources on this target. Although everybody in Italy claims to be worried for the needy segment of the population, no politician dares to abandon the universal approach, especially in the health and education sectors, because of the immediate political incentives, according to Jim Buchanan's Paradox (Buchanan, 1992);
- raising of the pension age and revision of the coefficients to take into account the increase of life expectancy;
- territorial reallocation and control of public health expenditure, as the present fair redistribution of financial resources does not produce equally efficient medical treatments.

The above economic policy measures fit the double aim of balancing public deficits and helping the recovery of the Italian economy. They answer a strong need for political responsibility,[7] but require unpopular policies and therefore tend to be indefinitely postponed even though they are extremely needed.

5. CONCLUDING REMARKS

The answer of the Italian State to the social and structural problems of capitalism has been weak, confused and contradictory, especially since the 1970s. The history of economic constitutions shows that the way towards models of acceptable societies is possible if past mistakes are not repeated. Finance and the market should be handled with caution and severity since, if not adequately controlled, at any moment they can destroy in a short time what has been built over a long period.

The malfunctioning of the Italian public administration has produced serious negative results in the country, most of all in the Mezzogiorno. Some of them are irreversible, like those produced by the mismanagement, after the 1970s, and the eventual collapse, in the mid 1980s, of public firms financed either by IRI or by the 'Cassa del Mezzogiorno', even though they had favoured economic growth and the economic unification of the country, for more than twenty years after World War II. Other negative results of the malfunctioning are temporary though significant in terms of the citizens' welfare losses, like those which hit the services for health, schools, higher education, justice and public transport. Other sectors which had experienced serious malfunctioning have found a way out through the control of independent authorities or more recently through the reform of the labour market and of the public administration. Faulty institutional arrangements give evidence that institutions matter. Italy shows a deep need of structural change to revert the absolute economic decline which is taking place in the country, while the accumulation of public debt keeps Italian economic policy in a stalemate. Among the legitimate State interventions we underline those aimed at filling the opportunity gaps and diluting the initial conditions differences. In this effort the State should find the support of social forces. An important step in the right direction recently has been the laborious introduction of the class action in Italy's legal system.

Policy models where the rules dominate political discretion have recently prevailed in other European countries. This attitude has a weight on the uneasy relationship between democracy and the market. The productive interaction between the market and democracy is legitimate only when corporations and financial institutions appreciate that their ambition cannot be limitless but prospers to the extent it serves the democratic imperative. Following the conventional wisdom, the deficit of democracy is associated with efficiency gains, since sovereignty reduces efficiency according with market theory. Free markets reflect a deficit of either economic theory or of political democracy in a society of unequals and the transaction costs are the trenches and the bulwark of vested interests. They may easily prevail over a weakened State sovereignty. In Europe and in the United States, many observers argue that the world economic crisis has favoured political power *vis-à-vis* market power, governments *vis-à-vis* business lobbies, and political intervention *vis-à-vis* economic liberalism. The bailing out process may make this thesis questionable, but there is no way out of the actual crisis without a renewed reliance of economic agents on national and international institutions. In order to make this work, the institutions have to manage a change of political incentives and select 'Bruno Frey anomalous' politicians (Frey, 1997).

The different speed of economic and political integration pushes EU national governments to tackle issues like energy, finance, climate, environment, security and immigration which spill over the national borders. Market fundamentalists complain about the results of referendums against European political unity, which can be read as clear signs of the survival of the electoral preference for sovereignty as a form of implicit original devolution to be maintained. In other words, the fact that European political unity has not yet been established shows a widespread demand for decentralization (Jefferson, Tiebout, Musgrave, Oates), outside federalism, on the issues which the European citizens want to be decided by the national government at a level closer to them than the supranational one.

NOTES

1. The subprime mortgage crisis has wreaked havoc on the lives of millions of people and has threatened to derail the US economy and economies around the world. Shiller blames the subprime crisis on the irrational exuberance that drove the economy's two most recent bubbles in stocks in the 1990s and in housing between 2000 and 2007. He shows how these bubbles led to the dangerous overextension of credit now resulting in foreclosures, bankruptcies, and write-offs, as well as a global credit crunch. To restore confidence in the markets, Shiller argues, bailouts are needed in the short run. But he insists that these bailouts must be targeted at low-income victims of subprime deals (Shiller, 2008).
2. Financial illusion consists of an erroneous collective evaluation of the target and consequences of public expenditure and of debt burden.
3. This ratio was 41% in 1970, grew to 121.8 per cent in 1994 and is now growing again from 106 per cent (2007) to 118 per cent (2010) because of the economic crisis.
4. The most relevant case of unfair distribution, as far as dimension is concerned, was given by social security, where pensions were generously distributed to different categories of people. It is difficult to change this situation since most of the existing transfer schemes are widely considered insufficient to cope with commonly shared needs.
5. Here the reference is to law 262 of 28 December 2005 'Disposizioni per la tutela del risparmio e la disciplina dei mercati finanziari'.
6. At that time, Guido Carli was Governor of the Bank of Italy.
7. The responsibility principle has often been recalled in the writings of José Casas Pardo (Casas Pardo, 2007).

REFERENCES

Buchanan, J.M. (1992), 'Public choice after the revolutions 1989–1991', *Economia delle scelte pubbliche*, **2–3**, 94–101.

Carli, G. (1976), *Intervista sul capitalismo italiano*, Tusin: Bollati Boringhieri.

Casas Pardo, J. (2007), 'Threats democracy faces: an overview', in J. Casas Pardo and P. Schwartz (eds), *Public Choice and the Challenges of Democracy*, Cheltenham, UK and Northampton, MA, USA: Edward Elgar, pp. 15–34.

Frey, B.S. (1997), 'Do people care about democracy?', *Public Choice*, **1**, 53–5.

Keynes, J.M. (1936), *The General Theory of Unemployment, Interest and Money*, New York: Harcourt Brace.

Niskanen, W. (1971), *Bureaucracy and Representative Government*, Chicago: Aldine.

Reviglio, F. (1994), *Meno stato e più mercato. Come ridurre lo stato per risanare il paese*, Milan: Mondadori, pp. 89–138.

Romagnoli, G.C. (1997), 'Some criteria for privatization in Italy', in M. Baldassarri et al. (eds), *The Privatization of Public Utilities: The Case of Italy – I*, London: Macmillan, pp. 35–51.

Romagnoli, G.C. (1999), 'Le funzioni economiche dello Stato in Italia', in N. Acocella, G.M. Rey and M. Tiberi (eds), *Saggi di politica economica in onore di Federico Caffè*, vol. III, Milan: FrancoAngeli, pp. 171–200.

Romagnoli, G.C. et al. (2008), 'L'Italia non deve rinunciare alla crescita', in C. Gnesutta, G.M. Rey and G.C. Romagnoli (eds), *Capitale industriale e capitale finanziario nell'economia mondiale*, Bologna: Il Mulino, pp. 17–38.

Shiller, R.J. (2008), *The Subprime Solution: How Today's Global Financial Crisis Happened, and What to Do about It*, Princeton, NJ: Princeton University Press.

Wolf, C., Jr (1979), 'A theory of the non-market failure: framework for implementation analysis', *Journal of Law and Economics*, **22**, April, 107–39.

13. Government bankruptcy of Balkan nations and the consequences for money and inflation before 1914: a comparative analysis*

Peter Bernholz

1. INTRODUCTION

> Where the payment of interest and the repayment of debts in self-inflicted devalued or ruined currency brings about an improvement of the fiscal situation, not an open but a veiled government bankruptcy takes place. Veiled government bankruptcy is the modern method of national bankruptcy. (Terhalle 1931, my translation)

If a government becomes unable to meet its obligations, there exist several methods by which to escape them. Either the debt or the interest on it are reduced more or less openly by government decree, or by raising the taxes on interest payments. Another method is to lower the debt's real value by inflation. This is all linked by a tautological 'unpleasant' *financial and monetary relationship* (Sargent and Wallace 1981). Historically, whereas a ruler like Philip II of Spain declared three open bankruptcies during the second half of the sixteenth century, the method of veiled bankruptcy has become more and more widespread during the last century. Philip did not touch the value of the Spanish currency, the 'piece of eight' (peso de ocho) which had established itself as a leading international currency and became the precursor of the dollar.

Still, veiled government bankruptcies reducing the nominal value of debts by inflation were certainly not unknown even before the last century of inflation following the demise of the gold standard. Thus a German encyclopaedia explained even before 1914 (*Meyers Konversationslexikon* 1907) that government bankruptcies may occur as follows:

(1) Repudiation of government debts, that is, an announcement that the state would not pay back the total or parts of its debt or pay interest

on them. Such a refusal often happened in earlier times when the government changed. The new government declared the debts incurred earlier to be illegal (some US states 1841, Denmark 1850, France during the revolution);

(2) Discontinuation of payments for an indefinite period;
(3) A unilateral reduction of interest . . . that is, without the creditors agreeing;
(4) A unilaterally introduced higher taxation of interest amounting to a hidden reduction of the interest rate, which can also occur by interest payments in debased coins or paper money;
(5) Issue of an excessive amount of paper money turned into compulsory legal tender. (Vol. 18, p. 807 f., my translation)

Point (5) obviously refers to veiled bankruptcy. The article goes on to mention, as recent examples, the government bankruptcies of Turkey (1875), of several countries in Central and South America (here Argentina 1890 should be mentioned), Portugal (1892) and Greece (1893). But other Balkan states faced the same problem in the decades before 1914: Serbia went bankrupt, and Bulgaria came near to bankruptcy. Only Romania proved to be more stable.

In the following we will undertake a comparative study of 'open' and 'veiled' government bankruptcies of Balkan countries before 1914, and of the relationship between national bankruptcy, inflation and devaluation. In doing so we have to differentiate between government debt expressed in national currencies and that denominated in foreign currencies, where the latter is mostly held by foreign creditors. Whereas the former debt can be reduced in real terms by inflation as long as the respective state has control of its currency, this is not true for the debt denominated in foreign money. Before 1914 most of this debt was expressed in terms of stable gold and silver currencies, like the French franc, the British pound and the German mark, which also scarcely fluctuated among each other because of the gold standard. It was different until the 1890s for Russia and Austria Hungary, which were on paper money standards for long periods during the nineteenth century.

2. DEVELOPMENTS IN THE OTTOMAN EMPIRE UNTIL 1914

We begin our comparative analysis by looking at developments in the Ottoman Empire before 1844; that is, before most Balkan states reached their full independence. As already shown by Pamuk (2004), the empire

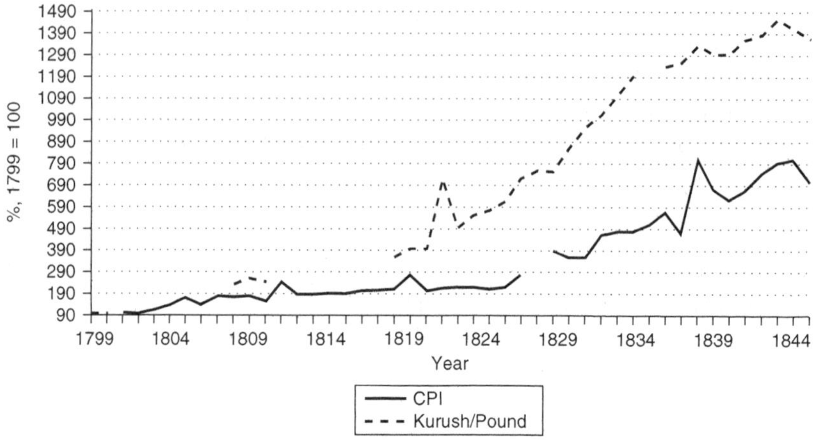

Sources: The development of prices and of some data for exchange rates have been provided by Sevket Pamuk in personal communication to the author, 2 January 2008. See also Pamuk (1999) and (2004). Most data for exchange rates are from Schneider et al. (1994), pp. 108–12.

Figure 13.1 Development of prices and of exchange rate for pound in Istanbul, 1799–1844

suffered from a substantial budget deficit during the first half of the nineteenth century, which was mainly covered by incurring domestic debt and by money creation. The latter led to substantial inflation and thus to a fall of the exchange rate (Figure 13.1). According to our definition the period is thus characterized by veiled bankruptcy.

Unfortunately no figures for government budget and the money supply are available. But we know that a substantial debasement of the kurush took place. A look at our figure also reveals that one of the hypotheses we want to test is clearly supported by the empirical evidence. With the flexible exchange rate to the pound as a result of the debasement, a substantial undervaluation of the Ottoman currency develops. The exchange rate moves up more quickly and more strongly than the price level.

In 1843–44 the situation changed dramatically. The government carried out reforms to stop the debasement of the currency and to balance the budget. Its efforts to stop the decline of the exchange rate proved to be successful, for the new parity with the pound could be maintained until the First World War (Figure 13.2). However, after two years the budget again turned into deficit (Figure 13.3). This meant, of course, that the deficit had now to be covered by raising credit, mainly by borrowing abroad, since the inflation tax was no longer available. But foreign loans were necessarily

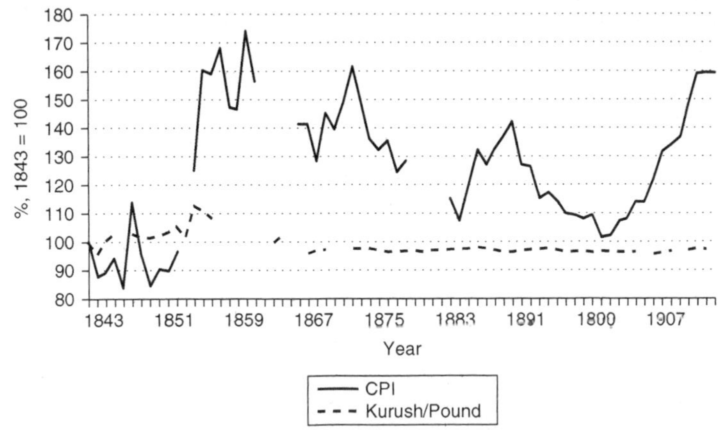

Sources: See Figure 13.1.

Figure 13.2 Development of prices and exchange rate for pound in Ottoman Empire, 1843–1914

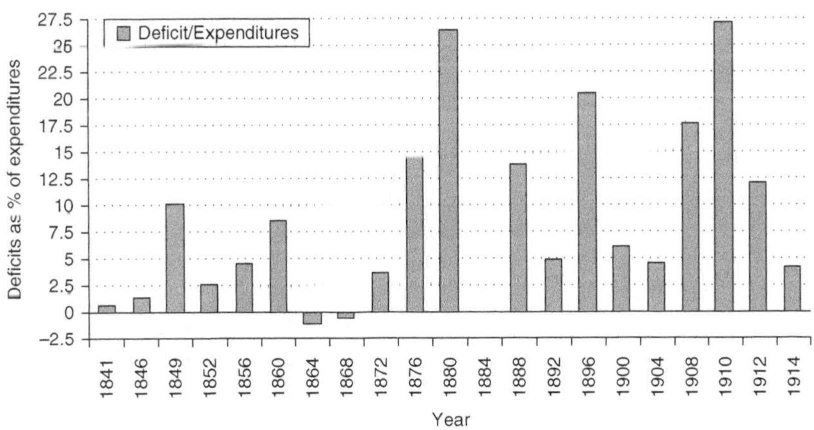

Source: Personal communication to the author by Sefket Pamuk, December 2007.

Figure 13.3 Ottoman budget deficit/expenditures, 1841–1914

denominated in stable foreign money, given the British gold standard. This meant that with ever increasing government debt, open bankruptcy of the Ottoman state could not be avoided in the long run. We will return to this event later, when we analyze the open bankruptcies threatening all

Balkan governments except Romania in the decades preceding the First World War.

We now turn to the development of prices and exchange rate as a consequence of these fiscal and monetary policies. According to our hypotheses we would now expect at least a removal of the undervaluation of the kurush compared to the British pound, and perhaps even an overvaluation since the Ottoman Empire suffered from a stronger increase of prices than the United Kingdom. And indeed, the price level moves strongly ahead of the stabilized exchange rate in the years soon after the reforms. This is quite in tune with other historical experiences. Subsequently we see a tendency of the price level to move towards the exchange rate, which seems to suggest a return to purchasing power parity. With the beginning of the new century, however, another rise of the price level can be observed. Does this mean that an overvaluation of the kurush was still present in 1913?

To answer this question we have to take up two points. First, the developments sketched in Figure 13.2 do not take into account that a substantial undervaluation was present in 1843, so that the stronger rise of the price level might just have removed this. Looking at the data we find that until 1913 the price level rose to 1291.89 and the exchange rate to 1376.63, with the base set equal to 100 for 1799. Given the empirical problems with the cost of living index and the selected base year, the small remaining 'undervaluation' of about 6 per cent may be just an artifact.

The second point refers to the development of price levels in the stable countries of the center, as they have to be taken into account for problems of purchasing power parities. I have looked up the figures for the cost of living index for Switzerland, and indeed, the above picture does not change. The Swiss index remained stable for all practical purposes in the long run. If we set the earliest figure for 1811 equal to 100, the index reached 100.58 in 1913.

So we can draw the cautious conclusion that either purchasing power parity was restored for the kurush before the First World War, or a slight undervaluation remained.

3. FISCAL AND MONETARY DEVELOPMENTS IN FOUR BALKAN COUNTRIES

We turn now to developments in Romania, Bulgaria, Serbia and Greece, and first have a look at the development of government budgets (Figure 13.4). We learn several facts from Figure 13.4. First, Greece and Serbia showed the most critical budgetary situations. Second, times of severe financial distress seem to occur for Greece around the 1880s and the late 1890s, and for

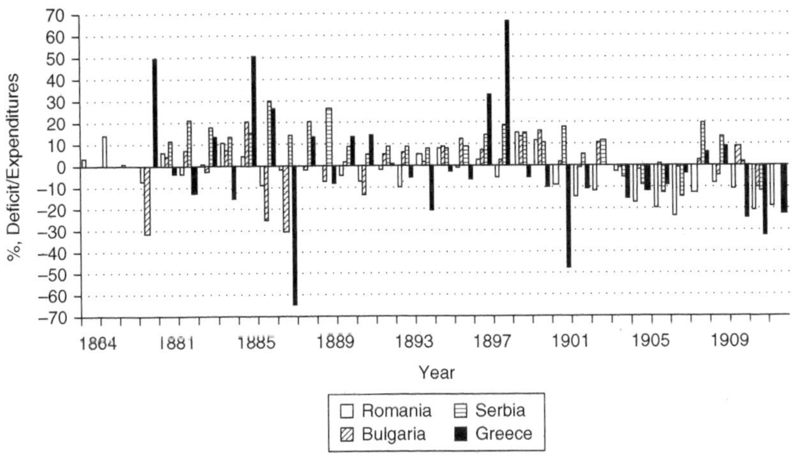

Source: Lampe and Jackson (1982), pp. 212 and 234.

Figure 13.4 Development of government deficits/expenditures in four Balkan countries, 1864–1912

Serbia around the early 1880s and around 1900. Third, Greece was experiencing the strongest budget fluctuations among the four countries. Fourth, the Bulgarian financial situation looks precarious around the late 1890s and the first years of the new century, but seems to be better than that of Greece and Serbia. Finally, Romanian government finances never became dangerous, since budget deficits were soon compensated by surpluses. Neither an open nor a veiled government bankruptcy ever threatened.

3.1 Romanian Developments

As a consequence of its sound government finances Romania was never motivated to manipulate its currency by debasement; its exchange rate could always maintain its parity (Figure 13.5). At first look, it seems that an undervaluation of the leu occurred, which should only happen according to our hypothesis if the Swiss rate of inflation were higher than the Romanian.[1]

This seems, however, not to have been the case (Figure 13.6). It may have been wrong to take 1887 as the base year, but we did so since no data were available for the exchange rates of the years before. With an assumed earlier stability of the rate[2] and taking 1877 as a base year, the red line would shift up strongly, suggesting an overvaluation of the leu, which diminished in time.

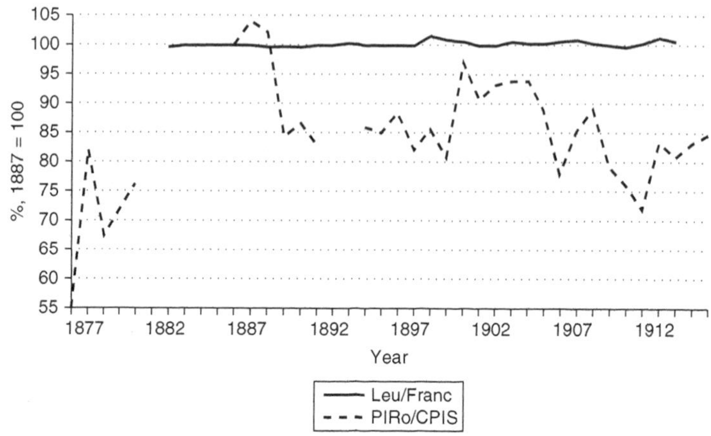

Sources: For prices see Figure 13.6. For exchange rates: National Bank of Romania, Reports of the Board of Directors to the General Shareholders Meeting, 1893–1915.

Figure 13.5 Development of purchasing power parity and exchange rate of Romania, 1877–1916

This would be in tune with our hypothesis, since the average annual rate of inflation in Romania was 1.4 per cent compared to −0.54 per cent for Switzerland. So we might again, as in the case of the Ottoman Empire, have in the end either some remaining overvaluation or an approach towards purchasing power parity, which would correspond to our hypothesis. We cannot be too certain about the result, since some deviations have to be expected, given the fact that for Romania we have only an unweighted arithmetic average of fourteen goods, mostly victuals. We also see greater fluctuations of the Romanian price index than of the Swiss CPI, which are probably caused by the higher volatility of food prices because of bad harvests alternating with good ones.

3.2 Greek Developments

Greek developments have been well described by Sophia Lazaretou (1995). She describes several switches of exchange rate regimes as a consequence of budgetary problems, leading on the one hand to veiled government bankruptcy and on the other to stabilization policies moving the exchange rate back to the old fixed parity. The periods of financial distress can be clearly seen by looking at the figures for accumulated deficits in terms of annual revenues (Figure 13.7). These are the years after 1833, the 1880s and early 1890s, and the late 1890s.

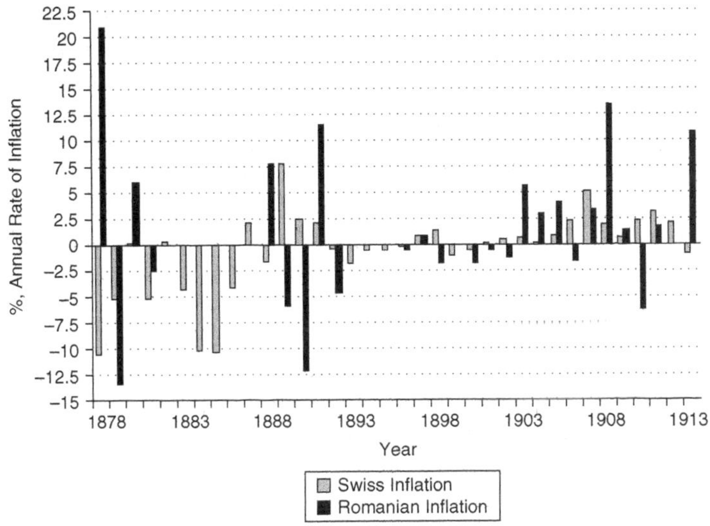

Note: An unweighted arithmetic average of 27 items has been used to calculate the Romanian inflation.

Sources: For Romanian prices: Postolache (1991). For Swiss cost of living index: Swiss National Bank: *Historical Time Series*, CD, 2007.

Figure 13.6 Romanian and Swiss rates of inflation, 1878–1913

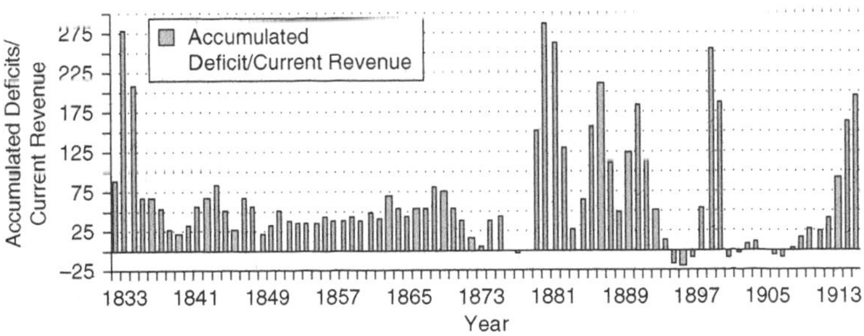

Sources: Lazaretou (1995), Table A1.

Figure 13.7 Greek government accumulated deficits since 1833

Financial stress develops again with the two Balkan wars and the First World War.

Given the work of Lazaretou (1995), our chapter can limit its analysis to the validity of the hypotheses for under- and overvaluation. As

Lazaretou reports, Greece suspended the convertibility of its currency four times from 1833 to 1914, but always returned to convertibility with an exchange rate fixed to the French franc at a parity of one to one before the First World War (Lazaretou 1995, Table 1, p. 30). All suspensions of convertibility were caused by the financing of excessive government deficits by money creation. The government reverted several times to open bankruptcy but also used money creation extensively to finance its deficits, and thus presumably also to reduce its domestic debt by inflation. The tendency of politicians and governments to incur deficits and to finance parts of them by money creation or debasement is a well known historical phenomenon explained by public choice theory (Bernholz 2003, Chapter 2). Inflation and the abolition of fixed exchange rates can thus only be prevented if the hands of governments are bound by strong institutional safeguards. But given the international gold standard, it can be observed that weaker peripheral countries, not only the Balkan countries, but for instance also Argentina and Brazil, always strove to return to a fixed parity. This has been explained as due to politicians seeking to follow the example of the more developed countries of the center (Bernholz 1987) and/or to restore their creditworthiness to foreign creditors (Lazaretou 1995, p. 48).

In testing the hypotheses for under- and overvaluation of the Greek currency we have unfortunately to limit ourselves to the period after 1877. Data concerning the development of food prices and of the exchange rate are only available from 1877, so that the earlier periods of distress, namely the years after 1833, cannot be examined. But the period from 1877 to 1914 casts at least some light on the validity of our hypotheses.

We have seen (Figures 13.7) that fiscal distress developed in the 1880s, stayed until the early 1890s and returned in the late 1890s. This corresponds with the development of the exchange rate (Figure 13.8). Until the mid-eighties it remained relatively stable near its parity. But afterwards the parity could not be maintained; the exchange rate became flexible, and moved up strongly by about 70 per cent. The price level followed more slowly, so that a substantial undervaluation developed. With stabilization policies setting in around 1900, the exchange rate fell more drastically than the price level and purchasing power parity was restored when the old fixed parity was reached. This corresponds to the hypotheses to be tested.

By contrast, the development from 1877 to 1887 seems to contradict the hypothesis that with a higher domestic than foreign rate of inflation, an overvaluation of the drachma should have developed. The price level fell, whereas the exchange rate remained relatively stable, which looks like an undervaluation. But this impression may be deceptive, since this

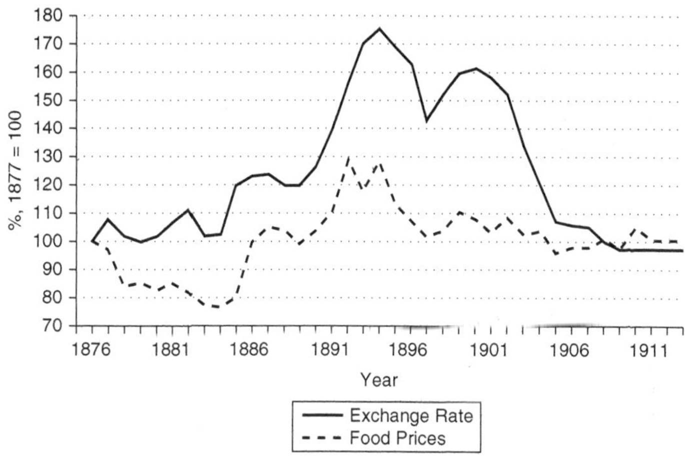

Note: Unweighted arithmetic average of food prices.

Source: See Figure 13.7.

Figure 13.8 Development of exchange rate and food price level in Greece, 1877–1914

development could be the removal of an earlier overvaluation. We cannot know as long we do not have figures for prices and exchange rates for the years after 1833.

3.3 Bulgarian Developments

Bulgarian fiscal developments were less favourable than those of Romania but better than those in Greece and Serbia (Figures 13.4 and 13.7). Periods of financial distress were limited to the late 1890s and the beginning of the first decade of the twentieth century, and again to the times of the Balkan wars. They were also far less severe than those of Greece (compare Figures 13.7 and 13.9). This is reflected in the development of the exchange rate after 1879 (Figure 13.10). In fact, parity could be maintained until 1914. With the price level falling in the early 1880s an undervaluation developed. When it began to rise after 1902, the undervaluation was first reduced and then turned into an overvaluation. Both events are quite in tune with our hypotheses. We will discuss later (Section 4) whether the financial distress beginning in the late 1890s led to problems with international creditors and whether it had something to do with an expansionary monetary policy.

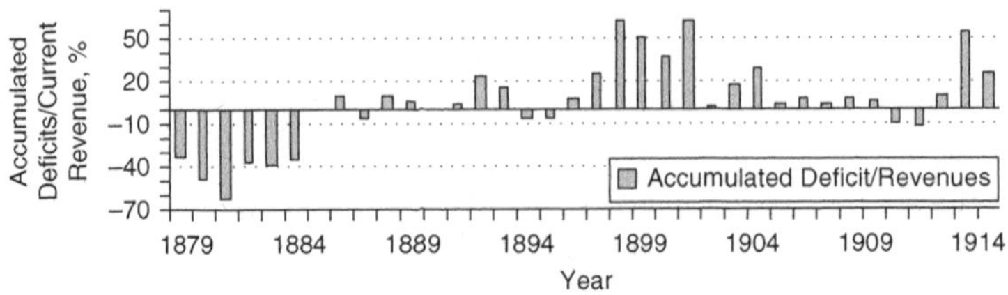

Source: Lampe and Jackson (1982), pp. 212 and 234.

Figure 13.9 Accumulated government deficits in Bulgaria since 1879

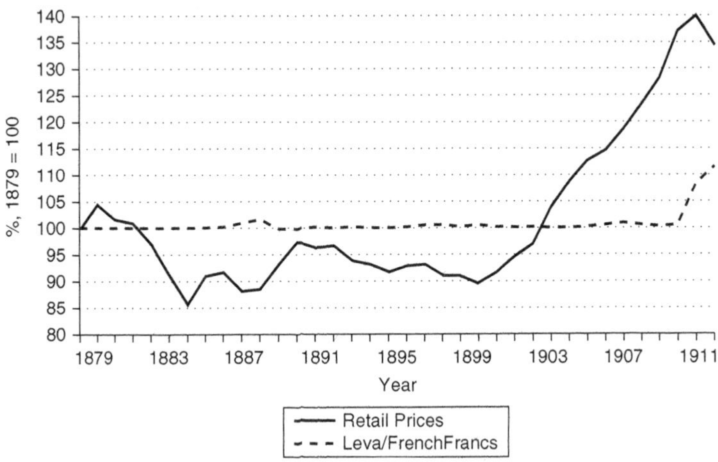

Note: Retail price index is based on 97 commodities.

Source: Personal communications to the author by Kalina Dimitrova and Martin Ivanov of the Bulgarian National Bank and the Bulgarian Academy of Sciences in 2007/08. For exchange rates see also Trifonoff (1930).

Figure 13.10 Bulgarian retail price index and exchange rate, 1879–1914

3.4 Developments in Serbia

As can be seen from Figure 13.11 there occurred three periods of fiscal stress in Serbia after 1881: the worst in the 1880s, then around the turn of the century and finally from 1909. Beginning in about 1901 we have a rigorous consolidation which even led to an accumulated surplus in the following years.

Unfortunately, exchange rates were only available to me from 1886. If we look at food prices, we cannot find evidence of an inflationary

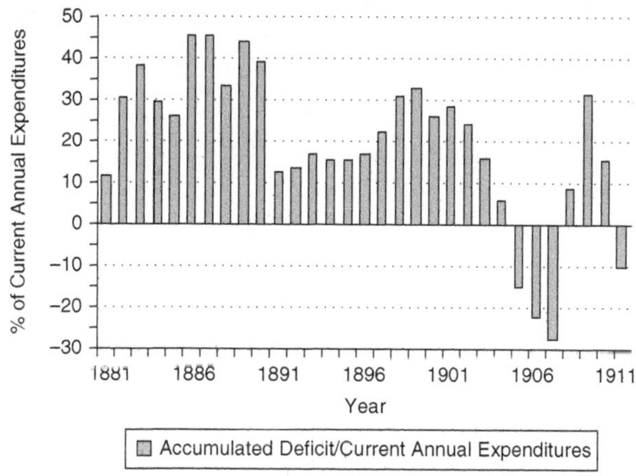

Source: Lampe and Jackson (1982), pp. 212 and 234.

Figure 13.11 Serbian accumulated deficit/current annual expenditures, 1881–1911

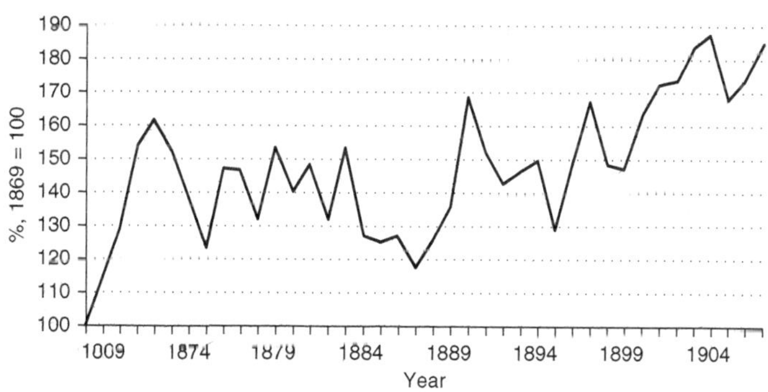

Note: Unweighted arithmetic average.

Source: Personal communication by Dragana Gnjatovic to the author, of data provided by Mr Sojic from the National Bank of Serbia.

Figure 13.12 Development of food prices in Serbia, 1869–1908 (arithmetic average of 14 food prices)

development in the 1880s (Figure 13.12), but this may be a consequence of the earlier rise by about 40 to 50 per cent in 1869 and the 1870s, which was maintained later. Around 1889 a reduction of the price level can be observed, which may be a consequence of the strong reduction of the

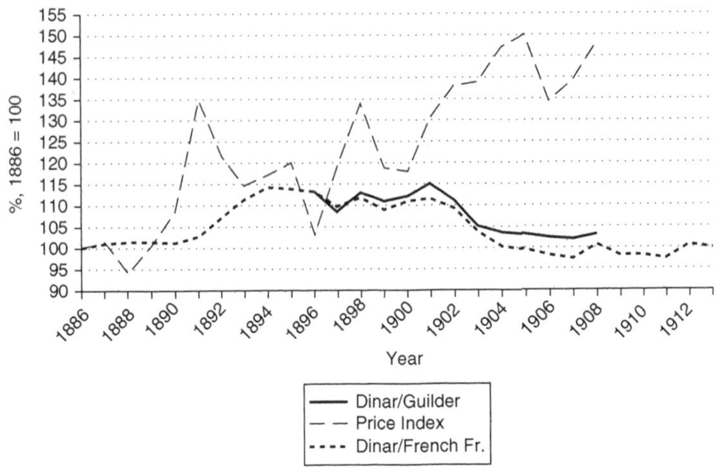

Note: The exchange rates for the French franc have been calculated by using the agio on metallic dinar. The exchange rate of dinars per Austrian guilder was set equal for 1896 to that of the French franc.

Source: For exchange rates for Austrian guilder: Statistical Yearbook for the Kingdom of Serbia, various issues; for agio on metallic dinar: Gnjatovic (1991), Table 6, p. 198. For prices: see Figure 13.12.

Figure 13.13 Development of price level and of exchange rates in Serbia, 1886–1913

accumulated deficit during that time. After that period, and certainly from the late 1890s, an inflationary trend can be observed again.

For the years from 1886 and 1896, respectively, exchange rates for the French franc and the Austrian guilder are available (Figure 13.13). They show that the exchange rate for the franc and the guilder, presumably expressed in paper dinars, since the agio or premium on the twenty dinar gold coin diminished even more, fell from 1894 until 1908. This probably reflects a move towards parity for the gold dinar, that is, towards full convertibility. In this sense a stabilization effort for the Serbian currency was undertaken. Together with the rising level of food prices this probably led to an overvaluation of the dinar, quite in line with the hypothesis to be tested. At least part of the divergence may be just a correction of an earlier undervaluation, but I believe that only a part of the divergence can be explained by such a correction, since in 1908 a premium of 20.26 per cent on the twenty dinar gold coin remained. It had fallen to this value from 23.1 per cent in 1894. This is a reduction by 12.3 per cent. By contrast the divergence of the development of food prices and exchange rate from 1896 to 1908 amounted to more than 50 per cent in 1908. However, these are just speculative judgments as long as we have no figures for earlier exchange rates.

4. OPEN BANKRUPTCIES OF BALKAN COUNTRIES

With a stable monetary policy and fixed exchange rates veiled government bankruptcy becomes impossible. The same is true if the debt or a large proportion of it is denominated not in the national but in stable foreign currencies. Foreign currencies were stable under the then prevailing gold standard. Given these conditions, an accumulation of debt at a rate higher than that of GDP must necessarily lead in time to open government bankruptcy. We have, therefore, to look into the respective experiences of the Ottoman Empire, Greece, Serbia and Bulgaria, all of which showed fiscal distress during periods in which they were striving for stable monetary

Table 13.1 Long-term European loans to Balkan governments, 1864–1911 (million French francs)

	Nominal amount	Effective amount	% Nominal interest	% Effective interest
1864–89				
Ottoman Empire (1876)	6182.5			
Romania (1864)	722.7	518.9	5.6	7.8
Bulgaria (1888)	76.8	71.4	6.0	6.5
Serbia (1876)	63.5	46.6	3.8	5.2
Greece (1833)	690.9	514.0	4.8	6.1
1890–1900				
Romania	1009.4	779.2	4.4	5.7
Bulgaria	150.0	131.2	5.8	6.6
Serbia	367.8	258.1	4.0	5.7
Greece (1893)	689.5			
1901–11				
Romania	951.8	880.0	4.9	5.3
Bulgaria	522.0	564.0	4.7	5.5
Serbia	555.0	476.0	4.8	5.6
Greece	55.3	44.2	4.0	5.0

Sources: Lampe and Jackson (1982), Table 7.7, p. 233. The 1876 figure for the Ottoman Empire and the 1893 figure for Greece are from *Meyers Konversationslexikon*, vol. 19, 1908, p. 829 and vol. 8, 1914, p. 310, respectively.

policies and had reached or were attempting to move towards fixed exchange rates.

As shown above the Ottoman Empire introduced stable monetary policies and a fixed exchange rate already beginning in 1844 (Figure 13.2). But at the same time government deficits remained sizable, so that the international indebtedness rose. As had to be expected, open government bankruptcy followed on 13 April 1876. After several years of negotiations the international debt was reduced from 250 to 106 million British pounds, and the interest rate to at least 1 per cent, but with an annual amortization of 1/3 per cent of this remaining debt (*Meyers Konversationslexikon*, vol. 19, 1908, p. 829). An international commission, the Conseil d'Administration de la Dette Publique Ottoman was created. It consisted of one private member from each of the following countries: Britain, Italy, France, Austria-Hungary and Germany. Several public revenues were pledged to serve the remaining debt and were administered and controlled by this commission (*Meyers Konversationslexikon*, vol. 6, 1904, p. 570). But in spite of these developments public finances did not improve much and, as we have seen, new fiscal distress arose in 1888, 1896 and from 1908 to 1912. In 1906 the international debt amounted to 129.1 million British pounds (*Meyers Konversationslexikon*, vol. 19, 1908, p. 822). These developments pointed to a renewed government bankruptcy, even if the First World War had not occurred.

We have already seen that Greece suffered from similar problems from the beginning of its new existence in 1832, as well described by Lazaretou (1995). Convertibility at par was already abolished in 1848 because of an overissue of banknotes. From 1895 a stabilization of monetary policies began which ended with a return to the old one to one parity with the French franc. Before this time Greece had not only reduced its real debt denominated in the national currency and increased its revenues by an inflation tax, but also accumulated increasing debts denominated in foreign currencies. This led to open government bankruptcy in 1893. At this time the government debt had risen to 598 million French francs and to 152 million devalued paper drachmas. The government reduced the interest rate on the foreign debt one-sidedly to one-third during the following years. But when the fiscal situation worsened even further because of defeat by the Turks in 1897, the Greek government agreed to a European Financial Commission similar to that instituted for the Ottoman Empire (*Meyers Konversationslexikon*, vol. 8, 1904, p. 310). Its members were mandated by the governments of Germany, France, Britain, Italy, Russia and Austria-Hungary. This commission had the right to control and to administer certain government revenues pledged for serving and amortizing the international debt (*Meyers Konversationslexikon*, vol. 6, 1904,

Table 13.2 Open government bankruptcies of Balkan countries

Country	Year	Reduction of debt	Reduction of interest	Foreign control
Ottoman Empire	1876	From 250 to 160 million pounds	To at least 1%	Yes
Greece	1893		By two-thirds	Yes
Serbia	1893		First no interest, then 4 %	Limited
Bulgaria	Near bankruptcy around 1900	New loan saved situation		

p. 571). It also imposed a moratorium on the issue of new banknotes and mandated the withdrawal of two million drachmas a year from circulation until the exchange rate reached par. These and other reforms led to more healthy monetary policies and to an increase of the exchange rate of the drachma until it had reached its original parity with the French franc in 1909. During this process the National Bank of Greece, led by the able Stephen Streit, was able to establish its independence from the government, whereas in 1891 the government had forced the Bank to lend it most of its gold reserves (Lampe and Jackson 1982, pp. 214 and 218 f.).

If we turn to Serbian developments, a similar pattern emerges. We observe periods of financial distress in the 1880s, around 1900 and around 1910 (Figure 13.11). The situation became so difficult in 1893 that neither public officials nor the interest on government debt could be paid (*Meyers Konversationslexikon*, vol. 18, 1907, p. 362). As a consequence the debts were consolidated into a new loan with an interest of 4 per cent, and a Serbian Autonomous Monopoly Administration was created in 1895. It controlled and administered several government revenues including those of the state monopolies with the purpose of serving the interest and amortization payments on the international debt (*Meyers Konversationslexikon*, vol. 6, 1904, p. 570 f.). The Serbian National Bank was able to reassert itself against the government, and in this process the money supply was reduced by three million dinars and further note issues were frozen until 1900 (Lampe and Jackson 1982, pp. 213 f.). As a consequence the exchange rate of the dinar rose substantially during the following years (Figure 13.13).

Let us finally consider the Bulgarian financial situation. It has already been shown that the exchange rate could be kept at par from 1890 to the outbreak of the First World War (Figure 13.10). Before 1914, financial distress developed only around the turn of the century. A new loan agreed on by parliament and prince in 1899 could not be obtained, first in Vienna and then in France. Thus the salaries of army officers and of bureaucrats were cut by 7 per cent in 1899, and 20–30 per cent of them were paid for two years in treasury bonds. The prince agreed to forego 50 per cent of the payments he received from the state, and the government was entitled to issue 40 million lev in treasury bonds. But the budgetary situation remained precarious, and led to additional (insufficient) savings by reducing the number of districts in 1901 and of the number of recruits in 1902. Thus it became necessary to convert government debts with the help of a new loan of 260 million lev in 1902. Only this new loan could help to bridge the remaining deficit (*Meyers Konversationslexikon*, vol. 3, 1903, p. 588 f.). However, the budgetary situation improved afterwards and no open government bankruptcy occurred.

5. CONCLUSIONS

Simple arithmetical relationships exist between government deficits and their financing in capital markets and through central banks and the money supply. High inflation has usually been caused by creating money to finance excessive government deficits. All inflations in Balkan countries before 1914 and that of the Ottoman Empire, as well as the abolition of fixed exchange rates (corresponding to monetary regimes based on gold or silver standards) were caused by veiled government bankruptcies. They usually led to an undervaluation of the respective currencies. If, however, fixed exchange rates were maintained or restored, a tendency towards overvaluation of the currency or a removal of the earlier undervaluation took place.

Open bankruptcies also occurred several times because of excessive deficits financed by incurring foreign debt denominated in stable currencies. In several cases they were combined with fixed exchange rates or motivated their restoration.

Unfortunately in a couple of cases a lack of data prevented a definite conclusion concerning the hypotheses tested.

NOTES

* I am grateful to Alina Blejan, Kalina Dimitrova, Dragan Gnjatovic, Martin Ivanov, Sophia Lazaretou and Sevket Pamuk for their help, especially in getting data on government budgets, prices and exchange rates.

1. To take the Swiss cost of living index for the comparison seemed to be adequate, since both currencies were fixed one to one to the French franc (Latin Monetary Union).
2. 14.4 guilders of Austrian currency were paid for 100 lei (equal to Walachian piasters) in Vienna in 1842 and 15 in 1863 (Schneider et al. 1991, p. 412). This suggests a long-term stability of the lei.

REFERENCES

Bernholz, Peter (1987), 'The implementation and maintenance of a monetary constitution', in James A. Dorn and Anna J. Schwartz (eds), *The Search for Stable Money*, Chicago and London: The University of Chicago Press, pp. 83–117.

Bernholz, Peter (2003), *Monetary Regimes and Inflation. History, Economic and Political Relationships*, Cheltenham, UK, and Northampton, MA, USA: Edward Elgar. Paperback edition 2006.

Gnjatovic, Dragana (1991), *Stari Drzavni Dugovi. Prilo ekonomskoj istoriji Srbije i Jugoslavije, 1862–1941*, Beograd: Ekonomiski Institut, Jugoslovenski Pregled.

Lampe, John R. and Marvin R. Jackson (1982), *Balkan Economic History, 1550–1950*, Bloomington, IN: Indiana University Press.

Lazaretou, Sophia (1995), 'Government spending, monetary policies, and exchange rate regime switches: the drachma in the Gold Standard period', *Explorations in Economic History*, **32**, 28–50.

Meyers Grosses Konversationslexikon (1903–1908), Vol. 3: Bulgarien; vol. 6: Finanzkontrolle; vol. 8: Griechenland; vol. 18: Serbien; vol. 19: Türkei, Leipzig und Vienna: Bibliographisches Institut, 807 f.

Pamuk, Sevket (1999), *A Monetary History of the Ottoman Empire*, Cambridge: Cambridge University Press.

Pamuk, Sevket (2004), 'Prices in the Ottoman Empire, 1469–1914', *International Journal of Middle East Studies*, **36**, 451–68.

Postolache, Tudorel (coordinator) (1991), *L'Economie de la Roumanie, Le XXe Siècle*, Academie Roumaine, Institut National de Recherches Economiques, Les Editions Expert, pp. 319–30.

Sargent, Thomas and Neil Wallace (1981), 'Some unpleasant monetarist arithmetic', *Federal Reserve Bank of Minneapolis Quarterly Review*, **5** (3), Fall, 1–17.

Schneider, Jürgen, Oskar Schwarzer and Friedrich Zellweger (1991), *Währungern der Welt I, Europäische und Nordamerikanische Devisenkurse, 1777–1914*, Teilband III: *Europäische Devisenkurse* (2nd Part). Stuttgart: Franz Steiner.

Schneider, Jürgen, Oskar Schwarzer and Marcus A. Danzel (1994), *Währungen der Welt, VIII*, Stuttgart: Franz Steiner.

Terhalle, Fritz (1931), 'Staatsbankrott', *Staatslexikon*, vol. 4, Freiburg im Breisgau: Herder, 1855 ff.

Trifonoff, P.I. (1930), *La Banque Nationale de Bulgarie et l'histoire de sa politique monetaire*, Lyon: Imprimerie BOSC Freres & Riou.

PART V

Extensions in Public Choice Theory

14. Regulator preferences and lobbying efforts in rent-seeking contests

Juan D. Montoro-Pons

1. INTRODUCTION

Standard public choice analysis of the political allocation of resources among competing interest groups has generated a growing literature on rent-seeking. In a typical rent-seeking contest[1] artificially created rents are allocated in the political market, and players compete for these, investing resources in a contest that resembles a lottery. In an imperfectly discriminating contest – as considered in this chapter – players devote efforts to increase the likelihood of obtaining rent. This leads to an inefficient allocation of resources, with the inefficiency measured as the overall amount of rent-seeking invested in by players.[2]

However, this insight ignores the mechanism by which rents are awarded. By assuming that only relative efforts alter the allocation of the rent, this rules out regulator preferences. These can, however, play a significant role. Some authors have incorporated ideology or political preferences into the analysis of lobbying, such as Martimort and Semenov (2007a, 2007b, 2008) from a theoretical standpoint, or McKay (2010) from an empirical one.

In this chapter regulator preferences over the outcome of a contest affect its outcome. To this end, players are located at some point on a one-dimensional range of support. This allows us to define the *distance* of a player to the position of the regulator who, in turn, can be influenced by this parameter, as well as by the resources invested by players when allocating the rent.

Note that one interpretation of this distance may be ideological. Some regulators are closer to particular interest groups than others. For instance, a left wing politician may be closer to unions than to firms; conservative press and media will more likely support conservative governments. In general, a politician may be ideologically closer to certain groups. In these cases, the ideological distance of an interest group can be a relevant trait to policymakers, as it gives them some control over the outcomes of contests, or because their utility depends on the player that obtains a rent.

There are many examples in which ideology plays a role in the political allocation of rents. For instance, in the allocation of radio or TV licenses, government decisions may be biased in favor of certain groups (again, those closer to the regulator). If decisions are biased from the onset, this will give an advantage to the rent-seeker closer to the position of the regulator, and to some extent will affect the process and the outcome of a rent-seeking contest. But ideology is not the only variable to take into account when thinking of proximity: social or cultural proximity may also be of importance. Canonization[3] in the Catholic Church may be easier and/or faster for those closer to the Vatican hierarchy.

However, biased contests are not necessarily the outcome of ideological preferences. Gual and Trillas (2006) analyze whether biased or asymmetric conditions should prevail in a context of markets opening up in telecommunications, favoring entrants relative to incumbents. In general, the authors claim, asymmetric contests may lead to regulators favoring certain competitors (rather than more competition).

In summary, when the allocation of a rent to an interest group confers some kind of power to it, the regulator may want to have some control over this power. In this case the more closely linked a group is to the regulator, the more capable she will be to control it or benefit from it. We do not claim that proximity – as described – is a feature present in all contests. However, we do think that there may be some situations in which it is of relevance.

This chapter considers the analysis of modified rent-seeking contests in which the regulator biases the outcome of a contest – modeled as the introduction of *a priori* winning probabilities for contestants. In terms of the cost conditions for rent-seekers the model can be neutral – i.e. it does not modify the results of standard rent-seeking models – or negative – i.e. it can increase inefficiencies. In the latter case, we allow for the explicit dissemination of information by interest groups as a means to counterbalance the regulator's behavior. To this end, we model the process as a two stage game: in the first stage interest groups send messages to the regulator; in the second rent-seekers allocate resources in the standard game. We show that in general there may be different qualitative equilibria at the first stage that, in turn, modify the amount of resources devoted to rent-seeking at the second.

The chapter is organized as follows. The next section develops a basic model in which interest groups compete for a rent in a setup where ideological proximity to the regulator plays a key role. Section 3 introduces relevant equilibrium issues and some comparative statics. Section 4 extends the basic model, by considering the role of information transmission which reinforces/counterbalances proximity. Finally the chapter ends with a discussion and conclusions.

2. RENT-SEEKING AND REGULATOR PREFERENCES: THE BASIC SETUP

This section develops a simple model in which two players compete for a rent – which they may value differently. A standard rent-seeking contest is considered. In it players invest resources in a political game in order to increase the likelihood of appropriating a rent.

The main difference lies in the consideration of the relative position of the players with respect to the regulator, as a relevant variable in the political allocation of the rent. Assuming that the regulator derives utility from proximity, then the standard rent-seeking setting may be biased in favor of the closest interest group.

In the most simple setup proximity is introduced in the form of prior beliefs about the outcomes of a rent-seeking game. Then interest groups are given an absolute advantage or disadvantage in lobbying, in terms of their position with respect to that of the regulator.

2.1 Interest Groups

Let us assume that there are two interest groups competing for a rent R_i in a rent-seeking game, with x_i, $i=1,2$, denoting rent-seeking outlays.

Consider that each group has a given position in a one-dimensional spectrum. Let the preferences of the regulator who allocates the rent be such that d_i measures the distance between any player and the politician. Assume, for the sake of convenience, that player one is closer to the politician such that $d_1<d_2$.

Consider that proximity biases the outcome of the standard rent-seeking game, such that it increases the probability of winning of player one. Think of the symmetric rent-seeking game – with equal risk neutral players – in which the rent is allocated with a 50% probability to each player. If the politician takes into account the position of both groups, then this probability will be modified in favor of player one, who will obtain the rent with a higher probability.

In order to model the combined effect of rent-seeking and relative position, a prior winning probability for player one $0<q<1$ is introduced. It is determined by the proximity to the regulator. Obviously, $1-q$ is the prior winning probability for player two. Given that player one is closer to the regulator than player two then $q>1/2$. Moreover, the closer the relative positions of both groups, the closer q will be to its limit value 1/2. On the contrary, the more extreme the position of group two with respect to the regulator – for any given position of group one – the closer q will be to unity. In brief, q maps proximity into a prior probability of winning the contest.

Combining the Tullock (1980) probability function,[4] with prior winning probabilities as in Gradstein (1995), posterior winning probabilities are

$$p_1(x_1, x_2, q) = \frac{qx_1}{qx_1 + (1-q)x_2} \tag{14.1}$$

$$p_2(x_1, x_2, q) = \frac{(1-q)x_2}{qx_1 + (1-q)x_2} \tag{14.2}$$

And the expected value of the rent for player i is given by

$$R_i^E = R_i\{f_i(x_i, x_j, q)\} - x_i \tag{14.3}$$

The problem player i faces is to maximize the expected value of the rent in (14.3).

2.2 The Regulator

In this setup it is explicitly assumed that the regulator has preferences over the outcome of the contest, and affects it by modifying prior winning probabilities. This is in contrast to the standard rent-seeking contest that implicitly assumes that the regulator allocates the rent according to relative rent-seeking outlays. Nevertheless, this modeling has several drawbacks, as van Winden (1999) notes.

In order to capture relative distance, it is assumed that policymaker utility is a weighted function of overall rent-seeking outlays,[5] according to the following specification:

$$U = U(\mu_1 x_1 + \mu_2 x_2), \tag{14.4}$$

with $U(\cdot)$ a concave and strictly increasing function.

Obviously, the weights of different players in expression (14.4) have to be consistent with their relative positions. Hence it is assumed that $\mu_1 > \mu_2$, which implies that the regulator values more one dollar spent in rent-seeking by player one than the same amount spent by player two; a preference that arises from player one being closer to the regulator.

Therefore, the regulator's problem is to choose a prior probability q that maximizes utility as per expression (14.4).

3. ANALYSIS OF EQUILIBRIUM IN THE SIMPLE MODEL

Let us consider the objective functions defined as per equations (14.3) and (14.4), and define rents as follows:

$$R_1 = R \text{ and } R_2 = aR \text{ with } a > 0 \tag{14.5}$$

In other words, a measures the degree of asymmetry in rents in the contest.

3.1 The Players

In the Nash equilibrium first order conditions state that any player will devote resources to rent-seeking up to the point where the marginal increase in the expected value of a rent is equal to marginal costs:

$$\frac{\partial p_i}{\partial x_i} R_i = 1$$

Given expression (14.3), Nash solutions for both players are given by

$$x_1^N = \frac{a(1 - q)qR}{(a + q - aq)^2} \tag{14.6}$$

$$x_2^N = \frac{a^2(1 - q)qR}{(a + q - aq)^2} \tag{14.7}$$

Second order conditions are

$$\Delta_i = R_i \frac{\partial p_i}{\partial x_i} < 0, \tag{14.8}$$

which always hold.[6]

Results on rent-dissipation are the same as those commonly found in the literature – see for instance Nitzan (1994). Note that the relative size of rent-seeking by the two players is given by

$$\frac{x_1}{x_2} = \frac{1}{a}, \tag{14.9}$$

as expected. Hence the individual amount of rent-dissipation depends on the degree of asymmetry of the contest.

Full differentiation of the first order conditions leads to the following derivatives:

$$\frac{\partial x_1}{\partial x_2} = -\frac{R}{\Delta_1}\frac{\partial^2 p_1}{\partial x_1 \partial x_2} = -\frac{x_2 - q(x_1 + x_2)}{2qx_2} \tag{14.10}$$

$$\frac{\partial x_1}{\partial q} = -\frac{R}{\Delta_1}\frac{\partial^2 p_1}{\partial x_1 \partial q} = -\frac{x_2 - q(x_1 + x_2)}{2(q-1)q^2} \tag{14.11}$$

$$\frac{\partial x_1}{\partial R} = -\frac{1}{\Delta_1}\frac{\partial p_1}{\partial x_1} > 0 \tag{14.12}$$

for interest group one, and

$$\frac{\partial x_2}{\partial x_1} = -\frac{aR}{\Delta_2}\frac{\partial^2 p_2}{\partial x_1 \partial x_2} = \frac{1}{2}\left(\frac{q}{q-1} + \frac{x_1}{x_2}\right) \tag{14.13}$$

$$\frac{\partial x_2}{\partial q} = -\frac{aR}{\Delta_2}\frac{\partial^2 p_2}{\partial x_2 \partial q} = \frac{q(x_1 + x_2) - x_2}{2(q-1)^2 q} \tag{14.14}$$

$$\frac{\partial x_2}{\partial R} = -\frac{a}{\Delta_2}\frac{\partial p_2}{\partial x_2} > 0 \tag{14.15}$$

$$\frac{\partial x_2}{\partial a} = -\frac{R}{\Delta_2}\frac{\partial p_2}{\partial x_2} > 0 \tag{14.16}$$

for group two. Except for expressions (14.12), (14.15) and (14.16), which all have a definite sign,[7] the rest of the expressions are ambiguous.

Note that the sign of expressions (14.10) and (14.13) – best response for a player to an increase in rent-seeking outlays by the other – is undefined. However it depends on q. At the limit, as q approaches 1, expression (14.10) is positive and (14.13) negative. For $q=1/2$ – both players have the same prior, i.e. the standard rent-seeking model – the sign of these depends on the rent asymmetry parameter a. Hence if $a>1$ expression (14.10) is negative and (14.13) is positive: an increase in effort by a competitor decreases the effort of player one but increases the effort of player two. In general, other things being equal,

- The larger the prior q the more likely that (14.10) will be positive, and (14.13) negative.
- The smaller the value of a, the more likely that (14.10) will be positive and (14.13) negative.

With respect to changes in q, expressions (14.11) and (14.14) show equally ambiguous results. An increase in the prior probability of winning a rent either increases or decreases rent-seeking outlays of player one. This, again, depends to a large extent on the valuation of the rent. The larger a is, the more likely it will be negative, and hence an increase in probability decreases group one's efforts. For group two, note that expression (14.14) will always be positive if $x_1 > x_2$, which is the case for $a<1$. If $a>1$, then expression (14.14) may be positive or negative depending on the prior probability, q. If it does not hold, it can still be positive for certain prior probability values of $q>q^*$. In fact in the next subsection we will see that maximizing outlays when $a>1$ implies setting q such that the elasticity of this group with respect to prior probability is null, i.e. rent-seeking outlays are perfectly inelastic with respect to q. In other words, if the rent valuation is not symmetric, then it is in the interest of the regulator to choose q such that expression (14.14) is zero.

3.2 The Regulator

The first order condition of the regulator is

$$U'\left\{\mu_1\frac{\partial x_1}{\partial q} + \mu_2\frac{\partial x_2}{\partial q}\right\} = 0$$

where U' is the first derivative of the utility function. This expression shows that the policymaker will increase (decrease) q up to the point where the weighted marginal increase in x_1 is equal to the weighted marginal decrease in x_2.

Given $U(\cdot)$ is a concave and strictly increasing function, it is trivial to show that the utility of the regulator will be maximum for a value q such that $X=x_1+x_2$ is maximum. Overall rent-seeking outlays will be maximized when

$$q^* = \frac{a}{1+a} \tag{14.17}$$

Note that (14.17) means that the policymaker will set q depending solely on the degree of asymmetry in the rent. This occurs, independently of the values of the rest of the parameters – and more specifically the weights μ_1 and μ_2. However this could be an inconsistent policy for $a<1$, i.e. $R_1<R_2$, as the optimal vaue for q will be less than 1/2. Should this be the case it is assumed that the regulator sticks to $q=1/2$.

How should we interpret the behavior of the regulator in this setup? Think in terms of a policymaker allocating a license for a monopoly among two alternative groups. To simplify the setting, let us assume that both groups face constant marginal costs, and that these are c_1 and c_2. The valuation of the license – the *Tullock rectangle* – will be larger for that group with lower marginal costs.

If player one has lower marginal costs, then $c_1<c_2$, and its rent will be larger: $R_1>R_2$ or $a<1$.[8] In this case $q^*<½$, see expression (14.17), but the regulator sticks to the standard rent-seeking model $q=1/2$, with prior probabilities equal for all participants. In this case the (in)efficiency of the process is not altered.

More interesting is the case in which interest group two has an efficiency advantage. In this case, with $a>1$, $q^*>1/2$: the regulator – which is a rent-seeking outlays maximizer – will alter the *ex-post* probability of players such that:

$$p_1 = \frac{qx_1}{qx_1 + (1-q)x_2} = \frac{\frac{a}{a+1}x_1}{\frac{a}{a+1}x_1 + \left(1 - \frac{a}{a+1}\right)ax_1} = \frac{1}{2}.$$

Hence the regulator equalizes the *ex-post* likelihood of obtaining a rent for both groups, even though the resources invested by interest group two are larger: $x_2=a\,x_1$. In this case the regulator requests larger efforts by the more efficient group. This is summarized in Result 1.

Result 1 In the biased rent-seeking game, if the inefficient competitor is closer to the regulator, it will grant it an advantage in rent-seeking. As a result, the contestants will overbid in the rent-seeking game.

Note that this setup is inefficient for two reasons. First, because independently of the relative efficiency of both players, the inefficient one has the same probability as the efficient one. Second, because rent-seeking outlays exceed those of a competitive contest, thus increasing the dissipation and thus the misallocation of resources in the political process.

4. AN EXTENDED MODEL: RENT-SEEKING AND INFORMATION TRANSMISSION

In the previously described model, interest groups choose their equilibrium outlays so as to maximize the *ex-post* probability of winning. The regulator, in turn, defines a value q^* that maximizes the effort of interest groups.

However, it is questionable whether the regulator holds all available information on the structure and parameters of the game. In the basic setup the optimal choice of q is dependent on a, which we assume is known to all players. If we relax this assumption, then agents can exploit the asymmetry of the game to their benefit.

In this section the role of information as a source of conflict is explored. Competition between both groups is modified so that players are allowed to send messages to affect the regulator's behavior. In this case, the predatory nature of competition can modify the efficiency results of the previous section.

4.1 Structure of the Modified Game

Now, let us begin by defining the structure of the modified game. Let us assume that there is an asymmetric information problem: while players know the value a, the regulator has only some prior belief about it. In the extended game, interest groups, by sending messages, play an informational role in public choice, as in van Winden (1999).[9] If messages spread information about the structure of the game and alter the outcomes of collective action, players can affect the net value of the regulation by sending them. Let us consider this point.

Let us assume that the game takes place in two stages. In the first stage the regulator announces a value for the parameter q and players try to affect it by sending messages.[10] In the second stage, where rent-seeking occurs, groups compete for the rent, given the underlying structure of the game – defined in the first stage.

In short, the structure of the game is as follows. Firstly, the regulator sets an initial value q in accordance with her preferences. Note that in order to make the optimal decision, the policymaker should be perfectly informed about the structure of the game and the relevant valuations of the players, i.e. a. However, this reflects the valuation of a given regulation for a player and can depend – among other things – on the efficiency and cost structure of the group. It is assumed, that the regulator has some expectation about a that is affected by the release of information by both groups.

Table 14.1 Payoff matrix for the first stage of the game: row is player one and column is player two

	Sends	Does not
Sends	$-m$ $-m$	B_2 B_1
Does not	A_2 A_1	C_2 C_1

Secondly, interest groups spread information – i.e. send costly messages – to alter the regulator assessment of a. A fixed unit cost m per message is assumed. The aim of players is to alter the equilibrium value q^*: while interest group one tries to increase it, interest group two tries to lower it. Hence messages have *opposite informational contents*. In this way, if either group is the only one sending a message, the information received by the policymakers is unambiguous. However, if both groups send messages, these contradict each other and their informational content leads to ambiguous outcomes.

For simplicity let us assume that the policymaker is *conflict averse*. By this, we mean that the policymaker believes a message if it is the only one received. However, if the regulator receives contradicting messages – i.e., both groups send messages – then the game is over and a rent is not allocated. One can think in terms of an ideological conflict in which conflicting messages reveal the arbitrary nature of the political allocation of rents and can, ultimately, affect in a negative way the utility of a regulator, by, for instance, reducing the likelihood of reelection in the case of politicians, or reducing the size of a budget in case of a bureaucrat.

Finally, note that messages are predatory in the sense that they try to overestimate the efficiency of the opponent. By doing so, interest groups diminish the opponent's prior probability in the game, as a consequence of the optimal selection of q. Hence, if the regulator holds some prior belief on a, the informational content of messages by player one will be $a'>a$, while those of player two will be $a''<a$. Let us assume then that the message is just a value for parameter a, such that group one sends a' and group two sends a'', with $a''<a<a'$. Additionally, a symmetric structure for messages is assumed, i.e. opposite messages consist of adding a differential h to the pivotal a value. Hence $a'=a+h$, and $a''=a-h$.

Payoffs in the first stage game can be described as in Table 14.1. In it, each player may or may not send a message to affect the policymaker. When both agents send messages the policymaker withdraws a regulation and payoffs are negative, being equal to the unit cost of sending messages m. When no agent sends a message, then equilibrium payoffs are given by the pair (C_1, C_2). When either player sends a message and the other does not, payoffs depend on the actual values of a and q and the nature of the messages, i.e. whether these are true or sent as a threat to deter competitors from sending.

Two alternative scenarios are analyzed: first, a setup in which a is the actual value defining the setup, i.e. the regulator expectations are right; second, a setup in which $a'<a$ will be analyzed. Note, in the first scenario the potential messages sent will be false ones, while in the second only one of the groups will be sending true messages.

4.2 Equilibria for Unbiased Regulator Expectations

In this setting it is assumed that the beliefs of the regulator are correct. However players have incentives to send messages to modify the optimal value of the prior probability q^*. By doing so, players underestimate their rent valuation or overestimate the rent valuation of the competitor.

One can analyze the equilibrium of this stage of the game by looking at the payoffs matrix. If player two sends a message, then the best reply for player one is not to send, as $A_1 > -m$. The same applies for player two if player one sends, as $B_1 > -m$. On the contrary, if player two does not send a message, then player one has incentives to do so, if $B_1 > C_1$. Similarly, if group one does not send a message, then group two will do so if $A_2 > C_2$. Assume that both conditions hold. Then the first stage defined by the payoffs matrix in Table 14.1 is a coordination game with two equilibria in which players should coordinate to take different actions: $\{S,D\}$ or $\{D,S\}$.

What are the payoffs of both players in the overall game? Before proceeding let us normalize the rent such that $R=R_1=1$. The payoffs of the game now without messages are:

$$C_1 = \frac{1}{4} \tag{14.18}$$

$$C_2 = \frac{a}{4}. \tag{14.19}$$

Figure 14.1 shows the equilibrium of the rent-seeking game when player one sends the message $a'>a$. In it, actual reaction curves are $r_i(x_j)$, while $r'_1(x_2)$ refers to the hypothetical (and false) situation a'. Point A is the equilibrium of rent-seeking outlays without messages. However player two's response depends on whether he actually believes the message. If he does, then he will consider $r'_1(x_2)$ as the relevant reaction curve for player one, and his best reply will be x_2^B. If this is the case, the optimal response

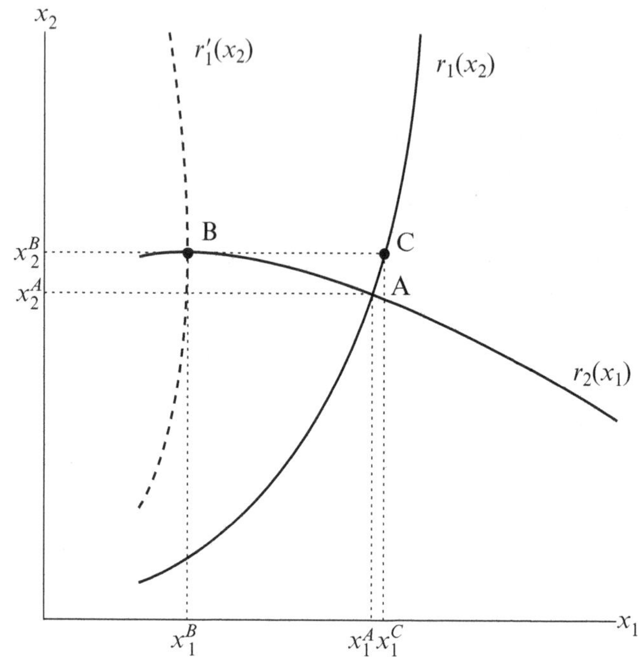

Figure 14.1 Equilibrium with player one sending a false message (a'>a)

of group one is point *C*, the actual best response, and rent-seeking efforts will be x_1^C.

Figure 14.2 analyzes the opposite situation. In it, group two sends the false message $a''<a$. The actual equilibrium is *A*, with player one not believing the message. However, if he does believe it, the relevant point for player one is *B*, in which case player two's best response is given by *C*.

Two comments are important. First, rent-seeking outlays differ depending on whether messages are believed or not. Second, given the shape of reaction curves the equilibrium of the game without messages is the point where both have a zero derivative:

$$\frac{\partial x_i}{\partial x_j} = 0.$$

which is where the regulator ensures maximum outlays. To announce $a'>a$ when it is not true increases q^*, shifting the equilibrium to a point where the slope of r_1 is positive and that of r_2 is negative. Conversely, announcing $a''<a$ changes the equilibrium to a point where the slope of r_1 is negative and that of r_2 is positive.

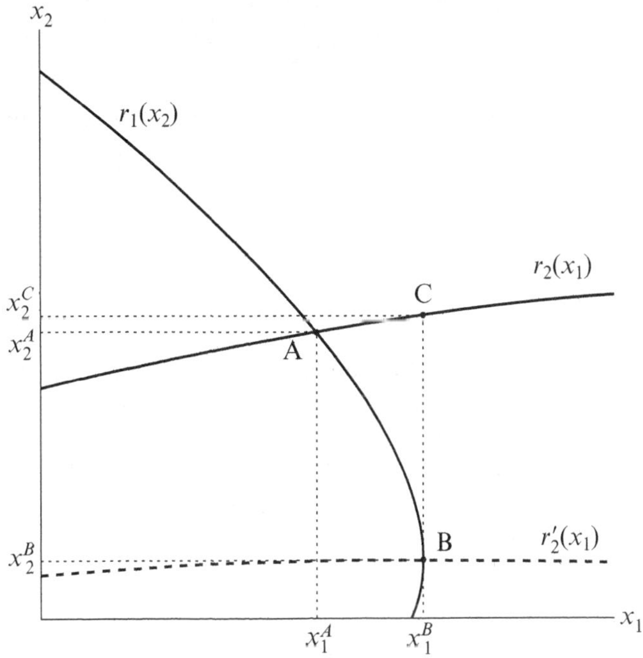

Figure 14.2 Equilibrium with player two sending a false message $(a''<a)$

How do messages affect payoffs? When player one sends a message and player two believes it, then the value of payoffs is:

$$B_1 = p_1 - x_1 - m \tag{14.20}$$

where

$$p_1 = 1 - \frac{\sqrt{a/a'}}{2} > \frac{1}{2},$$

and

$$x_1 = \frac{2a'\sqrt{a/a'} - a}{4a'} < \frac{1}{4}.$$

Note that – compared to the equilibrium without messages – player one will be better off in this case if m is smaller than the net gains. In this case player two gets

$$B_2 = \frac{1}{4}a\left(2\sqrt{\frac{a}{a'}} - 1\right). \quad (14.21)$$

On the contrary, if player two does not believe the message both players receive:

$$B_1 = \frac{a' + a}{a} - \frac{1}{4} - m \quad (14.22)$$

$$B_2 = \frac{a^3}{(a + a')^2} \quad (14.23)$$

Again equilibrium payoffs for the player that sends the message exceed those of the equilibrium without messages. Interestingly, it can be shown that there are no significant differences in payoffs in both cases: only for $a' >> a$ there is a disadvantage for the group believing a message.[11]

Now, let us turn to group two. If it sends a message and group one believes it we see that:

$$A_1 = \frac{3}{4} - \frac{a}{a + a''} \quad (14.24)$$

$$A_2 = a + \frac{a''}{4} - \sqrt{aa''} - m. \quad (14.25)$$

If player one does not believe the message

$$A_1 = \frac{a''^2}{(a + a'')^2} \quad (14.26)$$

$$A_2 = \frac{a^2}{a'' + a} - \frac{a}{4} - m. \quad (14.27)$$

Again it can be shown that the differences in payoffs are not significant unless $a'' << a$. In the rest of the setting it will be assumed that the player not sending the message does not believe it. One can interpret this assumption in two alternative ways. Implicitly we are assuming that competitors know the structure of the game although the regulator may not. Alternatively we can think of this scenario as part of an incomplete information game in which players are not sure about the structure of the game but have a probability distribution over the outcomes. Hence they assume a positive probability in this scenario of messages being false.

Now define ρ_i as the probability that group i sends a false message. Then a mixed strategy equilibrium exists and its solution is given by:

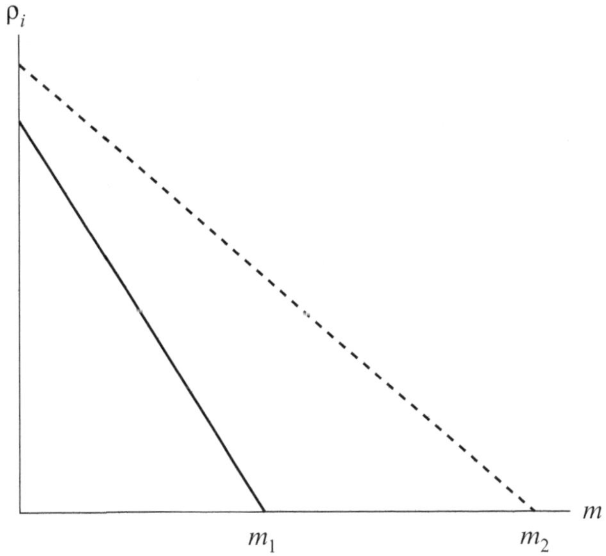

Figure 14.3 Boundary values for the probability of message sending in terms of unit cost m*: group one in solid black; group two in broken*

$$\rho_1 = \frac{C_2 - B_2}{C_2 - (A_2 + B_2 + m)} \tag{14.28}$$

$$\rho_2 = \frac{C_1 - A_1}{C_1 - (A_1 + B_1 + m)}, \tag{14.29}$$

with A_i, B_i and C_i as given above. Note that expressions (14.28) and (14.29) are defined in terms of the payoffs and of the cost of message sending. Hence a mixed equilibrium may or may not exist depending on m. From these expressions, player one will send a message if

$$m < \frac{B_1(1 - \rho_2) - C_1(1 - \rho_2) - A_1\rho_2}{\rho_2}. \tag{14.30}$$

Similarly player two will send if

$$m < \frac{A_2(1 - \rho_1) - C_2(1 - \rho_1) - B_2\rho_1}{\rho_1}. \tag{14.31}$$

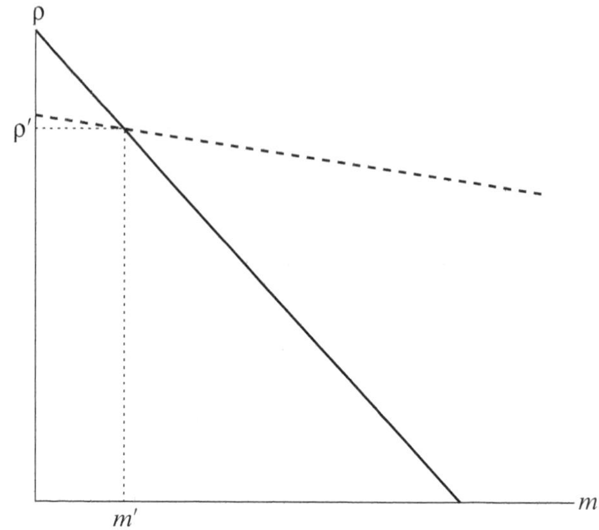

Figure 14.4 *Boundary values for the probability of message sending in terms of its cost: the case of crossing curves (large* h*): group one in solid black; group two in broken*

Figure 14.3 shows the set of feasible (m, ρ_i) combinations for both interest groups. Note that these lie below the lines which represent the boundary values (m, ρ_i). It shows that sending messages is compatible with greater message sending costs, m, in the case of group two – due to its efficiency advantage – than in group one. There are two elements that affect the feasible set:

- First, the actual asymmetry a. An increase in a decreases the slope (in absolute value) for both groups. As curves become flatter the probability of a message sending equilibrium declines.
- Second, the information contained in the message, i.e. the differential h. A larger differential, shifts both curves upwards and to the right. However, it also affects the relative slope of both curves such that for a large enough h, both curves cross – see Figure 14.4. Then player two has no clear advantage over player one in all the feasible range. In other words, for any message cost below m', player one has an advantage.

Expressions (14.30) and (14.31) define a maximum value m_i for each player, such that given a probability ρ_i that the opponent sends a message, for any $m>m_i$ the player will not. Note that the boundary (maximum) m_i values are given by the zero probability case:

$$m_1 = \frac{a' - a}{2(a' + a)},$$

and

$$m_2 = a\frac{a - a''}{2(a'' + a)}.$$

In general, m_1 and m_2 are upper bounds for all feasible values of m – those compatible with a positive probability ρ_i.

Finally the following conclusions apply in this scenario.

Result 2 There are three alternative message sending equilibria, for different message sending costs m_1 and m_2 such that:

1. for $m<m_1$ then both groups may send messages with positive probability.
2. for $m_1<m<m_2$ only group two sends messages with probability one.
3. for $m>m_2$ no group sends messages.

According to a threshold value h^* two alternative situations can be distinguished in the equilibrium in which both agents send messages.

Result 3 For every $h<h^*$, the mixed strategy equilibrium always implies $\rho_1>\rho_2$. On the contrary, for $h>h^*$, the mixed strategy equilibrium is compatible with $\rho_1\leq\rho_2$.

In other words, this result states that for a given cost m the probability of group one sending a message that is compatible with group two sending a message depends on the differential h. If it is small enough, for $h<h^*$, then $\rho_1>\rho_2$ and group two is willing to take a higher risk when sending messages, a situation which is shown in Figure 14.3. However if differential h is large enough, $h>h^*$, the equilibrium would be that presented in Figure 14.4. If $m>m'$ the previous result applies. However for $m<m'$ player one will be more willing to take the risk of disagreement, and hence $\rho_1<\rho_2$.

4.3 Equilibria for Biased Regulator Expectations

The second scenario is one in which the messages sent by one of the groups are true. Obviously, it cannot be the case that both players send true messages – as these are of opposite informational content. Therefore, we assume that player two sends true messages. Surprisingly this scenario is similar to the previous one with a minor change. Now the actual relative valuation of the rent is given by a'' while the regulator holds the expectation a. Hence, player one may send the (false) message a', with $a'>a>a''$.

Again the payoffs matrix are those in Table 14.1 with some modifications. Payoffs for both players sending messages remain unchanged. If none sends, then payoffs will be

$$C_1 = \frac{\sqrt{a}}{2\sqrt{a''}} - \frac{1}{4} \tag{14.32}$$

$$C_2 = 1 + \frac{a}{4} - \frac{1}{2}\frac{\sqrt{a}}{\sqrt{a''}}(1 + a'') \tag{14.33}$$

If player two sends a message then

$$A_1 = \frac{1}{4} \tag{14.34}$$

$$A_2 = \frac{a''}{4} - m \tag{14.35}$$

And finally, if player one sends – not believed by player two – then

$$B_1 = \frac{a'\sqrt{a}}{(a + a')\sqrt{a''}} - \frac{aa'}{(a + a')^2} - m \tag{14.36}$$

$$B_2 = \frac{(\sqrt{aa'} - (a + a')\sqrt{a''})^2}{(a + a')^2} \tag{14.37}$$

Note, in this setting there is an asymmetry in trustworthiness: player one's messages are not believed by two, while player two's messages are believed by one. Again, it is assumed that m is low enough so that we have two pure strategy equilibria: $\{S,D\}$ and $\{D,S\}$. Additionally, there is a mixed strategy equilibrium $\{\rho_1,\rho_2\}$, where ρ_i is the probability that player i sends a message.

Note that given the mixed strategy probabilities, the qualitative

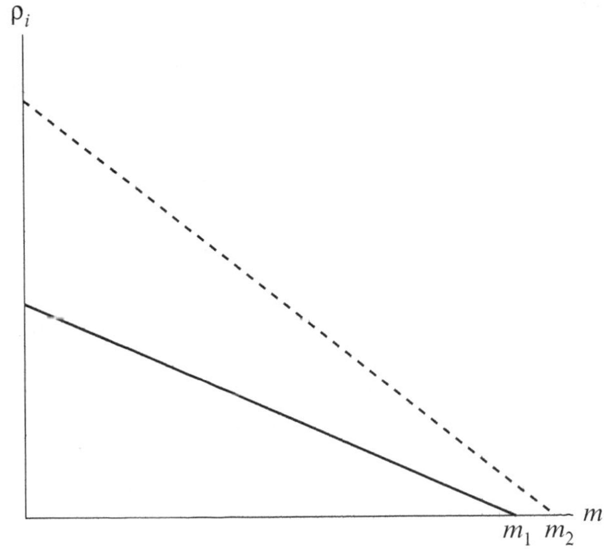

Figure 14.5 *Boundary values for the probability of message sending in terms of its cost: group one in solid black; group two in broken*

properties of the equilibrium change with m – the cost of sending messages. These are presented in Figure 14.5. Interestingly, the curve for player two always lies above that of player one. Both curves are affected by a and h. Increasing a decreases the absolute value of the slope of the curve of group two and increases that of group one. The former becomes flatter and the latter becomes steeper. All this leads to an increasing divergence of m_1 and m_2.

On the other hand, increasing h shifts both curves upward and reduces (the absolute value of) the slope of the curve of group one, but increases that of group two. This ensures m_1 and m_2 converge. In any case both curves only cross at $\rho_i=0$, leading to $m_1=m_2$.

Given this, Result 2 holds. However for a large enough $\bar{h}$, the advantage of player two, in terms of the higher costs of messages, vanishes. This leads to

Result 4 For $h \geq \bar{h}$, m_1 and m_2 converge leaving only two equilibria:

1. One for $m<m_1$, in which both groups send messages with positive probability.
2. One for $m>m_1$, without message sending.

Finally it should be noted that:

Result 5 The mixed strategy equilibrium always implies $\rho_1 > \rho_2$.

All in all, Result 5 implies that player two always takes more risk than player one in the biased expectations' setup.

5. DISCUSSION AND CONCLUSIONS

We have analyzed a model of rent-seeking in which a regulator affects the probability of winning a rent-seeking contest by assigning a prior probability to particular groups winning. This setup has alternative interpretations. It could reflect a policymaker's preferences for the different outcomes of the game, linking behavior with ideology. However this is not the only possible explanation and one could, alternatively, think of an initially biased game. In it, one of the players would have an advantage with the regulator seeking to maximize the resources invested in the political market.

If efficiency is the yardstick by which a rent-seeking contest is assessed, then the described model is at best as inefficient as a standard rent-seeking game. Rent-dissipation can be even greater when the player closer to the regulator places the lowest value on a rent. If one interprets this value in terms of the relative efficiency of rent-seekers, then a lower value implies a more inefficient use of regulation. Hence, the regulator introduces a new distortion into the process.

One interesting feature of the model is that it explicitly identifies the informational role of interest groups. These spread information by sending messages that ultimately aim at influencing the policymaker. This modified contest has been modeled as a two stage game: in the first stage interest groups try to alter the structure of a rent-seeking contest played out in the second stage. Disseminating information is a costly activity that interest groups undertake only if benefits outweigh costs. For a certain range of costs, the first stage becomes a coordination game in which players invest resources in altering the outcomes of the game with a certain probability. Here, three possible equilibria arise: one in which both players send messages, one in which only the most efficient player sends a message and one in which no player sends messages.

Interestingly, after introducing this stage, the rent-seeking game can be less inefficient if the cost of message sending does not offset efficiency gains. If this is the case, the model results in an unambiguous reduction in rent-seeking activities.

Finally, it should be stressed that the setup just described does not rule out influencing the regulator by targeting the public. In other words, information need not be explicitly sent directly to the policy-maker but could also be sent to the electorate. Related to this, if one assumes that a player can commit to a strategy, an interesting outcome emerges in terms of a regulator's policy function. Commitment will imply a sequential move in the second stage game and will significantly modify the outcome of the rent-seeking contest. Altering the second stage affects also the first stage with some clear consequences: if the interest group that moves first is the one with an efficiency advantage, then it significantly increases its *ex-post* probability of winning.[12] This affects the optimal choice of the regulator, which now takes into account not only the degree of asymmetry but also the relative weights of interest groups in its objective function, μ_i, which can be interpreted as the relevance of an interest group in the electorate, or its power to affect the political process.

NOTES

1. See for example Brooks and Heijdra (1989), or Nitzan (1994) for surveys on the standard literature.
2. This perspective departs from the original analysis by Tullock (1967). See also Tullock (1980).
3. The process by which an individual becomes a saint.
4. As Kooreman and Schoobeek (1997) show, the Tullock contest probability function is the only specification that satisfies some plausible conditions.
5. We follow Appelbaum and Katz (1986) by explicitly making the regulator's utility depend on rent-seeking outlays.
6. For group one it is $\frac{2(q-1)q^2x_2R}{(q(x_1-x_2)+x_2)^3}$. For interest group two it is $-\frac{2a(q-1)^2q^2x_2R}{(q(x_1-x_2)+x_2)^3}$. Both are negative.
7. These show a well known result, i.e.: rent-seeking outlays are positively related to the size of the rent.
8. This is the textbook case of a monopoly producing in the elastic part of the demand curve.
9. See also Potters and van Winden (1992).
10. These could be interpreted, using Congleton's (1991) terminology, as 'policy messages': messages that are sent in the short run in order to affect the behavior of the regulator which responds to a mix of both proximity – which can be understood in ideological terms – and self-interest.
11. This difference is significant whenever $a' > 3\,a$, which is a somewhat exaggerated message.
12. Several authors have analyzed the effects of sequential moves in a rent-seeking setting. For instance Dixit (1987), Epstein and Hefeker (2001), Johnson (1990), Lien (2002) and Linster (1993).

REFERENCES

Appelbaum, E. and E. Katz (1986), 'Transfer seeking and avoidance: on the full social costs of rent seeking', *Public Choice*, **48**, 175–81.

Brooks, M.A. and B.J. Heijdra (1989), 'An exploration of rent seeking', *The Economic Record*, **65**, 32–50.

Congleton, R.D. (1991), 'Ideological conviction and persuasion in the rent-seeking society', *Journal of Public Economics*, **44**, 65–86.

Dixit, A. (1987), 'Strategic behavior in contests', *American Economic Review*, **77**, 891–8.

Epstein, G. and C. Hefeker (2001), 'Lobbying and concessions: comparing Nash to Stackelberg games', *Public Choice*, **109**, 175–81.

Gradstein, M. (1995), 'Intensity of competition, entry and entry deterrence in rent seeking contests', *Economics and Politics*, **7**, 79–91.

Gual, J. and F. Trillas (2006), 'Telecommunications policies: measurement and determinants', *Review of Network Economics*, **5** (2), 249–72.

Johnson, P. (1990), 'Asymmetries in political entry', *European Journal of Political Economy*, **6**, 377–96.

Kooreman, P. and L. Schoonbeek (1997), 'The specification of the probability function in Tullock's rent-seeking contest', *Economic Letters*, **56**, 59–61.

Lien, D. (2002), 'Rent seeking and allocative efficiency: the case of bribery', *Pacific Economic Review*, **7**, 123–33.

Linster, B. (1993), 'Stackelberg rent-seeking', *Public Choice*, **77**, 307–21.

Martimort, D. and A. Semenov (2007a), 'The pluralistic view of politics: asymmetric lobbyists, ideological uncertainty and political entry', *Economics Letters*, **97** (2), 155–61.

Martimort, D. and A. Semenov (2007b), 'Political biases in lobbying under asymmetric information', *Journal of the European Economic Association*, **5** (2–3), 614–23.

Martimort, D. and A. Semenov (2008), 'Ideological uncertainty and lobbying competition', *Journal of Public Economics*, **92** (3–4), 456–81.

McKay, A. (2010), 'The effects of interest groups' ideology on their PAC and lobbying expenditures', *Business and Politics*, **12** (2), August, DOI: 10.2202/1469-3569.

Nitzan, S. (1994), 'Modelling rent-seeking contests', *European Journal of Political Economy*, **10**, 41–60.

Potters, J. and F. van Winden (1992), 'Lobbying and asymmetric information', *Public Choice*, **74**, 269–92.

Tullock, G. (1967), 'The welfare costs of tariffs, monopolies and theft', *Western Economic Journal*, **5**, 224–32.

Tullock, G. (1980), 'Efficient rent seeking', in James M. Buchanan, Robert D. Tollison and Gordon Tullock (eds), *Toward a Theory of the Rent Seeking Society*, College Station, Texas: A&M University Press, pp. 97–112.

van Winden, F. (1999), 'On the economic theory of interest groups: towards a group frame of reference in political economics', *Public Choice*, **29** (1), 1–29.

15. Cooperation in multilateral PDs: self-selected vs pre-defined groups

Viktor J. Vanberg

1. INTRODUCTION

This chapter is concerned with the issue of cooperative behavior in settings where adverse incentives exist. This is typically the case, for instance, in social dilemma situations of the Prisoner's Dilemma (PD) type. My specific focus will be on the issue of cooperative behavior in *multi*lateral PDs in contrast to *bi*lateral PDs. The 'multilateral' is meant to describe social settings that cannot be factored down into elementary bilateral relations between agents. Multilateral PDs in this sense are exemplified by the kind of collective goods problems involved in team production that, for instance, private firms, cooperatives, and clubs must overcome to be successful joint enterprises. In a generalized sense the term 'joint enterprise' is used here to include all joint activities in which a team surplus can be realized if all (or a sufficient number of) team-members cooperate, but which yields less than what the participants could realize in separate action if all defect.[1] In such joint enterprises a situation where all participants contribute is clearly preferable for everybody involved to a situation where all 'defect' or seek to free-ride, yet the PD-nature of incentives works against the cooperative outcome.

The contemporary discussion on cooperation among self-interested agents in PD-type settings has been strongly influenced by Robert Axelrod's (1984) study on the evolution of cooperation, a study that focused exclusively on interaction problems that can be modeled as repeated bilateral PDs. In later work on the evolution of norms Axelrod (1986) has extended his research to the study of cooperation in a multilateral PD-setting. Following Axelrod's methodology of comparing the payoffs earned by alternative strategies playing repeated PD games in tournament-type simulation experiments, Vanberg and Congleton (1992) have examined how adding an exit option to the 'cooperate or defect' choice in the standard repeated PD affects the viability of cooperative strategies or behavioral programs. In Axelrod's simulation experiments tit-for-tat turned out to be the most successful behavioral program in standard repeated PDs. The main result of the Vanberg and Congleton (1992) study was that in a repeated Prisoner's Dilemma with Exit (PDE)[2] a conditionally cooperative program that never defects but walks away from defectors (i.e. it always cooperates if and when it plays) outperformed competing programs, including tit-for-tat. While the analysis in Vanberg and Congleton (1992) was limited to pairwise interactions or bilateral PDEs, in Congleton and Vanberg (2001) the analysis has been extended to multilateral PDEs, with simulation experiments on the viability of alternative strategies in groups or 'teams' of three persons.

The purpose of the present chapter is to explore some of the more general theoretical aspects of the issues that are the subject of the above-mentioned studies. What will be examined, in particular, is the nature and significance of the differences that separate multilateral PDs from multi-person settings that can be disaggregated into bilateral PDs. A particular focus will be on the role that the availability of an exit option can be expected to play.

2. BILATERAL AND MULTILATERAL PDS

Robert Axelrod's 1984 study on the evolution of cooperation was based on the idea of comparing alternative strategies for playing repeated PD games in tournament-type simulation experiments. As noted, his original research focused on bilateral PDs,[3] and it generated the well known result, that tit-for-tat outperforms a wide range of competing behavioral strategies in such interactive settings. Tit-for-tat, the strategy that begins with cooperation and then 'responds in kind,' has long been known in the social science literature under the name of *reciprocity*.[4]

For the purposes of this chapter it is of particular interest to compare Axelrod's *The Evolution of Cooperation* (1984) with his later contribution 'An evolutionary approach to norms' (1986) in which he seeks to explore how a norm like 'not to cheat on an exam' can be expected to become respected, using, again, computer simulations as research tool.[5] In contrast to the former, the latter study is about a multilateral rather than a bilateral PD. It is concerned with a group-problem that cannot be factored down into two-party relations. There is no specific counterpart who is negatively or positively affected by a candidate's choice to cheat (to defect) or to be honest (to cooperate). Instead, the harm or benefits caused by such behavior affect everybody in the relevant group. And it is significant that reciprocity or tit-for-tat, while playing a central role in Axelrod's first study, plays no role at all in his later contribution. The reason for this should be obvious. In bilateral relations the principle 'to respond in kind' has an unambiguous meaning. This is, however, not the case where more than two persons are involved, except in situations in which all other parties either uniformly cooperate or uniformly defect. In multilateral settings with non-uniform behavior tit-for-tat is not a meaningful strategy.[6]

The difference between multilateral and bilateral PDs, reflected in Axelrod's two studies, is not, as one might be inclined to conclude, merely about the number of players involved. Whether or not a multi-person setting can be disaggregated into bilateral relations depends on the *nature* of the underlying 'problem of cooperation.' Two-person PDs can differ in this regard no less than many-person settings, though the difference is of little consequence in the two-person case. In regard to the nature of the underlying problem of cooperation one must distinguish, I submit, between what one may call *exchange PDs* and *joint enterprise PDs* respectively. By exchange PD I mean the kind of incentive structure that is exemplified by traders who face the choice of either dealing honestly (to cooperate) or cheating (to defect) in their exchange transactions. By joint enterprise PD, on the other hand, I mean the kind of dilemma situation that is illustrated by persons involved in a team project, who face the choice of either contributing their fair share to the team effort (to cooperate) or shirking (to defect).

As noted, behaviorally the difference between the two types of problems is not of much relevance, as long as the number of players does not exceed two. Where two persons interact, reciprocity or tit-for-tat can work as a mechanism of mutual behavioral conditioning and can help to promote cooperation, no matter what the nature of the dilemma is. The difference between exchange PDs and joint enterprise PDs becomes, however, apparent as the number of players grows beyond two. In the case of exchange PDs, an increase in the number of players beyond two does not change the nature of the underlying PD problem. As more players are added to an exchange setting – or in other words, as more traders enter a market – the dilemmas involved remain strictly bilateral. An exchange system, however large and complex, can be conceptually disaggregated into bilateral relations. By contrast, as the number of players involved in a joint enterprise increases beyond two, the nature of the underlying dilemma changes from a bilateral to a genuine multilateral PD that cannot be decomposed conceptually into separable bilateral relations. In other words, when we speak of the 'problem of cooperation' in many-person settings, it makes a critical difference whether we refer to exchange PDs or to joint enterprise PDs.[7]

Axelrod's 'Evolutionary approach to norms' (1986) is concerned with a problem that falls into the 'joint enterprise' category.[8] And, as already noted, in this study tit-for-tat plays no role whatsoever in generating cooperation. Instead, a critical explanatory role is played by assumptions about 'vengefulness' as an inherent disposition that makes persons willing to pay 'an enforcement cost without any direct return' (ibid.: 1100), not only to punish others whom they see cheating, but also to punish others for failing to punish defectors. It is instructive to reflect on the reasons for this contrast.

Where two persons interact their actions are necessarily 'targeted' in the sense that, whatever one of them does, it affects for good or ill the other. To respond to the other party's choice by cooperating, means to encourage whatever it was the other party did. To respond by defection means to discourage what the other did. Tit-for-tat can be viewed as a strategy that, in bilateral interactions, systematically rewards the other party for cooperating and punishes defection. Such a strategy makes perfect sense in dealing with an agent who can learn from success and failure. And reciprocity, the mutual playing of tit-for-tat, is nothing other than the pattern of mutual behavioral conditioning or reinforcement that results where two such agents meet.[9] It should be noted though, that the concept of reciprocity is commonly used in a more general sense, to include any strategy of conditional cooperation,[10] not just tit-for-tat as a strategy that responds *in kind*, answering defection with defection. While other strategies of reciprocity have in common with tit-for-tat that they are strategies of conditional cooperation (they cooperate only with cooperators), they differ in how they respond to their counterpart's defection. One such strategy (we may call it a retributive strategy) does not respond by defecting, but by some explicit punishing act. Another, which may be described as a defensive-moral strategy, responds to a counterpart's defection not with defection but with *exit*, i.e. by walking away from the interaction.

Whatever one may define as an equivalent to tit-for-tat for multilateral PDs,[11] because of its noted ambiguity one cannot expect such a strategy of reciprocity to play the same role in generating cooperation in multilateral PDs that tit-for-tat plays in bilateral settings. This is true for all strategies of conditional cooperation that, in their responses to other group members' behavioral choices, do not discriminate between cooperators and defectors. In multilateral PDs there is an apparent role to be played by programs that do discriminate, and that target their punishing response on defectors without discouraging other cooperators. This role can be played, for instance, by a retributive strategy, a behavioral program that, when faced with cooperators as well as defectors in a group, would continue to cooperate but would inflict, at a cost to itself, an explicit punishment on defectors. Such a strategy would obviously avoid the ambiguity of non-discriminating programs. And it would also avoid the ambiguity that is inherent in the use of the defection option as a punishing device because observers cannot easily tell whether it is motivated by the wish to punish or to exploit others.

The different strategies of conditional cooperation can be compared in terms of the protection that they provide against two kinds of error, analogous to the two types of errors in statistical testing. Type 1 error is to continue too long with an unteachable exploiter, type 2 error is to give up too early on a potential cooperator.[12] Tit-for-tat protects well against both errors. It signals one's willingness to cooperate and it protects against exploitation by allowing oneself to be taken advantage of only once. One of its drawbacks is the ambiguity inherent in its use of the defection option. While in bilateral interactions there is no ambiguity as to who is the addressee of tit-for-tat's defection, it is not unambiguously clear to others whether a player chooses to defect for his own protection or to exploit his counterpart. Others can, therefore, not know for certain whether the player is a punishing cooperator or an exploitative defector.[13] A retributive strategy that does not defect but imposes some explicit punishment on defectors avoids this ambiguity, though at a cost, namely the risk of continued exploitation and the cost of the punishing act. A defensive-moral strategy, one which never defects but walks away from defectors, is obviously applicable only where exit is feasible (Vanberg and Congleton 1992). It is a strategy that allows a player to realize the gains from cooperation with other cooperators, while protecting against exploitation. Like tit-for-tat, walking away from a defector provides a 'natural' protection against repeated exploitation, without the extra costs of retribution. The choice of the exit option, where available, allows a player to avoid the costly sequence of mutual defection that tit-for-tat may run into. The downside of this advantage is that an exiting strategy may give up too early on opponents who defect but could be conditioned into cooperation. This disadvantage is, however, of limited significance in settings where alternative partners for cooperation are easily available such that the effort to 'teach' a particular opponent may not be worthwhile. Conversely, where alternatives are not easily available or, in other words, where exit is costly, efforts to condition one's counterpart into cooperation may be worthwhile, making tit-for-tat and retributive strategies more promising than 'walk away' strategies.

An essential difference that separates multilateral PDs from bilateral interactions is the fact that the players' behavioral choices are no longer *targeted* in the sense noted above. As mentioned before, in multilateral settings tit-for-tat is not an unambiguous strategy, and the same is true, more generally, for strategies of conditional cooperation. Take the most elementary multilateral setting, a group of three players. What would a tit-for-tat player do in the second encounter if one counterpart did cooperate in the first encounter and the other defected? What would it mean to 'respond in kind'? To cooperate would mean to reward the defector along with the cooperator, and to defect would mean to punish the cooperator along with the defector. Whatever a tit-for-tat player does, the response that is appropriate for one of the counterparts is counterproductive with regard to the other.[14] Because the response is not targeted, it produces incentives as well as disincentives for cooperation, except in cases where both counterparts either cooperate or defect. A similar ambiguity exists for the program of conditional cooperation that exits from defectors, except, again, in cases where both opponents cooperate or defect. If they act differently, to walk away from the defector would mean, at the same time, to walk away from the cooperator, and to continue to cooperate with the cooperator would mean to continue to cooperate with the defector. Among the three above-mentioned conditionally cooperative strategies it is, obviously, only the retributive version that can *target* its punishment response on defectors, without discouraging, like tit-for-tat, cooperators by its own defection.

As for bilateral PDs we can also ask for multilateral PDs how alternative strategies of conditional cooperation can be expected to provide protection against the two types of errors, i.e. the error of cooperating too long with a non-convertible defector and the error of giving up too early on a potential cooperator. Because of its inherent ambiguity in multilateral PD settings, tit-for-tat can be predicted to perform poorly in both respects. Wherever it deals with counterparts who differ in their strategy choices, it gives mixed signals to cooperators as well as to defectors, providing incentives for cooperation to some, disincentives to others. In a setting with two tit-for-tat players and a strategy that defects in the initial encounter, the first two can easily end up mutually reinforcing each other's defection, even if the third strategy is one that could be converted to cooperation. Like tit-for-tat, a program that is confined to the non-targeted and non-discriminating strategies of cooperation and exit is unable to respond appropriately in settings where it faces counterparts with mixed responses. In contrast to tit-for-tat, it avoids becoming drawn into sequences of mutual defection, but it may walk away too early from potential cooperators. A retributive strategy would seem to be better prepared for handling multiple counterparts with differing strategies, because it can discriminate, in its punishment, between cooperators and defectors. Its main drawbacks are, however, first, that by continuing to cooperate despite other players' previous defection, it opens itself up for further exploitation and, second, that it bears the full cost of its punishing acts while the benefits that may result from converting defectors into cooperators are shared with non-punishing others in the group. In order for such a strategy to be individually advantageous, it would need to generate differential benefits to players who adopt it. It seems that the principal source of such benefits ought to be the enhanced prospects of ending up in successful, cooperative groups.[15]

3. MULTILATERAL PDS AND EXIT

The purpose of the previous section was to examine the principal differences that distinguish bilateral from multilateral PDs. In this section a closer look will be taken at the role that the availability of an exit option can be expected to play in multilateral or 'joint enterprise' PDs.

For the purpose at hand it is useful to draw a distinction within the 'joint enterprise' category that has some affinity to the exit issue, but needs to be distinguished from the latter, namely the distinction between, what we want to call, *self-selected* and *pre-defined* groups.[16] This distinction concerns the question of who are the principal beneficiaries of 'cooperative' activities. A group qualifies as self-selected or pre-defined relative to the activities that are viewed as 'cooperation' and 'defection.' If the potential beneficiaries of cooperation can be identified independent of, and prior to, any arrangement that may be instituted to promote cooperation, it is, in the sense the term is used here, pre-defined. By contrast, in a self-selected group the benefits of cooperation are limited to those who actually join the group. As an example, residents around a lake can be considered a pre-defined group relative to activities that may make for a cleaner lake. The same can be said for residents in a neighborhood relative to activities that deter crime in the area. In both cases the respective residents will benefit from whatever cooperative activities come forth, whether or not they are part of an organized effort that may be initiated for that purpose. By contrast, a group is, in terms of the chosen terminology, self-selected if there are no pre-defined beneficiaries, if a person can benefit from the cooperative activities in question only by joining a group organized around these activities. For example, members of a business partnership can be viewed as a self-selected group relative to activities that make the partnership economically successful. The same can be said about the members of a tennis club relative to activities that help to keep the club and its facilities functioning. In these cases the group of principal beneficiaries[17] is constituted by the joint enterprise, and whoever is not part of that enterprise is excluded from the benefits of cooperation.

As noted, the distinction between self-selected and pre-defined groups is conceptually different from the exit issue, even though there is a certain empirical affinity between the two, in the sense that one might expect self-selected groups typically to allow for easier exit than pre-defined groups.

This is, however, not necessarily so. Members of self-selected groups may choose deliberately to raise exit costs as a commitment device, in order to make cooperative gains possible that might not be available without such commitment. On the other hand, exit from pre-defined groups may be relatively easy, like, for instance, moving out of a particular neighborhood. One should expect the difference between the two types of groups to be of relevance for the dynamics of cooperation. Where the beneficiaries of cooperation are pre-defined, problems may arise – like hold-out or strategic bargaining – that are absent or less significant in self-selected groups. It would seem that to form a group of *n* willing cooperators out of a pool of *N* potential candidates ought to be easier, in general, than to secure cooperation among a group of *n* pre-defined beneficiaries who cannot be excluded from enjoying the fruits of cooperation, whether they contribute or not.

Typical examples of self-selected groups are *clubs* in the sense of Buchanan's (1965) theory of clubs[18] or *teams* in the sense of Alchian and Demsetz's (1972) concept of team-production.[19] Teams or clubs are social arrangements in which the benefits from cooperation are confined to the members of the club/team. It is the other members in the club/team who are the beneficiaries of a member's cooperation, and they are harmed by his defection (free-riding). The problem of cooperation in clubs or teams can be illustrated in terms of Gordon Tullock's (1985) parable for iterated PDs among self-selected pairs. Tullock suggests that one imagine a room with many players who can play, as pairs, an iterated PD game on computer terminals in separate booths along the walls of the room. In order to be able to play, players have to find willing counterparts. Each player remains free to walk away at any time from his respective counterpart. Tullock (1985: 1074) argues that under such conditions, where 'people voluntarily choose their own partners,' the prisoner's dilemma 'vanishes because the individual players have a strong desire to establish credibility so that they can play in future games,' and he suggests that such conditions are characteristic for trade in competitive markets. What Tullock describes illustrates the kind of setting that has been explored in Vanberg and Congleton (1992) for the repeated bilateral PDE, and it can be readily generalized to illustrate a multilateral PDE as examined in Congleton and Vanberg (2001). All we have to assume is that, instead of pairs, groups of *n* players out of *N* have to be formed who go into separate booths where they play, on *n* computer terminals, an *n*-persons PD, with the proviso that each player is free at any time to walk away from the group that he had joined, and to return to the pool from which new groups can be formed.[20]

The multilateral PDE version of Tullock's parable can be said to describe, like the bilateral original, the conditions that exist in competitive markets. More specifically, it describes the conditions under which joint ventures are established and carried out in a competitive environment where persons are free in their choices to join or not to join, and to remain or not to remain part of organized team efforts. Congleton and Vanberg (2001) report on simulation experiments that were meant to explore the survival prospects of cooperative programs in the kind of environment described by Tullock's parable, i.e. in an environment where interaction is essentially voluntary, where players can choose with whom they want to interact, and where they can walk away from undesirable counterparts. Their main result is that, at least for the case of the three-person PDE, and for the range of programs examined,[21] the addition of an exit option does, indeed, create a much more hospitable environment for cooperative programs. It allows, in particular, non-defecting programs, i.e. programs that cooperate whenever they play but walk away from defectors, to do quite well. Overall the results in Congleton and Vanberg (2001) suggest that the willingness to be a conditional cooperator can be a 'rational' disposition because it serves persons well who adopt it, at least under conditions of voluntary association. Self-selection of teams and the possibility of exiting from undesirable teams are effective instruments that allow cooperators to outperform their defection-inclined competitors.

The benefits from self-selection are, of course, greatly enhanced if players are able to mutually recognize each other's 'type' or behavioral program.[22] If cooperative and exploitative program-types can be recognized prior to the formation of pairs or teams, cooperation-inclined players would obviously team up with their likes only.[23] More generally, the benefits of self-selection increase with increasing reliability of type- or program-recognition. In the extreme case of perfect reliability only cooperative teams would form, while in the extreme opposite case of zero reliability, i.e. if cooperative and exploitative program-types cannot be distinguished at all in advance, the advantages of self-selection would be rather limited. Between these two polar cases there is, of course, room for considerable variation in the reliability of type-recognition. Increasing reliability tends to favor cooperation-inclined programs, while decreasing reliability improves the survival prospects of defection-inclined programs.

4. COOPERATION, MORALITY AND LARGE NUMBERS

If, as David Gauthier (1986) suggests, moral rules are typically about cooperation in PD-type settings,[24] one should expect that the distinctions drawn, in this chapter, between different types of PD situations, should

	Two players	More than two players
Exchange PD	Bilateral PD	Decomposable into bilateral PDs
Joint enterprise PD	Bilateral PD	Multilateral PD

Figure 15.1 Matrix 1

be of relevance for the prospects of 'morality' – in the sense of behavioral programs that never defect – to be viable. In this section I want to draw a few general conclusions that the above arguments imply for this issue.

A brief review of the relevant distinctions may be helpful here. Figure 15.1 classifies PD settings along two variables, in terms of the number of players involved (two or more than two), and in terms of the substantive problem, whether it is about cooperation in exchange or in a joint enterprise.

In the case of exchange PDs, the increase in the number of players beyond two does not change the bilateral nature of the underlying PD. Independent of the number of traders involved, an exchange network can always be disaggregated into bilateral transactions or relations. An increase in the number of traders does not transform the exchange PD from a bilateral into a multilateral PD. This is different for joint enterprise PDs. As long as there are two players involved, such PDs have the same bilateral nature as exchange PDs. Yet, as the number of players exceeds two, they become multilateral PDs with the consequences that we have discussed above. In other words, for bilateral exchange PDs the many-players case is of lesser systematic interest because it is decomposable into pairwise relations. On the other hand, the bilateral joint enterprise PD is of lesser significance because of its similarity to bilateral exchange. This leaves, as the two essential alternatives, the bilateral exchange PD and the multilateral joint enterprise PD.

	Multilateral PD/Joint Enterprise PD		
	Bilateral exchange PD	Self-selected group	Pre-defined group
Easy exit option	Exchange PDE	Club/team PDE	
No easy exit option			Class PD

Figure 15.2 Matrix 2

Figure 15.2 further distinguishes among sub-versions of these two cases in two ways, namely, first, according to whether or not an exit option is available, and, second, according to whether the respective group of players is self-selected or pre-defined. Among the feasible combinations I want to focus here on the three cases that are, for our present purposes, most instructive, namely exchange PDs with exit option (exchange PDEs), self-selected groups with exit option (club/team PDEs), and pre-defined groups without exit option (class PDs).[25]

It has often been argued that 'moral order,' i.e. a social state in which moral rules are widely, or at least tolerably, followed, has the characteristics of a public good in the sense that it is a preferable state for everybody, compared to an environment in which moral rules are generally disregarded, but that each person individually and separately has incentives to 'free ride,' i.e. to act unconstrained by moral rules and not to contribute to the enforcement of these rules. In an article 'Ethical rules, expected values, and large numbers' (1977; orig. 1965), J.M. Buchanan has made this argument, emphasizing that a person's interest in complying with ethical rules is systematically reduced as group size increases, and that in 'critically large groups' individuals face a large-number ethical dilemma:

> Each and every person may, of course, consider that he would be 'better off', in terms of his own evaluation, in a different world where the moral law is widely accepted as an overriding ethical rule. Yet, privately and voluntarily there is simply no means through which the single individual can choose to make this alternative state of the world more nearly realizable. (Buchanan 1977: 161)

Voluntary provision of the good 'moral order' should, therefore, be expected to be subject to the same adversities that impede the voluntary production of public goods in general, namely 'the tendency of each person who is a potential beneficiary from the commonly shared public good to choose, rationally, to remain a "free rider"' (ibid.: 163).

The analysis in Vanberg and Congleton (1992) and in Congleton and Vanberg (2001) suggests that the analogy between the public goods problem and the problem of moral order may need to be qualified, in the sense that not all moral rules may leave the individual person without any means to make a moral 'state of the world more nearly realizable.'[26] More specifically, the difference between bilateral and multilateral PDs, as well as the difference between self-selected and pre-defined groups, would seem to be of relevance here. It has been suggested (Vanberg and Buchanan 1994) that moral rules – i.e. rules of cooperation in PD-type settings – can broadly be classified into two types, called trust-rules and solidarity-rules, the former being rules that (primarily) apply to bilateral transactions/relations, while the latter apply (primarily) to multilateral PDs. Examples for trust-rules are 'to keep promises,' 'to be truthful,' or 'to respect property rights.' By contrast, solidarity-rules are exemplified by principles such as 'do not litter,' 'pay your taxes,' or 'do not shirk in team efforts.' To the extent that moral rules can, in fact, be classified in such fashion, we should expect trust-rules to be less affected by the large-number-problem than solidarity-rules, and, with regard to the latter, self-selected groups should be somewhat less vulnerable than pre-defined groups.

The essential difference between trust-rules and solidarity-rules lies, of course, in the difference that separates bilateral from multilateral PDs with regard to the 'targeted' nature of behavioral responses. A person's compliance with trust-rules directly benefits, and her violation of such rules directly harms the particular counterparts she is dealing with. The principal effects of her rule-compliance or rule-violation are concentrated on them, with little, if any, beneficial or harmful effects on others. By contrast, the beneficial or harmful effects of a person's compliance with, or violation of, solidarity-rules are not concentrated in this sense, but affect a (self-selected or pre-defined) *group*. In other words, and as noted before, in the bilateral settings to which trust-rules apply, a person has, to a significant extent, means to affect, through reward and punishment, the behavior of those she is dealing with, or – where exit is available – to choose the persons with whom she wants to associate, and to avoid those who do not accept, in their behavior, moral constraints.[27] That is, she has means to make, at least in her immediate environment, a moral 'state of the world more nearly realizable.' With solidarity rules, on the other hand, the control that a person can exercise in this regard by her individual and separate behavior is, obviously, much more limited. Yet there exists, clearly, a significant difference, in this regard, between the problem of cooperation in clubs/teams (self-selected groups with exit) and the problem of cooperation in classes (pre-defined groups). With regard to clubs/teams the person has some control over her own environment, because she can seek out clubs/teams with more cooperative members and avoid others. She has, in this sense, some means available to make a moral 'state of the world more realizable,' even though the choice among clubs/teams is clearly a less flexible instrument for that purpose than the choice among counterparts in bilateral dealings. For pre-defined groups or classes the analogy between the public goods problem and the problem of moral order is, apparently, more fitting than for the previous two scenarios. Here a person's means for creating, or finding, for herself, by her individual and separate choice, a moral environment are minimized.

Trust-rules allow for the formation of cooperative clusters or cooperative sub-groups – down to two persons – within larger populations of any size. In totally non-moral environments persons belonging to such clusters can realize differential benefits from following, among themselves, moral rules, benefits foreclosed to those who remain outside the 'moral network.'[28] The same is true, even if to a lesser extent, for what one may call *club-* or *team-rules*, that is, solidarity-rules applied to clubs or teams. The formation of cooperative clusters, or a sorting of moral and non-moral players, is possible here, even if with less flexibility, through self-selection and exit. Clustering is apparently ruled out, however, for what one may call *class-rules*, that is, for solidarity rules in pre-defined groups. There is no way for a sub-group of cooperators to realize differential benefits for themselves. Other class-members could not be excluded from whatever benefits their 'moral behavior' would produce, while they alone would be burdened by the costs of their cooperation. It is, to be sure, equally true for clubs or teams, that 'internal clustering' cannot generate differential benefits for the cooperators, since, whatever benefits their cooperative efforts generate they have to share with other club members who free-ride on their contributions. Yet, in the case of clubs or teams self-selection and exit provide moral players with some means to avoid being exploited by non-cooperating members.

5. CONCLUSION

In Vanberg and Congleton (1992) as well as in Congleton and Vanberg (2001) the problem of cooperation in PD-type settings has been approached as a matter of competition among alternative behavioral strategies, with a particular interest in the performance of *moral* programs, i.e. programs that cooperate whenever they play, but avoid defectors. The purpose of these studies has been to explore how such 'moral' programs perform, relative to potential alternatives, in settings where exit is available. The 'emergence of cooperation' is, in such a context, a matter of 'sorting' among players, and we found moral programs to do well where such sorting is possible at relatively low costs. This is most apparent in bilateral PDEs (Vanberg and Congleton 1992), yet the simulation results in Congleton and Vanberg (2001) show that this is also true, if to a lesser degree, for multilateral PDEs.

Because of their focus on competition among individual behavioral strategies the noted studies do not address the role of deliberate, organized efforts to enforce cooperative behavior in PD-type settings. As far as bilateral exchange relations are concerned, players' individual and separate responses are an effective instrument of conditioning others into cooperation and to avoid defectors, even though, of course, organized enforcement of ethical rules allows, as North (1990: 34f.) suggests, for a significant further increase in gains from trade, by extending the size of the market. Yet it would seem that organized enforcement should play a much more essential role in multilateral, joint enterprise PDs, especially with increasing group size. As has been noted above, the shift from bilateral to multilateral PD-type settings means that a player's individual and separate response loses its effectiveness as an instrument for conditioning other players into cooperation. It also means that the exit option loses some of its flexibility. Both effects will be enhanced as group size increases: a single player's individual and separate strategy choice is bound to become less and less significant, and exit becomes a less and less promising strategy, both because more attractive alternative clubs/teams may not be available, and because the costs of forming a new club/team increase.

Because of the reasons mentioned, explicit efforts to punish and discourage defection would seem to be an essential prerequisite to stabilize cooperation in multilateral PDs. Individual punishing strategies could produce such enforcement, and groups that include 'punishers' could clearly be more successful than groups that do not, yet this does not mean per se that punishing programs will do well in competition with others. Discouraging defection is a collective good that benefits all club/team members, including those who do the punishing, but non-punishing members benefit even more since they do not bear the costs of such actions. As group size increases, we should expect the collective goods nature of punishment to work increasingly against punishing programs. This implies that organized enforcement efforts should increasingly become an essential prerequisite for achieving cooperation in multilateral PD-settings.

The need for organized efforts to promote cooperation in multilateral PDs would seem to exist for self-selected groups no less than for pre-defined groups, but one should expect the former to be – other things (in particular group size) being equal – in a much better position to get such organized enforcement in place. Since, for self-selected groups, there has to be some 'constituting act' of setting up the club/team, one should expect the group at this point to be able to agree on some enforcement scheme, and to make such agreement a requirement for the admission of new members. The expulsion of non-cooperators may be one of the provisions of enforcenment. For pre-defined groups there are no explicit choices that constitute the group. The group is, by definition, pre-defined, prior to any effort that may be made towards securing cooperation. Agreement to some enforcement scheme can, obviously, not be made a requirement for group membership, nor can non-cooperators be expelled from the group. This makes achieving and securing cooperation much more difficult.

NOTES

1. The notion of a team-surplus can be interpreted in terms of Alchian's and Demsetz's (1972) theory of team production. In their study of multi-player PDs, Hirshleifer and Rasmussen (1989) speak of 'advantage to grouping' and of 'aggregation economies.'
2. Technically, with an exit option added the game is no longer a genuine Prisoner's Dilemma. Nevertheless, for reasons of convenience and because, apart from the exit option, the game is a PD, we found the use of the name 'Prisoner's Dilemma with Exit' (PDE) justified.
3. As Axelrod notes about his 1984 contribution: 'In this book I will examine interactions between just two players at a time. A single player may be interacting with many players, but the player is assumed to be interacting with them one at a time' (ibid.: 11).
4. For a classic argument on this issue see David Hume's (1967: Book III, Part II, Section V): 'Of the obligation of promises.' For a general review of the role of the concept of reciprocity or exchange in the social science literature see Vanberg (1975).
5. Axelrod (1986: 1097) notes about his later project: 'To investigate the growth and decay of norms, I have formulated a norms game in which players can choose to defect and to punish those they have seen defecting. The goal of the investigation is to see when cooperation based upon emerging norms will develop. Ultimately, the purpose is to learn what conditions favor the development of norms so that cooperation can be promoted where it might not otherwise exist or be secure.'
6. In situations to which the norm not to cheat on exams applies there is no specific counterpart who is negatively or positively affected by a candidate's choice to cheat (to defect) or to be honest (to cooperate). Cooperation in the sense of compliance with the norm 'not to cheat on exams' can, therefore, not be induced by strategies like tit-for-tat but requires the employment of other strategies. On this issue see e.g. Coleman 1990.
7. It is obvious from their discussion that Boyd and Richerson (1988) have a genuine multilateral PD in mind when they speak of 'cooperation in larger groups' (ibid.: 338) or of 'repeated interactions in larger groups' (ibid.). Yet, one cannot tell from such phrases *per se* whether they refer to exchange settings or joint enterprise arrangements. How the prospects for cooperation are affected when 'group size increases'

(ibid.) clearly depends, however, on whether we are dealing with one setting or the other.

8. The examination situation involves a collective good problem. The candidates share a common interest in the value of whatever certificate or degree they can earn by passing the examination. By cheating, a candidate can hope to improve his grade. Yet, cheating also tends to diminish the value of the certificate/degree. If all cheated, it would be worthless. It would seem most advantageous to be the only one who can cheat while all others are honest, and it would seem least attractive to be the only one who is honest while everybody else cheats.
9. For an interpretation of reciprocity as mutual behavioral conditioning see e.g. Homans 1974, pp. 51ff.
10. See e.g. Sugden (1986: 108) who defines 'strategies of reciprocity' as 'strategies that make a player's co-operation conditional on his opponent's co-operation.'
11. Boyd and Richerson (1988: 342) define such a strategy by the following rule: 'cooperate on the first move and then cooperate on each subsequent move if *a* or more of the other $n-1$ individuals in the group choose cooperation during the previous period.'
12. Programs of unconditional cooperation provide no protection against exploitative programs. Their principal drawback is that they cooperate too long with defectors.
13. Others cannot observe a player's strategy directly. What they can observe are behavioral responses, and from these responses they have to infer the underlying behavioral program. Since observed behavioral responses may be compatible with different general strategies, such inferences can only be conjectural (Vanberg 2002; 2004).
14. As Boyd and Richerson (1992) note, in the n-person PD, reciprocators who defect in order to punish defectors also penalize other cooperators in the group and induce, in turn, other reciprocators to defect. In order to explain how cooperation may be sustained in multilateral PDs, Boyd and Richerson take recourse in their analysis to strategies of retribution or '*moralistic* strategies which cooperate, punish noncooperators, and punish those who do not punish noncooperators.'
15. As Boyd and Richerson (1992: 171) note: 'According to contemporary evolutionary theory, cooperative behavior can only be favored by selection when social groups are formed so that cooperators are more likely to interact with other cooperators than with noncooperators.'
16. This distinction does not apply to exchange PDs since parties to an exchange transaction/relation are always 'self-selected' in the sense in which we define the term.
17. The phrase 'principal beneficiaries' is meant to allow for the fact that cooperative activities may have spillover benefits for outsiders as well.
18. Buchanan (1965: 1) characterizes clubs as 'consumption ownership-membership arrangements' in which goods are 'available for consumption to the whole membership unit' (ibid.: 3), and he notes that firms can also be considered as 'one form of club organization' (ibid.: 5n).
19. Alchian (1987: 1032): 'The "firm" . . . is a contractually related collection of resources of various cooperating owners. Its distinctive source of enhanced productivity is "team" production, wherein the product is . . . a non-decomposable, non-attributable value produced by the group.'
20. In Congleton and Vanberg (2001) the most simple case of a genuine multilateral PD is examined, with $n=3$.
21. The ten behavioral programs included in the simulation experiment included programs of unconditional cooperation and defection as well as a variety of programs that conditionally cooperated or defected, such as tit-for-tat, and also exiting as well as retributive programs.
22. On the issue of type-recognition in the context of PD games see Frank (1988: 56ff.).
23. This explains why reputation is such an important asset in settings where alternative potential counterparts for transactions or cooperative arrangements are readily available, as is the case, for instance, in competitive markets. As Hume (1967: 501) notes:

'There is nothing which touches us more nearly than our reputation, and nothing on which our reputation more depends than our conduct with relation to the property of others.'

24. Note that this is not the same as saying that *all* cooperative behavior in PD-type settings necessarily qualifies as 'moral' behavior in the ordinary sense of the term (a counterexample is cooperation in a cartel), nor does it imply that *all* moral rules, again, as commonly understood, are necessarily about cooperation in PD settings. All that is claimed is that typical examples of what is commonly viewed as moral behavior are about cooperation in PD-type situations.
25. The term 'class PD' is meant to indicate that membership of a group is not so much a matter of choice to join or not to join the respective group, but is pre-defined by possession of certain characteristics. This distinction is, to be sure, not entirely unambiguous since acquiring the characteristics that include someone in a particular class of persons may itself be a matter of choice. This applies, for instance, to the previously mentioned example of persons living around a lake, where taking up or giving up residence at the lake, is a matter of choice.
26. Buchanan points to the need for such qualification when he limits the analogy to cases where 'the potential benefits are genuinely nondivisible' (1977: 163), and when he suggests that things are different where there are 'possible means of factoring down complex interaction systems into small-group patterns' (ibid.: 168).
27. It is the possibility of avoiding defectors that encourages honesty in settings of repeated dealings and voluntary association. As Smith (1982: 538f.) has noted on this issue: 'Where people seldom deal with one another, we find that they are somewhat disposed to cheat, because they can gain more by a smart trick than they can lose by the injury which it does their character. . . . Wherever dealings are frequent, a man does not expect to gain so much by any one contract as by probity and punctuality in the whole, and a prudent dealer, who is sensible of his real interest, would rather choose to lose what he has a right to than give any ground for suspicion.'
28. The point that is of interest here has been nicely articulated by W.G. Sumner (1918: 95): 'Some say that a man cannot afford to be honest unless everybody is honest. The truth is that, if there was one honest man among a lot of cheats, his character and reputation would reach their maximum value.'

REFERENCES

Alchian, Armen (1987), 'Property rights', in John Eatwell, Murray Milgate and Peter Newman (eds), *The New Palgrave: A Dictionary of Economics*, Vol. III, Basingstoke: Palgrave Macmillan, pp. 1031–4.

Alchian, Armen and Harold Demsetz (1972), 'Production, information costs, and economic organization', *American Economic Review*, **62**, 777–95.

Axelrod, Robert (1984), *The Evolution of Cooperation*, New York: Basic Books.

Axelrod, Robert (1986), 'An evolutionary approach to norms', *American Political Science Review*, **80**, 1095–1111.

Boyd, Robert and Peter J. Richerson (1988), 'The evolution of reciprocity in sizable groups', *Journal of Theoretical Biology*, **132**, 337–56.

Boyd, Robert and Peter J. Richerson (1992), 'Punishment allows the evolution of cooperation (or anything else) in sizable groups', *Ethology and Sociobiology*, **13**, 171–95.

Buchanan, James M. (1965), 'An economic theory of clubs', *Econometrica*, NS **32**, 1–14.

Buchanan, James M. (1977), 'Ethical rules, expected values, and large numbers', in *Freedom in Constitutional Contract*, College Station, Texas: A&M University Press, pp. 151–68.

Coleman, James S. (1990), 'Norm-generating structures', in Karen Schweeres Cook and Margaret Levi (eds), *The Limits of Rationality*, Chicago and London: The University of Chicago Press, pp. 250–73.

Congleton, Roger D. and Viktor J. Vanberg (2001), 'Help, harm or avoid? On the personal advantage of dispositions to cooperate and punish in multilateral PD games with exit', *Journal of Economic Behavior & Organization*, **44**, 145–67.

Frank, Robert H. (1988), *Passions Within Reason – The Strategic Role of Emotions*, New York and London: W.W. Norton.

Gauthier, David (1986), *Morals by Agreement*, New York: Oxford University Press.

Hirshleifer, David and Eric Rasmussen (1989), 'Cooperation in repeated prisoner's dilemma with ostracism', *Journal of Economic Behavior and Organization*, **12**, 87–106.

Homans, George C. (1974), *Social Behavior – Its Elementary Forms*, New York: Harcourt Brace Jovanich.

Hume, David (1967), *A Treatise of Human Nature*, Oxford: Clarendon Press.

North, Douglass C. (1990), *Institutions, Institutional Change and Economic Performance*, Cambridge: Cambridge University Press.

Smith, Adam (1982), *Lectures on Jurisprudence*, Indianapolis, IN: Liberty Classics.

Sugden, Robert (1986), *The Economics of Rights, Co-operation and Welfare*, Oxford: Basil Blackwell.

Sumner, William Graham (1918), *The Forgotten Man and Other Essays*, New Haven, CT: Yale University Press.

Tullock, Gordon (1985), 'Adam Smith and the prisoner's dilemma', *Quarterly Journal of Economics*, **C**, 1073–81.

Vanberg, Viktor (1975), *Die zwei Soziologien – Individualismus und Kollektivismus in der Sozialtheorie*, Tübingen: J.C.B. Mohr (Paul Siebeck).

Vanberg, Viktor and James M. Buchanan (1994), 'Rational choice and moral order', in Viktor J. Vanberg, *Rules and Choice in Economics*, London and New York: Routledge, pp. 60–73.

Vanberg, Viktor J. (2002), 'Rational choice vs. program-based behavior: alternative theoretical approaches and their relevance for the study of institutions', *Rationality and Society* **14**, 7–53.

Vanberg, Viktor J. (2004), 'The rationality postulate in economics: its ambiguity, its deficiency and its evolutionary alternative', *Journal of Economic Methodology*, **11**, 1–29.

Vanberg, Viktor J. and Roger D. Congleton (1992), 'Rationality, morality and exit', *American Political Science Review*, **86**, 418–31.

16. Voluntary provision of public goods

Miguel A. Puchades-Navarro

1. INTRODUCTION

The standard theory of public goods shows that the market cannot efficiently supply public goods. The non-excludability of public goods prevents voluntary funding. As a result the supply of public goods cannot be based on voluntary gifts but on compulsory government exactions. However, in contrast to this conclusion, we actually find numerous non-profit institutions supplying a wide range of public and quasi-public goods; and in recent decades a large number of non-governmental organizations have emerged around the world.

How do economists bridge this gap between theory and evidence? The literature related to non-profit organizations has experienced significant growth, dealing with their operation, funding and performance. Two main arguments support the emergence of non-profit institutions: the unsatisfied demand and the private consumer model.

The existence of unsatisfied demand is at the core of theories explaining the establishment of non-profit institutions. Unsatisfied demand is a consequence of the failure of government in supplying some collective goods in societies with heterogeneous demand (Weisbrod 1975, 1988). On the other hand, private consumption models (Andreoni 1990; Bernheim 1986; Roberts 1984; Warr 1982) take into account consumer motivation to voluntarily fund non-profit organizations.

There is no conclusive empirical evidence about which kind of models better explain the role of non-profit organizations in the provision of public goods. The empirical results concerning the crowding-out effects of non-profit and government provision are contradictory (Nyborg and Rege 2003). Some studies suggest a 'dollar for dollar' crowding-out effect (e.g. Roberts 1984) while other analyses conclude that crowding-out effects are very small (e.g. Kingma 1989; Ribar and Wilhelm 2002). The problem is somewhat compounded by the fact that non-profit organizations offer a wide range of possibilities for supplying different kinds of goods to different consumers. The unsatisfied demand hypothesis may explain some activities of non-profit organizations, whereas altruistic motivations give a better explanation in many other cases.

However, these models do not explain significant differences in the size and the role of the non-profit sector among countries with a similar level of economic development. An unsolved question emerges: why is a particular collective good mainly supplied by private non-profit organizations in some countries, while in others the same good is primarily supplied by government? Differences in preferences would explain the larger or smaller provision of the public goods. However, preferences alone do not explain which type of provision occurs. We need to also understand the institutional setting, in order to explain what alternatives may arise.

This chapter advances a model in which private voluntary provision of public goods is a real alternative to public provision, assuming the hypothesis that individual behaviour is constrained by ethical and moral rules. Individuals choose between governmental or private voluntary provision as alternatives and determine the level of both governmental supply and voluntary supply of public goods through the political process.

2. FOUNDATIONS OF VOLUNTARY PROVISIONS OF PUBLIC GOODS

2.1 Clubs and Private Governments

Significant public choice literature dealing with non-governmental provision of collective goods has centred on the theory of clubs (Buchanan 1965). Many goods supplied by non-profit organizations embody the characteristics of club goods, and a number of non-profit organizations are actually clubs. Provision through clubs is an alternative to provision by government, and club provision should crowd out public supply.

However, club goods are a special case which is not applicable to voluntary provision[1] by non-profits in general. Exclusion is possible in many of the goods supplied by non-profits as well as for goods supplied by governments. In these cases, the presence of either significant externalities or a redistribution goal suggests not utilizing prices as a rationing or exclusion mechanism. The theory of clubs does not explain voluntary provision when institutions do not use prices or fees as a basic criterion of exclusion, and they fund themselves from voluntary gifts by donors who do not consume the good supplied.

In addition to clubs, rational consumers can organize themselves in order to improve their welfare, if they are unsatisfied with the government provision of public goods. This is the case of so-called *private governments*. Voters reject both broad-based tax increases and budget deficits, while at the same time demanding improved services. Private governments are voluntary, exclusive organizations that supplement services provided by the public sector (Helsley and Strange 1998). According to this approach, private governments appear because of public sector failure to provide public goods to consumers with heterogeneous preferences.[2] In this model, the government responds to private supply by reducing its provision of the collective goods, but the crowding-out effect is incomplete. The action of the public sector only partially offsets the private provision (Helsley and Strange 1998).

2.2 Altruism and Voluntary Funding

A basic assumption in the standard public goods model is that individuals only take into account the increase in the supply of public goods produced as a result of their own contribution. This individual behaviour leads to an underprovision of collective goods. The extent of such underprovision of public goods depends on the nature of utility functions (Cornes and Sandler 1986), but tends to rise as the size of a community grows.

The consideration of some altruistic behavioural patterns allows voluntary contributions to finance some level of public good provision. A selfish consumer only takes into account the benefits his own contribution has for himself; but individuals might have other motivations. People might care about others or ideas beyond themselves. Altruism can explain the voluntary funding of some charitable services. However, altruism cannot be considered a basis for adequate supply of public goods.

Applying a Cournot–Nash equilibrium to the pure altruism model results in the underprovision of public goods (Andreoni 1988; Warr 1982; Roberts 1984; Bernheim 1986). Moreover, the standard model of public goods and the altruistic behaviour model cannot explain different patterns of public or private provision found across countries (Andreoni 1988; Sugden 1982).

A different conception of altruism is based on the positive feelings of the contributors, which serve as the motivation to give. This is the case of the impure altruism model (Andreoni 1990), which considers voluntary contributions as a private good consumed by the donor. In this model, donors obtain some utility from the act of giving itself. Donors get a 'warm glow feeling' from their contributions. The impure altruism model explains voluntary contributions as the act of giving itself, which motivates donors to give, as long as their contributions increase their psychological welfare. These donors are indifferent about the kind of goods that their gifts finally finance because they derive some utility, even if their donations do not contribute to financing the production of any good. Contributions are not conceived of as an exchange for goods supplied, but rather as private goods, which themselves have a value. The fact that the main motivation to give is not related to output is in line with very low crowding-out effects identified in some empirical studies (Ribar and Wilhelm 2002).

In the same sense of the 'warm glow', social approval (Holländer 1990) or prestige (Harbaugh 1998) can also be considered as a motivation for voluntary contributions. These models are similar to the impure altruism model. Social approval or prestige are by-products of individuals' contributions, like the warm glow of Andreoni (1990).

Non-profit organizations can exploit the warm glow feeling in fund raising activities. But to the extent that such contributions are not related to the output of public goods, they cannot be considered a real alternative to the public provision of public goods.

2.3 Cooperation and Moral Norms

The underprovision in voluntary supply of public goods is derived from the assumption that individuals take the contributions of the others members of the community as fixed, and altruism does not overcome this problem. However, cooperative behaviour may allow an efficient private provision of collective goods to be obtained.

Cooperation can be based on the principle of reciprocity (Rabin 1993). Every individual benefits from contributions made; and the acknowledgement of this economic interdependence results in participants modifying (where possible) the behaviour of others. Cooperation has an externality which benefits every participant and which induces cooperation itself. According to the principle of conditional commitment, contributions by an individual depend on what the others do (Sugden 1984). In a model of social commitment, cooperative behaviour influences other members of the community, and voluntary contributions result in the private supply of public goods (Casas Pardo et al. 2001).

An implicit agreement supported by social norms might encourage cooperation, particularly in small communities. However, in large communities this social commitment may be too costly, as the rising transaction costs prevent such a complex mutual contract to evolve or be maintained in spite of its potential earnings.

Whether the contractual processes of political or economic exchange are excluded, the natural way to reach cooperation is via investing in some institutions which do not involve contractual attempts to modify the behaviour of the individuals. Ethical and religious principles may induce cooperative behaviour that is not necessarily grounded on reciprocity.[3] Without political or economic exchange, only ethics remains as a possible way of appropriation of the potential economic value that exists above and beyond ordinary policy (Buchanan 1991, 1996).

2.4 Honesty as a Behavioural Pattern

Fortunately, law is not the main mechanism to enforce peaceful co-existence. Ethical and moral constraints make people more determined to behave in a way that ensures the smooth running of the economic system. The idea of *honesty* may substitute pure altruism and enforce cooperation. In this sense, an individual subject to moral constraints does not pursue the well-being of others or fight against inequality. Honest people do not steal, they stop at the traffic lights and pay their taxes voluntarily. In addition, they obey the law principally not to avoid possible penalties but because they think it is their duty.

We define the honest consumer as following a Kantian ethic: that is, 'act like you think everyone should' (Gassler 1998). In order to modelize the behaviour of the honest consumer, we do not need to modify the standard utility function by introducing new variables. The honest consumer behaves rationally and he will try to maximize his utility. But the maximization rule operates under two constraints. The ethical constraint operates in addition to the budget constraint. In this way, honest consumers will be willing to reveal their real preferences for collective goods, be it by making voluntary contributions or paying taxes in the case of governmental provision. Moreover, the ethical constraint is compatible with voluntary agreements to supplement unsatisfied demand and with altruistic or warm glow feelings.

3. VOTING FOR GOVERNMENTAL OR VOLUNTARY PROVISION OF PUBLIC GOODS

Governmental supply of public goods is obviously a political decision. As long as voluntary provision is a real alternative, individuals will vote for public or private provision according to their preferences. In the absence of governmental provision of public goods, people may be willing to make voluntary contributions to private (non-governmental) provision.

Let us consider a community of n individuals $\{1, 2,\ldots j\ldots n-1, n\}$, arranged by their preferences for a public good G, with individual j as the median voter.

Assuming that the ethical constraint runs as described in the previous heading, an honest consumer does not exclusively take into account an increase in the supply of a public good as a result of his own contribution but also expects others to act as honestly as himself. Within a group of n individuals with a cooperative commitment, if an individual decides to donate an amount g to finance the provision of a public good G – provided that other members behave the same way – he expects an increase in supply of:

$$\Delta G = n \cdot g/C \tag{16.1}$$

where C is the per unit cost of supplying public good G (for simplicity, we assume a constant marginal and average cost C).

However, individuals may have heterogeneous preferences, so that each individual i is willing to make a particular voluntary contribution g_i. Consumer preferences can be represented as a standard consumer expenditure function.

$$g_i = \theta_i(G) \tag{16.2}$$

And in a community with n honest individuals, the output of a public good that can be supplied through voluntary contributions is

$$G^V = \sum_n g_i/C \tag{16.3}$$

The output level G^V fulfils the well known Samuelsonian condition for a Pareto-optimal provision of public goods, whenever all individuals behave honestly and ethical constraints avoid free-riding. In this case, ethical rules and cooperative commitments make it possible to optimal supply public goods.

The alternative to voluntary supply is tax-funded governmental provision. Let us assume that government collects a neutral tax T to finance public provision. Then, the public output supplied is

$$G^G = n \cdot T/C \tag{16.4}$$

Consider that, in a representative democracy, the preferences of the median voter determine the outcome. As the output fits the preferences of the median voter, a tax T must be equal to the contribution the median voter would be willing to make in exchange for the output G^G.

$$T = g_j = \theta_j(G^G) \tag{16.5}$$

The community faces these two alternative scenarios for supplying the collective good:

(a) Public provision: government collects a tax T and supplies a level of output G^G
(b) Voluntary provision: honest individuals finance an output level G^V through voluntary contributions.

Individuals do not know what the Pareto-optimum output is, nor do they try to maximize an aggregate welfare function. They just pay taxes or make voluntary contributions, and vote in the political process according to their own preferences.

An honest individual i will prefer – and will vote for – voluntary provision if $g_i < T$; otherwise, he will prefer public provision.

As decisions are made based on a simple majority, provision will be either governmental or voluntary depending on the position of the median voter in relation to the distribution of preferences for the public good.

As g_j is the voluntary contribution of the median voter and

$$\bar{g} = \sum_n g_i / n \tag{16.6}$$

the average contribution of all members of the community, voluntary provision will prevail when the distribution of preferences is such that $g_j < \bar{g}$.

On the other hand, if the distribution of preferences is such that the voluntary contribution of the median voter is greater than the average contribution, the outcome will tend to be governmental supply. In such a case, over-provision will occur.[4] Public output G^G is larger than the optimum level G^V.

These results can be graphically presented in a simple way. Let us consider three groups of individuals with different preferences: low demand, medium demand and high demand. It is assumed that the median voter belongs to the medium demand group.

Figure 16.1 explains a situation in which the collective choice process will lead to voluntary provision of the public good.

Standard demand curves for each group of consumers are shown in Figure 16.1 as *D1*, *D2* and *D3*. Consumers do not exchange public goods at a price per unit, but as tax or voluntary contributions in exchange for the overall level of output. However, for analytical purposes, consumer preferences can be summarized by a standard demand function instead of an expenditure function. Through a voluntary contribution g_i to finance the output G^V, in the end, consumer i pays a price per unit of the public good

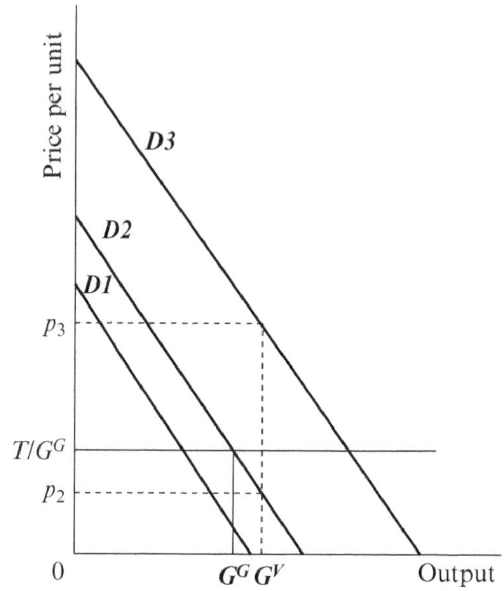

Figure 16.1 *Voluntary provision allows reaching an optimum output level* G^V*. Low demand consumers (*D1*) and medium demand consumers (*D2*) prefer voluntary output* G^V *rather than public output* G^G

$$p_i = g_i / G^V \tag{16.7}$$

And with governmental provision, the final price per unit resulting from paying a tax T is

$$p_t = T/G^G = C/n \tag{16.8}$$

The decision rule is really simple. Individuals will choose whatever is the cheaper option to obtain the public good. The median voter will follow this rule determining the outcome of the political process.

In Figure 16.1 G^V represents the Pareto-optimum level of output which can be obtained if every consumer behaves honestly, by contributing to finance output according to his real preferences. Individual contributions by high demand consumers would then be

$$g_3 = p_3 \cdot G^V \tag{16.9}$$

In a similar way, a medium demand consumer contribution would be

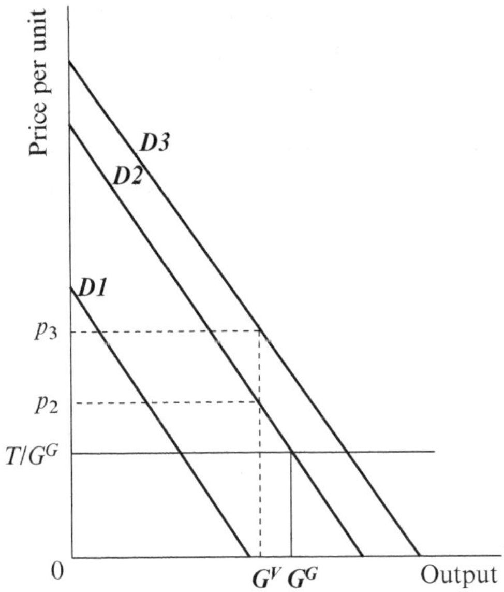

Figure 16.2 *Government supplies an output level* G^G *larger than the optimum* G^V. *High demand consumers (*D3*) and medium demand consumers (*D2*) prefer a government output* G^G *rather than a voluntary supply output* G^V

$$g_2 = p_2 \cdot G^V \tag{16.10}$$

and in the particular case presented in Figure 16.1, low demand consumers do not contribute at all. The sum of all contributions is equal to the total cost of producing the output

$$\sum_n g_i = C \cdot G^V \tag{16.11}$$

Note that, in this case, low demand consumers are not free-riders. Despite the fact that they consume and do not pay for it, they do not behave in an opportunistic way, but are revealing their true preferences.

The alternative to voluntary provision is public supply of an output level G^G, lower than the optimum G^V, and a final price per unit T/G^G higher than p_2, which the median voter was willing to pay with voluntary provision. Despite government adjusting public provision to the preferences of the median voter, the outcome will be voluntary provision as this leaves the median voter better-off.

Figure 16.2 presents a different structure of preferences leading to governmental provision. The optimum output level is, again, G^V, but both high and medium demand groups prefer governmental provision of output G^G. The outcome will be over-provision by government of the public good.

In the previous analysis it was assumed that all consumers behave honestly. However, free-riding cannot be completely avoided. The presence of opportunistic consumers, who are not willing to contribute according to their real preferences, modifies the outcome and the likelihood of voluntary provision.

Considering a share of the population $\varphi \in [0,1]$ behaving as free-riders, then the revealed demand for the collective good and the output voluntarily supplied decreases with φ.

$$G^R = (1-\varphi)\,G^V \tag{16.12}$$

Voluntary provision is still possible as long as $G^R \geq G^G$. The threshold proportion of free-riders which allows for voluntary provision is then

$$\varphi^* < 1 - g_j/\bar{g} \tag{16.13}$$

4. A VOTING GAME DETERMINING PUBLIC AND PRIVATE PROVISION

The model in the previous section presented a choice between two exclusive alternatives: public supply versus private voluntary supply of public goods. However, both alternatives usually occur concurrently. People pay taxes to finance public provision and make donations to non-profit institutions to finance private voluntary provision.

Consumers do not make calculations to maximize their utility function, but realize whether or not they are satisfied with the output supplied. Every individual knows how much he pays in total (tax plus donation, $T+g_i$) and he is able to evaluate whether his contribution is aligned with his own preferences.

An individual might consider that he is giving too much money in exchange for the output supplied. In such a case, he would like to reduce his total contribution, despite the fact that a lower contribution reduces the output supplied. On the contrary, a high demand consumer might feel unsatisfied if the output supplied is too low. Facing such subjective under-provision, an honest consumer is willing to raise his contribution in order to increase output. In this way, consumers may reveal their preferences for public goods without any special institutional arrangement.

In the political arena, people vote for higher or lower public output and taxes according to their preferences. In general, high demand consumers will vote for increasing taxes while low demand consumers will vote for cutting taxes. Voluntary provision arises from unsatisfied demand. Faced with a certain level of governmental supply of public goods, high demand consumers would prefer more output; they are therefore willing to make donations to non-governmental institutions in order to increase the level of output. This is not altruistic behaviour; nor is it grounded on any reciprocity criterion. Individuals reveal their preferences as they behave under ethical constraints.

We can model the behaviour of individuals as a two stage game. At the first stage, people vote according to their preferences. There are two political parties; the programme of one party is to increase a tax T to supply more public goods, and the programme of the other party is to reduce the tax. After elections the winning party implements its programme. At the second stage, individuals decide on their voluntary contributions.

A repeated game introduces a dynamic setup from an evolutionary perspective leading to equilibrium solutions. In an evolutionary process agents take decisions and react to variations in output levels supplied in each period, showing in this way how equilibrium is reached.

The dynamic framework of the repeated game is as follows:

We start in period k=0 with an arbitrary tax level, T_0, and a set of voluntary contributions $g_i.\{1...n\}$.

The next period starts in the first stage and elections take place. Agents take into account their total contributions (tax plus voluntary donation) and the output supplied in the previous period. Individuals vote for a political party according to their preferences (to increase or to reduce the tax). The winning party implements its political programme. The new elected government does not adjust the tax level to what the median voter actually prefers; it simply increases or reduces the previous tax level. We assume that there is a tax variation in each period, α_k, which depends on the extent of the electoral victory. That is, α_k is a function of the difference of votes of the winning party over the losing party. Therefore, tax level in period k is:

$$T_k = T_{k-1} \pm \alpha_k \tag{16.14}$$

At the second stage of the game agents adjust their voluntary contributions. An individual may be motivated to reduce his voluntary contribution if he considers himself to be paying too much for the output level supplied. On the other hand, an individual may believe that output levels should be increased and be willing to increase his voluntary contribution to increase supply. Agents take into account the current level of tax T_k and their previous voluntary contributions (if any). The voluntary contribution of an individual i, in period k, is:

$$g_{k(i)} = g_{k-1(i)} \pm \beta_i \tag{16.15}$$

where β_i is the change in voluntary contribution of individual i. We assume that β_i depends on the difference between output levels currently supplied and the output level an individual desires. Individuals do not adjust their new contributions to a level that would match their utility function; they just give up or cut down their donations according to subjective perceptions.

The game is repeated until equilibrium is reached, when taxation and the voluntary contributions remain unchanged in successive periods.

The game does not automatically lead to an equilibrium, but in consecutive periods government will adjust tax to a level preferred by the median voter, and individuals will adjust their voluntary contributions according to their preferences.

Equilibrium depends on the structure and distribution of individual preferences. But for every set of preferences there is not a single equilibrium point, and multiple equilibria may emerge because the median voter might crowd out tax and voluntary contributions. Given a set of individual preferences, there is a wide range of possible values of tax T and voluntary contributions $g_i\{1...n\}$ that fulfil the equilibrium conditions.

Equilibrium cannot be determined unless we give a functional specification of the distribution of preferences, the distribution of voluntary contributions, the initial tax and the evolutionary patterns of both tax and voluntary contributions. The repeated game allows us to show the dynamics of the process towards equilibrium and to focus not only on equilibrium states but also on dynamic issues, and how initial conditions affect the outcomes.

The model presents some preliminary results on the determinants of equilibria solutions:

1. Inequality of preferences. Ceteris paribus, the greater the inequality of preferences the greater the proportion of voluntary provision in the final equilibrium. Higher dispersion raises unsatisfied demand for high demand consumers. Accordingly they are willing to make larger voluntary contributions.
2. Median voter preferences. The position of the median voter in the distribution of preferences has a particular significance in determining the political outcome. A median voter demand that is greater than the

average demand function results in an equilibrium with a higher proportion of public supply; the opposite is the case when median voter demand is below the average demand function.

3. Initial tax level. The equilibrium depends on the initial situation. Given a distribution of individual preferences, a low level of taxes encourages individuals to adjust their contributions to voluntary funding. By contrast, starting with a high level of public supply tends to maintain it.
4. The pattern of voluntary contribution changes. Unsatisfied consumers are willing to make voluntary contributions but may also request raising the level of taxation. Depending on the ability of individuals to quickly adjust their contributions, voluntary supply may crowd out public supply and lead to an equilibrium with a larger degree of voluntary provision.
5. Free-riding. The model allows for the introduction of a share of individuals behaving as free-riders. Free-riding reduces voluntary contributions and private provision in favour of public provision. As the proportion of free-riders increases, voluntary contributions fall towards zero.

In general, equilibrium is determined by the distribution of individuals' preferences, by the initial set of tax and voluntary contributions, and by the ability to speedily adjust levels of taxation and donations. The outcome depends on preferences and initial conditions, as well as on the evolutionary path. Similar structures of individual preferences can lead to very different outcomes. History matters!

5. FINAL CONSIDERATIONS

Most models dealing with non-profit institutions consider either that they supplement public provision of some goods and services, or that they exist simply because altruistic people want to do good things. However, these considerations disregard historical evidence. Previously, when governments neglected the supply of such goods as charitable services, social security, medicare, education, cultural services, and so on, their supply was made through non-governmental, non-profit institutions – indeed, mainly religious institutions.

So, why did this institutional setup break down in favour of further governmental intervention? The increasing complexity of modern societies prevents that the supply of public goods is grounded on a voluntary agreement among individuals. The political process emerges as the only mechanism to reduce transaction costs and reach a broad social contract satisfying collective needs. However, cooperative behaviour among rational individuals should not be excluded. A set of widely accepted ethical and moral rules modifies the behaviour of rational individuals. An efficient voluntary provision of public goods may thus be possible as an alternative to public provision. Moreover, voluntary provision is a means to supplement public supply when unsatisfied demand remains in heterogeneous communities. So, public goods can be supplied by the public sector or by non-governmental organizations, or a mixture of both public and private supply.

In the political arena, individuals will vote for higher or lower taxes according to their preferences, and the relative position of the median voter will determine the outcome. Additionally, in a community with heterogeneous preferences, some agents will be willing to make voluntary contributions in order to increase the level of output of a public good. This is not altruistic behaviour. Donors cannot hope that all members make voluntary contributions but, assuming a large share of the population behave honestly, it is reasonable to expect the level of output to rise by more than any increase in an individual donor's contribution. The sum of individual voluntary contributions determines overall voluntary supply.

The members of the community reveal their preferences for public goods by voting to determine both taxes and public supply, and funding non-profit institutions. Individuals pay compulsory taxes and make voluntary donations; they know their total contribution and the total output level supplied, and they realize whether or not they are satisfied with an outcome; that is, if their contributions and the level of output fit with their own preferences. An equilibrium solution requires that median voters, in addition to high demand voters, adjust their voluntary contributions so that they do not consider themselves to be paying in excess or that the output level is too low.

For every set of preferences there is not a unique equilibrium solution. Since the tax level and voluntary contributions must be simultaneously determined, multiple equilibria may emerge. A change in the distribution of preferences may crowd out the supply of public goods from private to public provision, or vice versa. In this sense, the model can be useful to explain significant differences among countries, i.e. why non-profit institutions financed through voluntary contributions play an important role in supplying many public and quasi-public goods in some countries, whereas in others these goods are mainly supplied by government.

NOTES

1. Although becoming a member of a club is a voluntary action, the output of club goods is not financed through really voluntary gifts. In club goods, it is possible to exclude those people who do not contribute by paying either an admission fee or a utilization fee. Buchanan (1965) regarded clubs as non-government private alternatives for the provision of collective goods, but the model can be considered to be more appropriate for guiding the actions of local governments in this field than for explaining the workings and functioning of voluntary non-governmental organizations.
2. The private government can be considered a special kind of club. The collective good exhibits a type of imperfect or coarse exclusion (Helsley and Strange 1991). Specifically, with public provision, there is universal access; the collective good provided by the public sector is available to all consumers. This universal access may be the result of technical difficulties or institutional rigidities (legal guaranties of equal provision). In contrast, with private provision there is restricted access; the private supplement is available only to subscribers.
3. Analysing non-profit institutions we cannot leave out the ideological and religious dimension of a large part of them. This is a way to overcome free-riding problems in the presence of altruism (Collard 1987). It also explains why people form non-profit organizations to redistribute income to the poor, lobby the government on behalf of general causes and so forth.
4. Note that public output G^G only fulfils the Pareto-optimum condition if the preference of the median voter coincides with the average for all members of the community. That is, if $g_j = \bar{g}$, then $T = g_j$ and $G^V = G^G$. In such a case, the median voter is indifferent between public or private provision.

REFERENCES

Andreoni, J. (1988), 'Privately provided public goods in a large economy: the limits of altruism', *Journal of Public Economics*, **35**, 57–73.

Andreoni, J. (1990), 'Impure altruism and donations to public goods: a theory of warm-glow giving', *The Economic Journal*, **100**, 464–77.

Bernheim, B.D. (1986), 'On the voluntary and involuntary provision of public goods', *American Economic Review*, **76**, 787–93.

Buchanan, J.M. (1965), 'An economic theory of clubs', *Economica*, **33**, 1–14.

Buchanan, J.M. (1991), *The Economics of the Ethics of Constitutional Order*, Ann Arbor, MI: University of Michigan Press.

Buchanan, J.M. (1996), *Ética y progreso económico*, Barcelona: Ariel.

Casas Pardo, J., M.A. Puchades and A. Sajardo (2001), 'Volunteer nonprofits' provision of collective goods as a public choice decision', *DT 2001–2*, Instituto Universitario de Economia y Mercado, Madrid.

Collard, D. (1987), *Altruism and Economy: A Study of Nonselfish Economics*, New York: Oxford University Press.

Cornes, R. and T. Sandler (1986), *The Theory of Externalities, Public Goods and Club Goods*, New York: Cambridge University Press.

Gassler, R.S. (1998), 'Altruism and the economics of non-profit organizations', *Financial Accountability & Management*, **14**, 173–82.

Harbaugh, W.T. (1998), 'What do donations buy? A model of philanthropy based on prestige and warm glow', *Journal of Public Economics*, **67**, 269–84.

Helsley, R.W. and W.C. Strange (1991), 'Exclusion and the theory of clubs', *Canadian Journal of Economics*, **XXIV**, 888–99.

Helsley, R.W. and W.C. Strange (1998), 'Private government', *Journal of Public Economics*, **69**, 281–304.

Holländer, H. (1990), 'A social exchange approach to voluntary cooperation', *American Economic Review*, **80**, 1157–67.

Kingma, B.R. (1989), 'An accurate measurement of the crowd-out effect, income effect and price effect for charitable contributions', *Journal of Political Economy*, **97**, 1197–1207.

Nyborg, K. and M. Rege (2003), 'Does public policy crowd out private contributions to public goods?', *Public Choice*, **115**, 397–418.

Rabin, M. (1993), 'Incorporating fairness into game theory and economics', *American Economic Review*, **83**, 1281–1302.

Ribar, D.C. and M.O. Wilhelm (2002), 'Altruistic and joy-of-giving motivations in charitable behaviour', *Journal of Political Economy*, **110**, 425–57.

Roberts, R.D. (1984), 'A positive model of private charity and public transfers', *Journal of Political Economy*, **92**, 136–48.

Sugden, R. (1982), 'On the economics of philanthropy', *The Economic Journal*, **92**, 341–50.

Sugden, R. (1984), 'Reciprocity: the supply of public goods through voluntary contributions', *The Economic Journal*, **94**, 772–87.

Warr, P.G. (1982), 'Pareto optimal redistribution and private charity', *Journal of Public Economics*, **19**, 131–8.

Weisbrod, B.A. (1975), 'Towards a theory of the voluntary nonprofit sector in a three sector economy', in E. Phelps (ed.), *Altruism, Morality: An Economic Theory*, New York: Russell Sage Foundation, pp. 171–95.

Weisbrod, B.A. (1988), *The Nonprofit Economy*, Cambridge: Harvard University Press.

17. Awards play an important role

Bruno S. Frey and Susanne Neckermann

1. THE NATURE OF AWARDS

Awards in the form of orders, decorations, prizes, and titles, are predominantly non-material, but extrinsic incentives. They thus differ from both intrinsic incentives and extrinsic incentives in the form of money. Awards have existed in all centuries, and are used in all countries and in all areas of society, including the private sector of the economy.

There are major differences between awards and monetary compensation:

- The material costs of awards, consisting of a certificate or a small trophy, are typically low for the donors, but the value to the recipients may be very high.
- Accepting an award establishes a special relationship, in which the recipient owes (some measure of) loyalty to the donor. This is not true for monetary compensation.
- Due to their vague nature, awards are more adequate incentive instruments than monetary payments when the recipient's performance can only be vaguely determined.
- Awards are less likely to crowd out the intrinsic motivation of their recipients than monetary compensation.
- Awards are not taxed, while monetary income is.

In our view, these substantial differences make it worthwhile to analyze awards as a separate phenomenon. Nevertheless, economists have traditionally focused on monetary compensation and have largely disregarded awards.[1] Major reasons for this neglect may be:

- Awards may be considered to be *less efficient* incentives than monetary compensation, because they are not fungible and are difficult to apply marginally. Hence, the use of awards presents an error by the award giver that should be eliminated by the market over time.

- Awards may be the *result* of high motivation and success and not a contributing *cause*. While awards are sometimes bestowed on already famous persons to associate that person with the award-giving organization, the majority of awards do serve as incentives either directly or indirectly. Awards are direct incentives, when they are known to be handed out for a particular kind of effort, e.g. an award for best customer service in the next year. Awards serve as indirect incentives when they create role models.
- Awards may be thought to motivate only insofar as they lead to *future* material or immaterial *benefits*. Their impact on behavior can then be studied directly. Ginsburgh and van Ours (2003), for instance, show that winning the Queen Elizabeth musical competition, the best-known international competition for piano (and violin), significantly increases subsequent market performance of the artist. However, Huberman et al. (2004) demonstrate that people value status independently of any monetary consequence; they are even willing to incur material costs to obtain it.
- Economists may shy away from the study of awards because of serious data limitations. To our knowledge, there is no comprehensive list of awards spanning the different types and levels of awards in the various spheres of society (government, the arts, culture, media, sports, religion, academia, not-for-profits and for-profit enterprises), countries and time periods. Only partial, spotty and inconsistent evidence is available from scattered sources. This applies in particular to the many awards given by private institutions, such as non-profit organizations, clubs and firms. Orders given by monarchs or governments are somewhat better documented. In general, it seems to be impossible to measure the usage of awards from the supply side. There are hundreds of thousands, if not millions (and moreover a constantly changing set), of institutions bestowing awards in the various countries.

This chapter endeavours to empirically document the importance of awards in modern societies. Due to the serious data limitations addressed above, we construct our own data set. We believe that the best source of information on the awards received by an individual is the *International Who's Who (IWW)* by Neal (2006), which covers the most important personalities in each of the 212 countries included in the book. Entrants are asked to indicate the honors and awards they received. This enables us to challenge some popular – but as we shall show mistaken – notions about awards.

The next section presents five widely held beliefs about awards, and discusses their validity using the unique data compiled on the basis of the *International Who's Who*. The concluding section argues that it is important for economists to study awards.

2. HOW CORRECT ARE BELIEFS ABOUT AWARDS?

Five generally held notions about awards are challenged and analyzed using the data constructed on the basis of the *International Who's Who*. This data source provides information on the number and kinds of awards each person received as well as on person-specific characteristics such as nationality, job, age, and international mobility. A sub-sample of 82 countries was selected according to the availability of the basic country specific variables necessary for the statistical analysis. For these 82 countries a random sample of 50 persons per country was chosen. Where there were less than 50 entries, all the available entries were coded. With respect to awards, we collected the following information when available: source of the award (country of origin, foreign country, or international); award-giving institution (state, private organizations, non-profit organizations, university, media) and category in which the prize was awarded (social welfare, military, science, culture/art, sport, media, business, religion). This information allows us to construct the number of awards received per person.

Five Popular Notions

1. Awards are important only in monarchies

In the past, awards have mainly consisted in state orders, honors and decorations and have been closely connected to monarchies. In Spain, for example, the Golden Fleece (founded in 1430) is the most important and best-known Order, but there is also the Order of Carlos III, of Santiago, of Isabella the Catholic and the Laureate Cross of Saint Ferdinand.

Table 17.1 suggests that the link between monarchies and awards no longer holds nowadays.

The left-hand panel of Table 17.1 lists the countries with the ten highest average numbers of awards received per individual. Among those countries with the highest number of awards, seven are republics (the Anglo-Saxon countries Canada, Australia – we count them as republics – and New Zealand; and the European countries Poland, Hungary, Switzerland and Finland). Only two are monarchies (the United Kingdom and Spain). The table also lists information on the number of awards received for

Table 17.1 Average number of awards per individual per country

Total awards		Domestic state awards	
Mean	2.66	Mean	0.43
Variance	1.96	Variance	0.11
Top 10 countries in each category			
Canada	6.82	Poland	1.78
UK	6.78	France	1.32
Poland	6.16	Tunisia	1.05
Australia	5.66	Egypt	1.02
Senegal	5.30	Malaysia	1.00
Hungary	5.00	Finland	0.88
New Zealand	4.96	Canada	0.86
Switzerland	4.70	Portugal	0.84
Finland	4.64	Ecuador	0.83
Spain	4.20	Philippines	0.82
Information on 7 additional countries			
USA	3.80		0.22
Canada	6.82		0.86
UK	6.78		0.78
France	3.60		1.32
Germany	2.46		0.48
Spain	4.20		0.70
Italy	1.96		0.22

an additional set of seven countries deemed to be of particular interest. Americans living in the United States receive a considerable number of awards, more than in France and Italy. The data indicate that today awards are no longer linked to monarchies. Indeed, staunch republics such as France, the United States and Switzerland are on top of the list of the 82 countries in our sample.

It might be argued that the monarchic link of awards would become apparent when awards bestowed by the domestic state are considered. Column 2 of Table 17.1 shows that among the top ten countries, there is an even smaller number of monarchies (Tunisia and Malaysia) but eight republics. The United Kingdom and Spain drop out of this list. This suggests that, surprisingly, state awards tend to be even more popular in republics than they are in monarchies.

2. Awards are mainly used in the military sector

Judging from pictures appearing in the press of soldiers and officers having their chests covered with orders, decorations and medals, it might be concluded that most awards are received by the military. However, our data suggest that awards are not mainly a military affair.

Of the 82 countries in the sample, 49 countries contain individuals from the military sector in their sample of individuals drawn from the *IWW*. Averaged over these 49 countries, these people receive 11 per cent of the total number of awards. If one includes the remaining countries in the calculation, assuming that these exhibit zero awards per person in the military sector, this figure falls to 7 per cent. But in a few countries awards focus indeed on persons in the military. In Uganda, Paraguay, and Venezuela, for example, one third to almost one half of all awards (46 per cent, 38 per cent and 37 per cent, respectively) are given to people in the army. However, these countries are the exception rather than the rule. When considering domestic government awards only, the share of awards going to persons in the military sector is larger (15 per cent or 9 per cent depending on whether countries without military personnel in the sample are included in the calculation). However, this share is still far from being dominant.

3. There are few awards in academia

It might be expected that in academia intrinsic interest in scientific progress and/or monetary compensation would provide all the motivational drive needed and that awards are not necessarily held in high esteem.

In contrast to this notion, however, academia has an elaborate and extensive system of professional associations awarding a great number of medals. Nobel Prizes are certainly the most visible ones. Many prestigious fellowships exist in academies of science. Moreover, there is a complicated system of titles (not always connected to functions), such as that of lecturer, reader, assistant professor, associate professor with or without tenure, full professor, named professor, university professor, distinguished professor, etc. Honorary doctorates are another form of highly valued awards in academia.

Table 17.2 reports that almost one quarter of all awards (23 per cent) are given to individuals in academia.

Switzerland and Belgium lead with a share of 66 per cent of all awards going to individuals in academia. In Turkey the academic sector is also a major recipient (61 per cent). There are four additional countries in which half or more of the awards go into this sector (Netherlands with 56 per cent, Germany with 55 per cent, Australia with 53 per cent, and Nigeria with 50 per cent).

Column 2 shows the ten top countries listed according to the average number of awards received by the elite. These include the United States, and several other countries whose university systems count among the

Table 17.2 Awards per country going to individuals in academia

Share of total awards		Average number of awards	
Mean	0.23	Mean	3.76
Variance	0.03	Variance	7.62
Top 10 countries in each category			
Switzerland	0.66	Belgium	10.83
Belgium	0.66	Venezuela	10.00
Turkey	0.61	Switzerland	9.50
Netherlands	0.56	Japan	9.43
Germany	0.55	USA	9.43
Australia	0.53	Lithuania	9.17
Nigeria	0.50	France	8.50
Sweden	0.47	Poland	7.67
Israel	0.45	Argentina	7.60
El Salvador	0.43	Australia	7.50
Information on 7 additional countries			
USA	0.35		9.43
Canada	0.21		6.00
UK	0.19		6.50
France	0.28		8.50
Germany	0.55		3.37
Spain	0.06		1.71
Italy	0.42		3.80

leading ones: Belgium, Switzerland, Japan, France and Australia. But some other countries give much weight to bestowing academics with awards though their universities are not considered to be among the best (Venezuela, Lithuania, Poland and Argentina).

Our data suggest that it is mistaken to claim that awards are unimportant in the academic system. Individuals in the scientific sector, the place of rational discourse, are quite happy to receive awards.

4. There are few awards in the business sector

One may think that awards are rarely used in the corporate sector of a market economy. After all, employees in private corporations are used to seeing their performance compensated in monetary terms. Moreover, transactions in the market sector are typically considered to aim solely at realizing mutual material advantages. This would disqualify awards as they consist in a paper certificate or a small trophy with a value close to zero. Moreover, awards are inefficient as compared to monetary compensation as they are not fungible and competition should therefore drive them out of existence.

Table 17.3 Business awards

Average number of business awards per person		Average number of awards of a person in business sector		Proportion of awards in country handed out for business activities	
Mean	0.06	Mean	1.14	Mean	0.02
Variance	0.01	Variance	1.62	Variance	0.00
Top 10 countries in each category					
Canada	0.52	Canada	4.78	Saudi Arabia	0.21
Singapore	0.46	Venezuela	4.75	Korea, Republic of	0.15
USA	0.34	Israel	4.00	Singapore	0.15
Saudi Arabia	0.27	Luxembourg	4.00	Tanzania	0.14
Australia	0.26	Ukraine	3.60	USA	0.10
Korea, Republic of	0.24	UK	3.50	China	0.10
Philippines	0.20	Australia	3.43	Israel	0.09
Sweden	0.18	Nigeria	3.38	Pakistan	0.09
Turkey	0.16	Poland	3.00	Canada	0.08
Israel/ Switzerland	0.14	China	2.80	Turkey	0.08
Information on 7 additional countries					
USA	0.34		1.17		0.10
Canada	0.52		4.78		0.08
UK	0.04		3.50		0.01
France	0.04		1.50		0.01
Germany	0.06		0.47		0.03
Spain	0.06		0.33		0.02
Italy	0.04		1.14		0.02

However, already a casual observation of business practice suggests that awards and titles are very important. Consider Federal Express, which confers a host of awards, for individual as well as team efforts. These include the 'Circle of Excellence Award' which is presented monthly to the best-performing FedEx station, and the 'Golden Falcon' which is awarded to employees who go beyond the call of duty to serve their customers. Honorees of the latter award receive a golden uniform pin, a congratulatory phone call from a senior executive and ten shares of stock.

Column 1 of Table 17.3 shows that across all 82 countries, the average individual has 0.06 business awards. This number may sound small, but is quite sizeable considering the large number of politicians, artists and sportspersons in the *International Who's Who* that typically are not eligible for business awards, which lower the mean. The eleven countries with the highest number of business awards per individual in our sample comprise a broad variety of countries in terms of GDP per capita. The top 10 include some countries that are rich such as Canada, Singapore, the United States, Saudi Arabia, Sweden and Switzerland, but also some developing countries such as the Philippines and Turkey.

The second column of Table 17.3 indicates that in some countries, such as Canada, Venezuela, Israel and Luxembourg, business persons included in *IWW* on average indicate having received quite a number of awards (between four and five). China's business people listed in *IWW* receive a substantial number of awards, more than even the respective US business persons.

The claim made about the unimportance of awards in business is partly right (see column 3 of Table 17.3). Awards going to individuals active in business are shown to be of little importance in many countries such as Spain or Italy, but are very central in some of the economically most successful countries of the world, such as Singapore, the United States, China and Israel, with between 9 and 15 per cent of all awards. It may be conjectured that the picture will change in the future. An increasing number of countries may well adopt the practice of honoring business people with awards, thus imitating the economically particularly successful countries.

3. AWARDS PLAY AN IMPORTANT ROLE

The statistics presented in this chapter allow some interesting and unexpected insights. Awards are widely used in modern society and not solely in monarchies; they are predominantly in the civilian sector and are not mainly a military affair; and they are important in academia as well as in business. Hence, awards are worthwhile studying as they present a widespread empirical phenomenon that we currently know little about.

NOTE

1. Forerunners are Hansen and Weisbrod (1972), Besley (2005), and Frey (2005). A few isolated works discuss awards as incentives, e.g. Gavrila et al. (2005). For the case of corporations, Cueni et al. (2008) study the channels via which awards motivate and investigate the differences to monetary rewards. Malmendier and Tate (2005) as well as Neckermann et al. (2009) find that awards significantly affect the subsequent behavior of winners. Markham et al. (2002), Frey and Neckermann (2008), Neckermann et al. (2010), and Kosfeld and Neckermann (2011) show that award systems have a systematic incentive effect on performance in the corporate sector, and that managers rightly take awards seriously as incentive instruments.

REFERENCES

Besley, Timothy (2005), 'Notes on honours', mimeo, London School of Economics.

Cueni, Reto, Susanne Neckermann and Bruno S. Frey (2008), 'Awards as incentives', IEW Working Paper, Institute for Empirical Research in Economics, University of Zurich.

Frey, Bruno S. (2005), 'Knight fever. Towards an economics of awards', IEW Working Paper, Institute for Empirical Research in Economics, University of Zurich.

Frey, Bruno S. and Susanne Neckermann (2008), 'Awards: a view from psychological economics', *Journal of Psychology*, **216** (Special Issue), 198–208.

Gavrila, Caius, Jonathan P. Caulkins, Gustav Feichtinger, Gernot Tragler and Richard F. Hartl (2005), 'Managing the reputation of an award to motivate performance', *Mathematical Methods of Operations Research*, **61** (1), 1–22.

Ginsburgh, Victor A. and Jan C. van Ours (2003), 'Expert opinion and compensation: evidence from a musical competition', *American Economic Review*, **93** (1), 289–96.

Hansen, J. Lee and Burton Weisbrod (1972), 'Toward a general theory of awards, or, do economists need a hall of fame?', *The Journal of Political Economy*, **80** (2), 422–31.

Huberman, Bernardo A., Christoph H. Loch and Ayse Onculer (2004), 'Status as a valued resource', *Social Psychology Quarterly*, **67** (1), 103–14.

Kosfeld, Michael and Susanne Neckerman (2011), 'Getting more work for nothing? Symbolic awards and worker performance', *American Economic Journal: Microeconomics*, **3**, 1–16.

Malmendier, Ulrike and Geoffrey Tate (2005), 'Superstar CEOs', mimeo, University of Stanford, University of Pennsylvania.

Markham, Steven E., K. Dow Scott and Gail H. McKee (2002), 'Recognizing good attendance: a longitudinal, quasi-experimental field study', *Personnel Psychology*, **55** (3), 639–60.

Neal, Alison (ed.) (2006), *The International Who's Who*, London: Routledge.

Neckermann, Susanne, Reto Cueni and Bruno S. Frey (2009), 'What is an award worth? An econometric assessment of the impact of awards on employee performance', IEW Working Paper No. 411, University of Zurich.

Neckermann, Susanne, Reto Cueni and Bruno S. Frey (2010), 'Awards at work', Working Paper No. 411, Department of Economics, University of Zurich.

18. The optimal Babel: an economic framework for the analysis of dynamic language rights*

Bengt-Arne Wickström

1. INTRODUCTION

Language is certainly the most important means of communication in all human societies. At the same time, language is one of the most important aspects of an individual's personality, as well as of its social and cultural identity. These two aspects of language often find themselves in conflict with one another.

On the one hand, network externality properties of the communication aspect imply that the greater is the number of speakers of a certain language, the more useful is that language in communication; taking this to the extreme, it would be efficient to have only one single language for communication purposes.

Balancing this tendency is the desire of many individuals to preserve their language as a marker of identity. In a static perspective, language, like talents and other personal characteristics, can be seen as part of the definition, or initial endowment, of the individual. In a dynamic setting, however, the situation is slightly more complex. Here, we have to distinguish between dynamics within a generation and between generations. Of course, an individual can over its lifespan change its language, or acquire additional idioms. However, the more drastic changes occur between generations, where a language shift often happens over three consecutive generations: the members of one generation are unilingual in one language, their children grow up bilingual and their grandchildren unilingual in the second language.

The survival of a language, its implantation in the next generation, depends on many factors, one of which is the status of the language in society. This status is influenced by, among other things, the possibilities to use the language in various social areas or domains.

Whether a language receives an official status in any specific domain or not, is very often a political issue, and it is an instrument that can be used by those in power – be it a dominant majority or a political elite – to control and exploit those who are weak, whether they are underprivileged masses or ethnic minorities or both. An analysis of these aspects is closely related to rent-seeking and political, social and economic power. These are questions analyzed in positive economics.

One can also, however, look at the problem from a constitutional or normative perspective. One may look for acceptable allocations of rights according to some ethics criterion. The choice of rights for minorities can, for instance, be realized in a decentralized Wicksellian system based on the equivalence principle, where only (potential) Pareto improvements on some initial situation are to be realized within the community, or the desired allocation of rights may be governed by some other normative principles, such as the maximization of a (paternalistic) welfare function. These principles may or may not consider the effects on other external communities.

In this chapter the dynamic impact of assigning rights to certain languages is tied together with the Wicksellian view of an optimal allocation and contrasted with a more welfare-oriented approach. We set up a formal dynamic model of language evolution in Section 2 and then specify this model in Section 3 in order to analyze first the equivalence-principle approach in Section 3.1. Then in Section 3.2 it is shown that this approach causes negative externalities outside the ethnic community. Finally, in Section 4, it is demonstrated that in a paternalistic model of justice these externalities have to be relativized.

1.1 Language and the Allocation of Rights

One can distinguish between various characteristics of the goods enjoyed by the individuals in a society. The actual use of a language is an individual matter, giving benefits to the individual using it.[1] Whether a person chooses to use a certain language or not in a given situation, will to a large extent depend upon the constraints the person is facing. One important constraint is, of course, whether one is understood or not and manages to communicate. This can partially be determined by legal rights, forcing, for instance, public offices to accept the use of certain languages in doing official business. Ignoring associated costs, such rights to communication in a certain language can in principle be made available to all individuals to the same extent. Unlike many other rights, like the right to smoke in public places versus the right to enjoy fresh air at the same location, the right to use a certain language in a given setting is a non-exclusive right that does not per se exclude the right to use another language in the same setting.

My right to communicate with (and get answers from) a public office in Bislama, say, does not infringe on your right to use Volapük in doing your business with the same office.

Considering the costs of implementing a right, we note that in the dependency on the number of beneficiaries all possible degrees of economies of scale can occur. Having street signs in a certain language, involves only fixed costs, whereas the provision of elementary education is more or less proportional to the number of beneficiaries.

Here we are focusing on these legal rights and not on all the other possibilities to use a language outside the public sector. The latter possibilities are, of course, determined primarily by the number of speakers, but also by other factors, such as the domain in which a certain interaction takes place. In a comprehensive analysis of language rights and justice, these aspects would also have to be taken into account.[2] In this chapter, however, we limit the analysis to formal legal rights.

2. THE BASIC MODEL

2.1 Notation

Society at time t is made of a set N_t of all individuals born into society at time t as well as the set N_{t-1} of all individuals born at time $t-1$. That is, the set of individuals alive in period t is given by $N_t \cup N_{t-1}$. In other words, an individual lives two periods. At birth it is socialized into a certain language l, where the set of all languages under consideration is denoted by L.[3] The number of individuals of cohort t in language group l, that is, the number of individuals born in period t into group l, is written as n_t^{l0}. Since individuals live for two periods, the number of older individuals alive at time t is n_{t-1}^{l0}. This is also denoted by n_t^{l1}. The total number of individuals in group l at time t is then $n_t^{l0} + n_{t-1}^{l0} = n_t^{l0} + n_t^{l1} = : n_t^l$. Let the set of legally defined domains be D. The set of rights in effect at time t is a matrix r_t of zeroes and ones. The right to use language l in domain d in period t is then written as $r_t^{ld} = 1$ and the denial of that right as $r_t^{ld} = 0$. The propensity of individual i to pay for a certain allocation of rights, r, is written as $b^i(r)$.

This propensity to pay is, of course, only well defined in relation to a status quo. That is, we normalize the propensities to pay to be equal to zero at the status quo. Two polar choices are $\tilde{r} = O$, all r^{ld} are zero, and $\tilde{r} = I$, all r^{ld} are equal to one. The first case means that our benchmark is that there are no rights at all in effect and the second signifies that the benchmark is the existence of all possible rights in all domains for all languages.

Intuitively, one can say that, in the first case, we are born without any individual rights, and all rights have to be bought from society. In the second case, we are all born with all possible rights, and the negation of any right has to be bought from the beneficiaries of that right by the rest of society.[4] For the purpose of this chapter, we will assume the former, that is $b^i(O)$ is set equal to 0 for all i. The right to be able to use a certain language in a certain situation can for our purposes be looked upon as a non-rival good. The 'demand' or propensity to pay for this good will vary over the individuals. The sum of all individuals' propensities to pay will then give society's total propensity to pay for this specific right. A difference from the text-book case is that the rights are not continuous, but discrete non-rival goods. Of course, the individual propensity to pay will depend (directly or indirectly) on a number of exogenous factors such as income and prices, but also the availability of other language rights will enter the demand for any specific right to use a certain language.[5]

Let $c(r, n)$ be the costs to society that the realization of the rights allocation r causes. Again, this can only be sensibly defined in relation to the status quo. The costs will depend on a number of factors in addition to r. Especially, the number of individuals making use of the right is important. The function c is assumed to be concave in n^l if $r^{ld} = 1$ for some d.[6]

2.2 Dynamic Structure

It is reasonable to assume that the rights conveyed on speakers of language l in effect at period t influence the status of that language in that period and, hence, the choice of language of the next generation, that is the size of n^{l0}_{t+1}.[7] That is, we assume, that the parents, when they bring up their children, decide on socializing them into their own language or another (majority) language depending on the status of the own language compared to the alternative language(s) – the emotional, cultural aspect – as well as on the number of speakers – the practical, communication aspect. Hence, the distribution of the individuals on the different language groups, as well as the rights given to the speakers of the various languages will determine the size of the groups in the next cohort. That is, the distribution of the next cohort on the language groups is assumed to be given by a function g, such that

$$n^0_{t+1} = g(r_t, n^0_t), \tag{18.1}$$

with

$$\Delta_\xi n_{t+1}^{l0} := g^l(\bar{r}_t, n_t^0) - g^l(\mathring{r}_t, n_t^0) > 0, \text{ if} \begin{cases} \Delta r_t^{md} := \bar{r}_t^{md} - \mathring{r}_t^{md} = 0 \text{ for } m \neq l \\ \Delta r_t^{ld} = 0 \text{ for all } d \neq \xi \\ \Delta r_t^{l\xi} = 1 \end{cases} \tag{18.2}$$

$$l > \frac{\partial g^l(r_t, n_t^0)}{\partial n_t^{l0}} \geq 0,$$

where n_t^0 is the vector of all n_t^{l0}. The population dynamics is then given by

$$\dot{n}_{t+1}^{l0} := n_{t+1}^{l0} - n_t^{l0} = g^l(r_t, n_t^0) - n_t^{l0} \tag{18.3}$$

By setting $\dot{n}_{t+1}^{l0}$ for all l, we find a (in general) different steady state distribution of the language groups for any given allocation of rights in society:

$$n^{l0}(\bar{r}) > n^{l0}(\mathring{r}) \begin{cases} \Delta r^{md} := \bar{r}^{md} - \mathring{r}^{md} = 0 \text{ if } m \neq l \\ \Delta r_t^{ld} \geq 0 \text{ for all } d \\ \Delta r^{ld} = 1 \text{ for some } d \end{cases} \tag{18.4}$$

This dynamic structure is a crucial assumption of the model.

2.3 Efficiency

In analyzing the efficient allocation of rights, we look for Pareto efficiency. This can easily be realized applying the compensated-variation criterion.

Let N be the relevant set of individuals and suppress the time index. The aggregated propensity in society, denoted by b, to pay for any given allocation of rights, r, is then given by

$$b(r) = \sum_{i \in N} b^i(r). \tag{18.5}$$

This would have to be compared to the costs to society of providing these rights. The change in language rights from the status quo, $\bar{r}$, to r is an improvement according to the compensated-variation criterion if

$$\sum_{i \in N} b^i(r) > c(r). \tag{18.6}$$

By introducing compensation payments (or taxes), θ^i, we can formulate this slightly differently. The sum of the compensation payments covers the costs of introducing the rights – the introduction is feasible – if θ is in the set

$$\Theta^F(r) := \left\{\theta \Big| \sum_{i \in N} \theta^i = c(r)\right\}. \tag{18.7}$$

The net benefit to individual i of the allocation of rights r in comparison to the status quo is given by

$$a^i(r,\theta^i) := b^i(r) - \theta^i. \tag{18.8}$$

The necessary requirement that this allocation be a feasible (strong) Pareto improvement, is then that all a be positive, that is, that θ be in the set defined by

$$\Theta^P(r) := \{\theta \in \Theta^F(r) | a^i(r,\theta^i) > 0, \forall i\}. \tag{18.9}$$

A necessary and sufficient condition for the set $\Theta^P(r)$ to be non-empty is that the set

$$\Theta^E(r) := \left\{\theta \in \Theta^F(r) \Big| \sum_{i \in N} a^i(r,\theta^i) > 0\right\} \tag{18.10}$$

be non-empty. Clearly, $\Theta^P(r) \subset \Theta^E(r)$, and the condition $\Theta^P(r) \neq \emptyset$ is equivalent to condition 18.6. If 18.6 holds, we can always find a set of compensation payments such that every individual experiences an improvement on the status quo through the introduction of the allocation of rights r.

The Pareto-efficient allocations can then be found by maximizing the sum of the net benefits, denoted by S, over all possible allocations of rights subject to the feasibility constraint 18.7:

$$\max_r S, \text{ such that } S := \sum_{i \in N} a^i(r,\theta^i) \text{ and } \theta \in \Theta^F(r) \tag{18.11}$$

This can also be written as

$$\max_r \left[\sum_{i \in N} b^i(r) - c(r)\right]. \tag{18.12}$$

Denote the set of r solving 18.11 by $\hat{R}$. If $\bar{r} \notin \hat{R}$, then $\Theta^P(\hat{r}) \neq \emptyset$, and the efficient allocation can also be realized as a Pareto improvement on the status quo.

2.4 Rights, Fairness and Justice

The liberal theory of justice, also referred to as justice as fairness, basically takes the position that, in making normative judgments, an individual should be able to abstract from his or her own position in society in order to make decisions about just allocations of resources between all individuals. One should be able to 'put oneself into others' shoes'. This way of thinking goes back at least as far as antiquity. In Plato (1888, 1980) Socrates uses such an argument to justify to Crito why he would not be prepared to leave Athens even in the face of imminent execution. In modern times, Rawls (1971) has become the standard reference in the moral philosophy applied to the social sciences.

Fairness is usually defined as freedom from envy in combination with an efficient allocation of resources.[8] It is a well-known result, that fair allocations in many situations do not exist.[9] In other cases, one can also argue that the concept is not very relevant. If we are talking about exclusive rights, for example, any allocation is envy-free, since all individuals have the same right. However, some individuals might value the right more than others.[10]

In the case of non-exclusive rights, like the right to use a language of one's choice, this problem does not arise with the same severity. Also here one could argue that the right to use a certain language in a certain domain is the same for all and hence fair, just like the right to smoke in public places. However, a more reasonable point of departure is also possible. One can, as noted in Section 2.4.1 below, choose a status quo where each individual has the same right in relation to a language of their choice and then allow voluntary interchanges in the form of side payments for less rights. This would be in the spirit of fairness. This choice of a status quo with equal rights in this sense, however, is a priori a political issue independent of a strictly *wertfrei* analysis, and different choices have different implications.[11]

In this chapter, we will take as our status quo the absence of all rights and as a first-best optimum define compensation payments in $\Theta^P(r)$. A first-best optimum is then realized under the condition that all the externalities to be discussed in Section 3 are accounted for.

The problem becomes interesting, however, when certain compensation payments are impossible, restricting the feasible transfers to some politically-institutionally given set $\Psi, \Theta^P(r) \cap \Psi = \varnothing$. Here, some kind of trade-off between different individuals has to be defined. Such a definition will always be subjective and political, determined by the preferences of the policy-maker. This trade-off can be formalized with the help of a welfare function.

2.4.1 Efficiency versus equality

In order to address the issue of justice, as already noted, we need some standard of comparison between individuals. We will deal with the individual changes a^i from the given status quo and then discuss the criteria for the interpersonal comparison of these changes. The status quo is *per definitionem* just. This is the basic axiom of our analysis of just distributions. Limiting the analysis to only one sector of society – the allocation of language rights – we are implicitly assuming that injustices in other parts of society are of no consequence for the allocation of language rights. Contrary to the analysis in Section 2.3 it is now assumed that not all transfer payments are possible, but are restricted to some (institutionally given) set Ψ that defines the politically feasible payments. That is, restriction 18.7 is now replaced by

$$\theta \in \Psi \cap \Theta^F(r). \tag{18.13}$$

It is assumed that the vector of zeroes – no transfer payments – is in the set Ψ. Then, clearly, $0 \in \Psi \cap \Theta^F(r)$ and, by definition, $a^i(\bar{r},0) = 0$.

The welfare function needed to analyze the comparison over individuals, is defined to be a function of the a's, $W(a)$. Under the assumption that $\Psi \cap \Theta^F(r)$ is non-empty the maximization problem then becomes:

$$\max_r W(a) \text{ such that } \theta \in \Psi \cap \Theta^F(r) \tag{18.14}$$

Assuming W to be concave and additively separable in the a^i, that is

$$W(a) = \sum_{i \in N} \omega(a^i), \tag{18.15}$$

with ω a concave function, the maximization problem can be written as

$$\max_r \sum_{i \in N} \frac{\omega(a^i)}{a^i} a^i(r, \theta^i) \text{ such that } \theta \in \Psi \cap \Theta^F(r) \tag{18.16}$$

or

$$\max_r \sum_{i \in N} \beta(a^i) a^i(r, \theta^i) \text{ such that } \theta \in \Psi \cap \Theta^F(r). \tag{18.17}$$

By not making ω, and, hence, β, dependent on i, we assume that all individuals are treated symmetrically.

The function $\beta(a^i)$ is the policy variable of the planner determining the degree of inequality aversion, giving different weights to the individuals according to their net gains. If the planner is not concerned about distributional issues, all $\beta(a^i)$ are constant and identical, $\beta(a^i) = \beta$, and the maximization problem searches the efficient allocation:

$$\max_r \beta \sum_{i \in N} a^i(r, \theta^i) \text{ such that } \theta \in \Psi \cap \Theta^F(r). \tag{18.18}$$

This is equivalent to:

$$\max_r \left[\sum_{i \in N} b^i(r) - c(r) \right] \tag{18.19}$$

If all weight is given to the person with the lowest gain (or largest loss), the case of extremely egalitarian policy, we have:

$$\max_r \min_{i \in N} \{a^i(r, \theta^i)\} \text{ such that } \theta \in \Psi \cap \Theta^F(r) \tag{18.20}$$

The planner will minimize the loss of the biggest loser. In general, there is a trade-off between efficiency and equality and the choice of the function $\beta(a)$ determines the amount of trade-off that is deemed (politically) acceptable.

3. THE EFFICIENT ALLOCATION OF LANGUAGE RIGHTS

We will illustrate the analytical framework above with the aid of a simple example. In spite of its simplicity, the example suffices for our purpose in this chapter, which is to address the dynamic issue of rights allocation. We limit ourselves to two languages and two language groups, A and B. An individual i belongs to either group. Group A is the majority and B the minority, and we analyze the efficiency of providing full rights to the minority language in any of the domains D, denoted by $r^{Bd} = 1$, if the right is granted, and $r^{Bd} = 0$, if it is not. Assuming 'selfish' preferences, we let the propensity to pay for such a right for language B be $b^i = 0$, if $i \in N^A$, and $b^i > 0$, if $i \in N^B$. Further, let b^i be additive in the various rights:

$$b^i(r^B) = \sum_d b^i(r^{Bd}) \tag{18.21}$$

Let the size of the two groups be n^A and n^B, respectively, and the cost of providing the right, $c(r^{Bd}, n^B)$. The function c is assumed to be concave in n^B.[12] Let

$$b^{iBd} := b^i(r^{Bd})\big|_{r^{Bd}=1} \tag{18.22}$$

and

$$c^{Bd}(n^B) := c(r^{Bd}, n^B)\big|_{r^{Bd}=1}. \tag{18.23}$$

It will now, in a static setting, be efficient to provide the right in domain *d* if

$$S^{Bd} := \sum_{i \in N^B} b^{iBd} - c^{Bd}(n^B) \geq 0. \tag{18.24}$$

We can rewrite this condition as

$$n^B b^{Bd} - c^{Bd}(n^B) \geq 0 \tag{18.25}$$

or

$$b^{Bd} - \frac{c^{Bd}(n^B)}{n^B} \geq 0, \tag{18.26}$$

where b^{Bd} is the average propensity of the *B* individuals to pay for the right.

We can now order the domains according to the size of S^{Bd} with the highest value for $d = 1$ and successively lower (or same) value for increasing values of *d*. There will then be a critical value d^* such that, for all $d \leq d^*$, $S^{Bd} \geq 0$ and, for all $d > d^*$, $S^{Bd} < 0$. That is, it is efficient to introduce rights for language *B* in domains $1, 2, \ldots, d^*$ and not in domains $d^* + 1, d^* + 2, \ldots, D$.[13]

Since an individual is alive for two periods and the generations overlap, the problem is slightly more complex, however. In period *t* there will be both young and old individuals in the two groups. The size of the different groups is n_t^{A0} and $n_t^{A1} (= n_{t-1}^{A0})$ as well as n_t^{B0} and $n_t^{B1} (= n_{t-1}^{B0})$, respectively. Further, $n_t^l := n_t^{l0} + n_t^{l1}$. Correspondingly, we denote the propensities to pay for individuals alive in period *t* by b_t^{i0} and b_t^{i1}. Furthermore, the average propensities are defined as

$$b_t^{l0} := \frac{1}{n_t^{l0}} \sum_{i \in N_t^{l0}} b_t^{i0}$$

$$b_t^{l1} := \frac{1}{n_t^{l1}} \sum_{i \in N_t^{l1}} b_t^{i1}$$

$$b_t^l := \frac{1}{n_t^l} \left(\sum_{i \in N_t^{l1}} b_t^{i1} + \sum_{i \in N_t^{l0}} b_t^{i0} \right). \tag{18.27}$$

The total discounted aggregated net propensity to pay for realizing the right in domain *d* at time $t = 0$ can be decomposed into three effects. There is the one obvious direct effect and two indirect effects due to the fact that the future n^B changes and that the future r^B also might change as a consequence. The effect on the cost-benefit calculation of the introduction of the right in domain d at time t now becomes:[14]

$$\begin{aligned} \Delta_d S^B &= n_0^{B1} b_0^{Bd1} + n_0^{B0} b_0^{Bd0} - c^{Bd}(n_0^{B1} + n_0^{B0}) \\ &+ \sum_{\xi} \sum_{t=1}^{\infty} [n_t^{B1} b_t^{B\xi 1} + n_t^{B0} b_t^{B\xi 0} - c^{B\xi}(n_t^{B1} + n_t^{B0})] \delta^t \Delta_d r_t^{B\xi} \\ &+ \sum_{\xi} \sum_{t=1}^{\infty} \left[\left(b_t^{B\xi} - \frac{c^{B\xi}(n_t^B)}{n_t^B} \right) - n_t^B \frac{\partial}{\partial n_t^B} \left(\frac{c^{B\xi}(n_t^B)}{n_t^B} \right) \right] \delta^t r_t^{B\xi} \Delta_d n_t^B \\ &= S_0^{Bd} + \sum_{t=1}^{\infty} \delta^{\tau} \sum_{\xi} \left\{ S_t^{B\xi} \Delta_d r_t^{B\xi} + \left[\frac{S_t^{B\xi}}{n_t^B} - n_t^B \frac{\partial}{\partial n_t^B} \left(\frac{c^{B\xi}(n_t^B)}{n_t^B} \right) \right] r_t^{B\xi} \Delta_d n_t^B \right\} \end{aligned} \tag{18.28}$$

where $\delta \leq 1$ is a discount factor and the dynamics of n^B is given by

$$\dot{n}_{t+1}^{B0} := n_{t+1}^{B0} - n_t^{B0} = g(r_t^B, n_t^{B0}) - n_t^{B0} =: h(r_t^B, n_t^{B0}). \tag{18.29}$$

The analysis of the problem of finding an optimal allocation of rights, that is, finding a sequence of r_t^B that is efficient, can be divided into several cases. We can see it from the point of view of all – present and future – B individuals or from the point of view of only the B individuals alive in period t. We can also consider the effect on the A individuals, that is possible external effects due to the introduction of rights for language B.

3.1 Group-internal Considerations

If only the interests of the group are taken into consideration, there are two basic views to consider. One is that only the individuals alive at a certain time are to be counted in the decisions. This can be seen as close to a constitutional-economics analysis and is in the tradition of the equivalence principle. It is not unreasonable to assume that individuals will seek institutional set-ups leading to efficient allocations. This is the question asked in constitutional economics and it has its roots in the work of Wicksell. A more normative point of view takes also unborn generations into account. We will see that the results then can differ from the more egocentric view.

3.1.1 Cohort-centered analysis

The total aggregated propensity to pay for the right for language B in domain d at time t and $t + 1$ of the individuals living at time t, that is, the gross benefit to the individuals alive at time t of the right being in effect in periods t and $t + 1$, is now

$$\sum_{i \in N^{Bt}} b_t^{i1} + \sum_{i \in N^{Bt}} b_t^{i0} + \delta \sum_{i \in N^{Bt}} b_{t+1}^{i1} = n_t^{B1} b_t^{B1} + n_t^{B0} b_t^{B0} + \delta n_{t+1}^{B1} b_{t+1}^{B1}$$
$$= n_t^B b_t^B + \delta n_{t+1}^{B1} b_{t+1}^{B1}. \qquad (18.30)$$

The cost of providing the right at time t is $c^{Bd}(n_t^{B1} + n_t^{B0}) = c^{Bd}(n_t^B)$ and at time $t + 1$, $c^{Bd}(n_{t+1}^B)$, from the latter costs, however, in order to get the compensated variation, the propensities to pay of the next generation alive in period $t + 1$ have to be subtracted. From the point of view of the individuals living in period t, the cost-benefit calculation of the introduction of the right in domain d, equation 18.28, hence becomes

$$\Delta_d S_t^B = S_t^{Bd} + \delta \sum_{\xi} \left\{ S_{t+1}^{B\xi} \Delta_d r_{t+1}^{B\xi} + \left[\frac{S_{t+1}^{B\xi}}{n_{t+1}^B} - n_{t+1}^B \frac{\partial}{\partial n_{t+1}^B} \left(\frac{c^{B\xi}(n_{t+1}^B)}{n_{t+1}^B} \right) \right] r_{t+1}^{B\xi} \Delta_d n_{t+1}^B \right\}. \qquad (18.31)$$

In comparison to the static case, we have a second and third term due to the increase in n_{t+1}^B because of the increased status of language B caused by granting it the right in domain d in period t. We need to find a set of domains

$$\hat{D}_t = \{d \in D | \Delta_d S_t^B \geq 0\}. \qquad (18.32)$$

We note that $\hat{D}$ is not necessarily unique, since $\Delta_d n_{t+1}^B$ is a function of the whole vector r_{t+1}^B (not only of r_{t+1}^{Bd}). We can also define the set of domains for which the static criterion is satisfied:

$$D_t^* = \{d \in D | S_t^{Bd} \geq 0\} \qquad (18.33)$$

That is, using the static criterion, we have that $d \in D_t^*$ is equivalent to setting $r_t^{Bd} = 1$. Due to the concavity of c, we see that $n_{t+1}^B > n_t^B$ implies that $D_t^* \subset D_{t+1}^*$ and, hence, $\Delta_d r_{t+1}^{B\xi} \geq 0$ for all ξ.

Since the term after the minus sign in the square brackets of the third term of 18.31 is negative due to the concavity of c in n, the application of the static criterion to expression 18.31 implies that $\Delta_d S_t^B \geq 0$ and that $D_t^* \subset \hat{D}_t$. It is readily seen that it in general is a proper subset, since for small values of ξ the second and third terms will be strictly positive, allowing the first term to become negative without violating the dynamic criterion.

We can then conclude that the static criterion for introducing language rights is too restrictive, and, due to the dynamic structure of the problem, minority rights should go further than a simple static analysis indicates.

3.1.2 Intergenerational efficiency

The net future benefits are given by expression 18.28. In comparison to the analysis in Section 3.1.1, we see that the correction due to the intertemporal structure has increased, since the change in the number of individuals in the B group not only increases in the period after the introduction of the right, but, of course, continues to be bigger than in the alternative scenario – no right in period t – due to the dynamic structure defined in expression (18.2).

3.1.3 Steady state

We can also compare the steady states of intergenerational efficiency with and without a certain right in effect. To simplify things, we consider the situation with and without a right d. All rights in the sets $\{1, \ldots, d-1\}$ and $\{d+1, \ldots, D\}$ are assumed to be unaffected by the decision on d. Further, let $n^B(0)$ be the steady-state size of the B community without right d in effect and correspondingly $n^B(1)$ if right d is in effect. The criterion for keeping right d if it has been in effect is then $\Delta_d S^B(1) \geq 0$ with

$$\Delta_d S^B(1) = n^B(1)\left(b^{Bd} - \frac{c^{Bd}(n^B(1))}{n^B(1)}\right)$$

$$+\sum_{\xi=1}^{d}\left[\left(b^{B\xi} - \frac{c^{B\xi}(n^B(1))}{n^B(1)}\right) - n^B(1)\frac{\partial}{\partial n^B}\left(\frac{c^{B\xi}(n^B(1))}{n^B(1)}\right)\right]\sum_{t=1}^{\infty}\delta^t \Delta_d n^B(1). \tag{18.34}$$

and the criterion for not introducing right d if it has not been in effect is $\Delta_d S^B(0) < 0$ with

$$\Delta_d S^B(0) = n^B(0)\left(b^{Bd} - \frac{c^{Bd}(n^B(0))}{n^B(0)}\right)$$

$$+\sum_{\xi=1}^{d}\left[\left(b^{B\xi} - \frac{c^{B\xi}(n^B(0))}{n^B(0)}\right) - n^B(0)\frac{\partial}{\partial n^B}\left(\frac{c^{B\xi}(n^B(0))}{n^B(0)}\right)\right]\sum_{t=1}^{\infty}\delta^t \Delta_d n^B(0). \tag{18.35}$$

Since $\Delta_d n^B(1)$ and $\Delta_d n^B(0)$ could be assumed to be arbitrarily small and $n^B(1) > n^B(0)$, it is clear that the situation

$$\Delta_d S^B(1) > 0 > \Delta_d S^B(0) \tag{18.36}$$

is not unreasonable, making both allocations of rights efficient in the long run. In other words, the problem of finding an intergenerationally efficient allocation of rights is path-dependent. The analysis of the case of the cohort-centered analysis is, of course, totally parallel.

3.1.4 Discussion

The simple analysis in this section has demonstrated that the naive static criterion for determining the compensated variation of the introduction of language rights tends to underestimate the net benefits of the rights to the speech community. What our analysis tells us, is that a static analysis of the net benefits will lead to a too small set of realized rights, since the status effect on the language of the introduction of the right would not be sufficiently accounted for. *In nuce*, it is efficient from the point of view of a language community to introduce rights that go beyond the instantaneous cost-benefit calculations.

3.2 Global Considerations

In addition to the effects analyzed above, there is also an effect on the A group. If a right is introduced in period t and, as a consequence, the B group increases by $\Delta_d n^B_{t+1}$ in the subsequent period, then, by constant cohort size, the size of the next A generation, n^A_{t+1}, will decrease by $\Delta_d n^B_{t+1}$ and the aggregated propensity to pay for the right of language A in the next generation will also decrease. In the cost benefit calculus in the cohort-centered analysis, the young individuals in period t will hence suffer a loss in period $t+1$, giving us a total aggregated change to the A individuals alive in period t equal to

$$\Delta_d S^A_t = -\delta \sum_\xi \left[b^{A\xi}_{t+1} - \frac{\partial c^{A\xi}(n^A_{t+1})}{\partial n^A_{t+1}} \right] \Delta_d n^B_{t+1}$$

$$= -\delta \sum_\xi \left[\frac{S^{A\xi}_{t+1}}{n^A_{t+1}} - n^A_{t+1} \frac{\partial}{\partial n^A_{t+1}} \left(\frac{c^{A\xi}(n^A_{t+1})}{n^A_{t+1}} \right) \right] \Delta_d n^B_{t+1} < 0. \tag{18.37}$$

This loss would in a global analysis have to be compared to the gain to the B community, found in expression 18.31:

$$\Delta_d S^B_t = S^{Bd}_t + \delta \sum_\xi \left\{ S^{B\xi}_{t+1} \Delta_d r^{B\xi}_{t+1} + \left[\frac{S^{B\xi}_{t+1}}{n^B_{t+1}} - n^B_{t+1} \frac{\partial}{\partial n^B_{t+1}} \left(\frac{c^{B\xi}(n^B_{t+1})}{n^B_{t+1}} \right) \right] r^{B\xi}_{t+1} \Delta_d n^B_{t+1} \right\}, \tag{18.38}$$

and the total gain to society would be

$$\Delta_d S_t = \Delta_d S_t^A + \Delta_d S_t^B. \tag{18.39}$$

Since *ex hypothesi* $n_{t+1}^B < n_{t+1}^A$ and c is concave in n the change to the A community is negative, and the consideration of the externality implies a reduction in the number of rights put into effect in the B community. Indeed, $\Delta_d S_t^A$ is bigger in absolute value than the third term of $\Delta_d S_t^B$ and, since more rights are in effect for the A group, it can be considerably so. Hence, the use of the static criterion does not imply that $\Delta_d S_t > 0$. That is, what is efficient according to the static criterion, is not necessarily efficient if the externality is taken into account. Hence we would have to reverse the conclusions in the previous section. It can be efficient to introduce fewer minority rights than a simple static analysis would imply. We can find an 'efficient discrimination' of minorities.

4. WELFARE-OPTIMAL ALLOCATIONS OF RIGHTS

Returning to the problem in Section 3.2, we now modify the efficiency analysis and introduce the welfare function from Section 2.4.1. Firstly, we look at the problem when the costs of the rights are carried by the respective communities. Within the community everyone pays the same tax. Then, we analyze the situation when the costs are equally divided among all individuals in both communities.

4.1 Intracommunity Cost-sharing

Here, the set Ψ, defining the political restrictions, is given by

$$\Psi = \left\{ \theta | \theta^i = \theta^j = \sum_d \frac{c^{ld}(n_t^l)}{n_t^l}, \forall i,j \in N^l, l \in \{A,B\} \right\}. \tag{18.40}$$

The a's are

$$a_t^{Ai} = \sum_d \left(b_t^{Adi} - \frac{c^{Ad}(n_t^A)}{n_t^A} \right) \tag{18.41}$$

and

$$a_t^{Bi} = \sum_d \left(b_t^{Bdi} - \frac{c^{Bd}(n_t^B)}{n_t^A} \right) r_t^{Bd}, \tag{18.42}$$

respectively. The welfare function from equation (18.17) now becomes:

$$W = \sum_{t=0}^{\infty} \delta^t \sum_{i \in N} \beta(a^i) a^i(r, \theta^i)$$

$$= \sum_{t=0}^{\infty} \delta^t \left[\sum_{i \in N^A} \beta(a_t^{Ai}) \sum_d \left(b_t^{Adi} - \frac{c^{Ad}(n_t^A)}{n_t^A} \right) + \sum_{i \in N^B} \beta(a_t^{Bi}) \sum_d \left(b_t^{Bdi} - \frac{c^{Bd}(n_t^B)}{n_t^A} \right) r_t^{Bd} \right]$$

$$= \sum_{t=0}^{\infty} \delta^t \left[\beta_t^A \sum_d n_t^A \left(b_t^{Ad} - \frac{c^{Ad}(n_t^A)}{n_t^A} + \frac{V^{Ad}}{\beta_t^A} \right) + \beta_t^B \sum_d n_t^B \left(b_t^{Bd} - \frac{c^{Bd}(n_t^B)}{n_t^B} + \frac{V^{Bd}}{\beta_t^B} \right) r_t^{Bd} \right]$$

$$= \sum_{t=0}^{\infty} \delta^t \left[\beta_t^A S_t^A + \beta_t^B S_t^B + \sum_d (n_t^A V^{Ad} + n_t^B V^{Bd} r_t^{Bd}) \right] \tag{18.43}$$

Here, β_t^l is defined by

$$\beta_t^l := \frac{1}{n^l} \sum_{i \in N^l} \beta(a_t^{li}) \tag{18.44}$$

and V^{ld} is a measure of the heterogeneity of the l community defined by:

$$V^{ld} := \frac{\sum_{i \in N^l} (\beta_t^{li} - \beta_t^l)(b_t^{ldi} - b_t^{ld})}{n_t^l} \tag{18.45}$$

If the planner wants to redistribute in favor of the losers, the β's will be negatively correlated with the b's and V^{ld} will be negative.

The introduction of the right for speakers of language B in domain d at time $t \geq 0$ will affect welfare in various ways:[15]

$$\Delta_d W = \sum_{t=0}^{\infty} \delta^t \left[\beta_t^A \Delta_d S_t^A + \beta_t^B \Delta_d S_t^B + n_t^B V^{Bd} + \sum_{\xi} (V^{B\xi} r_t^{B\xi} - V^{A\xi}) \Delta_d n_t^B \right] \tag{18.46}$$

We first have the direct effect on the B community, $\Delta_d S_t^B$, and the externality on the A community, $\Delta_d S_t^A$, due to the change in n_t^B from time $t = 1$. This is the same phenomenon as analyzed in Section 3.2 above.[16] Given that $n^A > n^B$ and that rights are realized in all domains for the members of the B community, we readily see that for any two individuals $i \in N^A$ and $j \in N^B$, if $b_t^{Adi} = b_t^{Bdj}$ for all domains d, then $a_t^{Ai} > a_t^{Bj}$, since due to concavity

$$\frac{c^{Ad}(n_t^A)}{n_t^A} < \frac{c^{Bd}(n_t^B)}{n_t^B}. \tag{18.47}$$

A planner, wanting to redistribute in favor of the weaker individuals, will, hence, give higher weight to individual i than to individual j. If the distributions of the propensities to pay b are similarly distributed among the individuals in the two communities, then as a consequence $\beta_t^B > \beta_t^A$ and the negative externality on the A community will have a lower weight than in the corresponding efficiency problem in Section 3.2. This signifies that the term $\Delta_d S_t^B$ can take on lower values than in the efficiency case without making the change in welfare negative. That is, rights in more domains become acceptable in the paternalistic welfare analysis.

However, we have a negative effect due to the dispersion measure V. Since the planner wants to redistribute in favor of the losers, more weight will be given to the individuals with low values of b in the consideration of the right becoming effective in the new domain, which will tend to reduce the change in welfare and, hence, the likelihood of introducing the right.

Finally, there is the intertemporal effect of the introduction of the right causing an increase in n^B. This will not only affect the costs, which is already taken into account in $\Delta_d S_t^A$ and $\Delta_d S_t^B$, but also the heterogeneity measures within the two communities, negatively due to $V^{B\xi}$ and positively due to $V^{A\xi}$. We note that if the two communities are homogenous, that is, if $b_t^{Adi} = \beta_t^{Ad}$ and $b_t^{Bdi} = \beta_t^{Bd}$ for all i and d, then $V^{A\xi}$ and $V^{B\xi}$ are all equal to zero and the result is clear: by giving more weight to the relative losers, it is desirable to give more rights to the minority language, than what comes out of a pure efficiency analysis.

4.2 Universal Cost-sharing

We now assume that the costs of the rights must be distributed equally among all individuals, that is:

$$\Psi = \{\theta | \theta^i = \theta^J, \forall i, j \in N\} \tag{18.48}$$

The a's are then

$$a_t^{Ai} = \sum_d \left[b_t^{Adi} - \left(\frac{c^{Ad}(n_t^A)}{n_t^A + n_t^B} + \frac{c^{Bd}(n_t^B)}{n_t^A + n_t^B} r_t^{Bd} \right) \right] \tag{18.49}$$

for an A individual and

$$a_t^{Bi} = \sum_d \left[b_t^{Bdi} r_t^{Bd} - \left(\frac{c^{Ad}(n_t^A)}{n_t^A + n_t^B} + \frac{c^{Bd}(n_t^B)}{n_t^A + n_t^B} r_t^{Bd} \right) \right] \tag{18.50}$$

for a B individual. The welfare criterion from equation 18.17 then becomes:

$$W = \sum_{t=0}^{\infty} \delta^t \sum_{i \in N} \beta(a^i) a^i(r, \theta^i)$$

$$= \sum_{t=0}^{\infty} \delta^t \sum_{d} \left\{ \sum_{i \in N^A} \beta(a_t^{Ai}) \left[b_t^{Adi} - \left(\frac{c^{Ad}(n_t^A)}{n_t^A + n_t^B} + \frac{c^{Bd}(n_t^B)}{n_t^A + n_t^B} r_t^{Bd} \right) \right] \right.$$

$$\left. + \sum_{i \in N^B} \beta(a_t^{Ri}) \left[b_t^{Rdi} r_t^{Rd} - \left(\frac{c^{Ad}(n_t^A)}{n_t^A + n_t^B} + \frac{c^{Bd}(n_t^B)}{n_t^A + n_t^B} r_t^{Bd} \right) \right] \right\}$$

$$= \sum_{t=0}^{\infty} \delta^t \sum_{d} \left\{ \beta_t^A S_t^{Ad} + \beta_t^B S_t^{Bd} r_t^{Bd} + n_t^A V^{Ad} + n_t^B V^{Bd} r_t^{Bd} \right.$$

$$\left. + (\beta_t^B - \beta_t^A) \left[\frac{n_t^A}{n_t} c^{Bd}(n_t^B) r_t^{Bd} - \frac{n_t^B}{n_t} c^{Ad}(n_t^A) \right] \right\} \tag{18.51}$$

Here,

$$n_t := n_t^A + n_t^B. \tag{18.52}$$

We see that the welfare measure consists of several components, the well-being of the A community, weighted by β^A, the well-being of the B community, weighted by β^B, and a fiscal externality, weighted by $(\beta_t^B - \beta_t^A)$. We will look at the fiscal externality in more detail in the following.

If all β are identical, the fiscal externality disappears and the V become equal to zero. The expression reduces to

$$W = \beta \sum_{t=0}^{\infty} \delta^t \sum_{d} (S_t^{Ad} + S_t^{Bd} r_t^{Bd}) = \beta S \tag{18.53}$$

which brings us back to the efficiency criterion. If both communities are homogeneous, the expression becomes:

$$W = \sum_{t=0}^{\infty} \delta^t \sum_{d} \left\{ \beta_t^A S_t^{Ad} + \beta_t^B S_t^{Bd} r_t^{Bd} + (\beta_t^B - \beta_t^A) \left[\frac{n_t^A}{n_t} c^{Bd}(n_t^B) r_t^{Bd} - \frac{n_t^B}{n_t} c^{Ad}(n_t^A) \right] \right\} \tag{18.54}$$

The introduction of a marginal right in domain d at time $t \geq 0$ then causes a change in welfare equal to:

$$\Delta_d W = \sum_{t=0}^{\infty} \delta^t \left\{ \beta_t^A \Delta_d S_t^A + \beta_t^B \Delta_d S_t^B + (\beta^B - \beta^A) \sum_{\xi} \Delta_d \left[\frac{n_t^A}{n_t} c^{B\xi}(n_t^B) r_t^{B\xi} - \frac{n_t^B}{n_t} c^{A\xi}(n_t^A) \right] \right\}$$

$$= \sum_{t=0}^{\infty} \delta^t \left\{ \beta_t^A \Delta_d S_t^A + \beta_t^B \Delta_d S_t^B + (\beta_t^B - \beta_t^A) \frac{n_t^A}{n_t} c^{Bd}(n_t^B) \right.$$

$$+ (\beta_t^B - \beta_t^A) \sum_{\xi} \left[\left(\eta^{B\xi} \left(1 - \frac{n_t^B}{n} \right) - \frac{n_t^B}{n} \right) \frac{c^{B\xi}(n_t^B)}{n_t^B} r_t^{B\xi} \right.$$

$$\left. \left. + \left(\eta^{A\xi} \left(1 - \frac{n_t^A}{n} \right) - \frac{n_t^A}{n} \right) \frac{c^{A\xi}(n_t^A)}{n_t^A} \right] \Delta_d n_t^B \right\} \tag{18.55}$$

Here the elasticities η are defined by

$$\eta_t^{l\xi} := \frac{\dfrac{\partial c^{l\xi}(n_t^l)}{\partial n_t^l}}{\dfrac{c^{l\xi}(n_t^l)}{n_t^l}}. \tag{18.56}$$

We have assumed that no other right is changed as a consequence of the introduction of the right in domain d: $\Delta_d r_t^{B\xi} = 0$ for $\xi \neq d$. Again, the change in welfare is determined by three effects, a direct externality on the A community, which is negative with weight β^A, a direct effect on the B community, with weight β^B, as well as several fiscal externalities. Hence, in addition to the case in Section 4.1 we have the fiscal externalities. The first one is the obvious direct one; the A community contributes to the financing of the implementation of the right in domain d in the B community; an advantage for the B community and a clear disadvantage for the A community.

The second fiscal externality depends on the dynamic structure and has two components. Firstly, because of the increase in the size of the B community and the corresponding decrease in the size of the A community, a larger share of the public budget falls on the B community compared to the efficiency case in Section 3.2. Secondly, the costs of implementing all rights decrease in the A community, but increase per capita due to the convexity of the cost functions. Similarly, the implementation costs of the rights in the B community increase, but decrease per capita. Of course these fiscal externalities work in opposite directions in the two communities, which is reflected in the signs of the weights. The net effect is unclear and depends on the elasticities of the cost functions. If only fixed costs are encountered, the elasticities are zero and the effect is a negative one for the B community. If the cost functions are linear, the elasticities are equal to one, and the effect is a positive one for the *B* community, since, by assumption, $n_t^B/n < 1/2$.

Intuitively, in the first case the costs in the *A* community do not change, but the number of individuals decreases, and some of the costs are therefore shifted to the *B* community which increases in size. In the second case both the number of individuals and the costs in the *A* community decrease proportionally and correspondingly increase proportionally in the *B* community. Since the *A* community is bigger than the *B* group, the relief in the tax share of the *B* people due to the reduction in the costs of the implemented rights in the *A* community is greater than the increase due to the increase in the size of the *B* community. The contribution from the *A* community to the financing of the rights in the *B* community will then, by the corresponding argument, increase, since the size of the *A* community is greater than that of the *B* group.

In comparison to the analysis in Section 4.1 we see that the direct fiscal externality adds a further argument in favor of more rights for the minority, whereas the indirect fiscal externality via the dynamic effect in some cases relativizes this effect.

5. CONCLUDING REMARKS

In this chapter we have tried to examine systematically the factors influencing the normative arguments for the allocation of language rights to a linguistic minority from an economic point of view. We have seen that a simple static cost-benefit analysis has to be augmented in various directions. If there are dynamic implications of the rights assignment, strengthening the minority numerically, this brings an argument in favor of more rights for the minority. However, such a dynamic effect creates a negative externality for the majority, which more than compensates for the positive effect on the minority, delivering an argument for an optimal discrimination of the minority. If we leave the simple cost-benefit paradigm and introduce a redistributive policy in favor of the losers in society, these conclusions again have to be modified and there are arguments for giving less weight to the externality on the majority due to the dynamic structure. These positive effects on the minority are further strengthened in the presence of a fiscal externality on the minority, which will be compensated through more rights than in the previous case.

The scope of the study has been limited to rights in formal domains which can be regulated by legal means. The larger – and probably more important – issue of how to deal with linguistic discrimination in the market place, has been totally ignored. Also the question of what constitutes a legitimate minority, is not the topic of this chapter. Should recent immigrants be treated differently from minorities, whose ancestors have lived in a territory for numerous generations, often much longer than the majority population? A related question is: When does a newly arrived group become the legitimate majority in a territory and left-over members of the old majority a 'normal' minority? This opens up many interesting, contradictory and important questions, which can be approached and partially resolved by economic methodology. These are, however, the topics left for future chapters.

NOTES

* This chapter was begun during a visit to Dipartimento di Economia Pubblica, Facoltà di Economia, Università di Roma 'La Sapienza'. I would like to thank my hosts, especially Maria and Giuseppe Eusepi, for excellent and inspiring working conditions and a very pleasant stay. The importance of the topic of this chapter and the emotional character of language usage were illustrated in an interesting manner by the publishers of this volume. The chapter originally had a very short greeting and dedication to José/Josep Casas Pardo in the two languages of Valencia, Catalan and Castilian. This had to be removed, since languages different from English were used.

1. Of course, one person's use of a language might very well affect the well-being of the person being talked to, or might want to communicate with, producing an externality, be it positive or negative. The larger is the number of speakers of a language, the greater is the potential number of contacts and, hence, the benefit of the language to a person knowing it. This network externality is central in the analysis of the long-term dynamics and equilibria of language usage as a means of communication. This is analyzed by, among others, Selten and Pool (1991), Church and King (1993), and Güth et al. (1997), who look at the benefits of learning other languages in addition to the mother tongue, and Wickström (2005), where the possibilities of the survival of communities of native speakers are analyzed. The present analysis treats this property of language usage as part of the set of the exogenous constraints facing the individual and is, hence, a possible factor influencing its propensity to pay for a certain language right.
2. For more general analyses in this direction, the reader is referred to, for instance, Kymlicka and Patten (2003) and the references therein. For a more formal analysis, see also Van Parijs (2002), as well as the contribution of the same author in Kymlicka and Patten (2003).
3. For the purpose of this chapter, we ignore the fact that individuals can belong to several language groups at the same time. The assumption that each individual is associated with one language simplifies the notational problems considerably and does not detract from the principal points of the analysis.
4. For a further discussion of the choice of status quo the reader is referred to Wickström (2007), for instance.
5. The latter point can be partially operationalized as the 'linguistic distance' between the languages. See, for instance, the analysis in Ginsburgh et al. (2005) or Fidrmuc et al. (2005). These authors use such a distance as a measure of disenfranchisement. However, the propensity to pay will in general depend on other factors, as well. Especially the emotional attachment to the language seems to be important. Compare, for instance, the situation in Wales, where virtually every Welsh-speaker is bilingual in English, too – see, for instance, the statistics in Grin (1992) – or in the Basque country, where almost all speakers of Basque are bilingual in French or Spanish. Nevertheless,

the propensity to pay for an official status of the respective language seems to be considerable among its speakers.

6. For different assumptions on this function, see Wickström (2007).
7. The long-run effects of certain allocation of language rights would be part of the 'emotional' aspect in determining the propensities to pay. The designation of certain languages as 'official' in given domains gives them a higher status, which reduces the incentives of following generations to use the non-official ones, reducing the number of their speakers. This can also lead to a situation of diglossia where the domains of the official language are constantly extended at the expense of non-official languages. This, in turn, would give the speakers of the official language a head start in life. In the long run, it might even lead to the death of non-official languages. For a further discussion of this possibility, see Wickström (2005).
8. See, for instance, Foley (1967), Varian (1974), or Varian (1975).
9. Compare, for instance, Varian (1974), Pazner and Schmeidler (1974), or Pazner (1977).
10. Take as an example the right to smoke or the prohibition on smoking in a public place; both a smoker and a non-smoker enjoy the same right in both instances; hence, in either case, neither of them has any reason to want to exchange their societal position with the other one. Efficiency considerations would tell us in this case which right assignment is the efficient one, but the traditional fairness concept provides us with little guidance as to how to compensate the 'loser' in the efficient allocation of rights, that is, telling us what is a 'good' allocation of rights (and other goods) in this case.
11. This is discussed in some detail in Wickström (2007).
12. For different assumptions on this function, see Wickström (2007).
13. We are implicitly assuming that there is at least one domain, in which it is inefficient to introduce the right. Else, our problem becomes trivial.
14. Because of the discrete changes in n^B_{t+1}, this, of course, is a first-order approximation of the effect. However, higher-order effects cannot change the qualitative conclusions.
15. We are implicitly assuming that the changes in the weights β and the dispersion measure V due to the introduction of a new (marginal) right are negligible.
16. The difference is only that we are now looking at the effect on all future generations, whereas in Section 3.2 we limited the analysis to the individuals alive at time $t = 0$. The present analysis could easily be limited to the cohort-centered case, which would have no consequence for the qualitative results.

REFERENCES

Church, Jeffrey and Ian King (1993), 'Bilingualism and network externalities', in *Canadian Journal of Economics/Revue canadienne d'économique*, **26**, 337–45.

Fidrmuc, Jan, Victor Ginsburgh, and Shlomo Weber (2005), 'Economic challenges of multilingual societies', research report.

Foley, Duncan (1967), 'Resource allocation in the public sector', in *Yale Economic Essays*, **7**, 73–6.

Ginsburgh, Victor, Ignacio Ortuño-Ortín, and Shlomo Weber (2005), 'Disenfranchisement in linguistically diverse societies. The case of the European Union', in *Journal of the European Economic Association*, **3**, 946–65.

Grin, François (1992), 'Towards a threshold theory of minority language survival', in *Kyklos*, **45**, 69–97.

Güth, Werner, Martin Strobel, and Bengt-Arne Wickström (1997), 'Equilibrium selection in linguistic games: kial ni (ne) parolas esperanton?', in Wulf Albers, Werner Güth, Peter Hammerstein, Benny Moldovanu, and Eric Van Damme

(eds), *Understanding Strategic Interaction: Essays in Honor of Reinhard Selten*, Berlin: Springer, pp. 257–69.
Kymlicka, Will and Alan Patten, (eds) (2003), *Language Rights and Political Theory*, Oxford: Oxford University Press.
Pazner, Elisha A. (1977), 'Pitfalls in the theory of fairness', in *Journal of Economic Theory*, **14**, 458–66.
Pazner, Elisha A. and David Schmeidler (1974), 'A difficulty in the theory of fairness', in *Review of Economic Studies*, **41**, 441–3.
Plato (1888, 1980), Κρίτων, edited by J. Adam, Cambridge: Cambridge University Press. (Originally published as Κρίτων, *c*. 395 BCE.)
Rawls, John (1971), *A Theory of Justice*, Cambridge: Harvard University Press.
Selten, Reinhard and Jonathan Pool (1991), 'The distribution of foreign language skills as a game equilibrium', in Reinhard Selten (ed.), *Game Equilibrium Models IV*, Berlin: Springer, pp. 64–84.
Van Parijs, Philippe (2002), 'Linguistic justice', in *Politics, Philosophy and Economics*, **1** (1), 59–74.
Varian, Hal R. (1974), 'Equity, envy, and efficiency', in *Journal of Economic Theory*, **9**, 63–91.
Varian, Hal R. (1975), 'Distributive justice, welfare economics and the theory of fairness', in *Philosophy and Public Affairs*, **4**, 223–47.
Wickström, Bengt-Arne (2005), 'Can bilingualism be dynamically stable? A simple model of language choice', in *Rationality and Society*, **17** (1), 81–115.
Wickström, Bengt-Arne (2007), 'Fairness, rights, and language rights: on the fair treatment of linguistic minorities', in Pio Baake and Rainald Borck (eds), *Public Economics and Public Choice*, Berlin: Springer, pp. 81–101.

19. A theory of conversion to exclusive religious and political faiths

Mario Ferrero

1. INTRODUCTION

In ordinary usage, the word 'conversion' carries the connotation of an abrupt shift of behavior, whereby people are supposed to give up their old ways in one bound and thoroughly embrace an entirely new package of belief and behavior. The prototype example that may lie in the back of most westerners' minds is Saint Paul, who was thunderstruck on the road to Damascus. This prototype seems to fit conversion to Christianity no less than conversion to communism: in both cases, as soon as one has seen the light, one is no longer allowed to indulge the old beliefs and practices of heathen and bourgeois life, respectively. Conversion implies that there is no halfway house between the old and the new: one is expected to take a plunge into the new faith – to 'believe' it, literally. So conversion is first of all a matter of intentions, not conduct nor conviction. It is never an intellectual process of rational argument over competing doctrines and final choice of the best doctrine. The sympathizer may well read a book or attend a lecture about Jesus Christ or Karl Marx, but the decision is eventually made by the heart. Leaders of religious and political organizations have always known that while the heart may be perfect, the brain and the body are not, so the initial plunge must be followed up and strengthened by intense socialization in the new faith's tenets and gradual learning of the new practice. Ideally this will subsequently convince the neophyte that his/her initial leap was well taken, but the leap itself is made prior to the conviction. It is this first step that poses a problem for addicts to the rational choice approach. This chapter is an addict's attempt to provide a solution to this problem.

If one has to jump, it is because there is a yawning gap in the path. The gap is created by exclusivity: certain faiths demand and enforce exclusive dealing by destroying the intermediate opportunities of multiple membership. With those faiths, one cannot have it both ways: it has to be either in or out. So in its proper, strong sense, conversion occurs only to, or from, exclusive faiths, and reciprocally, exclusivity implies that joining can occur only in the form of conversion; a simple change of mind does not qualify as conversion. Two questions then arise: why do some faiths demand exclusivity and conversion, which is obviously costly to the prospective member? And why do some people – sometimes, very many people – take the exclusive deal and convert? The first question has been addressed by Iannaccone (1992, 1995), whose answer is that exclusivity, like other prohibitions and sacrifices, helps to deter free riding and raise participation and commitment among the membership. The second question has not, to my knowledge, been addressed by economists so far. Yet it is an important question: if exclusivity were always an inferior offer, exclusive organizations would not be viable; if, at the opposite extreme, exclusivity were always a superior offer, all the observed, viable organizations would demand it. Neither, however, is the case. Thus the consumers' reaction to exclusivity affects the form and outcome of the competition among rival faiths. This chapter offers a joint answer to both the questions above: exclusivity is a signal that the product is of superior quality; that is why some suppliers request it and some consumers are willing to accept it.

The next section defines the problem more accurately by looking at some important historical instances of exclusivity or, respectively, the lack of it. Section 3 sets forth the signalling theory of exclusivity and conversion. Section 4 tries to engage the evidence. Section 5 concludes.

2. EXCLUSIVE FAITHS: SOME ILLUSTRATIONS

Perhaps the benchmark setting for the problem of religious conversion is the Mediterranean world from about the third century BCE to the fourth century CE, where it first presented itself in known history.[1] The polytheistic religion of the classical world was a composite array of cults, in which supplicants made sacrifices and offers to different gods to propitiate good fortune in a strictly *quid-pro-quo* exchange relationship (Ferrero, 2008). The priesthood was a disparate collection of temple caretakers, who lived off the offers but were not supposed to be exemplars of moral behavior. Indeed, ethics was no part of ancient religion: the latter was just not intended to regulate personal conduct; the gods were powerful but not necessarily 'good'. And the believers were not a community: religious practice did not involve living together or sharing experiences with fellow believers. It was a strictly individual activity. Consequently, the notion that to embrace one cult one should forswear allegiance to all other cults was entirely foreign to the ancient frame of mind: conversion had no meaning in this world (Nock, 1933). In the course of time, new cults kept coming in from the East, and were lined up alongside the others for the supplicants to choose from. The system was one of unlimited tolerance of diversity, one which could in principle accommodate every newcomer – including two of the exotic Oriental religions: first Judaism and later Christianity.

The Jews and the Christians, however, rejected such an accommodation. They were unique in the ancient world in that they demanded exclusivity and offered membership in a community in return. The spectacular rise of Christianity from deviant Jewish sect to world religion has exercised generations of historians, biblical scholars, and sociologists of religion. There seems to be a broad agreement that the key factor in the Christian success was that the promise of man's salvation for the last times was backed and made credible by the tangible benefits of participation in a community that provided collective goods to its members. In this the Christians followed the earlier Jewish example, the key difference being that Judaism was always tied to ethnicity and imposed costly rites of admission, whereas Christianity from the beginning broke free of it (Stark, 1996).

If we put the ancient Roman case in comparative perspective, we see that conversion arises as an issue only on certain conditions. First, conversion implies faith, and not every religion is based on faith; some are based on ritual and propitiation of overarching powers. Secondly, the faith must be exclusive; thirdly, this faith must aim at propagation; and fourthly, this propagation must take place in a competitive environment. Ancient paganism is the prototype of a non-exclusive religion, one not based on faith. Judaism has been an unswervingly exclusive faith from the beginning, but while in Hellenistic and early Roman times it was actively and successfully proselytizing across the Mediterranean, roughly after the defeat of the second Jewish war it turned inward and gave up seeking conversions to this day. As another example of an exclusive but non-missionizing faith, Islam in its first two or three centuries functioned as the religion of the Arab conquerors and did not seek nor encourage conversion of the Jews and Christians of the Near East. Only in the tenth century AD did the pace of conversion to Islam gain momentum; concomitantly, the caliphate lost its religious authority and the ulama class emerged as the custodian of doctrinal interpretation (Berkey, 2003). Yet another example is a number of Protestant sects issued from the Reformation, such as the Amish and Mennonites, which seem content to reproduce themselves without expansion. As to competition, the early Christian situation has been unique in the history of Catholic Christianity. In the Roman Empire, the new religion came up against an established religion that had been in place for centuries, amid the mistrust, and often the hostility, of the surrounding society, and it had to face up to the challenge of many other new cults that also were blooming in the cracks of the traditional system. Fighting its way up from the bottom of society proved so hard that, in the later waves of expansion outside the empire, the church took the easier path from the top down whenever feasible: the Christianization of the Slavic, Germanic, and Scandinavian lands, as well as of Spanish and Portuguese America centuries later, was carried out by converting the ruler first, or by enlisting the strong arm of a Christian colonial power. Only in modern times, when the attempt to secure endorsement from the states of East Asia such as Japan and China disastrously failed, was the Catholic Church confronted once again with the challenge of competition – and in the event, its performance proved modest.

An important, perhaps counterintuitive point here is that monotheism is *not* necessarily exclusive nor does it necessarily require conversion. The monotheistic *theology* is of course, by definition, exclusive, but the corresponding *organization* need not be. For example, a number of new cults that contested the ground to the early Christians – such as Mithraism and Manicheism – were variants of the Zoroastrian religion of Iran and were actively proselytizing but did not insist on exclusivity. Similarly, the Gnostic varieties of early Christianity were based on initiation to esoteric knowledge and hence on self-selection; therefore outward, public behavior, including exclusivity of membership, did not matter. As another example, the very many Protestant denominations are not exclusive towards one another or towards other Christian brands: if one switches from one denomination to another this is not perceived by either party as 'conversion', only a change in emphasis or practice, since there is thought to be no authority on revealed truth beyond Scripture itself. So 'born again' Christians are not converts but revived, or re-activated, previously slumbering believers. By contrast, the Catholics still today view anybody joining them from anywhere, including from other Christian denominations, as converts, since it is a progress from error to truth. It follows that a rational theory of monotheism (see the impressive effort by Stark, 2001) is not, or not quite, a theory of exclusivity or of conversion.

Turning to political ideologies, they vary a great deal from the non-exclusive to the totally exclusive. Socialism, with its eldest child, communism, is perhaps the paragon of exclusive political faiths. Much like Christianity *vis-à-vis* ancient paganism (Engels, 1982, was the first to point out and elaborate the analogy), it promised a total overturning of society as its long-term goal, but backed this promise with the offer of a community that delivered tangible benefits to its members in the here and now. One might not mix: to join in meant to forsake all alternative options. The European political environment of the late nineteenth and early twentieth centuries was very competitive, but despite this – or possibly, *because* of this (see below) – the socialists held tight to the principle that a full member was altogether unlike an outsider, even if a sympathetic one, and that all kinds of awkward problems and difficulties posed by the competitors should not be compromised with them but met by an internal response – a 'socialist solution'. So they worked out – in the language of the day – a socialist solution to the agrarian question, to the nationality question, to the colonial question, to the women's question, to the religious question, and so forth. In this way they built up a counter-society within the larger society, one that spanned all conceivable institutions designed to cater to the full range of needs and problems of the membership. For this reason, repeated attempts by all manner of well-meaning intellectuals, picking what they thought was good in the socialist program and blending it with other ideas and proposals – a typically liberal attitude – were invariably met with scorn and hostility. Indeed, these 'fusion' products were regarded as even more threatening than the open enemies, and every effort was made to insulate the membership from them.

3. EXCLUSIVITY AS MARKET SIGNALLING

A good starting point is Iannaccone's (1995) useful classification of religions in terms of their response to risk. The quality uncertainty surrounding religious products is enormous, as claims cannot be conclusively evaluated ex ante and there is no effective mechanism for lodging complaints and seeking redress ex post. Religions have evolved two types of response to this extreme degree of uncertainty. One is collective production: there is a congregational structure that emphasizes participation and commitment by ordinary members and keeps down both numbers and salaries of professional clergy. To control the free rider problem associated with collective production, these religious organizations resort to costly demands on members – 'sacrifice and stigma' – whose functional purpose is to screen out the less committed members and to raise the opportunity cost of alternative activities for those who remain. These costs typically take the form of prohibitions or limitations of secular activities that would otherwise compete for members' time, effort, and resources. The other organizational response to the ultimate uncertainty inherent in religion is portfolio diversification. In societies in which there is at least a degree of religious choice, rational risk-averse 'investors' will minimize risk by holding a diversified portfolio of religious assets. Religions that cater to this sort of demand are made of specialized, fee-for-service producers, who sell their products to individual customers; there are no real 'members' to speak of. Since there is no collective activity there is no free riding problem, and therefore no limitation on outside activities. Customers of these firms will thus bear no cost for patronizing many different firms. Brand loyalty is here no higher than with secular producers. In contrast, congregational religions will accommodate the pressure to diversify in-house and take 'a department store approach to religion – comprehensive belief systems, cradle to grave services, extensive and varied social networks, and so forth' (Iannaccone, 1995, p. 289).

The problem of exclusivity comes in at this stage of the argument: if the demand for diversification is so great, how can churches resist it under competition? Iannaccone's answer is centered on different production technologies. Some religions produce private goods and lend themselves to diversification. Others rely on collective production as an uncertainty-reducing mechanism and hence have to enforce costly prohibitions of secular activities to reduce free riding. But if these prohibitions have the purpose of binding people to the religious group and isolating them from alternative activities, such a purpose would be defeated if people were allowed to participate in competing religions. Hence restriction on *secular* consumption necessarily entails restriction on alternative *religious* consumption. Thus in this view exclusivity – in different degrees – follows from collectively oriented religion.

There is no doubt that exclusivity deters people from diversifying and free riding. Exclusivity is in a sense the ultimate prohibition, as it goes to the heart of what religion is all about. The problem with this view of exclusivity as a tax on negative externalities is that it has difficulty in fully accounting for a competitive environment, as Iannaccone (1995, p. 294) himself acknowledges. Specifically, it explains why it may be rational for collective religions to *demand* exclusivity, but not why it is rational for people to *supply* it and convert; hence, it falls short of being a full theory of conversion in the sense defined above. It may well be true that for some people the high costs of exclusivity are more than offset by the benefits of a given communal religion, so self-selection in a large free market will ensure that virtually all exclusive religions draw at least some minimal following and survive. But explaining rapid, spectacular expansion among the adult population seems an altogether different matter. Recalling the early Christian and socialist examples discussed above, how are we to explain the quantum leap from paganism, or liberalism, to an exclusive faith by large numbers of people? Granted that, once in, many people will find that the benefits of membership are indeed worth the costs ex post, how can any sensible, not to say rational, individual bring himself to 'burn' all his religious assets and take a plunge into the unknown? In what sense is this rational on an ex-ante basis? There is a problem of moral hazard of unparalleled magnitude here: how can a prospective convert have some reason to trust that he's not just being cheated, or sold a lemon?

The theory of market signalling has the potential to provide an answer. In its basic formulation (Spence, 1974), the informed party that suffers from the other party's inability to observe product quality or productivity differences has an incentive to signal. To be credible, the signal must be costly to the signalling party; and to be successful, the signalling cost must be such that those who stand to gain from the lack of observability have no incentive to undertake it. In the standard illustration, workers of superior ability have an incentive to undertake schooling to signal their productivity to employers. This move succeeds if it yields a separating equilibrium, in which unit costs of education for the two groups and the amount of education are such that the high-productivity group undertakes it whereas the other group does not. In homogeneous groups where adverse selection is not an issue but moral hazard is, the signal becomes an initial sunk cost, much like posting a bond whose value can be recouped only through repeated trade in subsequent periods, thereby making the honest strategy profitable, as in models of price premiums on high-quality products (Shapiro, 1983; Klein and Leffler, 1981). In the price premium literature, the sunk cost can be either a conspicuous, non-recoupable expenditure, such as advertising or pure waste, or an initial investment in reputation. In all variants of the signalling mechanism, an important implication of the theory is that the necessary amount of signalling or sunk cost is proportional to the value of the hiding or cheating strategy, respectively: the more the low-productivity worker, the quack, or the low-quality seller stand to gain from undercutting quality or from hiding in the larger group, the larger and more expensive the signal will have to be to implement contractual compliance by, or separation from, them.

Let us now apply the insights of the signalling model to religion. Consider a competitive religious market with no barriers to entry and umpteen non-exclusive, 'private' religious firms servicing consumers, as in the Roman Empire. Suppose a collective, monotheistic religion enters this market without requiring exclusive membership. The organization offers a communal worship but incurs no cost from doing so. People will visit this group in their spare time, at no cost to them, and find the experience disappointing; communal life will be unrewarding precisely because nobody is putting in much effort or commitment. But these visitors will reason: this is just what we should have expected, for there is nothing to suggest that this new group should be any better than the others. In a large society the new group will nevertheless be viable because it will find some people especially willing to patronize it, but it will remain small.

Suppose instead that the new religion requires exclusivity. It incurs an opportunity cost from doing so: this is the value of the 'business' lost because of exclusivity. If the religion's success is measured by the number of members, this cost is proxied by the number of people who would otherwise join but are turned away because they are prevented from diversifying their religious portfolio. If this were all there is to it, the exclusive strategy would put the organization at a competitive disadvantage. But the people will notice that this group is willingly incurring a seemingly gratuitous cost, and they will reason: if this group behaves this way it must be because they are advertising a superior product and expect to recoup the initial cost through future 'sales'; if they were selling a lemon, they would just be throwing one-period business away. This expectation of superior quality is self-fulfilling: once they join in, the people find the experience rewarding and worth continuing, not because they gain access to the proof of the religion's ultimate truth – this they never will – but because they find a fulfilling collective life catering to their various needs and supported by high participatory effort. Thus the exclusive strategy pays back because prospective members think they have reason to trust a group which is posting a bond in advance of 'sales': the higher the value of the bond, the higher the trust. In turn, given the technology to enforce exclusivity, the opportunity cost of the exclusive strategy – the value of the bond – is the higher, the more diversified the portfolio of non-exclusive religious assets can be. Hence, in principle, a testable implication of this model is that, given that an exclusive religion is on offer, we should observe a positive correlation between a religious market's product assortment mix and the rate of conversion. Anyway, the signalling value of exclusivity as a sunk cost seems to be the key to the occurrence of conversions.[2]

Emphasizing the supply side of exclusivity, in addition to the demand side stressed by Iannaccone (1995), does more than simply yielding a richer description of the mechanism of conversion. If participation in competing religions is only a liability that detracts from a person's commitment to a particular group, and if this is the reason for prohibiting it, then the achievement of monopoly and the withering away of the competition can only be good for the group: there's virtually nothing left to prohibit. But if the group turns this liability into an asset that signals high quality and attracts the most committed people, as we are suggesting, then the value of this asset to the group cannot be independent from the existence and strength of the competition. When the religion has expanded so much that it includes most of the relevant population and the competition is in disarray, the effectiveness of exclusivity as an incentive mechanism is destroyed because the possibility of portfolio diversification is now minimal. In this sense, exclusivity is only one – perhaps the most important one – among the behavioral prohibitions considered by the sacrifice and stigma model: these too crucially depend on interaction with outsiders and so their effectiveness falls as the religion's membership increases. It follows that a religion in these straits will be likely to look for substitute incentive devices, such as doctrinal strictness, that are not subject to decreasing returns to size.[3]

The same approach can be applied to political ideologies. As with religions, it is not so much the content of the ideology as such as the distance of its goals and promises from the status quo that determines the signalling value of exclusivity. So the more revolutionary an ideology is, the more radical its departure from the status quo, the more incentive its proponents will have to require exclusivity and prevent diversification. When socialism first came up against liberalism towards the close of the nineteenth century, it had to convince its prospective constituency, the working class, that it was worth joining in. So the socialists built up step by step a theory of society and a political program that included everything – a department-store approach, in Iannaccone's (1995) terminology – and anathematized mixing or multiple membership at an obvious cost to themselves. If our argument is correct, this exclusive strategy is the key to understanding their success because the bond thus posted enhanced their credibility in the eyes of prospective members. Once in, workers found the experience rewarding not because the revolutionary claims were proven true, but because they benefited from the participatory environment of the socialist counter-society.[4] Thus the exclusive strategy paid off and conversions occurred on a mass scale.

There is, however, an important difference between religious and secular faiths. Unlike religions, whose theology can never be conclusively proven true or false, political ideologies sometimes do meet a definitive reality test: it is when an organization embracing an exclusive ideology succeeds in taking power and begins to implement the new social order, as with the socialist revolutions of the twentieth century. Then we should expect the signalling value of the exclusive ideology to collapse. It is a well-known and widely documented fact that people in communist states became ever more cynical and disillusioned with the regime's ideology: when subscription to the ideology is made mandatory for the whole population it no longer carries any cost, rather there is a benefit to pretending to believe it. The communist regimes grappled with this problem until the end, struggling unsuccessfully to devise a substitute for it.

Finally, a qualification is in order. The signalling theory set forth above lays claim to being a theory of the competition between a collective group and many private suppliers. All it does is to show that under some conditions, exclusivity is a superior strategy for the collective faith. However, it cannot, without qualification, readily extend to the competition between two or more collective, exclusive groups, such as Jews and Christians in the Roman Empire, or Christians and Muslims in the medieval Middle East, or socialists and fascists in modern European politics. Fully addressing this more general problem is beyond the scope of this chapter. Here it may be sufficient to note that confrontation between two exclusive groups necessarily breeds conflict, which can be resolved only if and when one group gains the upper hand and manages to enlist the coercive power of the state on its side. Thus the Christian empire repressed the Jews, the Muslim caliphate institutionalized discrimination against Jews and Christians, and the communists suppressed the fascists, and the fascists suppressed the communists, as soon as they took power in different countries.

4. SOME HISTORICAL EVIDENCE

4.1 Religions

The first, basic class of evidence in support of our theory is that monotheistic religions that do not require exclusivity have usually failed. An example is the philosophical monotheism of the ancient world. Greek and Roman philosophers recognized that worship of the traditional gods was just superstition and that one higher entity must lie behind the multiplicity of creation, but as Cicero famously maintained, the traditional religion was good for law and order and therefore should not be challenged. Unsurprisingly, this philosophical monotheism never reached beyond a tiny literate elite. The same can be said of the modern counterparts of the ancient philosophers, the English and French deists and freethinkers of the seventeenth and eighteenth centuries up to Voltaire and Hume.

It could be countered that neither the ancient nor modern philosophers ever aimed at a wide following, or offered a communal religious experience. But as mentioned in Section 2 above, other quasi-monotheistic competitors of the early Christians, notably the Gnostics, the Mithraists, and the Manicheans, who also did not insist on exclusivity, were collective groups and engaged in active missionizing. Yet they lost out and in the end disappeared without a trace.

The philosophers' monotheism was mainly negative and polemical, as it stressed that, insofar as different religions emphasized differences that were illusory and concealed the simple, common truth behind them all, they were all wrong. Others, however, tried a more positive approach to this conciliatory program, emphasizing that the different religions are all right. The Baha'i religion was founded in Iran in the nineteenth century with the stated aim of reconciling all the monotheisms to a common worship of the one and only God (Wikipedia). The Sikh religion was founded in early sixteenth century India to bridge the divide between

Hinduism and Islam (Wikipedia). Both were intensely communal and participatory, but given their basic assumption, neither prevented or discouraged its followers from participating in the traditional religions. In the end they both failed, becoming separate sects instead of meeting halls of the great established religions.

More speculatively, Buddhism arose in ancient India, in opposition to the established Hindu polytheism, as a way to man's spiritual salvation beyond the bounds of the material world, breaking the chain of endless reincarnations. In this, despite its non-theistic outlook, it was analogous to the Western monotheistic religions, while Hinduism was in many ways analogous to Greco-Roman polytheism. Thus the great Indian contest was in a sense a rehearsal of the Mediterranean drama. However, unlike its Mediterranean counterparts, Buddhism did not prohibit traditional Hindu worship; it only devalued it and stressed the benefits of its own doctrine and practice for those willing to go over to monastic life. In the end, despite its impressive initial spread, Buddhism was completely wiped out of India proper. Outside force is not a sufficient explanation for this extinction: Muslim rule cracked down on all Indian religions but Hinduism and Jainism survived; furthermore, Buddhism also disappeared from South India which was never subject to Muslim rule. Conze (1979) suggests that this dismal fate had much to do with Buddhism's inherent weakness as a religion of renunciation – another way of stressing the non-exclusivity of Buddhism.

We noted in Section 3 that if exclusivity is seen as a signal of high quality, then one should observe a positive correlation between the rate of conversion and the product assortment on offer in the religious market. In one of the very few quantitative studies of conversion, Bulliet (1979) finds that conversion to Islam in the medieval period reached a peak after the initial take-off and then slowly tapered off, so that the Muslim fraction of the population follows a logistic growth curve. Though admittedly this finding is compatible with other interpretations as well, it also supports our theory – with the complication, however, that conversion to Islam in the Middle East occurred not from a pagan religious portfolio but from previously established exclusive faiths, especially Christianity.

An interesting by-product of the signalling approach to exclusivity is that it suggests a natural explanation, over and above the obvious rents from monopoly, for the final resort to state religion and state-enforced prohibition of competing cults, as observed for example in the late Roman Empire. When most people are Christians, if there is a minimum critical mass for any religious firm to function, most such traditional cults are in disarray, so the opportunity cost – and hence the signalling value – of exclusivity is very low. Those who have not converted so far are even less likely to do so now. In the Roman case, these were the group who had the least interest in the collective religion and who, however, would have been most valuable to the church as officials and bishops: the literate upper class. Harassing these people by proscribing their traditional worship was a way of lowering their opportunity cost of joining the church (Ferrero, 2008). By contrast, in the Islamic Middle East, where Islam came down from above instead of rising from below, the Christian and Jewish communities were not so valuable to the new state religion and so their cult was never proscribed.

A final, testable implication of the model is that as the exclusive religion becomes dominant, and the value of alternative religious products declines, it becomes possible and profitable to accommodate the pressure for asset diversification *inside* the new religion to a greater extent than before. Thus the cult of Mary, the cult of the saints, the cult of relics, and other forms of 'polytheistic' worship within the framework of a monotheistic faith distinctly grew and multiplied after the Christian takeover of the Roman Empire. Something of the same sort seems to have occurred in Islam in the medieval Middle East (Bulliet, 1979).

4.2 Political Ideologies

Socialism has been discussed at some length in the previous sections. Here we will briefly touch on some of the other main ideologies of the modern era.

European fascism is an obvious candidate for analysis as an exclusive ideology.[5] Much like their socialist rivals, the fascists were attractive because they demanded rejection of all the moderate policies of their liberal opponents and offered instead a full range of doctrinal and institutional solutions to all social problems – one targeted to displace, and replace, the socialists' 'department store'. Again like the communist regimes, once the fascists were firmly in power the signalling value of their exclusivity rapidly vanished – so much so that in the last frenzied years of World War II, a renewed fascist republic sprang up in Northern Italy under German protection and tried to promote a return to the original, radical ideals of the fascist movement, allegedly lost to the conservatism of the pre-war regime.

Insofar as it rests its claims on the uniqueness of a particular 'nation', real or imagined (Anderson, 1991), nationalism is typically exclusive, and offers a counter-society and a comprehensive world view not unlike those of socialism and fascism – with each of which, significantly, it was often closely allied. So there will be a national art, literature and music, national labor unions and business associations, national leagues of artists, writers, youth, women, farmers, often a national church, and so forth. Multi-nationalism and multi-culturalism are anathema: exclusive commitment to the national cause is demanded. In the two great historical waves of nationalism – the nineteenth century in Europe and the twentieth century in the colonial world – nationalists were often revolutionaries rising up against the international status quo; when at last they achieved their goal of a nation state for their people, however, the ideology soon began losing steam and survived as a reserve tool which might yet prove handy to enforce discrimination against minorities inside the country or to support a confrontational attitude toward neighbors or rivals outside.

Liberalism provides an interesting testing ground for our theory. In its early days it was in total opposition to the old, absolutist political order, so it tended to be exclusive and to offer a full range of solutions to all kinds of social problems – witness the Jacobins in the French Revolution, or the Italian liberal revolutionaries of the nineteenth century. Liberals were militant fighters, often at great personal risk; as late as the 1920s the Italian liberal Piero Gobetti argued for a 'liberal revolution' against the rising fascist regime, which later had him killed. When, however, liberalism triumphed and became the basis of Western political societies, it gradually became a composite ideology picking something from all quarters and offering no collective activity beyond political propaganda at election times. In our approach, this is explained by the fact that with liberalism's victory, the signalling value of its exclusivity collapsed – but unlike religions, it had no ready substitute for it.

5. CONCLUSION

This chapter has argued that conversion to exclusive faiths is rational because exclusivity, in some circumstances, is a signal of superior quality that prospective members have good reason to trust. This signalling model of exclusivity seems capable of accounting for both the astonishing success of some exclusive faiths confronting non-exclusive belief systems, and the involution and decay that often set in when these same faiths completely defeat the competition and conquer political power.

The *prima facie* evidence on the rise of Christianity within ancient paganism and on the rise of socialism within liberal capitalism seems broadly to support the predictions of the model. The daunting task for future research is to test the model against the big stylized facts of the history of mass conversion to and from different religions across time and space.

NOTES

1. The first-ever monotheism seems to have been founded by the prophet Zarathustra towards the end of the second millennium BCE, displacing the original Indo-European polytheism. In time, Zoroastrianism became the state religion of the Persian empire, but exclusivity seems not to have been enforced – witness the freeing of the Jews from Babylonian captivity. Too little is known of this precedent, however, to make any firm statement. See the fascinating account of Kriwaczek (2004).
2. One might wonder, if exclusivity is such a good business strategy, why do competitors not follow suit and request it too? Simply because 'private' religious firms are not equipped to provide the collective goods that only make the high expectations towards the exclusive group self-fulfilling, so that the exclusive strategy would be disastrous for them.
3. This problem is analyzed in another paper (Ferrero, 2006).
4. Elsewhere (Ferrero, 2004) I developed a model of a revolutionary cooperative that engages in the production of tangible short-term benefits, or reforms, to support its long-term goals. The argument is here extended to ideologies.
5. Although in many ways an extreme example of a fascist regime, German Nazism cannot be included in this group because it was based on race, and race allows no conversion. Even if and when all ethnic Germans were 'converted' to the Nazi ideology, there still remained substantial groups of non-convertible people inside and outside the country – enough to feed continuing conflict and hence to keep Aryan exclusivity valuable.

REFERENCES

Anderson, B. (1991), *Imagined Communities*, rev. edn, London: Verso.
Berkey J. (2003), *The Formation of Islam*, Cambridge: Cambridge University Press.
Bulliet, R.W. (1979), *Conversion to Islam in the Medieval Period*, Cambridge, MA: Harvard University Press.
Conze, E. (1979), *A Short History of Buddhism*, London: Allen and Unwin.
Engels, F. (1982), 'Zur Geschichte des Urchristenthums' (1895), translated as 'On the history of early Christianity', in K. Marx and F. Engels, *On Religion*, Chico, CA, Scholars Press: American Academy of Religion, pp. 120–42.
Ferrero, M. (2004), 'Revolution or reform? Socialism's dilemma as a rational choice problem', *Homo Oeconomicus*, **21**, 251–82.
Ferrero, M. (2006), 'Exclusivity and strictness: a model of extremism in sects and universal religions', mimeo, University of Eastern Piedmont.
Ferrero, M. (2008), 'The triumph of Christianity in the Roman Empire: an economic interpretation', *European Journal of Political Economy*, **24** (1), 73–87.
Iannaccone, L. (1992), 'Sacrifice and stigma: reducing free riding in cults, communes, and other collectives', *Journal of Political Economy*, **100**, 271–91.
Iannaccone, L. (1995), 'Risk, rationality, and religious portfolios', *Economic Inquiry*, **33**, 285–95.
Klein, B. and K. Leffler (1981), 'The role of market forces in assuring contractual performance', *Journal of Political Economy*, **89**, 615–41.
Kriwaczek, P. (2004), *In Search of Zarathustra*, New York: Vintage Books.
Nock, A.D. (1933), *Conversion: The Old and the New in Religion from Alexander the Great to Augustine of Hippo*, Oxford: Oxford University Press.

Shapiro, C. (1983), 'Premiums for high-quality products as returns to reputations', *Quarterly Journal of Economics*, **98**, 659–79.

Spence, M. (1974), *Market Signaling*, Cambridge, MA: Harvard University Press.

Stark, R. (1996), *The Rise of Christianity: A Sociologist Reconsiders History*, Princeton, NJ: Princeton University Press.

Stark, R. (2001), *One True God: Historical Consequences of Monotheism*, Princeton, NJ: Princeton University Press.

Wikipedia (2009), 'Baha'i faith', available at http://en.wikipedia.org/wiki/Baha'i_Faith.

Wikipedia (2009), 'Hinduism and Sikhism', available at http://en.wikipedia.org/wiki/Hinduism_and_Sikhism.

Wikipedia (2009), 'Islam and Sikhism', available at http://en.wikipedia.org/wiki/Islam_and_Sikhism.

Index

Titles of publications are shown in *italics*.